THE

WORKS

OF

LEONARD WOODS. D. D.,

LATELY PROFESSOR OF CHRISTIAN THEOLOGY IN THE
THEOLOGICAL SEMINARY, ANDOVER.

IN FIVE VOLUMES.

VOL. V.

BOSTON:
JOHN P. JEWETT & COMPANY,
17 & 19 CORNHILL.
1851.

ANDOVER:
JOHN D. FLAGG,
STEREOTYPER AND PRINTER.

CONTENTS.

TWO SERMONS DELIVERED IN THE CHAPEL OF THE THEOLOGICAL SEMINARY.

TWO SERMONS DELIVERED IN THE CHAPEL OF THE THEOLOGICAL SEMINARY.

LETTERS TO YOUNG MINISTERS.*

LETTER I.

Brethren and Friends,

The subjects on which I propose to address to you several familiar Letters, are those which are always interesting to ministers of the gospel, and, as I conceive, specially so at the present day. I have been particularly inclined to an undertaking like this, because the time allotted to study in our Theological Seminary is so short, and the field of inquiry so extensive, that every subject, even the most important and difficult, must of necessity be passed over with only a partial consideration. But imperfect as the acquisitions are which students are able to make in three years, they are of essential importance to their ultimate usefulness. And it is among the valuable ends which are answered by a regular course of study in our Divinity Schools, that young men are led to a careful survey of the field which lies before them, and get a distinct view of the knowledge to be acquired and the good to be accomplished in the sacred office.

It is indispensable to the proper usefulness of a minister, that he should maintain a constant and lively interest in that which appertains to his great work, and that he should aspire after the most clear and Scriptural views of the principles of Christianity,

* First published in the Spirit of the Pilgrims, A. D. 1832.

and of the best way of teaching and defending them. His reputation and success depend in a great measure on his continued diligence in the improvement of his mind. Nothing can be more unsuitable for any minister, especially for one just entering on the sacred office, than to feel satisfied with his past attainments, and to be confident of the correctness of all his opinions. On the contrary, nothing can be more suitable for him, than frequently to make the inquiry *whether the views which he and his brethren entertain of the doctrines and laws of Christianity, and their methods of inculcating them upon their people, are agreeable to the word of God.* An inquiry like this should be carried into middle life, and even into old age. For we are never to imagine ourselves beyond the reach of error, or too old to be capable of higher acquisitions in knowledge. Great improvement may be made by those who have studied the Christian religion with the best advantages, and for the longest time, and who have preached it with the most remarkable success. Their success must indeed imply, that they have exhibited important truths with clearness and fidelity. But it certainly does not imply, that they are free from error; nor does it imply, that an entire freedom from error would not greatly increase their success. No minister then can refer to the length of the time he has studied and preached, or to the measure of his success, as a proof that his opinions are all correct, or that there is no fault in his manner of preaching. And it must certainly be looked upon as very unseemly for one, who ought to be humbled under a sense of his deficiencies, to wrap himself up in a fancied perfection, because God has put him into the ministry, or made the gospel preached by him a savor of life unto life to many. God often sees fit to honor his sovereign grace by employing those as ministers, and blessing their labors, whose knowledge is very defective, whose opinions are in many respects erroneous, and whose characters are marked with blemishes. This surely is no reason why we should think it of little consequence to strive after higher knowledge, more correct opinions, and a better character; though it is evidently a reason why we should be lowly in heart, and should remember continually, *that the excellency of the power which gives success to the preaching of the gospel, is not of man, but of God.* The way then is open for us to inquire, whether our own opinions, or the opinions of any other ministers are true, and whether any particular modes of preaching, ancient or modern, are conformed to the right standard, and suited, in the highest degree, to accomplish the great end of preaching. Religion never has been injured, and never will be, by free inquiry, conducted on right principles, and carried on simply for the discovery of the truth, though it has been and may still be injured by false arguments, and by bad passions. It may be injured, too, by silence, when we ought to speak; or by timidity, when duty calls for boldness; or by a slumbering confidence that all is safe, when we ought to be awake and at our post, remembering that there are more false opinions in the world than true, and more zeal against Christianity than for it.

Now when you seriously consider the errors, whether more or less flagrant, which are advocated at the present day, especially by ministers, you may sometimes be disposed to indulge anxious and desponding feelings, and to say within yourselves, *What will be the end of these erratic movements of the human mind?* My own heart has been no stranger to such feelings. Looking with lively emotions at *the cause of truth*, and believing that it involves the highest interests of man, I have found it no easy matter to maintain a quiet state of mind, when I have seen its prospects overcast. But there are considerations adapted to secure to us the perpetual enjoyment of inward quietness and peace. These considerations have been of special use to me, and they may be so to you.

The chief consideration is, *that God is the unchangeable Friend and supporter of the truth, and that he will sustain it, and finally cause it to prevail.* He loves the cause of truth with a strength of affection infinitely superior to what we are capable of, and takes an infinitely higher interest than we do, in its success. In his unsearchable wisdom, he may indeed for a time, suffer the truth to be obscured and suppressed, and error to triumph. But this temporary triumph of error will only prepare the way for its more signal overthrow. God doeth his pleasure among the hosts of heaven and the inhabitants of the earth. And is he not able, when he pleases, to confound error, and give prevalence to the truth? Take those false opinions which are most pernicious. To an alarming extent you see them believed and defended. Men of learning and talent, and, in some instances, of respectable character, are laboring, by all that is plausible and imposing in sophistry, and by artful appeals to the unsanctified heart, to propagate them far and wide. Now does the impious zeal and hardihood of these men, and their temporary success, occasion fear or disquietude? Think then of the omnipotence of God. How easy it is for him to restrain the propagators of error, and to prevent the evil they are striving to accomplish. By the agency of his Spirit he can renew their hearts, and bring them to love and zealously to promote what they now hate and labor to destroy. Or he can so operate on the minds of others, that the advocates of error shall lose their influence. He can so order it in his providence, that every examination and every discussion of the subjects in debate shall make known the darkness and deformity of error, and the lustre and glory of divine truth. He can raise up powerful defenders of the faith, whom no adversaries shall be able to gainsay or resist. Or, if it seem good in his sight, he can suffer error to prevail, till its evil consequences shall alarm even its adherents, and constrain them to turn from it with shame and abhorrence. The history of the church abounds with examples of this.

The same ground of comfort is necessary for us, and in some respects more necessary, in regard to *those errors which cleave to the minds of Christians.* Such errors excite painful emotions within us, because they are most unnaturally associated with the truth, and maintained by those who love the truth. But we have reason to think that there will ere long be a remedy for all these remaining errors of Christians. God will, we trust, impart to them in larger measures, the influences of his Spirit, and thus give them greater illumination of the understanding and greater spirituality of affection. And if he does this, the evil will quickly be cured. For error naturally retires from that mind, in which the light of the knowledge of divine glory clearly shines. Whenever God shall be pleased more abundantly to pour out his Spirit upon his ministers and people, and more fully to sanctify their hearts, they will at once attain to better conceptions of divine things, and will be happily freed from a variety of mistaken or defective views, which are sure to accompany lower degrees of sanctification.

You will find a Christian here and there, who is very tenacious of his mistaken opinions. He may contend for them because he is ambitious to be the head of a party. Or, through a misguided conscience, he may really believe his errors to be important truths, and so may contend for them to do God service. What shall be said of such a case? I reply, as to the individual himself who thus pertinaciously maintains wrong opinions from feelings of ambition, or from religious motives, — it may be that nothing can ever be done effectually to open his eyes, before the light of another world shall shine upon them. And others may be associated with him, or rise up after him, who will pertinaciously adhere to the same false notions. But the time will come, when those false notions will be exposed and rejected. The event is certain. Perhaps men of a more correct faith will be raised up, whose writings or oral instructions will cast such a light on the doctrines of divine truth, that error will be instantly seen by every one, and renounced as soon as seen. Or God may judge it best to let the error run on, till its hurtful consequences shall open the eyes of all to its deformity and mischievous tendency.

Are there any of you, then, whose hearts throb with fear, or are oppressed with gloom, on account of the errors which prevail? To such I would say, — remember that the Lord, who reigns over all, is an unchangeable enemy to error; and that, however great the subtlety with which it contrives to conceal itself, he will finally bring it to light, and expose it to contempt. And what is more; he will make the temporary prevalence of error the means of bringing his people to a more perfect knowledge and a more unwavering belief of the doctrines of revelation. That he has often done this, the history of the church shows. And that he will continue to do it, his promises imply. We have then solid reason quietly to commit the cause of truth to his almighty protection, and to cheer ourselves with the assurance that he will give it success. Long and dreary has been the time in which error has borne sway. But the bright and glorious day will come, in which truth shall reign through the world, and shall reign forever. Happy are they who discover and embrace the truth, and are active in its defence. The Lord will compass them with his favor as with a shield. As to error, all error, whether more or less flagrant, — we ought from our heart to be afraid of it, and to labor with the greatest earnestness to rid ourselves of it. For error is as really opposed to the character and will of God, as sin is. And they who would not be partakers in the evils of its overthrow, must not be found among its subjects or its allies. Away, then, with every false opinion, however zealously we or others may have contended for it, and however great the self-denial which the renunciation of it may require. If any one of our errors is dearer to us than others, it is just so much the more injurious; and giving it up will be a sacrifice more acceptable to God, and will do more to fit us for heaven.

This search for the truth and this endeavor to rid ourselves of error, is a work which ought to be pursued with unremitting diligence; and never to be given up as long as life lasts. In the day of adversity, and on the bed of sickness, we may still be growing in the knowledge of divine things, and detecting and renouncing errors which have been injurious to our spiritual interest. Happy they, who, with a humble reliance upon the grace of God, are thus intent upon the great work of curing the disorders, and promoting the health, beauty and vigor of their own immortal minds.

But in this momentous work, how could we proceed, and what hope could we have of success, were we left to the mere guidance of our own erring reason? In what uncertainty and error should we have been perpetually involved, had not God granted us his word to be a guide to our faith? And in consequence of the great ignorance that is in us because of the blindness of our hearts, how unable should we still be to come to a right knowledge of God's word and to a right faith in its heavenly truths, without the inward teaching of the Holy Spirit? With these helps, that is, the word and the Spirit of God, if there is a pious docility and diligence on our part, we shall not fail of success in our inquiries after the truth.

That the word of God is the only and sufficient rule of our faith and practice, is the grand principle for which Protestants have contended. This principle, universally received and acted upon, would put an end to error and division, and would ultimately bring all Christians to see the light and glory of divine truth.

But the right reception and use of this Protestant principle implies much more than is commonly apprehended. It implies a full conviction, that the Scriptures were written under the infallible guidance of the Holy Spirit; that they contain truth unmixed with error; and that they teach all which is necessary for us to know in our present state. It demands that our great and only inquiry should be, what did God intend to communicate to us by these writings; in other words, what is the meaning of the divine testimony; and that in determining what this meaning is, we should be free from prejudice, distrustful of ourselves, earnestly desirous of knowing the truth, and resolved to embrace it, how much soever it may oppose the prepossessions of our natural reason or the bias of our own heart. And it requires that we should apply ourselves, with diligence and prayer, to the business of interpreting the Scriptures by just and proper rules.

LETTER II.

Brethren and Friends,

As the close of the last Letter, I stated the Protestant principle, that *the word of God is the only and sufficient rule of our faith and practice*, and endeavored to show, in part, what is implied in rightly receiving and applying this principle.

There is one point of great importance, though often overlooked in practice, namely; that *as soon as we ascertain what God teaches us in his word, we have come to the end of our inquiry — we have attained to the knowledge of the truth.*

This is a principle so essential to believers in revelation, and so extensive in its influence, that I shall dwell upon it with more than ordinary care.

Suppose, then, I am desirous of learning the truth in regard to the duration of future punishment. Accordingly I apply myself to the study of the Scriptures, and find a variety of passages which represent the punishment of the wicked as endless. I am quite sure that if the sacred writers spoke of the happiness of the good in a manner exactly similar, no one would doubt that they meant to teach its endless duration. But the question soon rises in the mind, whether the everlasting misery of many of the human race is consistent with the benevolence of God, or with the atonement of Christ. What regard shall I pay to a question like this in ascertaining the meaning of the Bible? None at all. Suppose God had addressed me thus: *This subject hath depths which you cannot fathom. But for the glory of my justice and holiness, and for the benefit of my eternal kingdom, it is my purpose that the wicked, according to their proper desert, shall suffer a punishment without end.* Could any one doubt the fact? Now God does virtually address me in this manner. He plainly teaches this tremendous truth, although he knew all the difficulties which would arise in our minds respecting it. These difficulties he does not undertake to solve. He requires it as a most reasonable thing, and a proper expression of our confidence in him, that we should believe the doctrine which he teaches, notwithstanding its unsearchableness, and that we should believe it to be perfectly accordant with his infinite wisdom and goodness, though we may be unable to see how it is so. But should not the natural horror we feel at the thought of endless misery, and our strong desire that it may be prevented, have an influence upon our judgment as to the meaning of the Scriptures? To answer this, take another case. Our legislators make a law, that every murderer shall be put to death. The words of the law are plain and determinate. But men in general, especially criminals, feel a natural horror at the thought of such a punishment, and a wish that it might not take place. Ought such a feeling to affect the sense they put upon the law, and to lead them to say, *Such cannot be its meaning; it is too dreadful to believe?* Surely not. And for the same reason, the horror we feel at the thought of the endless punishment of impenitent sinners, and our desire that all may be happy, cannot be permitted to have any influence upon us in determining the sense of Scripture. We have no reason to think that God, in making his laws and arranging things in his moral kingdom, was influenced merely by such views and feelings as belong to ignorant imperfect beings. But to make the sense of his laws conform to our views and feelings, would be in effect to attribute our views and feelings, circumscribed, fallible, and disordered as they are, to his infinite mind. It would be saying, that he is subject to all our weaknesses, and is no more influenced by a regard to his own glory and the general interests of his kingdom, then we are. It would, in short, be making God altogether like ourselves. Hence our natural views and feelings as to the propriety or the desirableness of any particular doctrine should not influence our judgment as to the true meaning of the revelation which God has made.

If in the instance now before us, the question should be, whether the endless punishment of the wicked, *admitted to be a certain truth*, has anything in it inconsistent with the dictates of justice or benevolence; we might then direct our reasoning to that point, and might show that it is not inconsistent, and that no valid objection lies against it. But if the *truth* of the doctrine is the subject of inquiry; then we have nothing to do with the justice or utility of endless punishment *as viewed by us*, but must confine ourselves to the single question, whether the Scriptures reveal the fact. If, without any revelation, we were able, in our way of reasoning, to prove to our own satisfaction the justice and the necessity of endless punishment; still this could not be relied upon as the foundation of a confident belief. And after we had, by a process of general reasoning, come to the conclusion, that there must be endless punishment; if the word of God should declare against it, that conclusion of ours would stand for nothing. On the other hand, if we were wholly unable, by any reasoning of ours, to make out the justice or propriety of endless punishment, or to obviate the objections urged against it; this would be no sufficient reason why we should disbelieve it when made known by revelation. From our imperfect wisdom and benevolence we cannot determine what plans a God of infinite wisdom and benevolence will adopt, and how he will compass the ends he has in view.

This then is my position. If our inquiry is whether the wicked will in fact endure endless punishment; the testimony of God, and that only, must be consulted; and our understanding of the meaning of that testimony must not be influenced, one way or the other, by any reasoning of ours as to the consistency of such punishment with the divine benevolence or justice. For while we seem to be reasoning respecting *divine* benevolence and justice, we are in fact reasoning respecting our *own* benevolence and justice. And it is by no means certain, that those measures of government which would agree with such imperfect benevolence and justice as ours, would agree with the infinite benevolence and justice of God. But after we learn from the word of God that the punishment of the wicked will be endless; and after we have given full credence to the fact; it may then be proper and useful for us to attempt, with modesty and caution, to vindicate the divine conduct from the objections of unsanctified reason, and to show, as far as the case admits, that it agrees with acknowledged principles of justice and benevolence.

Take another example. God declared to Abraham, that he should have a son, and that his posterity should be as the stars of heaven for multitude. Abraham knew it was the declaration of God, and as such he believed it, though human reason might have urged strong and unanswerable objections against it. His faith rested simply upon the word of God. The only thing which his reason had to do, was to decide, *that every declaration of God must be true, and worthy of confident belief*, whatever objections may seem to lie against it. And he suffered no objections in the least to influence his mind as to the *meaning* of the divine declaration. This is the main point. Our faith must rest simply upon the divine testimony. It was this which distinguished Abraham's faith, and rendered him worthy of being held up as an example to all believers in after times. *He believed God.* The word of God was the basis and rule of his faith. His reason did nothing but apprehend and believe the divine testimony.

The principle which I have now endeavored to illustrate, would be exceedingly advantageous to ministers, as well as private Christians. We are prone to forget the high authority of God's word, and to treat it with irreverence and neglect. It is too much the fashion of the day, even among Christian ministers, to form opinions respecting the various doctrines and duties of religion, in the way of general reasoning. And if there is an occasional reference to the Scriptures, it is evident that they hold only a secondary place, and that their decision has less influence than the arguments suggested by human reason. In this way, we subject ourselves to a great loss of time, and to great uncertainty and perplexity on the subject of religion. We part with an infallible guide, and take one that is fallible. We give up the divine authority of revelation. And if by mere reasoning we arrive at the knowledge of the truth, and then believe it merely because our reason has discovered it; such faith is not so much the faith of a *Christian*, as of a *rationalist*.

But it is said that reason and philosophy are necessary in order to discover the meaning of God's word. And to show this, the declaration of Christ is adduced: "this is my body." But in this case the proper inquiries are,— *What was the occasion on which the words were spoken? What were the circumstances of the apostles to whom they were spoken? What object had Christ in view? What had been his manner of speaking? What sort of metaphors had he been accustomed to use? How would his apostles naturally understand his words?* Now this is not *philosophizing*. The apostles had no need of *philosophy* in order to understand this declaration of Christ, any more than they had to understand him, when he said, "I am the *vine;* ye are the *branches.*" Apprehending the meaning of figurative language is not, properly speaking, a matter of philosophical *reasoning*, but a matter of *common sense and feeling*. If *philosophy* should be applied to the declaration of Christ, "this is my body," it must relate to the propriety and utility of metaphorical language; and so must lead to an analysis of those principles of the mind which make such language natural, and which account for its effects. But the right understanding of metaphorical language and its proper influence on the mind is no more dependent on any reasoning of this kind, than eating and digesting food is dependent on our understanding the physiology of those parts of the body which are particularly concerned in eating and digestion.

I do not say that philosophical reasoning on the subject of religion is in all cases to be rejected. My position is, that it cannot be considered as necessary in determining the sense of Scripture. And I should suppose that any one must be satisfied of this, when he considers, that those to whom the sacred writers addressed themselves, were not philosophers, and that if philosophy was necessary to the right understanding of God's word, they were incapable of knowing the truth, and were tied down to unavoidable ignorance and error.* But neither Christ nor his apostles

* "The preacher is to make the truth of Scripture the burden of his communications to his people, because this is a message which can be *easily understood.* It is brought down to the comprehension of a common religious assembly. It is the *simplicity* of scriptural truth, which adapts it to all classes of hearers." — "But of all modes of communication, the language of metaphysical philosophy is the

ever represent philosophical knowledge, or a capacity for metaphysical reasoning, to be at all necessary to those who would learn the truths of religion. What they insist upon as necessary is, a humble, docile, and obedient disposition, and prayer to God for the teaching of his Spirit. "If any man will do his will, he shall know of the doctrine." — "If any man lack wisdom, let him ask it of God." Instead of giving countenance to philosophizing in religion, the sacred writers directly discountenance it. When some inquired, "*how* are the dead raised?" the Apostle did not give them *the philosophy of the resurrection.* The argument he used to confute their objection was *rhetorical*, not *philosophical.* He vindicated an important doctrine of revelation by an apt analogy taken from the natural world; — as Christ illustrated and enforced an important duty, by referring to the fowls of the air, and to the lilies of the field. If that reasoning which is strictly *philosophical*, may ever be used on the subject of religion, it must be for the purpose of illustrating a doctrine or precept already made known, and vindicating it against objections. In some cases, the philosophy of the mind may afford assistance in accomplishing these objects. And those men, who carry their habit of speculation too far, and are more in alliance with philosophy than with Christianity, may sometimes have their defective faith aided and strengthened by finding an agreement between the principles of mental science and the doctrines of revelation. But their faith would stand in no need of such help, if it relied,

---

least adapted to the understanding of an ordinary congregation. Philosophical preaching requires a philosophical audience." — "How is a plain man to arrive at a knowledge of religious truth, by the refinements of metaphysical reasoning? Suppose he makes the attempt. He has a new science to learn; a science abounding in nice distinctions; requiring an analysis of the faculties and operations of the mind; and embracing a knowledge of the relations of cause and effect, powers and susceptibilities, motives and actions. If he looks to the pulpit for instruction on these subjects, he is involved in the mysteries of metaphysical phraseology. His minister speaks to him in an unknown tongue. He finds that he has not only a new science, but a new language to learn." — "If metaphysical philosophy had been necessary to salvation, it would seem that the Bible would have given us a new metaphysical language."

President Day's Sermon on the Christian Minister's Commission.

as the faith of Abraham did, with unwavering confidence on the word of God. Besides; those Christians who rest their faith entirely on the divine testimony are, much more likely to have a correct understanding of that testimony, than those who rest their faith partly on that, and partly on the deductions of speculative reason. And it is very easy to see which kind of faith does the greater honor to the word and the veracity of God.*

---

* On the subject here under discussion, the views expressed by President Day in the sermon before referred to are so just and seasonable, that I shall quote a few more passages.

"The evidence of Scripture truth is the testimony of God himself. Here human reason has no right to interfere. It is bound to stand aside and hear what God the Lord hath said. Reason decides, indeed, and decides intuitively, that the word of the God of truth is to be believed. It is bound to submit implicitly to the divine declarations, whatever they may be. Here is the distinction between faith and mere reason. The truths which God reveals to us, may or may not accord with the opinions which we ourselves had formed. Their previous probability or improbability is, therefore, no ground on which we are to receive or reject them, when we find them in the word of God. It is not a sound principle of interpretation, to determine before-hand what doctrines *ought* to be found, or are probably found in the Bible, and therefore to make it speak a language in conformity with our pre-conceived opinions. The Scriptural evidence in favor of any doctrine is wholly independent on the probability furnished by reason alone without the aid of revelation. This evidence is the simple testimony of God. It is neither weakened nor strengthened by any previous opinion which we had formed on the subject revealed. The doctrines of metaphysical philosophy ought to have no influence in determining the doctrines of the Bible. If the language of Scripture is to be so explained, as to conform invariably to probabilities suggested by reason, then it is no revelation. It makes known to us no new truths. It can decide no controverted point. For each contending party will give the passages referred to as proofs, the meaning which accords with its own opinions. This is the great reason why the various denominations of Christians make, ordinarily, no approaches towards agreement in doctrine, by discussions which professedly refer to the Scriptures as a common rule of faith. In truth, each party, instead of making the Scriptures the only standard of belief, makes his own opinions, to some extent at least, the standard of Scripture. If the book of God is to be interpreted according to pre-conceived philosophical opinions, it will not be *one* Bible but *many*. It will be made to contain as many different systems of doctrines, as there are different schemes of philosophy brought forward to give a construction to its contents. It may be necessary, in interpreting the Scriptures, to take into consideration the opinions and modes of thinking of the classes of persons to whom they were *originally addressed.* The true point of inquiry is, how did *they*, if they were candid, understand what was said to them. How did the children of Israel understand Moses? How did the primitive Christians understand Christ and his apostles?

I have extended my remarks to such a length, because I conceive the point under consideration to be of primary importance, and because I think it would conduce in a high degree to our benefit as Christians, and to our usefulness as ministers, if we could bring ourselves to such a habit of mind as to make it our single inquiry, *what doctrine God has revealed in his word;* but never to make the inquiry, so incompatible with the character of Christians, *whether the doctrine which God has revealed is true.* You may perhaps think it needless to dwell longer on the general principle I have stated. But I am desirous of giving so clear an illustration of it, that no one can fail of understanding it aright. Let me therefore apply it to the question of Christ's character. This is a subject of pure revelation. Our inquiry is, what do the Scriptures teach? But a difficulty arises. *How can it be that Jesus Christ is God, when there is only one God, the Father?* What influence shall a difficulty of this kind have upon us in determining the meaning of the divine testimony? None. Suppose we are totally unable to reconcile the doctrine of Christ's divinity with the doctrine of the divine unity. What then? We are not required to reconcile them. Our business is to determine *philologically* and *historically* what the inspired writers taught, just as we determine what Athanasius or Arius taught. The only difference between the two cases, which I need to notice, is this; that the very doctrine which the inspired writers taught is the doctrine which we are unhesitatingly to receive as true; but as to the doctrine of Athanasius or Arius, we are to believe it or not, as we find it supported by proper evidence. The one is directly binding upon our faith; the other not. But the method of determining what doctrine was taught, is substantially the same in both cases. Now suppose you make it your object to inquire what doctrine Athanasius taught. Would you think it proper that your views of the consistency or inconsistency of his doctrine should influence you in determining what his doctrine actually was? You would look for the usus loquendi. You would take into view all the circumstances of the writer, and of the time when he wrote. But in ascertaining what doctrine he held, you certainly would not first inquire whether, agreeably to your mode of reasoning, the doctrine was philosophically correct, and then conclude that it was his doctrine or not, according as it agreed or disagreed with your notions. No enlightened and impartial man ever proceeded in this manner in determining what opinions were maintained by any *uninspired* writer. And no one can with propriety proceed in this manner in determining what doctrines were maintained by the inspired writers. Suppose a man should release his mind, as the German Rationalists have released theirs, from the idea that the sacred writers were inspired, and from all sense of obligation to believe what they taught. He could then pursue the question, what doctrines they taught, without being embarrassed with any reasonings about the consistency or inconsistency of those doctrines. So some of the most learned Rationalists have pursued it. And so ought we. Those Rationalists have in some important instances, decided, that the Scriptures teach the doctrines which we hold. In this we agree with them. But we go farther, and hold this sense of Scripture to be according to truth, and make it the foundation and rule of our faith.

But you ask, whether in determining the meaning of the divine declarations, we are not to have respect to the moral sentiments and feelings which are inseparable from the constitution of human nature. My answer is, that if in any case, we do this, it should be with great caution. If the divine declaration is unambiguous, and its meaning obvious, it is to be received on the ground of its own authority, whether it agrees or not with our moral sentiments and feelings; and for this plain reason, that our moral sentiments and feelings may rest on defective or partial views of things. God commanded Abraham to offer up his son Isaac as a sacrifice. Abraham had the same moral sentiments and natural feelings as we have. If his moral sense had been consulted, must it not have decided, that killing a man, especially a son, would be exceedingly unnatural, inhuman and wicked, and that a kind and merciful God would forever disapprove of it? How could Abraham then believe that God actually commanded it? Certainly he could not, if he had formed his opinion of the meaning of the divine declaration in the manner above mentioned. But he had one moral sentiment, which was paramount to all others, and controlled all others; and that was, that *whatever God says is right.* He knew that God commanded him to perform the deed. He consulted not with flesh and blood; he consulted not with his own sensibilities, as a parent; he consulted not even with the sentiments which belonged to his moral nature respecting the evil of slaying a man. Nor did he inquire how this command could be consistent with the previous promise of God, or with the command not to kill. He yielded entirely to the authority of God's command. He had higher confidence in God's perfections, than in the dictates of his own moral nature; — and he acted against all those dictates, except that one which was superior to all others, and which is indeed the highest moral principle proper to the human mind, namely; *that God is to be believed and obeyed.* In any such case, it is evident that an attempt to model the meaning of God's word according to our own speculative notions or natural feelings would lead us far astray, and that the right meaning of God's word is that which readily suggests itself to the docile, obedient, pious heart.

But after we have ascertained the doctrine of revelation, and have received it as the matter of our faith, the question often arises, whether such doctrine agrees with the common principles of reasoning, or with facts which occur in the natural or moral world. This may be a suitable inquiry, and we may sometimes find it advantageous to pursue it with all the means in our power. But the result of this inquiry is not to affect our belief of the doctrine revealed. If the doctrine agrees with the common principles of reasoning, or with known facts in the natural or moral world; this we shall consider a pleasing circumstance, and one which will enable us to silence the objections of unbelievers. This may be the case with the doctrine, taught in Rom. v. respecting the evils which are brought upon the posterity of Adam by means of his one offence. It is very easy to make out an analogy between this divine constitution, and events which continually take place. But this analogy is not the ground of our faith in the doctrine. For should we be wholly unable to make out any such analogy, we should still believe the doctrine taught by the inspired writers, *simply because it is thus taught.* And supposing that to be the case, instead of attempting to do what is beyond our power, it would become us frankly to acknowledge, that the doctrine differs from the deductions of reason in other cases, and has no analogy to truths otherwise made known. An acknowledgment like this is as consistent with our cordial belief of a doctrine made known by revelation, as it is with our belief of any principle of magnetism or electricity, which has no analogy to other principles in the science of physics. Such an acknowledgment should be made by every Christian, in regard to the Scripture doctrine of Father, Son, and Holy Spirit, and the doctrine of Christ's person, as including divine and human attributes. Refusing to make this acknowledgment, and attempting to find something among created beings which would be analogous to this peculiar mode of existence, has occasioned needless perplexity, and has done much to turn off the minds of men from the only true ground of Christian faith, *the divine testimony.*

But I have another remark, which, though it may seem very evident, deserves a careful consideration. The Protestant principle of making the Bible our only and sufficient standard requires that we should conform to it, both as to the *matter* and the *manner* of teaching.

I can best explain my meaning by an example. The sacred writers teach the important doctrine, that Christ made an atonement for the sins of men. But in what *manner* do they teach this doctrine? How do they set it forth? Sometimes they represent, that Christ *died for us;* sometimes, that he *died for our sins;* sometimes, that he was a *sin-offering*, that he *bare our sins in his own body on the tree*, and that *God laid on him the iniquities of us all;* sometimes, that he was *a propitiation for our sins*, that he *redeemed us*, that he *reconciled us to God*, etc. Now when we teach the doctrine of the atonement, this is the *kind* of representation we should make. The Scriptures use a great variety in the manner of exhibiting the subject; so should we. But how various soever the manner in which we exhibit the doctrine, we should keep our eye upon the manner in which it is set forth in the Scriptures, and should not only avoid whatever would be inconsistent with that, but should make it manifest, that we derive our conceptions of the doctrine, and our mode of teaching, from the Bible. If we undertake to explain it, and to reason upon it; our explanation and reasoning should be such as will correspond with the current language of the inspired writers; and such as will make it natural and congruous for us freely to quote that language, and intermix it with our own explanations and reasonings. In short we must make it manifest that we delight in the Scripture representation and Scripture phraseology, and consider it best suited to the nature of the subject; and on this we must build all our logic, and all our rhetoric. Now turn your thoughts to those preachers and writers who carry their fondness for philosophical investigation into the subject of religion, and see how they exhibit the doctrine of Christ's atonement, and then say, whether there is any appearance of their regarding the Bible as their only and sufficient guide. If they do so regard it, how comes it to pass that they seldom, if ever, set forth this principle of religion in the light in which it is set forth by the inspired writers? How does it happen that a doctrine, which always appears in the Scriptures so obvious, and so full of vital warmth and energy, comes in their hands to be so cold, and speculative, and lifeless, and so remote from common apprehension?

But perhaps a question may arise in the minds of some, whether the principle I have laid down will exactly hold at the present day; whether the change which has taken place in the mode of thinking, the prevalence of a new set of errors, the new systems of education, — in a word, whether the new circumstances of man, do not call for a change both as to the matter and manner of religious instruction.

To this I reply: that no change has taken place, which materially affects the subject under consideration. Man's relation to God, to the moral law, to Christ, and to his fellow creatures, — is the same now, as it was when the Scriptures were written. Man has the same faculties, dispositions, passions, appetites, — the same deceitfulness, and selfishness, and perverseness of heart, the same backwardness to feel and acknowledge his obligations to be holy, the same unwillingness to forsake his sins and come to Christ, and the same propensity to justify himself. Generally, the same false opinions prevailed formerly, as those which prevail now. What kind of error in regard to the subject of religion can be found at the present day, to which there is not some reference in the Scriptures? It is manifest, that not only the more flagrant errors, but all the slighter departures from the simplicity of the gospel, as to doctrine and practice, are more or less noticed and rebuked by the sacred writers.

It is also true, that the salvation provided for man, and the way of obtaining it, are subject to no change. The repentance, faith and obedience required, are always the same. Sinners in all ages and circumstances have the same need of the influence of the Holy Spirit. What Christ said to Nicodemus is as true and important now, as it was then. The renewal of sinners is the work of God in as high a sense at the present day, as formerly.

As therefore man's nature, relations, and duties, and other circumstances, so far as religion is concerned, are always the same; there can be no occasion for any material change, either in the matter or manner of religious instruction. If Christ and his apostles were to appear among us and to teach the doctrines and duties of religion at the present day; is there not every reason to think that they would teach the same things, and much in the same manner, as they did eighteen hundred years ago? Whatever changes have taken place in the world since the days of inspiration, there has been and can be no change, which materially affects the subject of religion; and what was true and important in doctrine, and suitable in the manner of teaching, in the time of Christ and the apostles, must be so now.

If we suppose it is left to our discretion what doctrines and precepts of the Bible shall be preached at the present day, and what omitted, or in what manner these doctrines and precepts shall be explained and inculcated; and if we suppose that the word of God is not to be taken as our standard in these respects; then we should consider ourselves at liberty, to omit in part, or altogether, the perfect obligation of man to obey the divine law, his depravity and ruin, the necessity of divine influence, the sovereignty of God's grace, justification by faith, the duty of obedience, self-denial, forgiveness of injuries, and any other doctrine or duty inculcated in the Scriptures; or if we should not wholly omit them, we should feel ourselves at liberty to receive them, and exhibit them to others, in a very different light from that in which the Bible exhibits them. And where should we stop? What limits could be set to our deviation from the principles contained in the word of God?

LETTER III.

Brethren and Friends,

Is has for years been a subject of inquiry with me, whether my own mode of preaching, and that which is common among evangelical ministers, is sufficiently *Scriptural;* whether, as to matter and manner, it is conformed, as much as it should be, to that inspired book which we profess to receive as our perfect and infallible rule; whether we have not adopted a manner of thinking and of preaching, which more or less sets aside the inspired volume; and whether in this way we do not dishonor the benevolent Author of revelation, deprive our hearers of the sincere milk of the word, and spend time and labor upon that which profiteth not. The result of my inquiries is a serious apprehension, that the literature of modern times, the endless variety of books which have been written on moral and religious subjects, and which contain a greater or less mixture of error with truth, the numberless controversies which prevail among Christians, and the want of a more diligent study of the Scriptures and of a larger measure of piety, expose us to the danger of being turned aside from the simplicity that is in Christ." This apprehension has respected my own case as really as that of any of my brethren in the ministry. Now if there is the least danger on this subject, it is important that we should be aware of it. For a small mistake among those who are set for the defence of the gospel, may be the occasion of great mischief to the church of Christ.

The remarkable success of the gospel, as preached by its ministers at different times, is no reason why we should suppress our fears, and abstain from such an inquiry as I propose. Any one who has been a careful observer of human nature, and who is at all acquainted with the history of the church, knows full well that a time of prosperity is a time of special danger. The same rain and sunshine which produce a plentiful harvest of wheat, may contribute also to an uncommon growth of tares. What season of unusual prosperity has the church ever enjoyed, which has not, through the corruption of man's heart, proved a season of danger, and an occasion of lamentable evils? In proportion then as God has been pleased to pour out his Spirit and revive his work, and to give enlargement to his people; just in that proportion have we cause to be awake, and to guard against the designs of our enemy, who is always plotting against the church, and is never better pleased than when he sees us lulled to sleep by prosperity. If any man shall look abroad upon the wonderful work of God which has been accomplished in our country by means of the word preached, and shall hence be led to say, *there is no longer any danger to the church, and any fears respecting the cause of Christ, are all out of place;* that man has to learn a most important lesson; and the sooner he applies for instruction to the word and providence of God the better. The inspired writers teach us to rejoice with trembling, to be vigilant, and to exercise a godly jealousy.

Allow me then to proceed with my design, and to remark particularly on the subject of man's *moral obligation;*—a subject very plain and simple in itself, but easily perplexed and obscured. My general inquiry is, whether this subject is not often treated in a manner which ill accords with our infallible standard.

What then is the doctrine of *moral obligation?* Expressed in the simplest, easiest manner, it is this: *We are in duty bound to obey the divine commands.* In other words, *we ought in all respects to conform to the moral law.* Or thus, *it is just and right that we should be what God requires us to be; and we are altogether inexcusable if we fail of this.*

I next inquire, what proof there is of this high obligation? And my answer is, that it is so evident and certain that, properly speaking, it does not need proof. There is nothing more evident. Let a man's heart be pure from sin, his conscience awake and active, and his affections holy; and let him, in this state of mind, look up, and see the glorious character of God, as exhibited in the works of creation, providence, and redemption; and then let him hear God announce the first and great command: "Thou shalt love the Lord thy God with all thy heart, and with all thy soul, and with all thy mind, and with all thy strength." Would that man need any argument to *prove* his obligation to love such a Being? Do the angels need to have it *proved* to them, that they ought to love the God of heaven? And when a sinner is renewed, and has a clear spiritual discernment and purity of heart, does he need to have it *proved*, that he is under obligation to love and obey God?

These remarks disclose an important principle, namely; that *the feeling of obligation is founded in the very constitution of the human mind;* that it is an ultimate fact in our moral nature. And this is only saying, that God has made us moral and accountable creatures; that he has so formed us, that we are the proper subjects of law, and have an inward consciousness that obedience is our duty, and that disobedience is totally wrong and worthy of punishment. Were it not for this constitution of our mind, no argument could ever convince us that we are under any obligation to love God; no increase of knowledge, no improvement of our faculties, no persuasion, could ever give us a *feeling* of such obligation.

As to the reality and extent of our moral obligation, and the vast importance of acknowledging and feeling it, I scarcely have words to express myself so strongly as I wish. That we are moral and accountable beings is, in my view, just as certain as our existence. And our eternal interests require, that we should have a deep impression of it. Our moral agency and moral obligation is not only certain, but *perfect.* Of course, it does not depend upon our character. Our being holy does not originate our obligation; nor does our being sinful destroy it. We are equally under law, and equally bound to obey it, whether our character is good or bad. The propriety of our being placed under law, and our obligation to obey it, depends upon those intellectual and moral faculties with which our Creator has endued us, and which we always continue to possess, whatever may be our character, or our external circumstances. Those who are to the last degree depraved, have still a perfect moral agency. It is indestructible. We can no more be rid of it, than of our existence. To whom did God give the law at Sinai? Of whom did he require obedience? Of perfectly holy beings? No; but of those who were sinful; for the most part, of those who were entirely sinful. And did Moses, who spoke in the name of God, ever intimate that there was to be any abatement of the high demands of the law on account of the sinfulness of man? Did the prophets, or Christ, or the apostles ever intimate such a thing? The fact is, no messenger of God, either under the former or the latter dispensation, ever gave a single divine command to any persons who were without sin. There was no opportunity for this. All whom the prophets, and Christ, and the apostles addressed, were sinners. And yet they required them to love God with all the heart, and to be perfectly and unceasingly holy. It was certainly just and right that men should comply with these requisitions. In other words, they were under obligation to love God and obey his commands.

This is always made evident by that influence of the Spirit which frees the minds of sinners from darkness and delusion, and causes them to know divine truth. They who are taught of the Spirit, are convinced of sin. They are sensible that they are and always have been under perfect obligation to love and obey God, and that they have no excuse for transgression. They acknowledge from the heart that the law is good, and that they ought to have kept it constantly and perfectly; that in disobeying the law, they have acted a most unreasonable and wicked part, and that they really deserve the punishment which the law denounces against those who transgress. All this sinners feel and acknowledge, when they are thoroughly convinced of sin, and judge of things according to truth. One who is only in part convinced of sin, feels and acknowledges this in part. His conscience is disturbed, but not fully awakened. He is so blinded by his selfish feelings, that he regards the very depravity which renders him ill-deserving in the sight of God, as an alleviation of his guilt. But thorough conviction of sin by the Holy Spirit sweeps away all these refuges, and brings the sinner, ashamed and trembling, to smite upon his breast, and say, *God be merciful to me a sinner.* Those who are thoughtless and quiet in sin have many false conceptions, which can never be removed, except by that Holy Spirit which Christ promised to convince the world of sin. On our part, if we would do that which is best adapted to convince men of sin, we must clearly explain to them the commands of the law and the gospel, and must urge them to immediate and constant obedience, as their reasonable service, and that which God absolutely requires. We must endeavor to persuade them to this by all the motives suggested by the word of God. And we must make it as evident to them as possible, that the delay of obedience is continued rebellion. If they excuse themselves because they are depraved, and say, you require too much; tell them that you only convey God's message to them; that you require only what he requires; that their complaints are against him; that their controversy is with their Maker. Show them the absurdity and presumption of supposing that God can abate anything of his demands upon them, *because they are sinners.* And never leave them to think that the long continuance and high degree of their sinfulness, or its early date, can have any other effect than to increase their guilt, and render them the more inexcusable. Address the commands of God to them with great seriousness. Show them that you consider these commands perfectly just; that you are in earnest when you inculcate obedience; that you regard them as under the highest conceivable obligation to obey the divine law in all its length and breadth, and as meriting the displeasure of God for failing to do this. In a word, show them that you heartily join with God, and approve of his high and spiritual commands *as addressed to sinners*, and of the sentence of condemnation which he pronounces against every one who disobeys.

As to the proper manner of exhibiting and inculcating moral obligation, we are to derive our lessons primarily and chiefly from the Holy Scriptures. We are to look much more than we have commonly done to the inspired teachers, as our models. They certainly had true practical wisdom, and their method of teaching was founded on just views of the human mind and character, and perfectly adapted to promote the highest good of the world. We are accustomed to celebrate the sacred writers, as affording the best examples of a just and impressive eloquence,—an eloquence suited to awaken conscience, and move all the springs of human action. Now we should act very inconsistently with ourselves, if after all our admiration of the Bible as a perfect model of what is eloquent and just and useful in the manner of teaching, we should not be careful to copy it. I earnestly hope that the extraordinary attention which is now given to the Scriptures by theological students, and by ministers of the gospel, will produce happy results, and that the common mode of preaching will become much more *Scriptural* than it has been. And I hope, too, that the growing attention to the Bible in our Christian community, and especially among the young, will contribute effectually to form such a taste, that no preacher can be acceptable to the public, unless he faithfully conforms to the infallible standard. Let us then seriously and patiently inquire, in what manner the momentous subject of our moral obligation is treated in the Holy Scriptures.

The first thing which occurs is, that the inspired writers do not formally *assert*, nor attempt by a process of reasoning to *prove*, our obligation to obey the divine commands, but assume it as a well known and acknowledged fact. In this they are fully justified; and in this we ought, certainly in all ordinary cases, to imitate them; because the feeling of obligation originally arises not from the force of arguments, but from the very constitution of our nature, and always exists in full strength when the mind is in a right state, and has the proper objects in view. It is as evidently proper, that a religious teacher should take it for granted that men are in fact moral and accountable beings, and under obligation to obey the divine law, as it is for a teacher of optics to take it for granted that his pupils have the sense of seeing; or for a teacher of geometry, that his pupils have the faculty of understanding. And in ordinary cases, why should it be thought any more necessary in moral and religious discourse, either to *prove* or to *assert* the fact, that we are accountable beings and under obligation to obey God, than in philosophical discourse to assert and prove that we are endued with various bodily senses and intellectual faculties, which render us capable of observing the physical world, and understanding philosophical truth? The teacher of natural philosophy says nothing, except incidentally, of these senses and faculties. He does not undertake directly to treat of them, and has no need to do it. Indeed he does not consider this to be within his province. He takes it for granted that we are what we are, and proceeds immediately to teach the principles of his science. The same with the mathematician. Euclid does not begin his system of geometry by affirming and attempting to prove, that we have eyes to see his diagrams, and a mind to understand his maxims and propositions. Should he affirm this and labor ever so long to prove it, he would make it no more evident to us than it was before. He has therefore nothing to do with this, but proceeds at once to give his maxims, and to lay down and demonstrate his propositions.

The inspired teachers generally act on the same principle. It is always manifestly implied in their instructions, that we possess the faculties of intelligent and accountable agents. But where do they directly *affirm* this? Where do they produce any *proof* of it? Nowhere. They take it for granted.

In order to get an exact idea of the manner in which the

inspired teachers proceed in regard to man's moral obligation, let us examine some of the great occasions on which truth is taught and duty enjoined in the Scriptures.

We begin with the giving of the law. The Lord descended upon Mount Sinai amid terrible thunders and lightnings; and Moses brought the people out of the camp to meet with God, and to hear his words. Now what did God say to them? In what manner did he inculcate their duty upon them? Did he begin by telling them that they had all the powers and faculties necessary to moral agency; that they were free, and accountable, and under obligation to obey? Nothing of this. "He spake all these words, saying, *I am the Lord thy God who have brought thee out of the land of Egypt, out of the house of bondage. Thou shalt have no other gods before me. Thou shalt not make unto thee any graven image. — Thou shalt not take the name of the Lord thy God in vain. — Remember the Sabbath day to keep it holy. — Honor thy father and thy mother,*" etc. He simply gave his law; simply announced his commands to the people. Their being under obligation to render obedience was asserted in no other way, than by merely giving the commands. No proof was given, as it was a well known and acknowledged fact. And how was it with Moses, who afterwards labored so particularly, and with an eloquence so powerful and moving, to enforce obedience upon the children of Israel? We have, in Deuteronomy, an account of his faithful and impressive address to the people, containing doctrines, precepts, warnings, threats, exhortations, and a recital of God's favors, and of their sins, in a great variety of forms. But where is the passage in the whole book, in which he asserted the fact of their moral agency, or gave them a description of those powers and faculties which constituted them moral agents, and made it just and proper that they should keep God's law, and be accountable to him for their actions? Let us peruse and re-peruse this remarkable book, till we are imbued with its contents. In this way we may do much towards learning the art of plain, pungent, affectionate, powerful, and profitable preaching. And it may be of some use to make the supposition, that Moses himself were now here, laboring among us as a religious teacher, and retaining the same views of man's obligation and man's sinfulness, and the same manner of setting them forth, which he had when he addressed the children of Israel after they had spent forty years in the wilderness. Might not his example correct some common faults in our manner of preaching, and give us a taste for greater seriousness, simplicity, and faithfulness? And if any of us, with our present habits, should stand forth and preach in his presence; what would he think of us? Would it not be a matter of wonder to him, that with all the advantages of the new dispensation, as well as the old, we had attained to no higher excellence? Let us more carefully study the Book of Deuteronomy, and more faithfully copy the model of sacred eloquence which it contains.

But we must consider other occasions on which truth was taught and duty inculcated.

Look then at the instances in which the prophets, from age to age, gave instruction, warning, reproof, and exhortation. Dwell upon those passages in their writings, where they undertook, with the greatest particularity, to teach men their duty and their guilt, and to urge them to repentance. Is there a single sentence which shows, that they ever stopped to assert and prove the doctrine of moral agency, or to inquire into the grounds of moral obligation, as ministers often do at the present day? Did they not always assume it as a thing too evident to need any proof, that man is a moral agent, and in duty bound to obey the commands of God?

Take a higher example still, that of Jesus Christ. Look at the manner of his teaching in his sermon on the mount. Read the beginning, and the middle, and the end of it. Read his parables; his conversations with his disciples; his addresses to unbelievers, to objectors, to cavillers. Never man spake as he spake. He is a perfect model. Who has studied this model as much as he ought?

Read also the addresses of Peter, of Stephen, and of Paul, in the Acts. Read the epistles, especially the Epistle to the

Romans, in a part of which the Apostle undertook to reason with those who made some of the doctrines of the gospel an occasion to excuse and justify themselves in sin. Where do any of these infallible teachers undertake to prove by metaphysical reasonings, where do they even *assert*, that those, to whom they gave instruction, were endued with the powers of moral agency, and that it was just and reasonable they should be under law? What reason have we to suppose, from what appears in holy writ, that they ever deemed it necessary or proper to assert and prove this? That man is in fact an intelligent and moral being, and a proper subject of law, is a truth perfectly plain and certain; and no affirmation or argument can make it more so. If a man has lost his natural consciousness of being a moral and accountable agent, there is little prospect of convincing him by philosophical reasoning. The degradation of his mind is of such a nature, that reasoning cannot remove it. To one who is free from this mental degradation, an inquiry into the grounds of moral obligation cannot be at all necessary. To pursue such an inquiry in any case is not the province of the preacher, but of the metaphysician. Yet while it is evident that the inspired writers do not make it their practice to prove or even to assert the fact, that we are moral agents, any more than they assert and prove that we have souls; it is also evident, that they have much to *do* with this fact. Whenever they address men, they address them as moral and accountable beings, and as under immutable obligations to obey the divine commands. And it is an object at which they constantly aim, to awaken in the minds of men a proper *sense* of this obligation. But by what means do they attempt to do this? Not, I repeat it, by asserting our moral agency; or by exhibiting the grounds of our obligation; (a business appropriate to the science of metaphysics, or mental philosophy;) but by holding up plain, obvious, certain truth; and this they do in a great variety of ways, giving to every one his portion. A few instances will show something of the Scriptural manner of awakening men to a sense of moral obligation.

Take then the case of David, when visited by the Prophet

Nathan. David had committed an offence against God, and greatly injured a faithful servant. But his conscience was stupefied, and he had no proper feeling of the obligation which he had violated. Nathan said not a word about conscience, or moral sense, or the grounds of moral agency; but he stated a case. There were two men, one rich, and the other poor. The rich man had exceeding many flocks and herds; and the poor man had nothing but one little ewe lamb. And the rich man spared to take of his own flocks to dress for a traveller, but took the poor man's lamb. David, looking at this deed as committed by another, and having his judgment thus freed from the bias of self-love, instantly pronounced the man who had done it worthy of death. Nathan then charged the deed upon David. "Thou art the man." David's conscience was roused; and with a penitent heart he said, "I have sinned against the Lord."

Jesus, with consummate skill, made use of the same principle in his parables. Always fixing upon the particular truth which was appropriate to the case, he presented it to view with great clearness, and in a manner perfectly adapted to guard against the blinding influence of passion, to suppress the disposition of men to self-justification, thoroughly to awaken their consciences, and to induce them to pass a just sentence upon themselves. There is no part of Scripture, from which we can derive more useful lessons as to the best manner of exhibiting the truths of religion in public and in private, than the parables of Christ. Let us study them again and again, and with increasing interest, for this very purpose.

When Peter addressed the Jews on the day of Pentecost, he did not go about to prove to them that they were moral and accountable beings, but by a proper exhibition of those truths which were specially applicable to their case, and suited to awaken their moral faculties, made them *feel* that they were moral and accountable. He charged them with crucifying Jesus of Nazareth, whom God had made both Lord and Christ. His discourse brought things to view which affected their consciences and their hearts, and led them to say, "Men and brethren, what shall we do?"

See how the Apostle Paul labors to awaken in the unbelieving and self-righteous Jews a sense of their violated obligations and their ill-desert. Instead of declaring to them that they have a conscience, he declares those plain and pungent truths which are suited to rouse conscience from its slumbers. Instead of telling them that they are intelligent moral agents, he endeavors to convince them that they are *sinners without excuse.* And what considerations does he address to them for this purpose? They are considerations adapted, not to an abstract intellect, but to the conscience and the heart. He says: "Therefore thou art inexcusable, O man, whosoever thou art, that judgest: for wherein thou judgest another, thou condemnest thyself; for thou that judgest doest the same things. But we are sure that the judgment of God is according to truth against them who commit such things. And thinkest thou this, O man, that judgest them who do such things, and doest the same, that thou shalt escape the judgment of God? Or despisest thou the riches of his goodness, and forbearance, and long-suffering; not knowing that the goodness of God leadeth thee to repentance? But after thy hardness and impenitent heart, treasurest up to thyself wrath against the day of wrath and revelation of the righteous judgment of God; who will render to every man according to his deeds." — "Behold, thou art called a Jew, and restest in the law, and makest thy boast of God, and knowest his will, and approvest the things which are more excellent, being instructed out of the law, and art confident that thou thyself art a guide of the blind, a light to them who are in darkness, etc. Thou therefore who teachest another, teachest thou not thyself? Thou that preachest a man should not steal, dost thou steal? Thou that sayest, a man should not commit adultery, dost thou commit adultery? — Thou that makest thy boast of the law, through breaking the law dishonorest thou God?"

This is only one instance of the plain, skilful, impressive manner, in which Paul labored to convince men of sin. Numerous other instances, equally striking, might easily be produced.

Go through the Scriptures, and you will find it a general fact, that those teachers who were endued with wisdom from above, labored to impress the minds of men with a sense of their obligation as moral agents, not by asserting the fact of their moral agency, nor by discoursing on the grounds of moral obligation, but by holding forth and applying those momentous truths, which were adapted to awaken their moral faculties, to convince them of sin, and lead them to repentance.

Now, brethren, what better can we do, than to make ourselves familiar with the manner in which Christ and his prophets and apostles treated this momentous subject, and to regard them as our models? Who is able to make improvements upon the honest, affectionate, and faithful manner of the inspired teachers? Happy shall we be if, by all our efforts, we come up half way to this exalted and perfect standard. Let us study the sacred volume with more intenseness of thought, and more of the spirit of prayer; so that we may have our habit of thinking, reasoning, and feeling, and our mode of teaching, formed on this divine model.

We come then to these results. The general and important fact, that man is a moral agent, and under perfect obligation to obey the divine law, is so evident and certain, that it needs no proof, and may properly be taken for granted by Christian preachers. Still, in consequence of the great spiritual blindness and stupidity which sin has brought upon the minds of men, much needs to be done to awaken them to a lively perception of their moral existence, and their high moral obligations. But what is the best manner of doing this? The inspired teachers labor to do it, not by directly asserting and proving that we have a moral nature, (which would be like asserting and proving to men whom you invite to see a picture or a landscape, that they have eyes, and are able to see; or to men whom you invite to a concert of music, that they have ears to hear;) but they labor to do it by a clear exhibition of the most important objects, — by an earnest and faithful declaration of the most plain, sacred, and moving truths. Let us pursue the same object in the same way, honoring the inspired volume, diligently following our infallible guide, and faithfully preaching God's holy law and the gospel of Christ, so that our hearers may never have cause to complain, that when they come as poor, perishing sinners, hungering for the bread of life, they are treated with a dry dissertation on the philosophy of the law, or the philosophy of the gospel.

NOTE.—As the remaining Letters in this series relate to subjects which have been particularly considered in a previous part of this publication, they are here omitted.

ESSAYS

ON THE

PHILOSOPHY OF THE MIND.*

NUMBER I.

MENTAL ACTS TO BE CLASSIFIED, AND REFERRED TO MENTAL FACULTIES. USE OF THE WORDS WILL, VOLITION, AFFECTION, AND VOLUNTARY.

IN this series of Essays on the *Philosophy of the Mind*, it is far from my design to bring forward the whole range of topics commonly treated in systems of mental philosophy. My design is to attend specially to those parts of the general subject, which have usually received a less degree of attention than they seem to deserve; — to those parts also which are attended with uncommon difficulties; — and most of all to those, which have an important bearing on moral and theological subjects. I shall do all in my power to free every subject which comes under discussion, from an indefinite and vague phraseology, and to present it in a clear and satisfactory light; and thus, so far as my honest endeavors shall avail, to promote a just mode of thinking and speaking, particularly among young ministers and theological students.

---

* First published in the Literary and Theological Review, 1834.

The philosophy of the mind is the knowledge and scientific description of *man*, considered as intelligent and moral. A careful attention to this point will frequently be of use in preserving us from confusion and mistake. Suppose we are perplexed in our inquiries respecting the nature and operations of the intellectual or moral *faculties;* the perplexity may often be removed by shifting our language and our mode of investigation, and making our inquiries relate to *man himself*, or to his *mind*, which is indeed *himself*, considered as intelligent and moral. The question in the more proper and exact form, is not, how does such and such a *faculty* act; but how does *man* act; or how does the *mind* act? What we call the faculties of the mind, are not so many different agents. There is only one agent, the *mind.* And when it is said, there are different intellectual and moral powers or faculties in the mind, the meaning is, that the *mind itself* acts in different ways, and so makes it manifest that it has *power* to act thus. It is in this way, that we come to consider the mind as possessed of different powers or faculties. But this point is of radical importance in mental science, and must be treated more at large.

To every one who carefully investigates the subject, it must be evident, that we are led to attribute different faculties to the mind, from the different classes of mental operations of which we are conscious. We perceive that certain acts of the mind have, in some respect, a resemblance to each other. The resemblance may be greater or less. For example; my mind recalls what is past. I have an idea of what I was acquainted with last year, or many years ago. The things recollected may, as to their own nature, and as to the times and circumstances in which they took place, be different; and the acts of the mind relative to them may in various respects be different, — may be strong or weak, pleasant or painful. In one respect, however, they are alike. *They relate to what is past.* With reference to this point of resemblance, this common relation, I give them a common name, *recollection.* To express each of these acts, I say, I *recollect*, I *remember.* The word relates to them all equally in that particular respect in which they are alike. The difference which exists among these acts of the mind in other respects, must be expressed in other ways. This word, recollection, or remembrance, expresses these mental acts only in that one respect, in which they have a common resemblance. After thus classifying these mental acts, which I denote by the word *recollection*, I take one step more; that is, I *attribute them to a particular faculty of the mind;* or I refer them to my *mind, as possessing a power or faculty to perform them.* In other words, I refer them to my mind, which I find to be so constituted, or to have such power, that it puts forth acts of recollection. To this power or faculty I give the name of *memory;* still ascribing the power and all its acts to *myself.* I say, I have the power or faculty to recollect. And as I find that I perform acts of recollection *permanently*, I speak of this faculty as permanent, and regard it as an essential attribute of my mind, and of other minds like my own.

I shall give one more example of this process in classifying our mental acts. I am conscious of certain actings or feelings of my mind towards others, which I call *affections;* and I give this general name to them, whether they have the nature of attachment, or aversion, and to whatever objects they relate. I do this, because, how different soever they may be in other respects, they all agree in this, that they are *feelings* of the mind or heart towards particular objects. With reference to this point of resemblance, I give them a common name, *affections* or *emotions*. And regarding myself as the agent, I ascribe to myself a power to exercise these affections. Or, if I regard myself as the subject of them, I consider myself as *capable* or *susceptible* of them. In this way I come to speak of myself as having a *power*, *faculty*, or *capacity* for the exercise of affections. And the word *affection*, which generally denotes the emotion of the mind, may be used, as it sometimes has been, to denote also the mental *faculty*. But this faculty has more frequently been called the *will*, or *heart*.

But the objects of science and the purposes of life cannot be accomplished, without making other and more particular classifications of those operations of the mind, which are called *affections*. If we should stop with a classification so general as this; how could we intelligibly point out the various kinds of emotions included in this large class? In what way could we make a distinction between love and hatred, desire and aversion, and other feelings which differ from each other? While conscious of a great difference, we should have no word to express it, but should be obliged to give all our affections the same name.

There is, then, an obvious necessity of making a more particular classification of these acts of the mind, and of having words appropriated to each of the classes. This brings us to the different *kinds* or *species*, included under the general head above given. The process here is the same as in forming the general class. We notice those emotions which imply *attachment* to an object, or *complacency* in it; and with reference to this point of resemblance, we call them *love*. We notice other emotions of an opposite nature, and call them *dislike* or *hatred*.

But we have occasion to go still further. Even those affections which are included under the name of *love*, are found to differ, in some important respects, from each other. If then we would be exact and definite in our discourse, and express just what we mean, we must make still more particular classifications. There is a set of feelings, called love, which aim at the welfare of intelligent beings, without regard to their moral character. To this set of feelings we give the name of *benevolence*. There is another class of feelings, which directly relate to the character of their object, and imply delight in it. These we call *complacency*. Some of the affections have such a relation to moral objects, as God, his law, and his government, that we may properly call them *moral* or *religious* affections, — retaining the general term, and marking the class by a particular epithet. Or we may include them under a name which is more common in religious discourse, and call them *piety* or *holiness*. Again; affections arise in our minds towards our natural relations; and these we call *natural* affections. These again we divide into *parental*, *filial*, and *conjugal* affections; and of the parental we make two classes, the *paternal* and *maternal*. Affections which regard *money* as their object, we denominate *avarice;* those which regard *honor* or *promotion* as their object, we denominate *ambition;* and those which regard the welfare of our country as their object, *patriotism*. On the same principles we form various other classes of affections.

I have given these examples for the purpose of showing how we proceed in classifying the mental operations, in giving names to the different classes, in referring them to the mind as the agent, and in ascribing to that agent a power or faculty adapted to such operations.

After proceeding thus far in the consideration of this subject, we can very readily detect the fallacy of what certain writers advance; namely, that the mind must have just so many faculties, and that they cannot be either more or less. They might, with equal propriety, say, the vegetable world must have just so many kinds of vegetables, and the mineral world, just so many kinds of minerals; and that they cannot be either more or less; and that air and water must have just so many powers, principles, or elements, and that these powers or elements cannot be either more or less. But who asserts anything like this in the physical sciences? Further improvement in these sciences has rendered it necessary that the classifications formerly made, should be multiplied. If any important facts are newly discovered, they must have a name. In some cases it may be, that certain facts or relations of facts have been observed, but have not been deemed of such consequence, as to require a particular and discriminating word to be applied to them; but in consequence of the progress of knowledge, it may be found necessary, for the purpose of reasoning correctly, and guarding against mistake, that those facts or relations should be carefully noticed, and marked with an appropriate word. In other cases, things heretofore classed together and denoted by a common term, may, in some important respects, be dissimilar; and this dissimilarity may lead to a new classification, which will of course be marked by a new name. And a further investigation of the subject may show that a still further classification is called for, in order that our language may be perfectly definite, and our reasoning freed from all uncertainty and confusion.

What has now been said of the natural sciences, is eminently true of the mind. Let any one begin by noticing a class of mental operations which have a common resemblance; call them *thoughts*, or *ideas*, and refer them to a faculty of the mind, which he denominates *understanding* or *intellect*. Let him proceed to another large class, which he calls *emotions*, *feelings*, *volitions*, etc. and refer them, if he pleases, to a power of the mind, to which he gives the general name of *will*. Let him comprehend all the mental operations in these two classes, and refer them to the *understanding* and *will*, as the all-comprehensive powers of the mind. But it will not be long before he will find this classification far too general for the purposes of science, or even of common discourse. The operations or states of the mind are so various, that he cannot sufficiently designate them by these general terms; and of course, he will have occasion to form various subordinate classes, and to distinguish them by particular terms. This process of classifying ought to proceed just as far as we discover new and more particular relations and differences of mental phenomena, and have occasion accurately to express them, either for the purposes of science or of common life. And the number of classes formed will, of necessity, be multiplied, in proportion to the advances we make in an exact knowledge of the mind. Accordingly, we are never authorized to affirm, that the classification of mental operations has proceeded to its utmost limits. Suppose we discover some new relations of our mental acts; or suppose it becomes necessary to take more particular notice of certain relations, which have before been known, though but slightly considered. Either of these circumstances will lead us to form a new class of mental phenomena, and to refer that class to a power of the mind, designated by a new name.

It should, then, be kept in view, that the classes which we form of mental acts, and the mental faculties to which we refer them, are to be multiplied more or less, according to the state of our knowledge, and as convenience requires. No other limits can be set to classification.

But in what way can the further classification which is found necessary, and which we have actually made in our own thoughts, be most conveniently marked? In regard to this, different methods may be pursued. First; a new word may be coined, to designate the new class. But this is frequently found inconvenient. Secondly; a word which has been applied to other subjects in a sense somewhat analogous, may be applied to the new class of mental phenomena, and when thus applied, may have a peculiar, technical, or scientific sense. This is very common, and no one considers it liable to objections. Thirdly; in case *two* words have heretofore been used to denote a larger and more general class of mental acts; one of the more particular classes formed, may be denoted by one of those words, and the other class by the other.

This last mode, or something like it, may be adopted, and has actually been adopted, in regard to the words *affection* and *volition.* Heretofore, these words were frequently used as nearly synonymous. And they are still used so by some writers. According to this, all the *affections* are acts of the *will*, i. e. *volitions;* and all the *volitions* are *affections*. Here the *will* is regarded as the general faculty, to which all the feelings, emotions, dispositions, and determinations of the mind are to be referred. And all these feelings, emotions, etc. are sometimes called *voluntary;* by which I suppose may be meant, that they are acts of the *will*, taken in the sense above mentioned. Now the practice of using the words *affection* and *volition* in so indeterminate a sense, has occasioned much needless obscurity and dispute. The fact is unquestionable, that the acts of the mind which have been thus comprehended under one class, and referred to one general faculty, are, in some important respects, different from each other. And disregarding this difference has often rendered language exceedingly vague, where it should be perfectly definite. This evil has been more or less felt by thinking men generally. And something has been done to remove it, even in common discourse. An attempt has been extensively made, and with considerable success, to divide this large set of mental acts into two classes, and to appropriate the word *volition* to one class, and *affection*, *emotion*, or *feeling*, to the other. Locke made this distinction expressly, and took pains to illustrate it. He spoke of it, however, not as a new distinction, but as one which was well understood. He says,* "We must remember that *volition* or *willing* is an act of the mind directing its thoughts to the production of any action, and thereby exerting its power to produce it." Again; "Volition being a very simple act, whosoever desires to understand what it is, will better find it, by reflecting on his own mind, and observing what it does when it *wills*, than by any variety of articulate sounds whatsoever. This caution of being careful not to be misled by expressions that do not enough keep up the difference between the *will* and several acts of the mind that are quite distinct from it, I think the more necessary, because I find the will often confounded with several of the affections, especially *desire*, and one put for the other; and that by men who would not willingly be thought not to have had very distinct notions of things, and not to have writ very clearly about them. This I imagine has been no small occasion of obscurity and mistake in this matter, and therefore as much as may be to be avoided. For he that shall turn his thoughts inward upon his mind when he *wills*, shall see that the *will* or *power of volition*, is conversant about nothing but *that particular determination of the mind, whereby, barely by a thought, the mind endeavors to give rise, continuation or stop to any particular action which it takes to be in its power*." Again; "We find in ourselves a power to begin or forbear, continue or end, several actions of our mind, or motions of our bodies, barely by a thought of the mind, *ordering* or as it were *commanding* the doing or not doing of such or such a particular action. This power which the mind has thus to order the consideration of any idea, or the forbearing to consider it, or to prefer the motion of any part of the body to its rest, and vice versa, in any particular instance, is that which we call the *will*. The actual exercise of that power by directing any particular action, or its forbearance, is what we call *volition*, or *willing*." And Locke speaks of that

* Essay on the Understanding, Book ii. ch. 21.

action, and that forbearance of an action, which is consequent to such order of the mind, as *voluntary;* and of that which takes place without such an order, as *involuntary.*

Abercrombie, in his work on the Intellectual Powers, says: "Simple volition is that state of mind which immediately precedes action. We will a certain act, and the act follows, unless it be prevented by external restraint, or by physical inability to perform it." And he represents *volitions* as arising out of the affections and desires.

This is a distinction which seems now to be generally made, especially when the object of discourse requires philosophical accuracy. It is a plain matter of fact, that there is a class of mental acts, which answer to the above description of *volitions;* and that there are other mental acts which answer to the sense now commonly given to the word *affections* or *emotions*, but do not agree to this description of volitions. So that there is a real foundation for making two classes of these mental operations. And it is clear that there must be two classes formed, and designated by distinct and appropriate terms, or we cannot express ourselves clearly and definitely. We have frequent occasion to speak of those particular acts of the mind which Locke, Abercrombie, and others, call volitions. Now suppose we call them *affections;* or suppose we call them *volitions,* — still using the word in the same sense with affections. How can we make ourselves to be understood, unless we go into a further explanation, and say we mean that class of affections or volitions which immediately precede particular mental or bodily actions, and which not only precede them, but ordinarily produce them? Now if we would consult convenience or correctness in our language, we must have some word appropriated to a class of mental acts, so numerous and important, and so distinguishable from others.

It is only in this way that we can free ourselves from the intolerable necessity of giving a particular description of those mental acts, whenever we speak of them, or a particular explanation of the word by which we denote them; — a necessity which will always lie upon us, unless those mental acts which are so clearly distinguishable from others, are formed into a class by themselves, and pointed out by a distinct word.

But by what word may this particular class of mental acts be most conveniently designated?

I have touched upon this question in previous remarks. And there can be no doubt as to the proper answer, considering that so much has already been done to settle the point, both by a prevailing usage, and by the authority of distinguished writers. The mental acts here referred to, may be called, and usually are called, *volitions*, or *determinations* of the *will;* while other mental acts formerly included, and by some still included under that name, may be called, and more commonly are called, *affections*, *feelings*, or *emotions*. To appropriate one of these words, that is, *volitions*, to one of these kinds of mental acts, and the other words to the other kind, is much more convenient, and much more according to the common mode of proceeding in other similar cases, than to invent a new word either for one or the other kind of mental acts. And it certainly makes the distinction much more plain and striking, than to apply the word *volitions* to both classes of mental operations, and then to go about to mark the different kinds of volitions by such epithets, as *immanent* and *emanent*, or by any other epithets. As there is so obvious and important a difference between these two sets of mental acts; the difference should, if practicable, be marked by different names, rather than by different adjectives applied to the same name. If we use the word *volition*, as Locke and Abercrombie do, and in conformity with prevailing usage at the present day; we denote the species of action intended, at once and very clearly, and then refer it to the *will*, as the faculty of the mind which is concerned in it. But if we call both these classes of mental acts, *volitions*, or acts of the *will*, we shall be obliged to distinguish the particular class intended, by such a hard and cumbersome phraseology, as *emanent volitions*, *imperative volitions*, *executive acts of the will*, etc. This might be tolerated, were there no other way. But as there is another way, and one perfectly convenient, and as custom has already done so much in favor of it; why should we not adopt it?

The ill consequences of neglecting to make the distinction above mentioned, are very obvious. Some things are true of those mental acts that I would call *volitions*, which are not true of those that I would call *affections*; and some things are true of the affections, which are not true of the volitions. Suppose now I affirm one of these things of *volitions*, using the word in the large sense, as comprehending affections. You see the matter is left in doubt. The truth or falsity of the affirmation depends entirely on the definition which I shall give to the word *volitions*. Take an illustration. Suppose I say, *animals eat flesh*. The affirmation is true of some animals, but not of others. To make the affirmation completely true, I must specify the animals that are carnivorous, and then confine the affirmation to them. Without this, whatever my meaning may be, my language is loose and vague. In like manner, I may assert a thing of *volitions*, taken in the large, indeterminate sense; but after I have made the assertion, I shall be obliged to tell what I mean by the word *volitions*, before any one can judge whether the assertion is true or false.

As an objection to the views above expressed, it may be said, that the inspired writers use the words, *will*, *choose*, etc. in a large, general sense, and that we may do the same. In reply to this, I remark, first, that the language of Scripture often requires explanation, and that the explanation is of no value, unless it is made in plain definite language. Secondly; I remark, that the inspired writers never intended to teach moral truth in a philosophical or metaphysical manner. When we undertake to treat of moral truth in this manner, we are no more obliged to confine ourselves to Scripture language, than astronomers are when they discourse scientifically of the bodies which compose the solar system. The inspired writers aimed to convey their meaning in the language of the times when they wrote. Our business is to find out what that meaning was, and then to express that meaning in language which is common and intelligible now; and, if our object requires philosophical correctness, to avail ourselves of philosophical discoveries, and of the exactness of philosophical terms. I might give many examples on different subjects, but shall content myself with one. Who doubts the meaning which the sacred writers affixed to the word in the original Scriptures, translated *bowels?* But who that is engaged in writing a system of mental philosophy, would now point out the emotion of *pity* by that word? In scientific use it belongs rather to physiology, or anatomy.

I remark, thirdly, that while the words *will*, *willing*, etc. are employed by the inspired writers with great latitude of signification, it is for the most part very easy to determine the sense in which they are used, from the circumstances of the case. These circumstances form a kind of definition of the word; that is, they show in what sense it is used. But amid the ever varying opinions, the controversies, mistakes, and ambiguous expressions, of uninspired men, the case is widely different. And we can never be sure that we rightly apprehend their meaning, unless they make known to us the specific and exact sense in which they use words.

These considerations, and others which might be offered, satisfy me, that the latitude of meaning which the Scriptures give to the words above mentioned, is no reason why we should not take pains to use theological and metaphysical terms in a uniform and definite sense. Indeed no man, who is at all versed in the discussion of religious or philosophical subjects, can need anything but his own experience, to convince him of the great importance of avoiding all ambiguity and vagueness, and aiming at perfect definiteness, in the use of language.

And if it is so necessary to classify the operations of the mind in order that the use of the words *volition* and *will* may be definite; there is the same necessity in regard to the word *voluntary*. This word seems to be applied by some, not only to that which results *from a volition*, taken in the more restricted sense, but to all the *affections*, certainly to the *moral* affections. See now what effect this produces. You say, for example, that *love to God* is a *voluntary affection*. But how do I know what you mean, seeing the word *voluntary* has different senses? According to one sense of the word, the affirmation, that love to God is a voluntary affection, would mean, that such love results, as a consequence, from a previous volition. Is this your meaning? If you say it is; I am still at a loss, because I do not know how you use the word *volition.* You may use it in the restricted sense of Locke and others, signifying a determination or thought of the mind, which "orders, and as it were commands" the exercise of love; a mere willing or choosing, for some reason, that love should exist. Or you may speak of volition in the larger sense, and make it synonymous with affection. How shall I know, unless you inform me, which of these senses you affix to the word volition? There is still another sense in which *voluntary* may be used, when applied to the affection of love to God. It may mean that love to God is a *free, unconstrained, spontaneous* act of the mind. Is this the sense you give to it? If you say, it is; I ask again; do you give it this sense uniformly? This cannot be; for you speak of the motions of the hands and feet as voluntary; and you surely cannot mean that these bodily motions are acts of the mind; and you will find that you can call them *voluntary* in no sense but this, that they take place in obedience to the will, or follow a volition. Some acts of the mind obey the will in the same way with bodily acts. To all these the word voluntary may properly be applied. Shall we then apply it thus? That is; shall we call those acts *voluntary* which follow a volition, and *because* they follow it? And then shall we immediately depart from this sense of the word, and apply it to those acts, which are not subject to the will, and do not follow our volitions? If we do so, the word can have no definite and settled meaning. Will you say, it is convenient to use the word voluntary in different senses, — sometimes to signify that an act of ours is *free* and *spontaneous;* sometimes that it is an act of the will, or a volition; and sometimes, that it is the *consequence* of a *volition;* and that the circumstances of the case will generally show which of these significations is intended? But suppose a case occurs in which I am really at a loss as to your meaning. When you say, that love to God is a *voluntary affection*, I may think your meaning to be, that love to God is dependent on an act of the will; that it arises in the heart in consequence of a previous volition. But I do not certainly know, and come to ask you whether this is your meaning. It now becomes important that you should explain yourself. For it is the opinion of some that moral affection must be voluntary, in the sense of being dependent on an act of the will. If this be true, it ought to be plainly asserted, and well understood. If it be not true, the mistake will have a bad influence. It therefore becomes important, that our minds should be set right as to your meaning. But if, instead of explaining your meaning, you continue in a loose, ambiguous manner to apply the word voluntary to moral affection; what will be the result, but that our minds will remain in doubt as to what you mean to assert, and will suffer all the inconvenience of not being able to find out the sense of your words? Why then will any one continue to make use of a word in such a way, that we may understand it to mean this thing or that, just as we please, or may not understand it in any sense? Is this consistent with frankness? Is it consistent with a just regard to the truth? Surely no man who has the habit of plain, honest dealing, will knowingly suffer others to be in doubt as to his meaning; much less will he continue to use an ambiguous word for the purpose of seeming to favor a popular opinion which he himself does not believe.

It is not within my present design to inquire whether love to God, or any other moral affection, is or is not *voluntary* in the prevailing and proper sense of the word. I have directed my remarks to one point; that is, the importance of classifying the different exercises of the mind, and of marking each class by an appropriate word. The importance of this I have endeavored to illustrate, by showing what consequences flow from the practice of treating a particular part of our mental exercises in too general a manner, and using the words *will*, *volition*, and *voluntary* in an ambiguous, vague sense. We cannot pursue the course of honesty and plain dealing, if we refuse to do what we are able, by intelligible and definite words and phrases, to convey to others the very meaning which we have in our own minds. If for example we declare, without any explanation, that love to God is a voluntary affection, while we do not believe the opinion to be true which we suppose others will derive from the expression; do we not violate the principle of Christian simplicity and uprightness? If indeed we do believe in our hearts, that love to God, or any other moral affection, is under the control of the will, and rises in the mind as the effect of a previous volition; then surely it is right that we should declare such belief. I may give another example, to illustrate the same thing. The obvious meaning conveyed by the phrase sometimes used, that sinners can love God *if they will*, is, that their loving God *will flow as an effect from a previous volition*, or that it will take place *in consequence of an act of the will.* Now if it is verily the opinion of any man, that love to God is produced in this way, it is right for him to say so. But if this is not his opinion, how can he consistently make use of a phrase, which will certainly be understood in this sense? Whether the opinion is true or not, will be considered in another place.

The uncertainty and mistake which will be sure to result from such an ambiguous, indeterminate use of the word *voluntary*, may be avoided by making a distinct class of those actions, bodily and mental, which flow from a previous choice, or are the consequence of volition, and distinguishing them by the word *voluntary*. The sense I have given to the word *voluntary*, is the sense which Locke and other writers generally give, and which it prevailingly has in common discourse. So that when it is applied, as it not unfrequently is, to the affections, the meaning is generally supposed to be, that the affections are under the power of volition, or move in obedience to the will. Let the word uniformly have this sense; and then, if a man affirms any action, either corporeal or mental, to be voluntary, we shall know what his meaning is. And if we doubt the truth of his affirmation, we shall readily see what is the question at issue between him and us, and can enter at once on the discussion of it, with a prospect of arriving at a right conclusion. But what good will it do to discuss the question, whether a particular affection is voluntary, while the meaning of the word is unsettled, and altogether ambiguous? In all sciences, and in none more than in the philosophy of the mind, the phenomena which are contemplated, should be carefully classified, and words should be used in a definite, uniform sense. If this were done, we should be rid of a great part of the obscurity, misapprehension, and controversy, usually occasioned by an ambiguous, vague manner of thinking and writing. The fact that words are often used loosely and variously in common discourse, and in books written for practical purposes, is no reason why we should not aim at something more definite and exact, especially in metaphysical discourse. Why should those who pretend to treat theoretically of the nature of the mind, be content with less clearness, definiteness and uniformity in language, than are found in the physical sciences? Those who write on these sciences have to contend, as really as we, with an indefinite loose way of thinking and speaking among the common people. But this does not hinder them either from carefully classifying the facts which occur in the natural world, or from applying words in a well defined and uniform manner to the different classes which are thus formed. When a new set of facts is discovered, of a different nature or different relations from those before known; they agree upon some particular term by which it shall be expressed. Nor is it ever made a matter of complaint, if they take a word from common discourse, and employ it in a new and peculiar sense, provided they do it judiciously and aptly. And after they have given proper notice of the sense which they affix to particular words; that sense is always put upon those words by others. This is notoriously the case in the different branches of Natural Philosophy. Why should it not be so in mental science? There is surely no science in which it is more important to avoid all looseness and indeterminateness in our language, and to speak with the greatest clearness and definiteness, and the greatest uniformity in the sense of our words.

It is also evidently necessary, that we should carry the classification of the *intellectual* operations and powers further than has commonly been done, and more definitely mark the different classes by appropriate words. The mind perceives things in the natural world, and is conscious of its own actions; and it has ideas of the relations of things, such as cause and effect, and of general abstract truths, such as the principles of mathematical, metaphysical, and moral science. Now it seems desirable that we should have a single word for the former class of these mental acts, and another for the latter; and that we should have distinct words for the different mental faculties developed in these different classes of mental acts. The word *understanding* might be used to denote the faculty to which the former class are referable, and *reason*, the faculty to which the latter are referable. It would manifestly do something towards clearing mental science of doubts and difficulties, if the operations of the mind to be classed under the word *understanding*, and those to be classed under *reason*, should be exactly defined and settled; so that we could distinguish between what is meant by acts of *understanding* and acts of *reason*, as really as we now do between what is meant by *seeing* and what by *hearing*.

It is unnecessary to extend these remarks to the other operations of the mind. My object is to expose the unsoundness of the opinion sometimes advanced, that there *are* and *must* be just so many faculties of the mind, and no more; and to show that if we would cultivate in ourselves and others a just and accurate habit of thinking and speaking, we must carefully notice the smaller as well as larger differences among the operations of the mind, and make new and more particular classifications, and employ new and appropriate terms to express them, as occasion requires; and that we must proceed in this way, till all the important relations among our mental acts, whether more obvious, or more minute and recondite, are distinctly and clearly marked. All this, which is desirable and necessary in regard to the operations of the mind generally, is specially so in regard to those which are of a moral nature, and stand in direct relation to divine objects. Here the want of a just and careful discrimination will expose us to dangerous mistakes. It is with an ultimate reference to the exercises or acts, which belong to us as moral and accountable beings, and to the general interests involved in them, that I have entered on the consideration of the present subject.

NUMBER II.

RECAPITULATION. DISPOSITION, INCLINATION, SUSCEPTIBILITY CONSIDERED.

THE remarks made in the previous essay on the manner in which mental operations are classified, and then referred to the mind as possessed of faculties adapted to the different classes of those operations, show clearly the truth of what I suggested at the beginning of the discussion, that what we call the *faculties* of the mind are not to be considered as distinct parts into which the mind is divided, and which, by being united together, constitute the mind, as different parts or ingredients make up a complex material substance. Locke well observes, that the ordinary way of speaking of the faculties of the mind is apt to breed confusion in men's thoughts, by leading them to suppose that the words denoting those faculties "stand for some real beings in the soul;" or, for "so many distinct agents in us, which have their several provinces and authorities, and command, obey, and perform several actions, as so many distinct beings; which has been no small occasion of wrangling, obscurity and uncertainty." The mind is a simple, indivisible, spiritual being. And when we speak of it as having different *faculties*, we do nothing more than to say, that the *mind itself*, a simple, immaterial being, performs so many different kinds of action, and of course has *power* to perform them. But what we call a power or faculty of the mind is no more a distinct agent, than the faculty of speaking or walking is a distinct agent. The faculty is not the agent, but *belongs to* the agent. It is the intelligent being, *man*, and he only, that acts, and acts in such a variety of ways. He thinks, desires, loves, hates, wills, and does all things else which are ascribed to his different faculties. I repeat it, that, strictly speaking, it is not the power or faculty that acts, but the person who is possessed of the power. We do indeed find it convenient, to keep up the usual expressions, and say, the *will chooses*, or puts forth a volition, *reason compares* and *judges*, etc. But after all, this is a loose way of talking, and far from being philosophically correct. For in strict propriety, it is the intelligent being, the person, that compares, judges, chooses, and performs all other mental acts; and from the fact of his acting in these different ways, we learn that he is *capable* of it, or has the *faculty* of doing it. We should keep this in remembrance. And when any obscurity or confusion arises from the more common modes of speech, we shall do well to dismiss them for a time, and adopt language which is strictly and philosophically correct. In this way we may in many instances effectually disentangle a subject under consideration, and obtain views of it which are clear and satisfactory.

These observations are as true, in regard to *moral qualities*, as in regard to actions. These qualities belong to the moral being, *man*. But in common discourse, we often ascribe moral qualities to particular faculties, and especially to the affections and acts. We say, the affections of the heart, the determinations of the will, and the voluntary actions, are good or bad, praise-worthy or blame-worthy. And it is sometimes represented, that all moral qualities are to be predicated directly of actions, and of actions only. But such representations cannot be literally true; nor can any thinking man seriously believe them to be so. Take an action which is morally wrong, and worthy of blame and punishment. Do we really blame and punish the *action?* When a man commits the act of stealing; do the civil magistrates condemn and imprison the *act?* When a man commits the act of murder, is it the murderous *act* that is put to death? The act itself began and ended perhaps in a moment. And even during that moment, it had no existence separate from the agent. Had we stood by, and witnessed the act of theft or murder, the real object of our disapprobation and abhorrence would have been, the *wicked agent himself*, the *thief*, the *murderer*. The agent has a permanent existence. And though many years may have passed away since the criminal action was perpetrated, the action itself having now no existence except in memory, and no action like it having been committed since, still we hold the agent responsible for it, and consider him to be as really worthy of punishment, as he was at the very time when he was engaged in perpetrating the criminal deed. We do indeed speak familiarly of the wickedness and ill-desert of the *act;* but, in strict propriety, wickedness and ill-desert can be predicated only of the *agent.* If we say, the *act* is wicked and ill-deserving; our real meaning is, that he who commits it is so; as our conduct clearly shows. All human actions and qualities are, then, attributable to man, the agent, and to him only. This view of the subject agrees with the practical judgment of all men.

When you read the life of Howard, and attend to the high commendations which the biographer bestows upon his *actions*, calling them *benevolent*, *philanthropic*, *humane*, *kind*, *self-denying*, *disinterested*, and *generous;* you understand him as commending *Howard himself*, and as applying all these honorable epithets to *him*, as the doer of these actions. In grammatical construction the epithets do indeed belong to his actions. But what of that? Your thoughts always fix upon Howard himself, as philanthropic, humane, self-denying, and disinterested. These attributes truly belong to a *person*, and to nothing else. And nothing else can be the real object of our esteem, gratitude, or love. When such qualities are predicated of actions, it is only in a secondary, relative sense, as the actions indicate the disposition or character of the person who performs them. To be *benevolent*, is to wish well to others. Does an action wish well to others? Has an action desire or volition? Can an action enjoy a reward?

I have dwelt so long upon this point, because I have been desirous of making it as clear and certain as possible; and because, though it seems perfectly obvious, and though conscience and common sense always hold it as a plain truth, it has often been overlooked; and men have reasoned about actions, as though the common phraseology, which ascribes moral qualities and relations to them, were literally and philosophically true.

In what light then are outward, visible actions to be regarded? I answer; so far as our moral relations are concerned, they are to be regarded principally as *indications of the character of the agent;* or, if you prefer it, as *giving* character, that is, *visible* character to the agent. To God, the character is known before those actions take place which manifest it to us. The searcher of hearts was perfectly acquainted with the internal character of Judas, or the qualities of his mind, before he did those things by which his character was developed. But his fellow men could not search his heart, and accordingly could not know his character, except as his actions made it visible. In like manner the children of Israel were put to various trials in the wilderness, *that they might know what was in them;* not that they might be made different from what they were, but that they might, by their conduct, discover their own real character, and make it manifest to others. The real, internal character of a man, his character as God sees it, essentially consists in what is usually called his *disposition*, *inclination*, or *propensity*. To say, a man has a benevolent *disposition*, or a disposition to do good, is the same as to say, he has a benevolent *character;* he is a benevolent *man*.

It has been common with those who have written on mental science, to use the word *disposition* or *inclination*, to express not only that current of affection of which we are directly conscious, but also that state of mind which precedes the exercise of affection, and which is developed by it, — and which becomes the subject of consciousness by being thus developed. The thing intended by the word *disposition* is, I think, as clearly apprehended, as anything which relates to the nature and attributes of the mind. If we attend to a few of the instances in which the word is commonly used, we shall find that no one can have any doubt as to its propriety, or any difficulty in understanding it; how abstruse and incomprehensible soever the subject may be, when treated metaphysically.

Take the case of Judas, at the grave of Lazarus. His mind, we suppose, was intensely occupied with a variety of thoughts and feelings, while he witnessed the events which took place on that memorable occasion. Perhaps he sympathized with the weeping friends, and was filled with astonishment at that omnipotent word which raised Lazarus from the dead. But whatever his thoughts and feelings might be, the real *character* of Judas was the same as at other times. He had an avaricious *disposition*. He might indeed have had, at the time, no thought of money, and no exercise of covetousness. Still he had a *disposition* or *propensity* to love money. The proof of this is, as soon as circumstances varied, and the thought of money arose in his mind, he had the same covetous desire, as before. Who can suppose that the *character* of that miser, or, which is the same thing, his *propensity to love money*, ceased, because his mind was, for a time, occupied with other things? The character of John was different. He had no such *disposition* to love money. If he had been tempted as Judas was, the temptation would have met with an opposite disposition, and would have been repelled with abhorrence.

Suppose another case. A man in prison has been long practised in stealing. His solitary confinement at night, his employment by day, and the religious instructions he receives, produce an apparent change, so that he weeps at the remembrance of his crimes, and resolves never to steal again. But the change is only apparent. There is no real alteration in his moral character. Now what is more common in such a case, than to say, he has in reality *the same disposition*, as formerly; and he will act it out, and make it manifest, as soon as tempting circumstances occur. The thing here intended by *dispostion*, is plainly something distinct from the present exercise of the mind.

Take the example of a decided Christian, whose mind is occupied with a mathematical demonstration, or engrossed with the reasoning and eloquence of a distinguished statesman, and whose thoughts are, for the time, wholly withdrawn from the subject of religion. We are accustomed to say, that whatever the present thoughts and feelings of such a man may be, he has a fixed *dispostion to love God*, or an habitual *principle of piety;* and that there is no need of a change in his disposition, or governing moral principle, in order to excite his love, his heart being renewed, and prepared to love, as soon as the object is seen. In this he differs essentially from an unregenerate man, whose enmity will be excited by a clear view of the divine character, and who, on that very account, is generally considered as having a disposition opposed to God, although he may not now have any conscious exercises of enmity.

Take the case of affectionate parents, who have now no thought of a beloved absent child, and of course no exercise of affection towards him. But they have what is called a *disposition* to love their child, a *principle* of parental affection. In this respect, they differ widely from those parents who are "without natural affection." They may all agree in this, that they are now wholly occupied with other subjects, and have no present thought or feeling respecting their children. But there is an essential difference in character. These parents have a kind, affectionate *disposition;* but those have not. If you doubt this, you may soon have your doubt removed. Let the parents first mentioned see their child returned from a long absence, or receive a letter from him, and their hearts instantly overflow with emotions of love and joy; while the other parents, in like circumstances, are unmoved.

There are two men, one of whom has always shown himself to be *mild* and *gentle*, the other, *irascible* and *violent*. What is more common than to say of the first, he has a mild *temper*, a *disposition* to bear affronts and injuries with meekness, or, that he is *inclined* to feelings of gentleness and kindness; and of the other, that he has an irritable *temper*, or a *propensity* to be angry and violent? And we say these things of them without respect to any present exercises which indicate what their disposition is. The existence of the particular disposition which is attributed to them, is, I admit, inferred from past exercises of it; but the disposition is believed and declared to exist, when there are no exercises of it. It is indeed spoken of with relation to future exercises, and as the ground of them; for when we predicate a disposition of any one, we do it on the supposition that he will have certain feelings hereafter, if circumstances occur which are suited to excite them.

Suppose one example more. There are two judges, one of whom we say has a corrupt *disposition*, a *principle* of selfishness, and is *inclined* to take bribes; and the other of whom we say has a firm *principle* of honesty and honor, an *integrity* of *heart*, an *uprightness* of *disposition*, which no temptation can turn aside. And yet these two judges may now be engaged in business which gives no exercise to their moral principles, and may for the present exhibit characters equally spotless and fair. There is, however, an obvious and important difference even now, lying not in present action, either corporeal or mental, but in what we call disposition, or moral principle.

The various cases here mentioned, together with the ideas commonly entertained and the language commonly employed respecting them, lead to the following conclusions.

I. *That the disposition, inclination, character,* or *principle, is discoverable in no other way than by the actions which flow from it.* This is true of the attributes of the mind universally. Nothing which belongs to the mind, not one of its faculties, and not even its existence, is ever known to us in any other way, than as it is developed by action. A spiritual agent must indeed exist, with all his essential attributes, in order to action. But how can such existence and attributes be known to others of the same nature, or even to himself, except by mental action? God, who creates the mind and all its powers, does indeed perfectly know them, without waiting for any disclosure to be made by action. But this is one of God's prerogatives. We are capable of nothing like it.

II. The fact, that the disposition of the mind is known only as it is developed by action, is certainly no proof that it does not *exist previously* to action. It is never made an argument that the mind itself, or any one of its essential attributes, does not exist, that there is no way in which we can be conscious of its existence, except by its operations? Will any one deny that Milton, and Pascal, really had minds, and superior mental powers, before they exhibited them in action, because their minds and their mental powers could not then be known, even to themselves? It will be admitted, that what a man does, and what he acquires, are to be considered only as *developing*, *strengthening*, and *improving* the faculties which he previously possessed, not as *originating* them. Why is not this equally true in regard to the *disposition* or *inclination* of the mind? What should we think of one who should deny that the mind of a human being has within itself a disposition or tendency to the exercise of *compassion* or *parental love*, because the time has not yet come for its exercise?

III. It is a truth commonly believed and acted upon, that *the particular feelings and actions of a man are connected with his disposition*, or the character of his mind, *and result from it as consequences.* I would now limit the proposition to those feelings and actions which occur as a matter of course. Such feelings and actions, I maintain, are connected with a man's disposition, and result from it as consequences. Judas's treatment of Christ plainly resulted as a consequence from his covetous and dishonest disposition. Peter's conduct in the judgment-hall doubtless resulted from the rashness and violence of temper, or the fear of suffering, which were natural to him, and which he had not yet completely overcome. The first emotions of pity, or of parental love, which arise in the mind of a man, are always regarded as resulting from his natural disposition. Saul of Tarsus, in his unrenewed state, had a proud, self-righteous, and violent disposition, and from this, in the circumstances in which he was placed, flowed his feelings and conduct towards Christians. Paul, the regenerate man, the penitent believer, had another disposition, — a disposition to love and obey Christ, to compassionate the souls of sinners, and to labor and suffer for their good; and from this holy disposition resulted his feelings and conduct as an Apostle. And after his holy disposition was known to himself and others, it was natural for him and them to conclude that, in all ordinary circumstances, such would be his feelings and conduct. Whatever may be said of certain extraordinary cases, this connection of our feelings and actions with our previous disposition must be considered as a fact in all common cases; and especially in those cases where particular feelings and actions may be anticipated as a matter of course.

I do not, however, mean by these remarks to imply that the disposition or propensity of our mind is the only cause of our feelings and actions. For this disposition, without the influence of outward motives, that is, without the influence of circumstances suited to call it forth, would never produce the effects referred to. The feelings and actions must be regarded as effects flowing from the combined influence of the dispositions of the mind, and of all the circumstances which bear upon them. So that when we say, a man's disposition is such as will cause these or those particular feelings, and lead to these or those actions, the meaning must be, that such a disposition will have such an influence when the appropriate circumstances occur.

Let me here advert, in few words, to a very obvious distinction between what we call *powers* or *faculties* of mind, and what we call *disposition.* The mental faculties which belong to a man qualify him to act in various ways, but do not account for his acting in any one particular way, rather than others. A man possessed of distinguished intellectual faculties, may be an eminent statesman, or merchant, or a minister of the gospel, or highwayman, or pirate. He is able to excel in anything which he undertakes. But from his ability to do so many things, we cannot infer that he will do any one particular thing, rather than another. I name to you a young man of brilliant talents, and I ask you what course a young man of such talents, under the influence of auspicious circumstances, will be likely to pursue. You say, you cannot tell, unless you know something of his *disposition*, or the *tendency* of his mind. Here is the distinction I have in view. By his powers or faculties, a man is made able to pursue many different courses, right and wrong. His disposition leads him to pursue one particular course, rather than another. Hazael had powers of mind sufficient to enable him to use his authority to the benefit or the injury of the people. It was his *disposition* that led him to those acts of barbarity which the prophet predicted. And we shall find it to be true universally, that whenever we would form an opinion as to the conduct which we are to expect from any one, we make it our chief object to determine what his *disposition* is.

I have intended to say nothing on this subject which would militate against the well known fact, that in many cases, a man's feelings and actions are at variance with the disposition which he formerly had. His disposition may have changed; and his new disposition may as strongly prompt him to a new course of affection and conduct, as his former disposition prompted him to his former course. This is the case with every one who is renewed by the Spirit of God. Besides; there may be *different* dispositions or propensities at the same time, — propensities which may clash with each other. In this case, one or the other of the propensities will prevail, according to its comparative strength, and the influence of circumstances. And was it not so with our original parents? They had evidently possessed from the first, a disposition to reverence and obey God. But that right disposition had not acquired confirmation, and was liable to be overcome by other propensities belonging to their bodily or mental constitution, when acted upon by temptation, and when the effectual aids of divine grace were withheld. When our first parents apostatized, what did they do but follow those propensities of theirs which were excited and rendered powerful by temptation, their pious disposition not being sustained and rendered predominant by divine influence? I make no account here of the common difficulties which pertain to the introduction of evil; nor would I advance anything confidently on that mysterious subject. All I would suggest is, that our first parents, when they sinned, did follow their inclinations, or did act according to their propensities; — not indeed according to their pious inclination which had previously governed them, but according to those other inclinations which had, up to that time, been kept in subjection, but which, under the influence of temptation, came to oppose and overcome their disposition to obey God, his effectual grace being withheld. Their pious disposition was in fact overcome; and it was evidently overcome by other propensities within them, acted upon and strengthened by temptation. From these inferior propensities, thus excited and rendered predominant, their disobedience flowed.* And what intelligent agents, possessed of the same attributes, and being in all respects in the same state inwardly, and the same circumstances outwardly, would not have acted in the same manner? I hold it to be a truth too plain and certain to need proof, that causes perfectly alike, acting upon subjects perfectly alike, will produce like results.

IV. When we attribute a predominant disposition to a man, our meaning is, that he has a principle of action which is likely to *continue*, and to unfold itself in the same way as heretofore; though not that it is absolutely immutable in all possible circumstances. Man is subject to change. Our confidence in him must of course have limitations. But so far as our confidence in any one goes, it rests on the supposed permanence of his present disposition. If we have no reason to think that a man who has exhibited a right character, will continue to feel and act as he has done, we consider him as fickle, and unworthy of our confidence. We never look upon past conduct as evidence of character, and we scarcely speak of a man as *having* a character, except on the supposition that his present state of mind will continue and will act itself out as it has done. Let a man make ever so clear an exhibition of love and kindness at the present time; still you would not confide in him as a friend, and would not ascribe to him, even now, the disposition of a friend, if you should expect that the next feelings of his heart would be feelings of enmity. Without some degree of permanency in a man's state of mind, he cannot have what is called *character*, — cannot be properly denominated either a friend or an enemy. Whenever any one is denominated thus, the idea is involved, that, in ordinary circumstances, he will continue to be what he now is.

---

* See Dwight's Theology, Serm. 27, 4th head.

It is evident, that the continuance of the same feelings and actions in any person results *chiefly* from the continuance of the same disposition, or state of mind, though I do not by any means exclude the influence of outward circumstances. But there are strong reasons against supposing, that the continuance of the same kind of affections and conduct is owing *principally*, much less *entirely*, to outward circumstances. One reason is, that we find the same kind of affections and conduct under a great diversity of outward circumstances. Tender parents will love their child, whether he is virtuous or vicious, — whether he affords them pleasure, or occasions them trouble and sorrow. They will love him, whatever their love may cost them. A miser continues to love his money, whatever changes may pass over him. He loves it in health and sickness. His heart cleaves to it in the hour of death, though he knows it can never be of any use to him. The unrenewed sinner will continue to disobey the divine law, whatever motives may be set before him, and in whatever outward circumstances he may be placed. The true Christian will continue to feel and act as a Christian. Neither life nor death, nor things present, nor things to come, can hinder his love to his Saviour. It is so with the man of true integrity and virtue. No temptation can prevail upon him to swerve from uprightness, and to do a dishonest deed. Now surely this continuance and uniformity of feeling and conduct cannot be owing chiefly to external circumstances. For these circumstances are exceedingly various; and if they had a governing influence, we should suppose the effects would vary accordingly. To account for the uniformity of feeling and action which takes place in such circumstances, we must refer to a uniform and stable cause. And if this is not found in anything extraneous to the mind, it must be found within the mind itself. It does indeed appear to be true, that in all instances in which the feelings and actions are the same, there is, in some important respect, a uniformity of *mental view*, and that the uniformity of feelings results from this. But this very uniformity of mental view, from which uniform feelings arise, must itself result from a uniform state of mind. The man who continues to have the same prevailing *apprehension* of things, evinces that he continues to have the same prevailing disposition or state of mind. So it is with the mental view of the unrenewed sinner, of the Christian, of the miser, of the upright man, and of all who have a fixed character.

But there is another reason against supposing, that uniformity in the affections and conduct is owing chiefly to the influence of outward circumstances; namely, that *in the same circumstances the affections and conduct of different men are essentially different, and even opposite.* Nothing is more common than to find that, while everything extraneous to the minds of two men is the same, the feelings which they uniformly have towards a particular object are different, — those of one, feelings of attachment; those of the other, feelings of aversion. This difference of emotions, so constant and uniform, cannot be accidental. It must have a cause; and a cause as uniform as the effect. But the cause cannot lie in the outward circumstances, as they are *alike.* It must then be found within. But the minds of both are equally possessed of reason, conscience, will, self-love, and all the natural powers and capacities. The cause or occasion of these different feelings must therefore lie in the habitual disposition or state of their minds; — a thing obviously distinct from their natural powers. Two men, one of them a sincere Christian, the other, a violent opposer of religion, are informed of the conversion of a sinner. The one is filled with emotions of pleasure; the other, of displeasure. To what is this owing? Common sense answers, — *to their different dispositions.* And the connection between their prevailing dispositions, and the emotions which arise in their minds in view of such an event, is so close and certain, that if you know beforehand what their dispositions are, you are ready to predict what those emotions will be. You know a man like David Brainerd, and are fully acquainted with his predominant disposition. I ask you, what emotions will be excited in his mind, when the conversion of a sinner, or the success of a benevolent enterprise is mentioned? You say, emotions of joy. And you ground this affirmation upon what you know of his disposition, or the habitual state of his mind. But you know another man, like Voltaire or Hume. What feelings will *he* have, when you mention the same things to him? You say, feelings of hatred and scorn. And you say this, because you know his disposition — his character — the habitual state of his mind. You believe that such feelings will flow from such a disposition of mind, as certainly as that figs will grow from a fig-tree, or as an effect in any case will flow from a cause. This is a practical principle; and you act upon it in the most important concerns. You do not apply to a man, whom you know to be like the infidel Paine, for money to send the Bible to the destitute; because you are satisfied what feelings such an application would excite in a man of such a disposition, and how he would treat you. But there are men, whose prevailing disposition is manifestly such, that you may be sure beforehand, that they will have feelings of approbation excited by any benevolent object, and will take pleasure in doing what they can to promote it. Thus you act and *must* act on the belief, that one man has a disposition or state of mind, which will insure benevolent feelings and actions in view of a benevolent object, and that another has a disposition, from which will arise feelings of an opposite nature. This principle governs you in all your intercourse with your fellow-men. If you give up this principle, your knowledge of men will be of no use. The principle I have endeavored to illustrate, is plainly implied in the common conceptions which men entertain, and the common language they employ. *Disposition*, *inclination*, *bias*, *habit*, *propensity*, *principle*, and other words of like import, are in good use among all men, and will be so, as long as the world stands. We cannot speak intelligibly without them. And what is called *disposition*, *heart*, *principle* or *habit* of mind, will always be referred to as that which chiefly accounts for the specific emotions arising in the minds of different men, and for the voluntary actions which they perform. Thus evangelical men believe, that unholy affections will uniformly arise in the minds of unrenewed sinners; and will result from their *depraved disposition*.

I have said, we cannot speak intelligibly on this subject without the word *disposition*, or *inclination*, or some other word of like import. All men are in the habit of referring to that state of mind which such a word expresses, as the circumstance which accounts for it, that particular, specific affections arise in the mind of any one in view of a particular object. But how shall we refer it intelligibly? We cannot point it out by the word *power*, or *faculty;* because a man's having a power or faculty, as the words are commonly understood, only renders him *capable of acting*, but does not influence him to act in one particular way, rather than another, or even to act at all. We cannot point it out sufficiently by the mention of a previous act of the mind; because we know that, under the influence of new circumstances, men are often led to a train of feelings, purposes, and actions different, in some respects, from any which have appeared in them before. And we never consider a particular act, whether bodily or mental, as evidence of what a man's future actions will be, any further than we can determine what his prevailing *disposition* is. In order, therefore, that we may speak intelligibly and truly, we must have a suitable word. And if there were no such word, as *disposition*, *inclination*, etc., now in use, we should find it necessary forthwith to make a word, for the specific purpose above mentioned.

In common discourse, and in the Scriptures, the word *heart* answers the purpose referred to, as it generally designates the *source* of the affections. Thus in Mark 7: 21, "From within, out of the *heart*, proceed evil thoughts, adulteries, fornications," etc. And if we should use the word *affections*, to denote the *capacity*, *power*, or *capability* of the mind, as well as its *acts*, we should be supported by good authority. The mind is often said to be endued with *affections*, as permanent attributes. And when we speak of exercising or eliciting, cultivating and improving, strengthening and elevating the *affections;* the word is used, in many cases at least, to point out not so much the actual feelings of the mind, as its *capability* or *habit* of feeling. So it is with the word *passions*. So it is with *imagination*, which sometimes denotes a *power* or *faculty*, and sometimes an *exercise* of that power. So it is even with *memory*. Though it more commonly signifies a *faculty* of the mind; it sometimes signifies the *exercise* of that faculty, the same as *remembrance*. This is true of the word *disposition*. It may denote either an actual feeling or emotion towards an object, or the previous aptitude of the mind to the exercise of such emotion. We are familiar with this variable sense of the word *Will*, denoting now the *power* of the mind, and now the *act*. There are many other words which have this twofold use. And this is a case in which, generally, we are not in the least exposed to mistake. For in good writing or speaking, the circumstances make it manifest, whether a word is intended to point out a faculty or an act.

The general remarks which have been made on the words *disposition*, *propensity*, *principle*, etc., are coincident with the opinions of Edwards and Dwight, who have, in a high degree, the confidence of the churches. With these authors agree other standard writers generally.

In the following quotations, we have the views which Dr. Dwight very plainly expressed on the subject.

"I do not deny, on the contrary, I readily admit, that *there is a cause of moral action in intelligent beings, frequently indicated by the words Principle, Affections, Habits, Nature, Propensity, Tendency, and several others*. In this case, however, as well as in many others, it is carefully to be observed, that these terms indicate a cause, which to us is wholly unknown, except that its existence is proved by its effects. We speak of *human nature as sinful*, intending *not the actual commission of sin, but a general characteristic of man, under the influence of which, he has committed sins heretofore, and is prepared, and is prone, to commit others*. With the same meaning in our minds, we use the phrases, *sinful propensity, corrupt heart, depraved mind;* and the contrary ones, *holy or virtuous disposition, moral rectitude, holiness of character*, and many others of the like import. When we use these kinds of phraseology, we intend that a reason really exists, although undefinable and unintelligible by ourselves, why one mind will, either usually or uniformly, be the subject of holy volitions, and another, of sinful ones. We do not intend to assert, that any one, or any number, of the volitions of the man whom we characterize, has been, or will be, holy or sinful; nor do we, indeed, design to refer immediately to actual volitions at all. Instead of this, we mean to indicate a state of mind generally existing, out of which holy volitions may, in one case, be fairly expected to arise, and sinful ones, in another: such a state as that, if it were to be changed, and the existing state of a holy mind were to become the same with that of a sinful mind, its volitions would thenceforth be sinful; and *vice versa.* This state is *the cause,* which I have mentioned; a cause, the existence of which must be admitted, unless we acknowledge it to be a perfect casualty that any volition is sinful, rather than holy. This cause is what is so often mentioned in the Scriptures, under the name of *the heart:* as when it is said, 'The heart is deceitful,' etc. I have already remarked, that the cause is unknown, except by its effects."

The view of Edwards on this general subject may be learnt from what he says as to the new principle which is given in regeneration. "By a principle of nature in this place, I mean that foundation which is laid in nature, either old or new, for any particular manner or kind of exercise of the faculties of the soul; or a natural habit or foundation for action, giving the person ability and disposition to exert the faculties in exercises of such a certain kind. So this new spiritual sense is not a new faculty of understanding, but a new foundation laid in the nature of the soul for a new kind of exercises of the same faculty of understanding. So that new holy disposition of heart that attends this new sense, is not a new faculty of will, but a foundation laid in the nature of the soul for a new kind of exercises of the same faculty of the will."

I might also refer to Abercrombie, and other respectable writers on mental philosophy, who speak of a right and a wrong state of mind as antecedent to moral exercises, and as having a principal influence in determining what emotions shall arise in the mind.

I shall not here inquire, what views we are to have of the moral nature and relations of this tendency or propensity of the mind to sin. For the present I have meant to consider such a propensity simply as a fact. And respecting this there is a remarkable agreement among men of sense, whether learned or unlearned.

The words, *susceptible* and *susceptibility* have of late obtained a remarkable currency. That we may judge of the correctness of the prevailing use, it is necessary to determine their exact signification. According to Johnson, *susceptible* means — *capable of admitting; disposed to admit; susceptibility; quality of admitting;* tendency to *admit.* Webster defines *susceptible* thus: *capable of admitting anything additional, or any change, affection, or influence, — tender, capable of impression.* And he gives *susceptibility* a correspondent sense. When it is said, the mind has various *susceptibilities*, the meaning is, that it is *capable of various states of feeling; capable of exercising, and disposed to exercise, various emotions; that it has the quality of receiving, or an aptitude to receive, various influences or impressions.*

In order to a right understanding of this subject, let the following things be considered.

First: There is no way to ascertain what susceptibilities we possess, but *by experience;* that is, by being conscious of the sensations and emotions which actually take place in ourselves. How could we know that we are susceptible of love and pity, of anger and revenge, if we had never been conscious of these feelings? What reasonable man ever attributes to the mind any capacity or tendency, which has not been developed by mental acts? As we think, reason, and remember, we know that we have corresponding faculties; and as we love and pity, hate and fear, we know that we have corresponding susceptibilities. How do we know that we are susceptible of *pity?* From the fact that we have had the emotion. But in what circumstances, or under the influence of what causes, have we had it? I answer; when we have witnessed or imagined cases of suffering. We have never had the feeling of pity on any other occasion. We contend, then, that we are susceptible of this feeling in the circumstances above mentioned, and in no other. Pity cannot be excited, except by the actual view or the thought of suffering in a fellow creature.

Suppose a man placed under all the influences suited to make him pleased with the melody and harmony of sounds, and continued through a long life in such circumstances, without the least emotion of pleasure in hearing the most exquisite music. We should say, that he is not susceptible of pleasure from music.

Again. Suppose a man, who has long been in a situation most favorable to the cultivation and development of parental affection, to be an utter stranger to any feeling of the nature of parental love. If we should find any one in this state, whether he came into it by the original structure of his mind, or by the practice of intemperance and cruelty; we should say, he is "without natural affection," he has no susceptibility to parental love.

These examples are introduced to show what is commonly meant by the word under consideration, and when it is suitable to speak of a person as *destitute* of a particular susceptibility. A susceptibility to a particular kind of emotion, is that state or quality of mind, which gives rise to such emotion, when fit occasions occur. But when on the fittest occasions, and under all the variety of circumstances, a person remains a total stranger to it, never having anything of that nature arise in his breast; we say, he is not *susceptible* of it.

But, suppose another case. Let a man be sick of a malignant fever, and consequently incapable, while in that state, either of the pleasure of eating, or of any proper appetite for food. If we should say of such a sick man, that he is *susceptible* of an appetite for food and of the pleasure of eating, we should say it hypothetically; meaning that he has a constitution from which such an appetite and such pleasure will arise, when he is in a sound and healthy state. His disease is all that prevents.

All that is necessary in such cases, is, to keep in mind the conditions on which the particular feelings or actions referred to, depend, or the circumstances which are indispensable to their existence; and when we would express ourselves with exactness, to ascribe the susceptibility to a man, on those conditions.

These remarks will aid us in answering the question, whether man, in his fallen, unsanctified state, has all the moral susceptibilities which belonged to him originally in his state of innocence, and which would belong to him now, if he should be sanctified; or, to be more specific, whether man, while he continues unrenewed, is susceptible of love to God, and other holy affections. Those who hold the doctrine of total depravity are agreed in believing, that man, while unrenewed, is wholly destitute of holiness; that however favorable the circumstances of his education; however numerous and powerful the motives to piety which are held up before his mind, and with whatever skill and fidelity they may be presented, and however long the trial may be continued; he will never, while unrenewed, have any holy affection. Now this being held by all concerned, what difference can remain except as to the use of words? The only question would seem to be, whether we can properly speak of depraved man while unrenewed, as *susceptible* of holy affection.

Here let it be kept in mind, that we are speaking of man's *moral* state, and are using words in a moral sense. Accordingly if any one says, that man is susceptible of holy love *without the renewing of the Holy Ghost*, his meaning would evidently be, that man, depraved as he is, *may* have holy love in his heart *without the sanctifying influence of the Spirit;* and of course, that a man's having holy affection is no proof that he is renewed by the Holy Spirit, and consequently, that man's being in his natural, unregenerate state is no certain proof that he is destitute of holiness. Now all this is directly contrary to the word of God.

If by man's being susceptible of holy affection in his unrenewed state, be meant only, that he possesses all the natural faculties which are necessary to the exercise of holy affection, and that nothing more is necessary, but that God should give him a new heart, or should renew him in the spirit of his mind; — in this sense he is doubtless susceptible of holy love. But this would be using the word in an uncommon sense, and in a sense not suited to the subject. The fact is, that when the word is used in its moral signification, and it is said, that unregenerate man is really *susceptible* of love to God, it is implied, that he may have such love in his unregenerate state, and even that he has a tendency, or an aptitude, to holy love. This obvious implication of the word is a sufficient reason why we should not affirm, without qualification, that man in his natural state is susceptible of holy affection,—that he is as susceptible of it as one that is renewed. Does not any such representation as this tend to make the impression on the minds of men, that there is no essential difference between the moral state of the regenerate and the unregenerate, and thus to set aside the necessity of a moral renovation by the special influence of the Spirit.

NUMBER III.

THE language sometimes used in books and in common discourse implies, *that man is entirely under the control of his will; that his volitions guide and regulate all his bodily and mental powers.* According to this representation, the will possesses the chief attribute of a despot, and man is very much in the condition of a slave. Be it so, that the master that governs him is his *own* will. If the power of that will is absolute, and subject to no limitation or check from truth or reason, who can be sure that it will not exercise as severe and merciless a despotism over him, as any power extraneous to his mind? And would not any man think it a less calamity to be subject to an unreasonable despotism that is distant, than to one that is always near; to a despotism *without*, than to one that is *within?*

It is my present object to ascertain what is the fact respecting the power of the will. The office of the will must be considered an important subject in mental philosophy; it is important too in a practical view. For if any one attributes to his will an agency, either more or less extensive than actually belongs to it, he will be liable to serious mistakes in the regulation of his own mind and conduct.

The kind and extent of power belonging to the will must be determined by an appeal to our own *experience and consciousness.* No hypothetical or a priori reasoning can be relied upon. We ought never to inquire what power we should suppose the will would have, or what power it must have, in order to make man a responsible agent. Any such inquiry might lead us to conclusions materially at variance with the truth. Our whole inquiry is, what do we learn from consciousness and experience? Accordingly, every man is qualified to investigate the subject under consideration as far as his own experience extends. There may be questions relative to the power of the will, on which a person of little experience, or one who has not been duly attentive to the operations of his own mind, will not be able to form a correct judgment; as a man is incompetent to judge respecting the operations of the magnetic or the electrical power, in any cases which have not fallen under his notice. Suppose now a question arises respecting the power of the will in cases in which I have had no experience, or in which I have neglected to learn the proper lessons of experience. Here I am an incompetent judge; and if I would form a just opinion, I must avail myself of the requisite knowledge by referring to the experience of others. This view of the subject is of special importance, and is suited to check the overweening confidence of some who have had but a limited experience, and have withal been too little observant of the operations of their own minds.

I will endeavor to remember these remarks myself; and though I must of necessity proceed in this discussion primarily on the ground of my own experience, I will readily admit, even at my advanced age, that my experience may be defective. The voluntary power belonging to me may not have been so perfectly developed, as in some others; or if it has been, I may have failed to notice its developments so carefully, or to recollect them so exactly, as others. And it may be suitable for every man to admit that the faculty of will, as found in him, may have less original power, and less acquired expertness, than in others, so that no one may be able to come to a right conclusion on every part of mental science, without availing himself of the experience and consciousness of his fellow-men. This is the case we well know, in all parts of physical science. How long and attentively soever any man may have observed the course of events in the natural world; he will find himself, in many cases, totally unable to judge from his own personal knowledge, what the laws of nature are, and so will be obliged to supply the defects of his own experience by the experience of others. In the study of natural science, men do this constantly, and why is it not the dictate of modesty, and of wisdom too, that something like this should be done in relation to our present subject? If the facts which have occurred in our experience, are not sufficient to teach us the whole extent of power belonging to the will, why should we not gladly avail ourselves of any well attested facts which have occurred in the experience of others?

It will be kept in mind, that I use the words *will* and *volition* in the restricted and exact sense in which they are used by Locke, Reid, Abercrombie and others, and in which I have before explained them.

I shall now pursue the inquiry, *what power belongs to the will?* I begin by saying negatively, the will has no power to alter the laws of nature, either in the material or spiritual world. For example, gravitation is an established law of all material bodies, and we have no power by our volitions to set aside or modify this law, or to direct or vary any events which stand related to it, except by availing ourselves of its influence. What man in his senses ever attempts to do this? Again, it is a law of nature that vegetables spring up and grow from seeds, under the influence of heat and moisture, and that animal life is sustained by food, and destroyed by continued abstinence, or by poison; and who has power by an act of the will, to make it otherwise? The same is true as to the laws of the spiritual world. It is a law of the mind, that the ideas of sensible objects are first excited by having those objects presented to the senses; that knowledge, in the higher sense, is acquired by study; that the regular action of the mind requires a sound state of the brain, etc. Now we have no power, by any act of the will, to alter these laws of the mind, or to produce any mental action, except in conformity with them.

Again, it is found to be a law of the mind, that the affections are excited in view of suitable objects, and that the influence of external objects is according to the character and state of the mind. And who has power to make it otherwise? What man of sense will ever attempt to interfere with these settled laws? If through ignorance we should think we could move our hearts to love or hate by the mere force of volition, without having a suitable object before us, or if we should think that, with an object in view, we could, by a volition, excite any affections in ourselves, except in accordance with the character and state of our minds, we should soon be convinced of our mistake.

These remarks are made to illustrate the position, that we have no power, by a *volition*, to contravene the laws of nature, whether as to matter or mind, and no power to accomplish anything, except in accordance with those laws. The whole range of our voluntary agency is confined within these limits.

This brings me to the business of showing, positively, what is the power or influence which belongs to the will; or more properly what power we ourselves have by the acts of our will. This may be briefly described thus. By availing ourselves of the laws of nature, we can voluntarily produce an endless variety of effects. In this way we can secure a harvest, promote bodily health, cure diseases, improve our intellectual and moral faculties, and obtain the advantages and comforts of life.

It evidently follows, that the greatest extent of voluntary power requires a complete knowledge of the laws of nature. Knowledge is power only as it enables us to avail ourselves of these laws. If we are ignorant of them, how can we turn them to any useful purpose? Without a knowledge of the laws which regulate events in the physical and moral world, we are utterly unqualified to act our part as intelligent, accountable beings. Without a good degree of this knowledge, all our efforts would be made at random, and the result would be altogether uncertain, and so the motives to exertion would be inefficacious.

Our voluntary power, considered in this light, manifestly admits of an almost unlimited increase. Take the power we have, by an act of the will, to direct our attention to one thing or another, and to fix and detain our thoughts on any particular subject. We are conscious of possessing this power now in a certain degree. But we may not be aware to what a vastly higher degree it is capable of being increased by suitable exertion. The power possessed by such men as Newton, Locke, and Edwards, to confine their attention steadily, and for a long time, to a particular subject, and to exclude all thoughts pertaining to other subjects, was acquired by diligent and continued efforts. Other men may acquire the same. And if a man had his mind raised to the highest improvement of which it is susceptible, he would possess this power in such perfection, that he could, without difficulty fix his thoughts on any subject he might choose, with the utmost intenseness, uninterruptedly, and for such length of time as the case should require. The voluntary control which we commonly possess over our thoughts — what is it, compared with that to which we might attain? No man, however conscious of present inability thus to command his thoughts, has any right to conclude that his inability cannot be effectually removed by the diligent, persevering discipline of his own mind. It is the same here, as in regard to the voluntary control, which a man, by long use, acquires over his bodily motions. No one, however great the activity and adroitness which he has acquired, can say, that he has raised his voluntary power to its highest possible limits.

And yet it is a law of our nature, and doubtless a wise and benevolent one, that this voluntary power should be extended over a part only of our bodily organs. Our sensations are, in themselves, all involuntary. When the proper objects are presented, the sensations follow without any act of the will. Indeed the will has no power to prevent them. The action of the heart, of the blood, and of the digestive organ is also involuntary. The continued life and growth and health of the body, instead of being under the control of volition, result from their appropriate physical causes. Over these causes our will has an influence, though that influence is very limited. But if the appropriate causes exist, the effect takes place without any dependence on the will; while it is on the other hand equally true that, without those causes, the will can do nothing towards producing the effect. Who that has been at all observant of the laws of his nature, ever attempts, by a direct act of his will to increase or diminish the pulsations of his heart, the circulation of his blood, or the growth or health of his body? All the voluntary power which we possess in these and many other respects, is *indirect*, i. e. it operates through the medium of other things which we can in some measure control. I say in *some measure;* because it is evident that our bodily state is in a great degree dependent on causes over which we have little or no power. So that it would be contrary to fact to say, that man has anything like a *complete* power, either direct or indirect, over all his bodily organs.

But the most important question still remains, namely, what voluntary power we possess over *our affections*. This must be ascertained in the same way as our power in all other respects, — by an appeal to our own experience and consciousness. We have already seen, that the affections are called forth, or excited, by a view of proper objects. Whether these objects are denominated motives, occasions, or causes, it matters not. They are the uniform and immediate antecedents of the affections. No act of the will comes between the view of a proper object and the excitement of an affection. Should we attempt to thrust in a volition here, it would be out of place, and wholly ineffectual. Let an affectionate parent look upon a dear child who has been long absent. Does his heart wait for an act of the will to kindle its love? Or if for some reason he should do so strange a thing as to will not to love; would his heart obey? Or if the same parent should hear of the death of his child, would he wait for an act of the will to cause sorrow to fill his heart? And if he should put forth a volition not to feel sorrow, would his heart be obedient? The same as to the pious affections of a regenerate man. When the glorious character of God is presented to his view, he loves and adores. He does it at once, without any influence from an act of the will. Indeed if a man in such a case should find any occasion for an act of the will to excite his love, it would prove his heart to be in a bad state. If the goodness of God and its manifold fruits are contemplated by a man of right spirit, grateful emotions will spontaneously arise. And if he turns his thoughts to the evil of sin, his abhorrence will at once be excited. In all such cases, it is the nature or quality of the object he contemplates, and not an act of his will, that excites the emotions. In other words, the affections of the heart, whether of one kind or another, do not depend on a volition as their proximate cause, but on the presentation of a fit object.*

If the principles which we have laid down are correct, it will be easy to settle the question, *whether the affections are voluntary.* We usually call those things voluntary, which take place in consequence of a volition, or of which a volition is the uniform and immediate antecedent. It is not common to speak of anything as voluntary, because it follows *indirectly* from a volition, or because an act of the will has an influence upon it through the medium of something else. By a voluntary act, Whately says, "we take a medicine which quickens the circulation of the blood:" but we do not, on that account, call the quicker circulation of the blood voluntary. "So also, though we cannot by a direct effort of volition excite or allay any emotion; we may by a voluntary act, fill the understanding with such thoughts as will" have this effect. But is it according to common usage to call such an effect *voluntary?* As the affections are not the *immediate* or *direct* result of volition, it is clear they are not *directly voluntary.* You may say they are *indirectly* voluntary, because a volition operates upon them and controls them indirectly. But even this indirect influence of the will is by no means essential to the excitement of the affections.

* As the practical views which occupy several pages of this Essay, together with the quotations from Whately and other writers, are, for substance, contained in the Lectures on moral agency, they are here omitted.

The affections are not generally excited in this way. For fit objects or motives are very often brought before our minds, without any volition or thought of ours. But in these very cases, the affections are of the same nature, and stand in the same relation, to the objects which excite them, as in other cases. Yet they do not result from a volition either directly or indirectly. That is, they are not excited by volition, nor are those objects which do excite them, brought before the mind by a volition. Any man who will reflect on his own past experience will find, that in instances too many to be numbered, those objects have been presented before his mind, without his choice, and not unfrequently thrust upon him contrary to his wishes, which have nevertheless elicited the deepest and strongest emotions.

On this point, are not some distinguished writers chargeable with an oversight? They allow that the affections are not excited directly by an act of the will, but by a view of fit objects, in other words, by proper motives. Still they call the affections *voluntary;* and they hold *all* the moral affections to be so,— overlooking the obvious fact that, in a multitude of instances, if not generally, the objects of the affections are brought before our minds without any volition of ours, and that in such instances no act of the will has any influence on the affections in one way or another. This fact however is not to be considered as having any influence in regard to the *nature* of the affections.

In a former number I endeavored to show, that the affections which any one exercises in view of the various objects or motives which come before him, will be according to his *disposition, character, or state of mind.* There is no truth more confidently believed, or more uniformly acted upon, by men of practical wisdom, than this, and none which is capable of more satisfactory proof from Scripture and common experience. Ministers of the gospel especially, have it exemplified before them continually in the different effects which the same truths produce upon men of different habits or states of mind. But this is a truth, which most writers on mental philosophy overlook, taking it for granted, that all men are in such a state that moral considerations or motives, if contemplated in earnest, will excite right affections. Dr. Wardlaw, in his Lectures on Christian Ethics, has clearly shown how frequently this mistake is chargeable upon the most eminent writers on moral philosophy, and what mischievous influence it has on their reasoning. Abercrombie, also, has distinctly, though rather incidentally, recognized the principle which I have advanced, and has shown that he attaches great importance to it. He says, that "moral causes, that is, truths and motives," operate "with a uniformity similar to that with which physical agents produce their actions upon each other." But he says, "they require certain circumstances in the man on whom they are expected to act." He then mentions those circumstances. "It is necessary that a man be fully informed in regard to" the moral causes intended; "that his attention be directed to them with such a degree of intensity as shall bring him fully under their influence as statements addressed to his understanding." Here many philosophers would stop. But not so this author. He proceeds to say, that another thing is necessary in order that truths and motives, however clearly presented and however intensely considered, may produce a right effect upon a man. This necessary circumstance is, "*that there be a certain healthy state of his moral feelings*, — for this has a most extensive influence on the due operation of moral causes." The position I maintain is, that whatever we or others may do to bring motives before us, or to direct our attention to particular objects, *the emotions excited will be according to the state of the mind.* The objects presented to view, and other external circumstances which may in many instances be more or less under the control of the will, are indeed a part of what may be called the complex cause of the emotions. But the influence of whatever is external, and even the influence of our intellectual perceptions and the dictates of conscience will, after all, be according to the predominant disposition or state of our mind. If a man of an impure disposition, has certain objects presented to his eye or his thoughts, either by his own voluntary act or not, will not impure feelings be excited? His willing, in those circumstances, to be free from wrong feelings and to have right ones, will not control the movements of his heart. With such objects before him, and such a state of mind, he will have such emotions. "To the pure all things are pure; but to them that are defiled nothing is pure." Thus we see how it happens that a man is so often disappointed in regard to his own feelings. He voluntarily turns his attention to particular objects, or puts himself in particular circumstances, because, for some reason, he wishes to have certain emotions. But instead of the emotions desired, others of a different kind arise, and he thus finds that an act of his will can have no influence to elicit affections which are contrary to the state of his heart. It may sometimes be the case, that a man of a covetous disposition, may wish and labor to acquire riches, for the purpose, among other things, of curing his covetousness, and making his feelings kind and generous. But he is disappointed. His riches, when acquired, have no effect but to increase his covetous desires. Why is this? Because his external circumstances and his own thoughts and wishes, have an influence upon him *according to the character or state of his mind.* This well known principle, this law of our intellectual and moral nature, is taught in the Scriptures. When Christ says, "a good tree will bear good fruit, and a corrupt tree corrupt fruit," and that it cannot be otherwise, he says it to illustrate the principle that a man's feelings and actions will be according to his mental state or character. We can, indeed, excite a great variety of affections in ourselves by the exercise of our voluntary agency in the manner above described; but they will all be consonant to our predominant disposition. Take the case of confirmed hostility to the Christian religion, such as appeared in the leading infidels of the last century. Was it in the power of the most convincing arguments or the most persuasive eloquence to produce in their hearts, while unchanged by the Holy Spirit, the affection of true love to Christ and his religion? Take the case of an inveterate miser. Can you present any motives before him which will produce in his heart a sincere affection for the word of God, and a readiness to give away his treasures to the destitute? Take the case of the wicked at the last day. Their attention will be powerfully arrested by the most excellent, glorious, and moving objects. But they will have no right feeling. Amid all the light and glory of that day, they will have no emotions but those which correspond with their sinful disposition. Satan is a moral agent of high intellectual powers. Now suppose he could be admitted into the heavenly world, and see all that the angels see and enjoy. What would be his feelings? They would be feelings of hatred, envy, and remorse. Whence this difference between the feelings of Satan and the feelings of Gabriel, in view of the same objects? Whence, but from their different states of mind?

The principle which I have endeavored to illustrate, is often exemplified in the experience of sinners under awakenings of conscience. They are conscious that their affections towards divine things are sinful; and from their natural dread of misery and love of happiness, they in a sense desire such affections as God will approve, and, for the purpose of producing them, they apply themselves to a diligent and serious consideration of the character of God, the merciful interposition of the Redeemer, the holy law, and the precious blessings of salvation. But if the renewing of the Holy Spirit is withheld, they will have no right affections. Those divine objects which they contemplate, will, through their perverseness, be the occasion of exciting dislike and opposition in their hearts, and so prove "a savor of death unto death." "He that loveth is born of God," and this implies, that he only who is born of God, loveth. No considerations however mighty, no motives however powerful and touching, if unaccompanied by the renewing influence of the Spirit, will ever have power to produce any right affections in unregenerate men. "Except a man be born again, he cannot see the kingdom of God." And it is equally true, that except a man be born again, he cannot have holy affections; for the want of this is all that prevents his seeing the kingdom of God. If now we say or do anything to lead sinners to think, that any voluntary agency of theirs, or any power of excitement or persuasion which they can use with themselves, or which others can use with them, will ever bring them truly to love God, or believe in Christ, without the new creating agency of the Spirit; we practise a dangerous delusion upon them; and in this way, we show too, that we ourselves labor under a great mistake, and that we forget *the desperate wickedness of the heart.* Such is the state of the posterity of Adam, that if they become holy, their holiness will not be "from the will of the flesh, or *the will of man*," not from any disposition or voluntary agency of theirs, but from the Spirit of God; and the whole of their salvation will result, not from any works of righteousness which they have done, but from the purpose and grace of God. Christian ministers should remember this, and should learn to rely wholly upon divine power and mercy for the conversion and salvation of sinners.

I cannot close this number without remarking distinctly on the mistake of those writers on mental philosophy, who make up their systems without recognizing the peculiar facts which are disclosed in the Scriptures, and in the history of the church. No system of mental philosophy can be considered as complete, which overlooks any of the *principal* phenomena which the human mind has exhibited. But the time would fail me to speak of all those writers on intellectual and moral philosophy, who entirely neglect the peculiar mental operations and states so fully disclosed in the Scriptures, and whose systems are just what they would be, if man had no natural alienation from God, and just what they would be, if there were no such thing as conviction of sin, and regeneration by the Holy Spirit, and a warfare, throughout the life of Christians, between the law of their sanctified mind and the law of sin in their members. I shall give a single example of the fault referred to. Writers very properly notice it as a law of the mind, that the affections are elicited by a view of proper objects; and then, without considering that man is morally depraved, they represent the clear exhibition of divine truth to the understanding, and the serious consideration of it, as all that is necessary to call forth right affections, overlooking that special divine influence, which is the only efficient cause of holiness in the heart of man. Now this is as palpable a mistake as it would be in writers on health, to represent that wholesome food is all that is necessary to promote vigor and activity in those who are sick. If there are any facts which ought to be made prominent in a system of mental philosophy, surely they are those which are made prominent in the infallible word of God. For does not he who made and redeemed the soul, know what are its powers and capacities, its dispositions and states, and the laws which govern its operations? And can any one who believes the Scriptures, especially any minister of the gospel, deem it proper to disregard those preëminently important facts which result from man's apostasy, and from the work of Christ and the Holy Spirit in man's salvation? These facts, and the laws of the mind respecting them, which are all involved in sound Christian experience, are as certain and as worthy of consideration in a system of mental philosophy, as the laws of the understanding, of the memory, of conscience, or of the natural affections. And a system which overlooks the former is as defective and as much at variance with the truth, as one would be which should overlook the latter. There is no right mental philosophy, but that which has its chief foundation in the facts revealed in the word of God. The sacred writers, taught by their own experience, and by the Divine Spirit, understood the true philosophy of the human mind, and spoke and acted according to it. And if we would understand it, and apply it to its proper uses, we must learn to think and reason, to speak and act, as they did.

NUMBER IV.

In the last Article on the Philosophy of the Mind, I inquired what influence the *acts of the will* have over the *affections*. If the distinction which I have made between the acts of the will and the affections, is kept in mind, this inquiry will be intelligible and important. If not, what does it amount to? If the affections are considered as acts of the will, then the influence which the acts of the will have over the affections, is the influence which some acts of the will have over other acts of the will; and the influence which the *will* itself has over the affections, is the influence which a faculty has over its own acts. And what is the influence which a faculty has over its own acts, but simply its putting forth acts? And what is putting forth acts, but acting? To say then, that the will exerts an influence over its own acts, is the same as to say, that the will *acts*. If it is anything more, what is it?

This way of considering the affections as acts of *the will*, is, as we have seen, attended with a manifest inconvenience. For if you call the affections, as well as volitions, acts of the will, then you include under the same head two classes of mental acts which are essentially different, one class being in themselves morally good or evil, and the other not. And you yourself recognize the distinction, when you speak of the affections being influenced by the acts of the will. For surely you do not mean to speak of the influence of one thing over another, when both of them are of the same kind. And if they are not of the same kind, how can we discourse about them without confusion, if we include them both under the same name? Those who call the affections acts of the *will* are obliged to divide the acts of the will into two classes, and to mark these classes by distinct epithets, the constant use of which would be cumbersome. But if you omit them, and call both classes *acts of the will* merely, how can you discourse about them with clearness? I speak particularly of philosophical discourse, in which precision and exactness are necessary. The same as to the word *voluntary*. If you make it include not only those bodily and mental acts which follow a volition, but the volitions themselves; you must say in each case in what sense you use it, or you will expose others to mistake by using it ambiguously. You say the moral affections are *voluntary*. But do you mean, that the moral affections are *consequent* upon a *volition?* You reply, no. Why, then, do you use an expression, which, according to its ordinary meaning, would convey that sense? If you mean merely, that the affections belong to the *moral faculty*, which has generally been called *the will*, and if, when you say the affections are voluntary, you mean, that they are of a moral nature, and that we are answerable for them; I acknowledge that this may be well enough for the purposes of common discourse among those who understand the word *voluntary* as you do. But as most men would understand you to mean, that the affections move *in obedience to a volition*, the expression would generally occasion a mistake.

The reason why it is supposed by many, that we can be accountable for nothing except what is *voluntary*, has already been suggested. In regard to our external, visible actions, and certain mental actions, it is true, that we are accountable for them only as they are voluntary, that is, subject to the control of the will. From these we get an impression that *all* the actions which we are accountable for, are voluntary, and under the influence of this impression, we frame our language, and then apply it to quite another kind of actions, that is, the affections, and call *them voluntary*; not to denote that they are controlled by a volition, but merely that they are of a moral nature; and that we are accountable for them, *as we are for those bodily and mental actions which depend on a volition.* I would not be strenuous about a particular word. But it is certainly important to avoid ambiguity, and to mark those things which are different by different words. And as I have often noticed the confusion of thought which arises from using the words, *will*, *volition*, and *voluntary*, in a loose indefinite manner, I shall adhere to the sense in which these words have already been explained, and to which there is a manifest leaning in the minds of common people.

No doubt some readers have had a difficulty arise in their minds respecting the position which I have taken. If it be so that our affections are not under the direct influence of the will, and often not under even its indirect influence, then how are we accountable either for the one or the other?

Here our proper business is to show what is *the fact* in regard to the influence of the will over the affections. Is it true, that we exercise our affections because we *will* to exercise them, and *as* we will to do it? If we find it to be the case, that our affections are thus controlled by a volition, then we will admit the fact, and make it a part of our system of mental philosophy. But suppose the fact to be, that our affections are not governed by an act of the will. Is not this to make a part of our philosophy? Or will you say, that it cannot be so, and that, if we are accountable for our affections, we must be able to control them by an act of the will? Examine the subject then thoroughly. If after all, you find the fact to be as I have stated, will you still say, *it cannot be, and if we are accountable for our affections, we must be able to govern them by a volition?* But suppose you find that your saying this, will not make it so, and the stubborn fact still comes out to view, that our affections are not under the control of volition. What will you do now? Will you turn caviller, and say, *why doth he yet find fault?*

While you are contemplating the fact, that the affections are not controlled by volition, take care not to overlook another fact, which is attended with the highest kind of evidence,—the fact that you are a moral and accountable being, and that you are good or bad, praise-worthy or blame-worthy according as your affections are. You know this intuitively. Unless your moral nature is totally perverted, you are as certain of it, as of existence. And it would be no more unreasonable and foolish for you to doubt your own existence, than to doubt your moral and accountable agency. You are in truth a moral agent, and are accountable for your affections, whatever may be the manner in which they are excited. The constitution which God has given to the mind, must be perfectly right, and the very fact above stated, which is sometimes thought inconsistent with moral agency, is doubtless essential to it. If the affections, instead of being excited by suitable objects, were governed by a mere act of the will, there would be an end of rational and accountable agency. The ground-work of moral good and evil would be taken away.

In making out a system of mental philosophy, our single inquiry must be, *what is matter of fact?* How that which we find to be fact, can be reconciled with moral agency, is another question, and no more belongs to us, than the question, how the magnetic power can be reconciled with gravitation. If, however, any one takes upon him to assert, that the fact which I have insisted upon in regard to the affections, is inconsistent with moral agency, it will be incumbent on him to prove his assertion. And I should hope, that an attempt to do this would convince him of his mistake. Every man is most certainly chargeable with a mistake, who supposes that perfect moral agency is inconsistent with anything which we find to be a fact in the constitution of the mind. The laws of the mind are not only consistent with moral agency, but essential to it. These laws it is our object, as philosophers, to discover. And if we would be successful in our inquiries, we must proceed without shackles. We must be governed by no prepossession. We must have no such impression as this, that the affections *must* be governed by the will, or we cannot be moral agents. An impression like this would certainly prove an embarrassment, and would prevent an impartial regard to evidence.

The supposition, that we are more accountable for our volitions, than for our affections, is wholly unwarrantable. It rests on the assumption, that our volitions are in themselves moral acts, and that our affections are not so. But, in truth, what is there in the class of mental acts called volitions, which leads you to consider them morally good or bad, more than the other class, called the affections? Do you say volitions are more properly our own acts than the affections? But how does this appear? Are not loving and hating as much our own acts, as willing and choosing? Do we not exercise as high a degree of activity, in the former, as in the latter? Is there anything in ourselves or in others, which we more spontaneously pronounce to be right or wrong, praiseworthy or blame-worthy, than the affections? Some appear to think, that if we only give the name of *volitions*, or *acts of the will*, to the affections, the difficulty is relieved at once. But does it alter the nature of mental acts, or make us more accountable for them, to call them by a particular name? Are not the mental acts referred to, perfectly the same when you call them *affections*, as when you call them *acts of the will?*

But I must come to the chief object of the present number; which is to show, that instead of the affections being under the direct influence of the volitions, just the opposite is true, namely, *that the volitions are under the influence of the affections;* and that, instead of the affections deriving their moral character from any acts of the will, *all acts of the will derive their moral character, so far as they have any, from the affections.*

To illustrate the first of these points, I shall adduce a few examples. And if we find what the laws of the mind are in a few instances, we know what they are in all instances of the same kind.

I ask then, why does a Christian *will* or *determine*, to devote a part of his property to the cause of benevolence? And why does a pious youth *choose* to quit his secular business, and prepare for the ministry? And why does a Christian, when duty requires, *choose* to suffer persecution for the name of Christ? What is it, in each of these cases, that *influences* a Christian thus to *will*, and thus to act? Obviously he does it under the influence of his pious *affections*. He does it, because he loves Christ and the souls of men. This is the *motive*, which leads him to such a volition. It is equally evident, that a wicked man's volitions arise from his affections. Why did Judas *will* to betray Christ? Because he had a selfish, avaricious, resentful heart. It was *fear* which influenced Peter to deny his Lord. *Ambition* prompts a Cæsar and a Napoleon to engage in war. It is a fact perfectly familiar to us, that the particular determinations of the will, whether right or wrong, are influenced by the affections. The affections including the emotions and passions, are eminently *the principles of action*. Without these, how could we act at all? And without *moral* affections, how could we perform moral acts, or have any volitions which are of a moral nature? If the acts of the will do not flow from the affections, why may it not be, that a man who has no love to God, will choose to labor and suffer for God just as much as if he had love? And why may it not be, that a person whose heart is full of benevolence towards his fellow men, will choose to treat them, and actually treat them, with unkindness and cruelty, just as though he had the opposite affection of hatred. If the affections do not govern the acts of the will, you can never anticipate what your voluntary conduct will be, from your knowledge of your own heart. If you are a parent, and have a strong and tender affection for your children, you cannot conclude from this, that your treatment of them will be different from what it would be, if your heart were full of spite towards them. Is it not perfectly clear, that all our expectations as to the voluntary acts of men, proceed on the principle, that their determinations and consequent actions will be influenced by their affections? And do not all our attempts to influence their determinations and acts proceed on the same principle? Do we not always endeavor to move their affections, in order to influence their determinations? The acts of the will, and the conduct resulting from them, are the natural utterance of the heart. They are the way in which the affections act themselves out. And without this efficacy of the affections, there is no conceivable way in which we can put forth acts of will. If any man will watch the operations of his own mind, and attend to those maxims of practical wisdom which flow from experience and observation, he will find abundant evidence of the principle, *that the affections govern the acts of the will.* Whatever external objects are presented before us, our affections are the real ultimate motives, which influence us in our volitions. That we have a motive or reason for our choices, is implied in the fact, that we are rational; as it will be seen on a moment's reflection, that our willing anything without a motive, (if such an absurdity can be conceived of,) would imply the want of rationality. This subject is treated particularly by Edwards in his treatise on the Will; and his main position in opposition to the notion of a self-determining power of the will, is supported by arguments, unanswered, and unanswerable. The principle which I maintain, is clearly implied in our moral and accountable agency. For we could never regard a volition, which should take place without any motive, as either morally good or evil. An essential condition of a moral act would be wanting. If you require proof of this, I produce the fact, that there never was a moral agent, whose will was self-determined in the sense above suggested. And that this is a fact, I show by appealing to every man's experience and consciousness. If you deny the fact, I shall require you to produce some instance, in which a moral agent put forth a volition, or determination of will, without any motive. And if you should produce yourself, as the moral agent who has done this; I should regret that you think so meanly of yourself, and should do you the honor to say, you are mistaken.

If it is necessary to consider this matter further, I would ask the reader, whether he would think it a desirable thing to be able to put forth acts of will which should be wholly uninfluenced by the affections. Would you regard it as a privilege to will and to do what is contrary to every affection and disposition of your heart? Would it gratify you to be so constituted that, while all your affections move towards God, and delightfully rest in him, your *will* might put forth choices in opposition to him, and so lead you to open disobedience? Such might be the result, if your will should break loose from the control of the affections, and put forth its acts in some other way. What distraction would be so dreadful as this? To reduce man to such a condition, his rational and moral constitution must have an unheard of shock. Happily for us, our intellectual and spiritual constitution is secured against such a calamity as this, by the appointment and ever-present agency of the being who made us.

The other point mentioned above, namely, that *the character* of every volition depends on *the character of the affection from which it proceeds*, is equally evident. If our volitions are the result of a *moral affection*, we necessarily consider them of a *moral nature*, whatever may be the outward object acting on the mind. For the outward object can get access to the will and influence its acts, only through the affections. It is the affection which comes in contact with the will, and determines the character of its acts. If the affection which prompts the volitions, is right, *they* are right, that is relatively; and a relative rightness is all they can have. If the affection is wrong, the volitions flowing from it are also wrong. And when I speak of volitions in this way, as flowing from the affections, I mean to include the mental and bodily acts which are connected with the volitions, and which are, on that account, called voluntary. And on the other hand, when I speak of these mental and bodily acts, I mean to speak of them as implying a volition, and as resulting directly from it.

The principle which I here advance, that the character of our volitions is according to the character of our affections, is nothing different from the common maxim, that our conduct is right or wrong according to our *motives*. For the motives of our conduct ultimately consist in the affections. This principle is acted upon continually and instinctively, whether men judge of their own conduct, or that of others. You see a man contribute to a charitable object. You immediately approve of the act. You say it is a good deed. Why? Because it appears to spring from a good motive, that is, a benevolent affection. But if you find that the action, which appeared so benevolent, really proceeded from a selfish, base motive; you change your mind as to the action, and as to the choice of the will to perform it. You cannot but judge of these according to the inward motive that prompted them; or, to speak more exactly, you cannot but judge of the *person* according to the affection which he exhibits in his conduct. Take another case. Suppose your first impression is, that a man *wills* and *acts* from a bad motive. You accordingly feel disapprobation. But if you afterwards discover that you made a mistake, and that his motive was good, you at once change your mind as to the character of the volition and act, or rather, as to the character of *the man*.

The judgment which we form in such a case, is founded on the immutable principles of our intelligent and moral nature. We cannot judge our own volitions, or the volitions of others, to be either praise-worthy or blame-worthy, without referring to the governing motive. Every sentiment of approval or disapproval in regard to the acts of the will looks ultimately to the inward motive from which they spring. The Scripture confirms the truth of this position, when it represents *love* to be the whole of what is required of us as duty. Various voluntary actions are indeed required, but they are required as expressions of love. If any volitions or voluntary acts of ours could be morally right, separate from affection, how could it be true, that all the law is comprised in the precept requiring love?

There are important points of a practical nature, resulting from the foregoing discussion.

First. In our addresses to our fellow men, we should avoid every expression which implies, that their affections depend on a volition, or spring directly from it. This would be inverting the established order of mental operations. We have seen, too, that the goodness of our volitions, which is only a relative goodness, presupposes the goodness of an affection, and flows from it; and we should avoid every representation which implies the contrary. If we teach, that a sinner's loving God depends on his *willing* or *resolving* to love, or if we exhort him to *resolve* or *determine* to love, as the way in which he is to exercise love; we violate the order which the Author of our being has established, and attempt to put a kind of force upon the mind, and to bring it to act contrary to its own unchangeable laws. It is under the influence of this mistake, that persons awakened to serious and anxious reflection, so often waste their time, and misapply their faculties, in striving to bring themselves to love God, and to believe in Christ, by merely *willing* or *resolving* to do it.

If you ask, then, what shall sinners be directed to do? I answer, *just what God requires.* His commands are perfectly reasonable. They require that, and that only, which it is right for men to do. These commands are to be the matter of our directions. If God commands sinners to believe in Christ, we are to announce this command to them, and to direct them and endeavor to persuade them to perform this duty. If he requires them to love him with all the heart, we, who are his messengers, are to require them to do the same. What should we direct them to do, if not to obey the divine commands? Now, if God does not direct sinners to *will* or *determine* to love him, as something distinct from actually loving him, why should we? Do you ask, how they can love without first *willing* or *resolving* to love? It would be more proper to ask, how they can do it *by* willing or resolving to do it, seeing the affection is not excited by the power of a volition. If we wish to bring men to exercise holy affections, we must exhibit the proper objects, or present the proper motives of such affections. And if men are convinced of the importance of right affections in themselves, and really wish to exercise them, let them fix their minds intensely upon the proper *objects*, and diligently contemplate the proper *motives*, instead of relying upon the direct influence of an act of the will to excite the affections. If we have a clear view of spiritual objects, if our attention is duly awakened, and directed to the great motives to holy love which the word of God presents, and if the moral state of our minds is right; there will be no occasion for an act of the *will* to intervene, in order to excite our love. A perception of the objects is all that is necessary. As soon as we see the glorious character of God, we love him. The affection flows forth spontaneously in view of that object. If, when we contemplate such an object, no love is kindled, and we resort to an act of the will to excite the affection, we give conclusive proof that our heart is not right. And we know it would be totally unsafe to rely for the renewal of the heart either on external motives, or on the power of a volition, as that great work is effected, not by "the will of the flesh, nor by the will of man," but by the Spirit of God.

You may say then, the efforts of ministers to exhibit divine truth and to persuade sinners to repent, and the efforts of unregenerate men to bring themselves to repent, are, according to this view, wholly in vain, and that we are reduced to a state of inaction and despair. The objection seems to amount to this; unless ministers can convert sinners by instruction and persuasion, *without the effectual operation of God*, their labors are in vain; and unless sinners can convert themselves, or bring themselves to repent, by their own voluntary efforts, *without the special influence of the Spirit*, they are reduced to a state of inaction and despair. As to ministers, one word will be sufficient. If they have received the testimony of the sacred writers, they know and feel, that "neither he that planteth, nor he that watereth, is anything;" that they cannot, of themselves, turn sinners to God, and that their labors would forever be in vain, were it not for the promised influence of the Holy Spirit. It is their dependence on the special operation of God, that encourages and animates them in their work, and fills them with hope that their labors will not be in vain in the Lord. As to the tendency of the views which I have exhibited to reduce sinners to a state of despair, I have but a few things to say here. First, the requisitions of the law and the gospel are all right, and sinners ought immediately to comply with them. Secondly, those who refuse to comply, are wholly without excuse, as there is nothing which hinders their compliance, but the obstinate wickedness of their hearts. Thirdly, if instead of requiring holy love, we should require of them a *volition* or *resolution* to love, and if instead of requiring cordial and holy obedience, we should require a *determination* to obey; this would be taking upon ourselves the fearful responsibility of essentially varying the divine requisitions; inasmuch as a volition or resolution of sinners to love and obey is entirely a different act from loving and obeying, and neither implies love and obedience, nor produces it. If we direct sinners to such a volition or resolution to love, as the means of exciting love, we commit an obvious mistake, and involve them in the danger of spending their time in fruitless efforts to do what they ought to do at once. If their hearts are right, they will love God, without trying to love. But if we direct sinners to a volition or determination to love God, as a *substitute* for love, and as that which will answer the divine requisition, for a time at least, without love; we commit a still greater mistake, and expose them to still greater danger.

As to the despair of impenitent sinners which is spoken of, what is it but an obstinate refusal to obey the holy command which God gives them, and to accept the gracious offer of eternal life which he makes? They despair, because God will not be pleased with anything short of what is right, that is, holy obedience. They say, require anything of us which we can do in our unregenerate state, and we will do it. With such a heart as we have, and from a regard to our own happiness, we can wish and resolve to repent and to love God. And this we do. But if you say, this will not answer, and insist upon our exercising holy affection, which we cannot do in our unregenerate state; you reduce us to a desperate condition, and we know not what course to pursue. Permit me to say in reply, that the condition of sinners, is in fact a dreadful one, and so far as relates to any thing which they, of themselves, will ever do to obtain salvation, it is *desperate*. And the sooner they are made sensible of this, the better; so that they may give up every hope, except in the sovereign mercy of God, and may find rest to their souls by trusting in an almighty Saviour. We cannot vary the directions which Christ and his apostles give to sinners, and which require them to love God and obey his word without any delay. We cannot accommodate our instructions to the depraved hearts of men; nor can we admit, that their depravity is any kind of excuse for their refusing to repent and obey the gospel. And we cannot substitute any volition or resolution arising from a selfish heart, in the place of that love which God requires. Instead of contenting ourselves with requiring of sinners any act which is destitute of holiness, because *they* are destitute of holiness, we must in the name of God, enjoin upon them the duty of *becoming holy;* not the duty of *resolving* to love God and believe in Christ, but the duty of actually *loving* and *believing;* and must charge them with being highly criminal, and altogether inexcusable, if they do not immediately perform this duty. And we must tell them, and endeavor to make them feel, that just so far as they find it difficult or hard to love God, or to believe in the Lord Jesus Christ, they show themselves to be exceedingly sinful, and deserving of the divine displeasure. And it seems to me unquestionable, that what we do, by giving instruction and by urging gospel motives, for the direct purpose of bringing sinners to *repent*, to *believe*, and to *love*, will be much more likely to accomplish the great object aimed at, than any efforts we might make to excite them to the performance of those acts which fall short of repentence, faith and love.

Secondly. The principle which I have maintained respecting the influence of the affections over the acts of the will, furnishes an easy and satisfactory explanation of what the Scripture says as to the bondage of sinners, and what the old writers say as to the slavery of the will. The sacred writers represent, that the wicked are in a state of *servitude*, and that none are *free*, but those who belong to the kingdom of holiness. To be in a state of *servitude* or *bondage* in the Scripture sense, is to be under the dominion of sin, to be governed by depraved affection. To be *free*, is to be free from the bondage of *sin*, and be under the dominion of holiness. The old divines spoke of freedom and bondage in the same sense. And unless you keep this in mind, you will be liable to mistake the meaning of many of the best writers of former days. When they asserted that since the fall, the human will is deprived of its *freedom*, and is under *bondage*, they meant something very different from what is meant at the present day, when it is asserted that *free will* belongs to all men alike, whether good or bad. *Freedom of will*, as now commonly understood, is an essential property of a moral agent. But freedom of will was formerly understood to be the property of those only who are the followers of Christ, and denoted freedom from the dominion of corrupt affection. In the controversy which took place respecting *free will* in the time of Luther and Calvin, and afterwards, those who maintained the freedom of the will, denied the natural and entire depravity of man. They held that the will is not naturally under a wrong bias, not subject to a sinful heart. Those who denied the freedom of the will, held that man is by nature depraved, that all the acts of his will, while unregenerate, are influenced by his corrupt heart, and that none enjoy freedom from the slavery of sin, but those who are brought into "the liberty of the sons of God." According to this use of the words, which fully corresponds with the Scripture use, our saying that the will of every natural man is *enslaved*, would mean, not merely that his will is governed by his *affections*, (which is common to all whether good or bad,) but that it is governed by *sinful* affections. And our saying that the will of those who are holy is *free*, would mean, not that their will is free from the dominion of the affections, (which is not the case with any,) but that it is free from the dominion of *sinful* affections. And it is certainly with very good reason, that the degraded state of those who are in subjection to depraved affection, is called *bondage* and *slavery;* and that the happy state of those who are delivered from the dominion of depraved affection, and whose will is brought under the dominion of holiness, is called *freedom* and *liberty*.

Finally; as it appears that the determinations of the will, and of course all the voluntary actions, are governed by the affections, and as the state of the affections is the basis and the substance of character; we see how indispensable it is, that we should have *the renewing of the Holy Ghost*. The great and essential work of the Spirit is, *to rectify the state of the affections*, *to renew the heart*. This work is not effected by any efforts of our fellow-men, nor by any acts of our own will. It is specially, preëminently the work of the Holy Spirit. Thus we see that the philosophy of the mind, rightly understood, teaches the same humiliating truth with the Scriptures, — that we are in a state of moral ruin, utterly lost, and that there is no help for us but in God.

NUMBER V.

HOW THE AFFECTIONS ARE INFLUENCED BY PREVIOUS AFFECTIONS.

I HAVE already endeavored to show, what influence the will has upon the affections, and the affections upon the will. I shall now attend to *the manner in which our affections are influenced by antecedent affections*.

It is indispensable to the right understanding of this subject, as well as of many other subjects in mental philosophy, to consider, that *the operations of the mind generally result, not from any one cause exclusively, but from various causes combined.* We are taught by experience, that a particular operation or state of mind follows a particular cause; and to this cause we are accustomed to refer it. And it may be that this cause has not only a real and uniform influence, but a chief influence. And we may direct our attention to this influence only; and so may be ready to conclude, that nothing else has any influence in causing the mental operation or state. Whereas, a further consideration of the subject may show, that this operation or state results from a variety of causes, some near and some remote.

It seems hardly necessary to remark, that when we use the words *cause* and *effect*, and other words of similar import, in relation to the mind, we are to give them a meaning correspondent with the nature of the subject. It is perfectly according to common usage, to apply these words to the mind as well as to the material world, although not in precisely the same sense. And why should any one suppose, that it is not as admissible to make this use of the words *cause* and *effect*, as to take any words which have been applied to body, and apply them to mind? Who would object to our using the word *move*, and its derivatives, to denote an influence exerted on the mind, because they also denote an influence on matter? An adherence to such a principle would lead to an entire revolution in our modes of speech, and would divest language of its greatest beauty and force. Be it so, that the use of words for which I now contend, is metaphorical. It is not, therefore, any the less just and suitable. The propriety of such a use of the words *cause* and *effect* appears in this, that there is as real and uniform a relation between cause and effect in *mental* science, as in *physical*. A *cause* is that from which an effect flows, — that which has an influence to produce an effect. An *effect* is that which flows from something else as its cause, or is produced by the influence of a cause. Now, that which we call a *mental* or *moral cause*, has an influence as real and certain as a physical cause, although the *nature* of the cause and effect in the one case is exceedingly different from what it is in the other. Do you say, there is so wide a difference in the nature of what we denominate cause and effect in the two cases, as to expose men to mistake, if we employ the same words in both? The difference, I admit, is obvious and entire. And this very circumstance is sufficient to prevent all mistake.

We sometimes speak of cause and effect in a *mixed* sense, — a mental cause being connected with a bodily effect, and a bodily cause with a mental effect. Numberless phenomena of this kind are involved in the connection of body and mind. There is a mutual influence. A volition, which is a mental act, causes a bodily act; and an affection of the body often causes a mental act.

We now proceed to the subject introduced above, namely, *the manner in which our present affections are influenced by those which occurred in past time.*

One way in which a previous affection has an influence upon present affections, is *by being distinctly recollected.* When brought by an act of memory before the mind as an object of contemplation, it becomes, like any other object of attention, a means of exciting present affections. It is, however, *only one* of the means, — one of a variety of things which operate as causes of present affections. Those very emotions which arise in view of a past affection, may result in part, and even chiefly, from other causes. And those other causes may greatly modify the appropriate influence of the recollected affection; so that the emotion which that recollected affection produces, may be very different from what it would be, if that were the only cause concerned. The cause which operates in this case, is a *complex* cause, and the principal part of it is the state or habit of the mind. Indeed, the recollection of past affection may rather be considered as the occasion of bringing out the affection which naturally results from *the state of the mind.* It is this which determines the particular influence of the external motive. If an intelligent being has a holy state of mind, it is the law of his nature, that in all ordinary circumstances, outward objects will excite holy emotions; and that if he has an unholy state of mind, outward objects will excite unholy emotions. So in the natural world. Heat will harden or soften, according to the *nature* of the substance on which it acts. This general principle is as true in mental science as in physical; although the causes and effects in the one are, in their nature, so different from what they are in the other. The relation of our affections to the divine law, and our being worthy of praise or blame on account of them, does not imply that they arise in the mind without appropriate moral causes.

It is not meant by any of the remarks above made, that the affections always flow on in an unbroken series, and that no cause whatever can interfere to prevent this; for, although the state of the mind and the outward objects commonly acting upon it, naturally tend to this result, there may be extraordinary causes which will mingle their influence with these, so that the series of similar emotions will be broken, and those of a different kind excited. For example, a moral agent, under the influence of strong temptations, changes from holiness to sin; and a sinner, under the special influence of the Holy Spirit, becomes holy. But the occurrence of these changes under the operation of extraordinary causes does not prove, that a continuance of the same affection is not likely to result from the ordinary causes above mentioned, namely, the *state of the mind* and *outward motives*. Nor does it prove that these ordinary causes may not, in due time, become so powerful, as to preclude any change in the character of the affections. Unquestionably this will be the case both with the holy and with the unholy in the future state.

In the second place, the affections we exercise have an influence in regard to subsequent affections, by means of their influence on the state or habit of the mind; or, upon the mind's aptitude to the exercise of particular affections. That there is such an aptitude or tendency of the mind to put forth certain emotions rather than others, under the influence of the same external objects, is a fact well known. This aptitude shows its highest power, when a particular object excites an affection most readily,

9*

most frequently, or most strongly. The natural tendency of any affection which is exercised, is to increase the aptitude of the mind to the exercise of the same affection. This tendency may be counteracted, or its effect varied, by other causes. But every exercise of mind, taken by itself, plainly has this tendency. Thus benevolent emotions give the mind a greater aptitude to the same emotions. The consequence of every act of love to God, supposing us free from all opposite influences, is, that we shall be more *apt* to love him hereafter. It is on this principle that Christians grow in grace. Every exercise of holy love has a good influence upon their character, in proportion to the purity and strength of the exercise. A few holy exercises, in which all the intellectual and moral energies are roused to intense action, contribute more to the growth and confirmation of a holy principle and habit, than thousands of exercises which come from a divided or sluggish heart. The same is true of malevolent affections. The emotions of anger and revenge naturally tend to increase the aptitude of the mind to the same emotions; and this effect will be in proportion to the strength and violence of the antecedent emotions.

But *this natural tendency of our affections*, like that above mentioned, *is frequently modified by other causes.* A particular affection may be attended with such circumstances, that it will be followed by a less aptitude to the same affection than existed before.*

A due consideration of the statements above made will help us to account for that low, earthly state of mind, that spiritual blindness and death, which Christians so often have occasion to deplore. This state is to be considered in connection with its causes. It is in a great measure to be traced to what has been faulty in us in times past. Every sinful feeling which we have heretofore exercised, has left its stamp upon our hearts. That moral state which we lament, is to be regarded as resulting chiefly from the general current of our moral feelings in past time. Every vain thought, every proud, resentful, or unkind feeling, every corrupt desire,

* Several illustrations of this principle, together with its practical uses, are here omitted, as they are for substance contained in the Lectures on moral agency.

which has lodged within us, has had an influence not limited to the time when it took place, but reaching to all following time, and helping to constitute our permanent habit. Thus our present condition may truly be regarded as a kind of index to the antecedent states of our mind, — the sum of the impressions made upon us by the affections we exercised the previous moment, the previous hour, and day, and month, and year, and all previous time. How often have we learned by experience, that our feelings through the week have an effect upon us on the Sabbath, and our feelings on the Sabbath, through the week? How evident it is that the thoughts and feelings indulged in childhood and youth have an effect upon character, in manhood, and even in old age! The wrong states of mind of which we are at present conscious, and which may sometimes appear unaccountable, are, in many cases, owing to what took place ten, twenty, or even fifty years ago. And it is not to be doubted, that the state in which the wicked will find themselves in the future world, will be the fair result of all their dispositions, thoughts, affections, and actions, during the time of their probation. With what awe should we be inspired, when we contemplate this constitution, which God has given to our immortal minds! With what fear and trembling should we consider the fact, that an unholy affection, exercised in early childhood, will be followed by a sinful, impenitent life, and a sinful and miserable eternity, unless the grace of God interpose to turn things from their natural course.

REMARKS ON CAUSE AND EFFECT.*

I HAVE read with no ordinary interest, the Essay in the last number of the Repository "on Cause and Effect, in connection with Fatalism and Free Agency. The Editor says, the name of the writer is withheld, on account of very peculiar circumstances. As there are no such circumstances in my case, I shall offer remarks on the Essay in my own name. The writer of the Essay may be one, for whom I entertain a very sincere esteem and affection. I choose to think that he is so; and it will be most agreeable to my feelings to proceed in my remarks with the apprehension distinctly in my mind, that the anonymous author of the Essay, who has given such evidence of ability to write well, possesses also a sincere love of the truth, a full conviction of the narrow limits of human intelligence, humility, candor, reverence for the Scriptures, and every other quality which belongs to the Christian character. Such an apprehension may have a salutary influence upon what I am to write, and it will at least render my employment in writing pleasant.

After all, *my concern will be with the subject.* And while I shall take the liberty to call in question some of the principal positions which I find in the Essay, it will be my endeavor to guard scrupulously against everything which would be unjust or disre-

* First published in the "Am. Bib. Repository," 1840, in reply to "An Essay on Cause and Effect in connection with Fatalism and Free Agency." See Am. Bib. Rep. for Oct. 1839.

spectful to the writer. Indeed I shall refer to the Essay chiefly as an occasion of introducing several topics, which require special attention at the present day.

As the subject under consideration is of a philosophical or metaphysical nature, the following remarks are intended for those, who have a capacity for metaphysical inquiries, and who have so far attended to matters of this kind, that they are prepared to begin where the present discussion begins, without any pains on my part to explain the common principles of mental science.

But I should hardly deem it proper to busy myself in preparing remarks upon the topics here introduced, were it not that they have a bearing upon some very important principles of revelation.

Let it, however, be remembered, that our mode of thinking on this subject cannot alter the facts in the case. If all the men in the world should happen to think, that our being *uniformly* influenced in our volitions by motives, and our choosing *invariably* according to the *strongest* motive, is inconsistent with free moral agency, it would not make it so. Should they be ever so confident, that moral necessity, as explained by Edwards, Day, and others, is the same as fatalism; still it would not make it the same. If it is a law of our nature, that our volitions invariably follow that which is, on the whole, the strongest motive; then, whatever may be our speculations, this law will stand and we shall conform to it in practice, and shall choose and act under the influence of the strongest motive, without the least infringement of our rational or moral freedom. I think the writer of the Essay does himself act on this principle, though against his speculative theory. There were reasons, I suppose, for and against his publishing his Essay; and probably he will find, on reflection, that these reasons were very carefully weighed, and that the most important reasons finally prevailed. So also there were, doubtless, reasons for and against his giving his name to the public. But the special reasons which he had against it, were unquestionably the most weighty in his mind; otherwise, I could not account for it, that he deliberately chose concealment. And who can doubt, that in all important cases which shall occur hereafter, he will thus weigh the reasons for different determinations, and decide according to that which is, in his view, the strongest. And I am greatly mistaken, if he ever finds, that choosing and acting invariably according to this principle, will interfere at all with his free agency, though his theory might lead him to think that it would. Rational beings will choose and act according to the laws of their intelligent and moral nature, whatever speculative theories they may form in their waking or sleeping hours. The laws of the mind are too firmly established to be shaken by our notions.

I am gratified that the author of this Essay, and some other late writers, make a distinction between *desire* and *volition*. It is a source of no small confusion in Edwards's Treatise on the Will, that he considers all the *affections* and *desires* as acts of the *will*. It is, however, manifest, that Edwards himself departs from this large sense of the word, and brings out the distinction which is now contended for, whenever he speaks of the desires or affections of the mind as among *the motives to volition*. For surely the *motive* to volition, and *volition* itself, cannot be the same thing.

I am gratified also, that the writer says distinctly, what Locke and others have been careful to say before, that " the Will is not a separate existence, to which qualities and actions can be ascribed. It is the mind itself which is moved by desire or motive, and the Will is the power which the mind has to choose which of several coëxisting desires shall be gratified."

The writer says ; " The point at issue is simply this : Is volition connected with a previous desire or motive as a producing constitutional cause ? " The affirmative he thinks is *fatalism ;* the negative, the doctrine of *free agency*.

The writer takes commendable care to inform us very definitely, what he means by a " producing cause, " and how we are to discover its existence. He maintains, that according to the doctrine of free agency, " there is *no invariable* rule of volition, " — " no *fixed* connection between any class of desires and volition ; " that " desires or motives are only the *occasional* causes, which enable the mind to exercise its inherent power of action, itself being the producing cause of its own volitions." He says too, "the only method of proving anything to be a producing cause is to show, that, in given circumstances, there is an *invariable rule* of change, so that when a cause is put in these circumstances, a certain change *invariably* follows. It is the *unfailing constancy* of the result, that enables us to detect the real producing cause. The philosopher, in experimenting to detect causes, is continually seeking to learn *which one* of the various circumstances cannot have a substitute, — *which* must be invariably an antecedent." He says the same again. "The only method of proving a thing to be a *producing* cause, is to establish the fact that it is an *invariable* antecedent."

Our author makes his meaning still more evident by his quotations from Priestley, and the use he makes of them. Priestley says, in common with Edwards, and other distinguished writers: "There is some fixed law respecting the Will; — it is never determined without some motive of choice; and motives influence us in *some definite and invariable manner*, so that volition or choice is constantly regulated by what precedes it. And this *constant* determination of the mind, according to the motive presented to it, is all I mean by *necessary* determination. *Through all nature, the same consequences invariably result from the same circumstances.*" Now our author says, "no intelligent defender of free agency will admit this." And his object in quoting it is to show what he means by fatalism. If we assert, that volition is invariably preceded by the strongest motive, or by that which, at the moment of choice, "seems most agreeable," he says we are fatalists.

To this allegation of the author I now invite the reader's attention.

I cannot but notice, that the author here and there gives an incorrect statement of the question at issue. He represents the doctrine of moral or philosophical necessity as implying, that "there is a *particular kind* of motive which is the invariable antecedent of volition." He says: "every one allows that motives of *some sort* are invariably antecedents to volition. This is taken for granted; and then the admission is used as if it were conceded that a *particular kind* of motive were the invariable antecedent. As if a man should claim, that *sowing of some sort* is always an antecedent to all kinds of harvest, and when this is allowed, should assume that the sowing of *wheat* is the invariable antecedent of all kinds of harvest." But neither Edwards nor any other respectable writer ever maintained such an opinion, or reasoned in such a manner. No one can believe what is so obviously contrary to experience, as this, that volition uniformly follows a *particular kind* of motives. One particular kind of motives consists of those which are derived from the appetite of hunger and thirst; another kind, of those derived from the sense of hearing; another, from the sense of seeing; another from a regard to property; another from the love of promotion or praise; another, from love to God. The *particular kinds* of motives are past numbering. Now who ever entertained the idea, that our volitions are all influenced by a *particular kind* of motives? It is as unnecessary for the author to disprove this, as to disprove the other thing he mentions, namely, that *sowing wheat* will produce all kinds of harvest.

The author speaks as though *a particular kind* of motive and the *strongest* motive were one and the same thing. He says,—"as if it were conceded that a particular kind of motive (i. e. the strongest,) were the invariable antecedent." But the strongest motive is sometimes of one kind, and sometimes of another. To one man the love of honor is the strongest motive; to another man, the love of wealth, to another the love of Christ. In many cases, various kinds of motives are combined to make the strongest. Now it is matter of wonder to me, that the author should think he is opposing a position which any one has maintained, when he affirms again and again, "that there is no particular class of motives which are invariable antecedents to volition," and that we have power to choose and do choose sometimes in one way, and sometimes in another way; that is, sometimes according to one class of motives, sometimes according to another. Nothing is more certain, than that we do choose in these different ways.

And why? Is it not because sometimes one particular class of motives is the strongest, and sometimes another class?

The author says, "The point at issue is simply this: Is volition connected with a previous desire (or motive) as a producing cause?"— which seems to imply that *desire* and *motive* are words of equal import, or that all motive consists of desire. But the point at issue might be more properly stated thus: whether volition is connected with a previous desire, *or any other motive*, as its invariable antecedent or cause.

The author seems to suppose that the asserters of moral necessity hold, that all the changes in the mind are caused by something ab extra; and in opposition to this notion, refers to the eternal mind, which before creation acted without any ab extra cause. But the doctrine of Edwards and others agreeing with him, is not that the changes or acts of the mind result wholly from causes extraneous to the mind. By motive Edwards means "the whole of that which moves, excites, or invites the mind to volition;" including not only "the views of the mind, but the state, frame, temper or habit of the mind." These do indeed, generally at least, refer to things without the mind. But mental acts are prompted mainly and ultimately by what is within the mind. An apostle teaches that a man is tempted and drawn into sin by his own unholy *desire*, (James 1: 14, 15). And is not affection to Christ and the desire to please him the great motive to obedience with every believer? And how can we form any other conception of God, than that he chooses and acts from his own perfections; that before anything else existed, he had a reason or motive for his determinations and actions in the wisdom, righteousness, and goodness of his own nature. No one can doubt that the mind itself is, in the strictest sense, an agent; that it has inherent powers of action; and that it really exerts its powers in a great variety of volitions and other exercises; and that the grand ultimate motive, by which it is influenced to all these is *within itself;* that is, its own dispositions, desires, habits, etc. We all hold to this, so that it is unnecessary to spend time to prove it. But it is time to proceed to the prominent principle of the Essay.

I shall first inquire how far the author contributes to overturn his own system. For whatever he does towards this result will prevent the necessity of labor on my part.

The author expressly admits "that mind never will choose, except to gain some good;" "that motives of *some kind* are indispensable antecedents of volition;" that "every one allows that motives of *some sort* are *invariably* antecedents to volition." Here then is one of the laws of our intelligent nature. *Motives of some sort are invariable and indispensable antecedents to volition.* This is a point in which we are all agreed. Volition cannot take place without a motive. How great soever the inherent power of the mind, and how various soever the acts of which it is capable; here is a manifest *limitation* of its power. A man has no power to put forth a volition without a motive. To choose in this way would be contrary to the nature of the mind. Though our author says in some parts of his Essay that "there is *no invariable* rule of volition;" he could not but see and acknowledge, that there is, *this one* invariable rule. Now does he, or any other candid person, complain of *this invariable rule* of volition? Does he complain that the mind is tied up to this constitutional principle, — that it must, in all its choices be influenced by motives? But what follows from the admission of this principle? It follows that motive, motive of some sort, is what he calls "the *producing cause* of volition." For he says again and again, that "the only method of proving a thing to be a producing cause, is to establish the fact, that it is an *invariable antecedent.*" Here we have an invariable antecedent, that is, *motive;* not *one particular class* of motives, but *motive of some kind.* And motive of some kind, being the invariable antecedent, is, according to the author's own showing, "the producing cause of volition." And such a cause he considers incompatible with free agency. Is it then so soon come to this, that our author, with all his dislike to fatalism, is according to his own account of the matter, a fatalist?

Our author, it seems, has no fear that free agency will be destroyed or impeded by being confined to this invariable rule, namely, that volition must always have a motive of some sort.

He holds that a free agent is placed under this invariable influence of motive; that without motive he cannot put forth a volition, — not merely that he cannot have a volition in this or that particular way, but that he cannot have it in any way; that his will cannot act at all. Such is the principle the author admits. And if there is any one who doubts the truth of this principle, let him look carefully into his own mind, and determine for himself by a fair trial, whether he can put forth a volition without any reason or motive. If he fails of being satisfied with one trial, let him proceed to a second, and though the effort may possibly put his mind into a very odd condition, and may occasion something of an unpleasant distortion; let him persevere, till he clearly finds out, whether his rational, moral nature is really tied to the principle above mentioned, namely, *that motive is, and must be an invariable antecedent of volition.*

But the connection of volition with the *strongest* motive, — *this* is regarded by the author as destructive of free agency. That we are governed in our volitions by motives of some kind, and of some degree of strength, is admitted. But to be governed invariably by the *strongest* motive, — this is looked upon as *fatalism.* I confess it is difficult for me to account for this view of the subject; and I am quite inclined to have a little free conversation with the nameless author. Permit me then to ask; why do you object to being *invariably* influenced in your volitions by that which is, on the whole, the *strongest* motive, while you are willing to be influenced by motives of some kind? Can you think it a privilege to be influenced by a *weaker*, rather than a *stronger* motive? to be governed in your voluntary actions by reasons of *less* weight, and those which *appear* to you of less weight, rather than by those which are, or appear to be of greater weight? Or would it be a better law of the mind, that we should study variety in this matter, and should sometimes choose according to what we consider the strongest motive or the most powerful reason, — sometimes, according to what we consider a weaker motive; and sometimes, for the sake of variety, and to display our unshackled, inherent power, according to what really appears to us the weakest motive of all? — When you wish, in any case, to know what to choose, would you think it proper to deliberate, at one time, in order to ascertain what is the strongest reason or motive, so that you might choose according to that; at another time, to hit upon a reason or motive of inferior force, so that you might choose according to that; and at another time, to get at a reason or motive the weakest of all, so that you might evince your unfettered freedom by choosing according to that? Can you recollect any instance in your past life, in which you did really choose and act in accordance with a motive which appeared to you to be, on the whole, of less weight, than another motive which you rejected? And if any one should presume to charge you with acting on this principle, and with habitually preferring what you regarded as a less reason or motive to what you regarded as a greater; would you not look at him with astonishment, and ask him, whether he really thought that a rational being could act so preposterously? Or if it should in fact be found, that you have a habit of acting, occasionally at least, in this way, methinks your friends would be very much perplexed. For if at any time they would induce you to determine upon a particular course, how would they know, whether they could best succeed by urging the strongest reason, or the weakest?

After all perhaps it is not the particular object of the author to maintain, that any man does actually reject what seems to him, on the whole, the strongest reason, and actually choose according to what he regards as the weaker reason; but that a free agent has *power* to do so. Now if it should become evident, that it is a law of our rational nature to choose and act according to what we regard as the strongest reason or motive; then a power to choose and act contrary to this, would be a power to subvert the very constitution of the mind, and to divest ourselves of our rationality. Can any one think that we have such a power; or that such a power, if it could exist, would be desirable? The law of the mind for which Edwards contends, is that which makes us *rational beings*, and makes us so *permanently*.

But although the author holds that the strongest motive cannot be the antecedent of volition invariably without destroying free agency; he allows that it may be so *occasionally*. He thinks that a free agent may choose *once*, and *again*, yea *frequently*, according to the strongest motive. What he denies is, that we can do it *constantly*, and yet be free. But if we can choose once, and twice, and frequently in this way, consistently with free agency, it proves clearly, that there is nothing in the *nature* of such a choice, which interferes with our freedom. If there were anything in its *nature* and *circumstances* inconsistent with free agency; then we could never, in any instance choose in this way, without setting aside our freedom. And according to this we should be obliged, in order to be free, to choose always according to the *weaker* motive; that is, the *weaker* motive must be the invariable antecedent of volition. But I suppose the author would think, that such an invariable antecedent as this would interfere with freedom as much as any other. He insists that there can be *no* invariable antecedent of volition consistently with freedom; that volition must sometimes follow motives of one kind, and one degree of strength, and sometimes of another kind, and another degree of strength. Certainly then it may sometimes, yea, frequently, follow the strongest motive. Indeed, according to the author's opinion, following the strongest motive *ever so often*, will not hurt our free agency, unless we do it *invariably*. Now, if our choosing according to the strongest motive to-day and to-morrow will not take away our freedom; why should it take away our freedom to choose in this way the next day and the next following? If we may, consistently with our free agency, choose according to the strongest motive, two-thirds of the time, what is there inconsistent with free agency, in choosing in the same way the rest of the time? If a part, even the greater part of our volitions may consistently be put forth in this manner; why not all of them? Will the author look into this matter with some special care?

But suppose that a free moral agent is completely in a right state of mind; that he judges correctly respecting all the objects of affection; that his desires in every case correspond with the truth, and that he forms a just estimate of the comparative weight of the motives presented before him. Such a man, the author declares, will uniformly govern his choice by the strongest motive. He says that, "in all cases where the strongest desire coincides with the decisions of the judgment, — the mind chooses to gratify the strongest desire." That is, in all cases where the disposition and habits are right, a moral agent chooses in conformity with the strongest desire or motive. The strongest motive, in all such cases, is the invariable antecedent of volition. But this *invariable antecedence* is a fearful thing, and is proof of a "producing cause;" and a "producing cause" overthrows free agency, and constitutes fatalism. Now as Jesus Christ was perfectly holy; — as his strongest desire always coincided with the decisions of judgment; he always chose according to the strongest motive. Here, then, was that invariable antecedence of the strongest motive, "that invariable rule of volition," which is proof of a producing cause; and a producing cause takes away freedom. If, then, the scheme of the author is true, our Saviour was not a free agent, but acted under the influence of fatalism. And as all the angels in heaven conform to this rule, they too are all destitute of freedom. And inasmuch as Christians in this life conform to the same rule in proportion as they are holy; in the same proportion must their free agency be impaired. And when they become perfectly holy, they will invariably choose according to the strongest motive, and of course will lose all their freedom.

Such is the author's theory; and such the assistance which he very candidly affords us in exposing it. If the theory were true, what an alarming influence it would have! See to what an extent it would sweep away the free agency of free agents! As the strongest desire or motive is the invariable antecedent of volition with all perfectly holy beings, and as this cannot consist with free agency; Christ, and the innumerable multitude of angels, and the spirits of just men made perfect, are all entirely destitute of freedom. Christians are all so in a degree, and will be so wholly by and by. Moreover, as the author allows that *all* men *sometimes* choose according to the strongest motive; how can he avoid the conclusion that, so far as they do this, they are all deprived of free agency? And he further says, that with *all* men motive of some sort is the invariable antecedent of volition; which invariable antecedence of motive is proof of a producing cause, and this sets aside free agency. Where then, in heaven or earth shall we look for free moral agents? Or if any remain, we see how much they are in danger of losing their freedom, by becoming holy, that is, by bringing their desires to coincide with the decisions of judgment, so that they may constantly choose and act according to the strongest motive.

The *consequences* of adopting the theory of moral agency, set forth in the Essay, are fearful, in proportion to the importance of the principles which it tends to undermine.

The theory implies, that a free moral agent must be free not only from force or coercion, but also from any *invariable rule of action*. It assumes that the invariable antecedence of the strongest desire, or motive, to volition, is irreconcilable with free agency. If we are influenced in our volitions in this invariable manner,—if the choices, which the mind makes, are constantly dependent on antecedent causes; it follows, as the author of the Essay thinks, that those antecedent causes are "producing" efficient causes, and that our choosing according to them is a law of our nature; and of course, that we have no power to put forth volitions in a different manner, as this would be contrary to a law of our nature. And if we have no power to choose and act differently, we are under a necessity of choosing and acting as we do; and this he says is fatalism, and precludes accountableness. This I suppose is the course of thought with all who adopt the principle of *contingent volition*, as commonly understood. This principle has been sufficiently examined by Edwards, Day, and others. It is manifest, that this principle of contingent volition is the basis of the philosophical theory of moral agency which is adopted by numbers at the present day, and substantially by our author. And see what a sweeping influence it has in his mind in regard to our emotions, desires, etc. These, he says, result from "constitutional producing causes." "It is God who, by the constitution of the mind and the ordering of his providence, decides what desires shall exist." We cannot prevent them. The objects which awaken desire, are the causes of desire in such a sense, "that no other effect could follow without a change in the nature of things." Of course, the author regards our desires, emotions, etc., as in themselves, no part of free accountable agency. According to the principle of the Essay, all those affections, emotions, and desires, which arise spontaneously in the mind in view of their appropriate objects, are excluded from the supervision of the moral law. For how can they belong to the catalogue of moral exercises, when they arise in the mind *invariably* in view of their proper objects, and do not wait for the bidding of the will?

On this notion respecting our emotions and desires, which obviously results from the principles of the Essay, and which the author expressly maintains, I have a few remarks to offer.

My first remark is, that *it stands in direct and palpable opposition to the authority of God's word.* His law requires *love*, and forbids all those emotions and desires which are contrary to love. Love is doubtless an affection or emotion of the mind; and doubtless it arises in view of suitable objects; and, if the heart is right, arises *invariably*, when those objects are presented before it. Nothing is necessary to excite love in a holy mind but the sight of a holy object. And is not love to God a *holy* emotion? The desire of the heart for God, for holiness, and for heaven, — is it not a *holy* desire? And does it not arise spontaneously in the mind of a holy being, when those objects are presented to his view? Even when the objects are brought before him without any previous design or thought of his, are not the same emotions excited? Take also a moral agent of another character. Take a man who is unregenerate, and who has that carnal mind which is enmity against God. When such a one turns his attention to God, and sees him in any measure as he is; does not the feeling of dissatisfaction and enmity spontaneously arise? While he remains in his natural state, can he, by the power of his will, prevent it, and call forth the affection of love, and so be subject to the law of God? How is it with pride, envy, revenge, covetousness, impure desire, and other affections, which, as Christ informs us, come forth from the heart? In a state of unregeneracy does not one or the other of these arise spontaneously in the mind, just as the disposition happens to be, when the appropriate object is presented to view? Is not this the case with the *moral* affections, as much as with the *natural?* If I rightly understand the author, he would admit the facts here mentioned. But does not his theory imply that they are no part of moral agency? As unrenewed men *invariably* have wrong affections and desires, and as perfectly holy beings *invariably* have right affections and desires, in view of moral objects, these right and wrong affections and desires must all be excluded from the catalogue of *moral* exercises. Such is the obvious principle of the Essay; and does it not directly contradict the word of God? If there is anything which the moral, spiritual precepts of the divine law undertake to control, it is the *affections and desires of the heart.* What is the love required by the two comprehensive precepts of the moral law, but an *affection* of the heart? What is hungering and thirsting after righteousness, but *desire?* The Greek *επιθυμια,* generally translated *desire,* denotes both good affection and desire, and bad. When it denotes bad desire, it is often translated by *lust.* And who needs to be told that Christ and the apostles speak of the affections and desires, and the passions too, (*πάθη,* Rom. 1: 26. 1 Thess. 4: 5,) as belonging to moral character? These are the inner man, upon which the eye of God is specially fixed. The theory which would free us from responsibility in regard to these, or would represent them as not in their own nature morally good or evil — who can reconcile it with the current language of the New Testament? How could Christ and the apostles have spoken as they did, if they had entertained such an opinion, as is expressed in the Essay?

Secondly. The theory above described is contrary to *the dictates of conscience.* Every man, not blinded by prejudice, disapproves of his disorderly affections and desires, and condemns himself on account of them. He is conscious that it is sinful to *gratify* them. But why should it be sinful to *gratify* desires which are not sinful? It is a common sentiment, that the sinfulness of men is great, in proportion as their depraved passions and desires are awakened suddenly and strongly in view of forbidden objects. Suppose any one is instantly filled with revengeful feeling at the thought of his enemy, or with envy at the thought of his superior, or with covetous desire at the thought of money, or with pride and vanity at the thought of himself; and suppose these feelings rise to great strength and violence. Is not *he* the man that we look upon as uncommonly wicked?

And if the theory is opposed to the consciences of men generally, it is more decidedly opposed to the *spiritual experience and consciousness of the devoted Christian.* He knows that he is holy or unholy in the sight of God, according to the nature of the emotions and desires which are awakened within him in view of moral objects. And if any scheme of philosophy contradicts this sentiment, he knows it to be wrong. If he finds that his state of mind is such, that the contemplation of worldly pleasure, wealth, and honor instantly kindle within him what the Apostle calls the lust of the flesh, the lust of the eye, and the pride of life; — especially if he finds, that these desires are *unawares* burning within him; he concludes that his heart is indeed very corrupt, and he learns how important it is, that such an one as he should fly from temptation, and should watchfully guard against everything which would bring any tempting object before him. And the more spiritual a Christian is, the more quick is he to discern and to condemn the first motions of the sin that dwells in him, — the first and feeblest actings of unholy affection or desire. Tell him your philosophy teaches, that he is not culpable for unsought, unlooked for emotions of pride, envy, covetousness, revenge, or impurity; his deep consciousness replies, that your philosophy is false. He sees and knows, that these emotions, in whatever way excited, are, in themselves, morally wrong, and contrary to that spiritual law, which extends its authority over all the thoughts and feelings of his heart. In view of his inward pollutions, he exclaims: *Behold, I am vile!* and his earnest prayer is, that his heart may be cleansed by the grace of God.

Thirdly. The theory advanced in the Essay is contrary to *the principles of philosophy*, even those which seem to be implied in the Essay. The author mentions it as a point of essential importance in his theory, "that the mind alone is the real producing cause of its own volitions." By this I suppose it is meant, that the mind itself *acts* in willing, and that the volition is *wholly* the mind's act; that the mind is the agent, and the only agent that puts forth its volitions. If anything different from this is meant, I know not what it is. The author says, "all sin arises from that power of free agency, which makes the mind the sole producing cause of its own volitions." Now does not the power of free agency equally make the mind the producing cause of its own *emotions*, *affections*, and *desires?* Is not the mind as *really active* in these, as in its volitions? Is it not as *intensely* active? Are not affections and desires mental actions of as high an order as volitions? In what can the rational and moral faculties be more truly or more intensely active, than in loving God with all the heart and soul and mind and strength? And as to the hungering and thirsting after righteousness spoken of by our Saviour,—is it not truly an *act* of the mind? And is not the mind as much the *author* or *cause* of it, as of any other mental act? Does not every Christian speak of it as his own act, when he says, "*I love* the Lord." "Thou knowest that *I love* thee." Is it not therefore evident, even according to the principles of the Essay, that affection and desire are as truly of a moral nature, as volition? And it is plain, that volition itself derives its moral nature from those affections and desires of the heart which prompt it, and is regarded as good or bad, according to the goodness or badness of those inward motives.

The doctrine of the Essay in regard to our emotions and desires is widely different from that which has been held by the great body of learned divines and philosophers. Those who insist that all morality is comprised in the acts of the *will*, include the affections and desires among its acts.

Is it said, for the purpose of showing that we are not answerable for our desires,—"that it is God, who, by the constitution of the mind and the ordering of his providence, decides what desires shall exist?" And does he not in the same way decide what *volitions* shall exist? The author of the Essay ascribes to God "the power to prevent any given volition, by removing an object of desire, or by substituting some other in its place." He holds that no volitions can take place without motives, and that all motives are under the ordering of God's providence. Now if all this agency and control of God over *volitions* does not interfere with their moral nature, nor hinder us from exercising free agency in them; why should we suppose that the same divine agency prevents our free agency in the exercise of *affection* and *desire?*

An appeal is often made in the Essay to the consciousness of men. I join in this appeal. If a man has in his heart an emotion of love to his fellow-creatures, and a real desire for their good; is he not conscious that the emotion itself is *right?* Or if the emotion of hatred, envy, or revenge rises in his heart; is he not conscious that the emotion is wrong? Does he not disprove of it as *really*, as he does of a definite determination to injure others, or even of an injurious act? And does not the explanation which our Saviour gives of the moral law, Matt. 5: 27, 28, 43, 44, correspond with these remarks?

And yet, according to the principles advanced in some parts of the Essay, the emotions and desires of the heart are not to be regarded as possessing a moral nature, or as appertaining to moral character. And why? The answer I suppose must be, that *they certainly and invariably* rise in the mind, when fit objects are presented to view. The writer holds, that this circumstance shows that our desires are not free, moral, accountable acts. But he gives no proof. I maintain that this circumstance does not show this, and that the theory of the author on this subject is wide of the truth. I have endeavored to show, that the theory is not only destitute of proof, but is opposed to the true sense of the moral law, which reaches to the desires and feelings of the heart; that it is opposed to the consciousness of men, especially of good men; and that it is opposed to the principles of philosophy, even those contained in the Essay.

It is the common doctrine of evangelical ministers and Christians, that there is a certain, invariable connection between the apostasy of Adam and the sinfulness of all his posterity; that *his* sin is the invariable antecedent of their sinful disposition, volitions and conduct; that it is the divine constitution and the law of our nature, that every one who is born of human parents, will be a sinner, and that this law is *invariable.* Now according to the theory of the Essay, this "invariable antecedence," is proof of a *producing cause;* and the existence of such a producing cause excludes free agency. According to this theory, therefore, one of these two things must be true; either that native depravity, and all our sinful volitions and actions, being the invariable consequence of Adam's sin, is a matter of fatalism, entirely precluding free, accountable agency; or else that there is no such invariable connection between Adam's sin and the sin and condemnation of his posterity, and that the doctrine, universally held by evangelical Christians, and taught by Paul, is not true.

And what would become of the doctrine of *election and efficacious grace?* The doctrine implies, that the repentance of all who are saved, invariably follows the purpose of God and that influence of the Spirit which is given to carry his purpose into effect. Now the author cannot consistently admit that the repentance and faith of sinners certainly and invariably follow this divine purpose and influence; because the invariableness of such an antecedent cause would preclude the free agency of those brought under its influence. The agency of men in repenting, believing and obeying, cannot, according to this theory, be free agency, if it is the certain, invariable effect of the purpose and agency of God. And to secure to men their freedom in this concern, the author, to be consistent, must hold, that there is no invariable connection between this divine cause, and the repentance of sinners, and that it is impossible for God to exert such an influence upon those who are chosen to salvation, as will certainly and invariably bring them to repentance, without violating their free agency; and then he must hold that, to guard their freedom from infringement, their conversion must be left uncertain, so that it may follow the purpose and agency of God, or not, as their sovereign will shall decide.

The same as to the doctrine of *perseverance.* If God should exert such an influence upon the regenerate, as invariably to secure their perseverance in holiness; then according to the theory of the author, they would lose their free agency. Hence, every one who embraces the theory and is consistent, must take care not to ascribe to God an influence which *certainly* and *invariably* causes perseverance, and must not *pray* for such an influence, as such prayer might endanger their free agency.

How manifest it is, that the theory which we have considered, is opposed *to the most devout dispositions and prayers of good men.* What do sincere Christians desire and pray for so earnestly, as for such an influence of the Holy Spirit, as will certainly and invariably secure them from sin, and lead them to persevering love and obedience? But if God should answer their prayers, and should give the influence which they seek, — if in their love and obedience they should act under so powerful an ab extra cause, a cause so efficaciously producing holiness; then, according to the Essay, they would lose their free agency. Now I think, that every humble, pious man will be inclined to say, I desire no such freedom as would exclude the effectual operations of the Holy Spirit. Let this divine cause govern me invariably; let it direct and control my understanding, my heart and my will, certainly and entirely. I crave it as the choicest blessing, that God would work in me both to will and to do, so that, in consequence of his influence, I may uniformly will and do what is pleasing in his sight. Let my agency be constantly and wholly governed by the almighty agency of God. Then I shall have a freedom truly precious, — freedom from the bondage of sin — freedom from the influence of my own perverse will and desperately wicked heart, — the glorious freedom of the children of God.

I shall here briefly answer the brief questions at the close of the Essay.

1. "In what does fatalism consist?"

But why does the author put this question at the end of his

Essay, after he has so fully and confidently answered it himself? The fundamental doctrine of fatalism is, he says, that we choose and act invariably according to the strongest motive, or that the strongest desire or motive is the certain and constant antecedent of our volitions.

2. "What are the different forms of speech in which the doctrine is expressed?"

These will be found in the books, mentioned below, in which the doctrine is taught.

3. "Is there any difference in the real meaning conveyed by these forms?"

This any discerning man can determine who has time to make the comparison.

4. "Is not fatalism a most pernicious doctrine in its tendencies?" — Answer. The author has settled this also. — "And does it make any difference in the evil, whether it is taught by a wise and pious man, or by the sceptic?" — Answer. It is, in some respects, evidently worse for a pernicious error to be taught by a wise and pious man, than by a sceptic.

5. "What are the books in which fatalism is taught, and by whose influence and authority are they sustained?" — Answer. According to the author's notion, it is taught in Calvin's Institutes, the Westminster Confession of Faith and Catechisms, the works of Edwards, West, Smalley, Bellamy, Dwight, Day, Beecher, and such like. And the doctrine which the author calls fatalism, is sustained by the influence of almost all the Presidents of our Colleges, almost all our Theological Professors, almost all the Ministers and Christians in New England, almost all the Old School and New School Presbyterians, and almost all the orthodox of other denominations.

The additional remarks which I shall make, will be arranged under several distinct heads.

The first subject which I shall examine is, *the power of a contrary choice.*

Many writers regard this as a matter of great importance; and some of them suppose, that the power referred to is frequently denied. As there is really much indefiniteness and obscurity in the disputes which are carried on respecting this subject; we should do what we can to make it clear and definite. Let us then inquire what are the points in which all candid men are agreed; so that we may avoid needless controversy, and may fix upon the real question at issue.

First. All agree that we have the power of choice. Every man certainly knows that he has this power, because he often exercises it. In the common course of human affairs, different things are proposed to us. We compare them, and then determine or choose between them, so that we can no more doubt that we have the power of choice, than that we have the power to think or to walk, when we are actually thinking or walking.

Secondly. It must be evident to all, that the way and the only way, in which our power of choice is acted out, is in the choices we really make. We never exercise our power by choosing differently from what we do choose. This may be called a *truism*. But it is *true*. However great our power of choosing differently from what we do, we never, in any instance whatever, exercise it. This is clear.

Thirdly. All must agree that we cannot at one and the same time make two choices, the one opposite to the other. However great our power of choice, we have no power to do this. If we should *wish* to do it, we could not. And when any one asserts, that we have the power of a contrary choice, he cannot really mean, that we can make the choice we do, and at the same time another choice opposite; for example, that we can choose to go north, and at the same time choose to go south. No one, who understands the import of words, can mean to assert such an absurdity. And I must suppose it an inadvertency, that the anonymous writer uses language which seems to imply this. Priestley says: "In any given state of mind, with respect both to *disposition* and *motive*, two different determinations are impossible." The anonymous writer rejects this; of course he holds, as we should suppose, that a man in the same state of mind with respect both to disposition and motive, may make two different and opposite determinations, and may do it at the same time. But I think he cannot really mean this ; and if not, what is the point of difference ?

Fourthly. All agree that *we have power to make different and opposite choices at different times and in different circumstances.* Our choice at one time is in fact different from what it is at another time. An unrenewed sinner chooses to disobey God and enjoy the pleasures of sin. The same person when renewed by the divine Spirit, chooses to obey God and forsake the pleasures of sin. The power thus to vary our choices under the influence of different motives, objective or subjective, evidently belongs to all men.

Fifthly. It is a point in which all will agree, that, in any case, we might have made a different choice *instead* of the one we did make, *if we had been disposed to do it, or had found sufficient inducements.* A man who chooses the life of a farmer, might have chosen the life of a mariner, if he had been so inclined, or had found sufficient inducements. This, I apprehend, is the meaning of those who say, that we might have chosen, or had power to choose, differently from what we did ;—not that we might at the same time have made another and opposite choice in *connection* with the one we made ; but that we might have made another choice *instead* of it, *if we had been disposed to do it,* or *if our inducements had been sufficient.* These are the necessary conditions of choice ; and without them choice cannot be. If a man should tell us that he put forth an act of mind which he called *choice,* without any inclination or inducements, we should say, he mistakes the meaning of the word.

Sixthly. All agree that *we may hereafter make a choice contrary to what we now make.* There may be such a change in our views, feelings, and circumstances, as will naturally lead to a change in our practical determination.

Seventhly. Whenever we make a wrong choice, all agree that we *ought* to have made a different choice, and that our not doing it was our own fault. There are in truth motives or inducements of such intrinsic value, that we ought to be influenced by them to a right choice; and if in any case we do not make such a choice, it is not because we are not *free* agents, but because we are *sinful* agents, — not because we are destitute of any of the endowments of moral, accountable beings, but because we are inclined to pervert those endowments; not because we have no power to choose, but because the power we have is under an evil bias.

Eighthly. I suppose there is a general agreement in this also, that a man does himself determine the influence which external motives shall have upon him, *by the dispositions and habits of his own mind*, or by *his own inward character*. A good man, by his pious dispositions, determines the influence which gospel truths shall have upon him. It is because he "has an honest and good heart," that the motives presented in the Scriptures excite his love, and lead him to obedience. Our Saviour asserts this connection between the state of the heart and the voluntary conduct, when he says, "A good man out of the good treasure of his heart bringeth forth good things; and an evil man out of the evil treasure of his heart, bringeth forth evil things." We expect a man will have love, pity, generosity, or the opposite, excited by the objects placed before him, according to his prevailing disposition. And if any one judges on any other principle, we say, he is ignorant of human nature.

If any one inquires whether we have not *power* to choose contrary to our inclinations and to the inducements presented before us; I reply, that we doubtless have power to choose contrary to *some* of our inclinations, and some of the inducements placed before us. But have we power to choose and act contrary to *all* our inclinations, and to *all* the inducements placed before us? Did any man ever learn that he has such a power by acting it out? If not, how does he know that he possesses it? Can any man think such a power desirable? If he had it, would he ever exercise it? And of what value is a power which is never to be exercised? A power to choose according to our inclinations and desires, and under the influence of rational inducements, is a possession of great value. But a power to choose independently of all our inclinations and motives, and contrary to them, is a power to do an absurdity; and a power to do an absurdity is itself an absurdity.

But some appear to think that, in every case, choice and voluntary action might have been contrary to what it was, *supposing all the motives, external and internal, and all the circumstances of action, to have remained perfectly the same.* They think this is the main point, and that it is the very thing implied in the power of a contrary choice. In reference to this, I cannot do better than to quote the words of an author, who was no advocate for the scheme of moral or philosophical necessity, but who judged according to common sense and consciousness. The author referred to, (Dr. Whately,) says: "If nothing more is meant," (that is, by the doctrine of necessity,) "than that every event depends on causes adequate to produce it, — that nothing is in itself *contingent, accidental, or uncertain,* but is called so only in reference to a person who does not know all the circumstances on which it depends; and that it is absurd to say anything could have happened otherwise than it did, supposing all the circumstances connected with it to remain the same; then the doctrine is undeniably true, but perfectly harmless, not at all encroaching on free agency and responsibility, and amounting to little more than an expansion of the axiom, that it is impossible for the same thing to be and not to be."

But if I have rightly understood the writer of the Essay, he holds that this very principle, which Whately says is undeniably true, and perfectly harmless, is the essence of fatalism. The doctrine which he represents as the opposite of free agency, and the great doctrine of fatalism, is, *that in the moral world, as well as the natural, the same consequences invariably result from the same antecedent circumstances.* It is manifestly implied in what he and others advance on this subject, that they mean to speak of the antecedent circumstances as *the same in all respects.* All the dispositions, habits, and desires, everything intellectual and moral, and everything extraneous to the mind,—in a word, the mind itself, and everything which can have an influence upon the mind, are to be regarded as perfectly the same. Now my position is, that when this is the case, the same consequences invariably follow. And I hold, with Whately and others, that this is self-evident, and that to assert the contrary is absurd. If any man thinks that he has the power actually to make a contrary choice when all the antecedent circumstances are the same; I must request him to think again. And if he still insists that he possesses such a power, it is no more than reasonable to call upon him for proof. Let him give an instance, in which he has in some way exercised it, or if he never has done it, let him do it now, and thus end the controversy. But if, though a man really has this power, he never has exercised it and never will exercise it, then, after all, the existence of the power does not amount to much, and does not in the least interfere with the doctrine, that the same consequences do in fact result from the same antecedent circumstances. In this point of view, the question whether a man has the power, is of no weight. For if he has it, but never uses it, the result will be the same as though he had it not. And so, according to the Essay, the *existence* of the *power of the contrary* being never exercised, would do nothing to shut out fatalism,—because, notwithstanding such a power, there may in fact be an invariable constancy in the result of moral causes.

I hardly know how to account for it, that the author of the Essay and some other writers should represent free agency as consisting in the power of a contrary choice. The power and the only power which we really use, is the power to choose and act as we do. We can indeed make a different choice at another time and in other circumstances. But have we power to make a different choice at the very time that we make the choice we do? Let it be that we have such a power. I say that we cannot *use* it, except by choosing at the very time differently from what we do choose. But how can this be? At the very same time that we choose to speak the truth, how can we use the power of a contrary choice, and choose to speak falsehood? Now, how strange it is, that any one should represent free agency as consisting in a power, which, if it should exist, would never be used, and the use of which would imply a contradiction? Does moral agency consist in the power to cause the same thing to be and not to be, or to cause a thing and its opposite to be at the same time? — a power to make a particular choice and a contrary choice at one and the same time? The choices I make and the actions I perform are the choices and acts of a free moral agent. And the power to choose and act *as I do*, is all the power that is necessary to my moral agency. Who can reasonably wish for more power, than that which he exercises in the variety of choices he makes, and in all the variety of his actions?

As an exemplification of the general principle which I maintain, take the words of Christ: "If any man love me, he will keep my words." Obedience is the invariable consequence of love. And disobedience is the invariable consequence of the want of love. "He that loveth me not, keepeth not my words." — But has not a man who is now destitute of love, *power* to *obey?* Yes, on the proper condition. He cannot render a true obedience to Christ, *without love*. That any one should *choose* to obey, and actually obey, when he has no love, is contrary to the nature of obedience. His power to obey is then *conditional*, and the conditions are such as arise from the nature of the mind, and the nature of voluntary action. These conditions are often expressed, and, when not expressed, are understood. And practical men understand them alike. When they wish to induce a man to make a choice different from what he has made, instead of appealing to the absolute power of the will, they labor at the well known conditions of the new choice. In this way, and in this way only, they hope to succeed. There are uniform laws in the moral world, as well as in the natural; and to attempt to accomplish anything irrespectively of those laws, would be as unwise and fruitless in one case as in the other.

I shall take the liberty to close my remarks on this subject by a few quotations from a writer, whom no one can charge with the want of enlightened, patient, profound thought, or of a clear, discriminating judgment on metaphysical subjects.

"Those who plead for contingent self-determination, or adopt a theory which implies it," says President Day, "often claim to themselves the exclusive right to be considered the advocates of liberty. If this assumption be conceded to them, it ought to be distinctly understood, according to which of the numerous meanings of the term, liberty is peculiar to their system. Those who believe in the dependence of volitions upon motives as well as agents, are also decided advocates of liberty. But they do not engage to give their sanction to every strange or even absurd combination of ideas, to which any philosopher may think proper to annex the term, however contrary it may be to the signification of the word as sanctioned by common usage. It is agreed on all hands, that with respect to external actions, we are free, when we *do as we will;* when there is such an established connection between our volitions and our actions that the latter invariably follow from the other. When we will to walk, we walk, if we are free. — Now is internal liberty, or liberty of the will, the direct *opposite* of this? Does it imply that there is no dependence of our volitions on antecedent feelings; that however ardently a man may love God, this has no controlling influence over his purposes and executive acts?"

"According to the advocates of independent self-determination, liberty of the will implies a *freedom to either side.* This is otherwise expressed by saying, that whenever a man acts freely he has *power to the contrary.* — Cousin says: 'An action performed with the consciousness of power not to do it, is what men have called a *free* action.' — 'Liberty — belongs to acts which we perform, with the consciousness of doing them, and of *being able not to do them.*' In a certain sense this is undoubtedly true. In reference to *external conduct*, a man is free when he does as he wills. But does liberty imply, that when a man wills a certain act, it is no more likely to follow than the contrary act; that there is no established connection between what he does, and what he wills to do; that with the *same volitions* his actions might be different?"

"But the advocates of a liberty to either side, would probably consider it as relating not so much to external conduct, as to acts of the will. Cousin says: 'Liberty exists in the pure power of willing, which is always accompanied by the consciousness of the power to will the *contrary* of what it wills.' But in what sense is it true, that man has the power to will the contrary of what he actually wills? He has such power, that with a *sufficient inducement*, he will make an opposite choice. But has he not power, you ask, to choose otherwise than he does, even though it be certain that he will never exercise that power unless there is some change in his feelings, or in the motives before him? A correct answer to this question must depend upon the extent of meaning here given to the word power. A man may have *some* power, and not have *all* power; that is, he may not have all that upon which the result depends. If the word power be used in its broadest sense, as including not only opportunity, knowledge, capacity, etc., but *motives of all kinds;* it is not true that a man has always equal power, that is, equal inducements, to opposite volitions."

"But if the word power be here used according to its more common acceptation, so as *not* to include motives and the state of feeling, this is not inconsistent with such a strength of inclination, as will certainly prevent any contrary volition. A man has as much power to speak the truth, *if he will*, as he has to utter falsehood. And he has as much power to *will* to speak the truth, *if his feelings are so inclined*, as he has to will to lie. But has he a power which will determine him to will one way, while his feelings are wholly inclined to will the contrary way? In many cases, there may be conflicting emotions in a man's mind, and therefore *some* power of motive in opposite directions. But when he comes to a decision, are the motives on the opposite sides always equal? Is it not the preponderance of one over the other which turns the scale? The man who wills in a particular way, under the influence of certain feelings, might undoubtedly will differently, *under a different influence*. But while the same mind continues in precisely the same state, in the same circumstances, and under the same influences of every kind, has it power to will in opposite directions; or if it has this power, will it ever use it?"

"If in asserting a power to contrary volitions, nothing more is intended, than that a *different influence* might occasion an opposite decision of the will, this is not inconsistent with the dependence of volition on the state of the heart, external motives, natural sensibilities, acquired propensities, etc. The younger Edwards, a strenuous advocate for the certain connection between volitions and their causes, admits that the power of acting implies, at the same time, a power of not acting. But he takes special care to guard his admission against the inference, that our volitions are independent of the influence of motives. — 'Moral necessity,' he says, 'is the certain or necessary connection between *moral causes and moral effects;*' — 'and there is no moral necessity in the case, unless the connection be real and absolutely certain, so as to insure the existence of the effects.' And his father says: 'Moral necessity may be as *absolute* as natural necessity; that is, the effect may be as perfectly connected with its moral cause, as a natural necessary effect is with its natural cause.' — 'As it must be allowed that there may be such a thing as a *sure* and *perfect* connection between moral causes and their effects; so this only is what I call by the name of moral necessity.' According to these writers, then, a man may have a *natural* power to make a contrary choice, although, at the same time he is *morally* unable to do it; that is, he is under the influence of such motives, as will infallibly prevent him from thus willing. It may be thought by some, that, by a *purpose* or *resolve*, we have power to give our volitions a contrary direction. But do we form purposes independently of all motives from without and from within? Will the same influence operating upon precisely the same state of mind, lead to opposite purposes and volitions?"

"If we pass from our purposes to our *affections* or *emotions*, shall we *here* find the liberty to either side? It is manifest that *different objects* may produce different feelings in the same mind; and the *same* objects will produce different feelings in different minds. But while the same objects are viewed in the same manner, by a mind continuing in precisely the same state of susceptibility, will the affections excited by these objects be so changed, as to become of an opposite character? Or does the state of the mind itself become contrary to what it was before, without any cause whatever?"

"Will it be said, that our volitions are *partly* contingent, and *partly* dependent on something preceding; that there may be *some* influence from motives, and at the same time a power of acting in opposition to motives? To this it may be answered, that if the very nature of liberty of will implies freedom to either side, then so far as this is controlled, and our volitions are determined by the influence of motives, by the state of the affections, or by anything else, liberty is impaired. The saint in heaven, who is under the influence of such motives as invariably excite in him holy volitions, has not the liberty of which we are now speaking!"

"Why have metaphysicians given to the terms liberty and power, when applied to the will, a meaning so different from that which they bear in customary use, and in reference to external conduct? In common language, a man enjoys liberty when he does *as he wills;* that is, when there is a *fixed connection* between his acts and his volitions. Whatever interrupts this connection, impairs his freedom. But according to some philosophers, liberty of will requires that there should be *no* dependence of our *volitions* upon anything preceding, for being as they are, rather than otherwise. External liberty consists in a man's acting uniformly, according to his *will.* Does internal liberty imply, that he frequently wills in *opposition* to his *supreme affections?* When we say that a man has power to the contrary external action, we mean, that *if his will were different*, the action would be different. But some who speak of a power to contrary volitions, seem to mean, that under the *same* influence, and in the *same* state of mind, the volitions may be different. It is a power of contingence, a capacity of being subject to accident. Is not the term power, as it is frequently used, a mere '*metaphysical sound*,' which is to produce its effect, not by any distinct signification in the connection in which it is introduced, but by association with feelings excited by the word, in cases of a very different nature?"

"Liberty is commonly considered a *privilege.* But what privilege is conferred by the liberty of contingence, — a freedom of our volitions from all influence of motives, — of argument, and persuasion, and affections? Suppose a man were to be endowed with a will which should put forth volitions wholly at random, without any regard to his feelings; that if these should urge him ever so strongly to go one way, his will would determine he should go in an opposite direction; that however much he might be pleased with obeying God, his volitions would lead him to disobey; would this be the perfection of liberty? Or suppose his volitions should spring up without any cause, or reason, or influence whatever, either from without or from within; would this be the most desirable condition of his being?" *

A *moral* agent is one who performs actions which are of a *moral nature*, and are related to a *moral law*. But what is a *free* agent? The word free is relative. Taken in a good sense, it denotes the absence of something undesirable. A citizen of the United States is *free*. From what is he free? He is not free from the authority of law, nor from the power of rulers. He is not free from restrictions as to the use of his property, or as to the business he shall pursue. In various respects his personal liberty is limited. Yet notwithstanding these various and sometimes unwelcome restraints, we say he is a *free man*. But from what is he free? He is free from a despotic government. He is free from the power of a king who rules, not according to just and equal laws, but according to his own absolute will. He is free from oppression, and from all unnecessary and unreasonable restraints. In the Scripture sense, a man is free, who is free from the dominion of sin, and has the liberty of the sons of God.

But in the case now under consideration, freedom is spoken of as an attribute of an intelligent, accountable being. Here freedom is freedom from whatever would prevent moral, accountable action. And here we form our judgment, not by an abstract intellectual process, but by *consciousness* and *common sense*. We *know* that we are moral, accountable agents. We *know* also that we have the freedom which is necessary for those who are the subjects of law. We are free from compulsion or force. We *do*

* See Day on the Will, Sect. 4.

what we *choose*, and we *choose* as we are *inclined*. We are not free from law, or from obligation to serve God. And we are not, in our voluntary conduct, free from the influence of our inclinations and desires, nor from the influence of external objects. In our unrenewed state, we are not free from the control of a deceitful and wicked heart. If we are Christians, we are not free from the influence of pious affections. And whether we are Christians or not, we are not free from the established laws of the mind; and one of these laws we learn from experience to be, that the executive acts of the will, called volitions, follow our inclinations and desires. That we should have a choice or determination, not conformed to our inclinations and desires, is inconceivable. Such a thing never did exist, and never can. It is indeed true that our choice and our voluntary conduct often have an effect, direct or indirect, upon our subsequent affections and desires; and this discloses another important practical principle. But who does not know that the very choice or determination of mind, which thus influences subsequent affections and desires, does itself spring from affections and desires already existing? Nor is this anything strange. In many cases we find that the same thing is the effect of a preëxisting cause, and the cause of a subsequent effect; and that this last effect becomes the cause of another effect, and so on. No man can be a watchful observer of human affairs, without perceiving such a concatenation of causes and effects in the common course of providence.

The doctrine that our volitions proceed from our affections, is thought by some to be liable to objection with regard to the case of Adam. How, it is asked, could he be influenced in the act of his will to disobey, *by his affections*, or *the state of his heart*, when his affections were holy? I answer; while his affections all remained holy, he could not disobey. But he was mutable, and the affections of his heart, which were once holy, became sinful. And it agrees with common experience, that sinful affections of heart should lead to voluntary transgression. But *how* did his heart change from holiness to sin? I answer; he certainly did change, and the change must have begun somewhere. As I never experienced such a change myself, and as I am unable to look into Adam's mind and trace the process of thought and feeling which took place when he became a transgressor, I cannot tell *how* he changed from holiness to sin. This lies beyond my knowledge. But as the inclinations, affections and desires of the heart are evidently the chief springs of voluntary action, it would seem very probable, that the change in Adam's character commenced in his heart, and that his sinful heart led to the act of disobedience. And it is certainly no more difficult to show *how* his affections became corrupt, and how these corrupt affections led to voluntary transgression, than to show how he could choose to transgress, while the affections and desires of his heart were all pure, and how this choice, proceeding from a sinless heart, could be sinful; in other words, to show how voluntary transgression could take place without any wrong feeling in the heart prompting to it. If, to escape this last difficulty, it should be said, that the first act of Adam's will to transgress, was an *ultimate fact*, and so not to be explained or accounted for, I could with equal propriety say, that the change of his heart, under temptation, from a pure to a corrupt state was an ultimate fact, admitting of no explanation.

If the case of the first transgression is treated *metaphysically*, there is no escape from difficulties. The common theory is no more encumbered with them, than any other, and therefore the existence of insolvable difficulties cannot fairly be urged as a valid objection against it. It may be that the theory of divine truth in relation to this matter has mysteries not to be explained, and depths which no finite mind can fathom. But after all, it *may* be, that there is nothing in this subject, which necessarily occasions any special difficulty. The difficulties which generally perplex us, *may* be owing to something wrong in our habits of thinking, and particularly to our undertaking to judge of that which is of a spiritual nature, by our speculative faculties. It may be that the views which David had of his own misconduct, when he wrote the 51st Psalm, were not only just and true, but the only views which were fit and profitable for him. The same may be said of Peter, when he went out and wept bitterly. It may be, that he then entertained the only right and proper views of his own offence. All the truth and all the philosophy, which justly belongs to any transgressor, may be contained in the humble, contrite confession; *I have done wickedly;—against thee, O God, have I sinned: I abhor myself. The Lord is righteous, and I am justly condemned.* We know that this is enough for the purposes of salvation, and it may be that, in regard to *all* important purposes, this is the end of the matter. As it is a concern of conscience and the heart, it may be, that any attempt to work out the problem in a speculative, philosophical manner, is not only needless, but hazardous; and that he who never makes the attempt, and is content to treat the subject merely in a penitent, devout and practical manner, is in the surest way to understand the truth, and to keep his mind effectually closed against the encroachments of error. And the time may come, when the wise and good man, instead of coldly inquiring after the *philosophy of sin*, will be wholly occupied with confessing and forsaking it, with seeking forgiveness for it, and watchfully guarding against it. And if we could have access to Adam, and could ask him to give us an exact account of his apostasy, it may be that, after all he has learnt in the world of spirits for five thousand years, the beginning, and middle, and termination of his story would be, that he was made in the image of God, and was under perfect obligations to obey his commands, but that he yielded to temptation and became a sinner. And it may be, that he would wonder at *us, philosophizing sinners*, that we should have so much trouble of a speculative, metaphysical kind, respecting our depravity, and so little of a spiritual kind, arising from a sense of the moral evil that is in us, and of our ill desert as transgressors.

I do not mean to discard mental philosophy, as a science. It is certainly conducive to the great end of our being, to turn our attention to the nature of the immortal mind, and to observe the established principles or laws which govern its operations. But mental philosophy, as a science, must be founded upon the facts of consciousness. It must take those facts *as they are;* just as the science of physics takes the facts in the natural world as they are, and builds upon them. Now our spiritual consciousness teaches us, that we are the proper subjects of law, and that we are accountable to God for our conduct, and are deserving of praise or blame according as we conform or not to the rule of right. This then is a *fact* settled forever, and not on any account to be called in question. Whatever we find the laws of mental action to be, this fact remains. It is a first principle. What then shall we think, if a man comes forward and says, if the laws of the mind are so and so, we cannot be moral, accountable beings? We tell him, the proper inquiry is, whether such *are* the laws of the mind. If, on a careful examination, we find them to be so, this can never justify us in setting aside the great fact *that we are accountable beings.* We cannot infer from one well-known truth, that another well-known truth, is not a truth. Whatever we find to be metaphysically true as to the nature of the mind or the mode of its acting — whether the necessarian scheme, or the opposite, or some one still different, proves to be the right scheme — the important truth remains in full force, and will remain forever, *that we are moral agents, justly accountable to God for our conduct, and are praise-worthy or blame-worthy, according as we obey or disobey the moral law.* Let us then no longer create to ourselves difficulties and perplexities by arraying the decisions of the speculative understanding against the decisions of conscience. Let us judge by our speculative faculty on speculative subjects, and by our moral faculty on moral subjects — never suffering one of these to interfere with the other. In this way, the decisions of each may become more clear and satisfactory, and the disputes which are carried on by speculative reason, respecting the affairs of conscience, may all come to an end. And as to the difficulties which have been accumulating of late in regard to moral agency — it may be that they are chiefly factitious or imaginary; and if so, they can be best removed, not by *encountering* them but by *dismissing* them.

Why should there be any objection to *moral necessity?* Writers explain it to be the certain connection between moral causes and their effects; or, the invariable influence of moral causes. Moral causes are the inclinations, affections, and desires of the heart, together with the objects to which they relate. The language is scientific, and has its use in philosophical treatises, and even in popular discourse. The sacred writers frequently use language which implies all that is meant by *necessity* in this case, and they sometimes use the very word, and in the sense which scientific writers affix to it; as Paul says, a *necessity* is laid upon him to preach the gospel; and Christ says, that there is a *necessity* that offences should come, and that his death is an event which *must* be. Similar language is often used in common discourse, in which it is expected, that a meaning will be given to words correspondent with the nature of the subject. Now as scientific use agrees with Scripture use, and with the prevailing use in common discourse, what valid objection can be made against it? If we interpret the language relative to this subject according to the acknowledged principles of interpretation, giving it a meaning corresponding with the nature and circumstances of the case, how easily should we rid ourselves of difficulty? And is it a mark of candor and enlargedness of mind, to indulge a prejudice against modes of speech which have long been in good use, or to insist upon fixing a meaning upon them, foreign to the manifest design for which they are employed?

President Edwards and others say, that "*moral necessity* may be as *absolute* as natural necessity; that is, a moral effect may be as perfectly connected with its moral cause, as a natural, necessary effect is, with its natural cause." The truth of this must be evident, if we look at particular instances of moral necessity. The moral perfections of God are moral causes. The effect connected with them or resulting from them, is holy, and benevolent action. Such a being as God *cannot* do *wrong*. He *must* do *right*. To suppose that infinite, immutable righteousness and goodness will lead to anything but *right* action, is absurd. The sincere love of believers to Christ is a moral cause, and is invariably connected with obedience, as its effect. "He that loveth me keepeth my words." The effect follows from the very nature of love. It cannot be otherwise. If we know that any one truly loves Christ, we know that he will obey Christ. And if any one does not obey, we know he does not love. The *carnal mind* is a moral cause, and is certainly connected with its effect, which is transgression of God's law. They in whom this cause exists, Paul says, "cannot be subject to the law," and "cannot please God." Disobedience *must* follow from the carnal, selfish heart, as certainly as any natural effect follows from a natural cause. These things are very plain. Now because *right* or *wrong* action is the *certain* result of moral causes, does it follow that the action is neither *right* nor *wrong?* Because moral causes produce their effect as certainly and invariably as physical causes, does it follow that the effect is a physical effect? Because there is as *real* an influence in the one case as in the other, does it follow that the influence is of the same nature? It does certainly result from the corrupt passions and desires of man, that offences will take place. There is a *necessity* for this. So the original word *αναγκη* signifies. Matt. 18 : 7. But can we conclude that this necessity is of the same nature with *physical* necessity? Or can we conclude that the offences which flow from it are destitute of a moral nature, and deserve no blame, because this is the case with the effects of a *physical necessity?* Here is the great mistake. And if any one falls into this mistake, he will be likely to go wrong on the whole subject. It certainly is a mistake. It is not true, that if the influence of moral causes is as invariable, as the influence of physical causes, the *effects* must be of the same nature with physical effects. It certainly is not true, that because the unquenchable love of Paul's heart had as certain an influence to lead him to preach the gospel, as the power of steam has to propel an engine, therefore he was no more praise-worthy for preaching, than an engine is for moving. Because the infinite perfection of God does as certainly result in holy and benevolent action, as the power of gravitation produces its appropriate effect, and because it is as really impossible for God to lie, as it is for gravitation to produce an effect contrary to its nature, it certainly does not follow that holy action in God has no more excellence or praise-worthiness, than, the effect of gravitation in material bodies. Moral and physical causes are in their nature entirely different. The fact that they are all *causes*, does not make them the *same* causes, or *like* causes. If moral causes have an influence which is equally powerful with physical causes, and which equally prevents or takes away all resistance, this does not alter the nature of the causes, nor the nature of their influence, nor the nature of the effects produced. To suppose that it does is the great mistake. If any one makes this mistake, he may easily correct it, if he will lay aside the technical language which occasions the difficulty, and speak of cases where moral causes exist and operate, in plain, common language, and for practical purposes — if, instead of saying that God acts under the influence of *moral necessity*, he will say, his actions flow from his infinite wisdom and goodness — if instead of saying, that *Christians* are influenced by a moral necessity, he will say, their love and gratitude to Christ, and their benevolence to their fellow men, are motives which influence them to pious and benevolent actions — and if, instead of saying, that *sinners* act as they do, from a moral necessity, he will say, they act from the selfishness, the pride, and the desperate wickedness of their hearts. By contemplating these common and well known facts, as *expressed in common language*, all unprejudiced men might become satisfied. And why should not *scientific* men be equally satisfied, when the same facts are expressed in scientific language? But if any of us have a dislike to the scientific language of Edwards and others on the present subject, let us take care that we do not impute to them a meaning which never entered their minds, and that we do not deny or overlook what is plainly a matter of fact, whether it is expressed in common or in scientific language.

The word *fatalism* denotes the opposite of the doctrine, *that we are free, moral, accountable beings, under the government of a wise, righteous and benevolent God and are either praise-worthy or blame-worthy for our conduct.* It may be proper and useful then, to consider it as including these several points.

Now in order to satisfy ourselves whether the doctrine of *moral necessity* involves fatalism, we must have a clear conception of what moral necessity is. And it will be just and right to consider it to be what its most intelligent advocates represent it to be ; that is, *the certain and invariable connection of moral causes and moral effects.* The doctrine implies that all the external voluntary actions of men, and all their inward affections, purposes, etc., result from motives operating in or upon the mind. Now, does *moral necessity, thus explained, involve fatalism, or lead to it? Does it imply the particulars which go to make up fatalism?* *

All that belongs to the doctrine of moral necessity, as stated by Edwards, appears to me to be a matter of *direct consciousness.* I am sure that I act in the manner described; and I am sure that I am a free, moral, accountable being, because I do act in this manner. I want no support for the doctrine, but my own consciousness. And whenever I have been embarrassed in my reflections respecting it, it has been the consequence of my mistaking the import of the terms by which the doctrine is expressed, or of my suffering speculative reasoning, to interfere with the decision of consciousness.

I ask those for proof, who affirm, that the theory of moral necessity is *incompatible* with free, moral, accountable agency. Let them show in what respects it is incompatible. Let them bring forward some instance in which a free moral agent ever did deliberately act otherwise than according to that theory.

President Day cites the remark of Cousin, that "the theory of Locke concerning freedom tended to fatalism;" and then he says: "Calling in the aid of an odious appellation, is a very convenient and summary mode of confuting an opponent. It has a special advantage when the name which is substituted for argument, is so indefinite and mysterious, that the reader is in no danger of discovering its meaning. Fatalism is commonly understood to be something heathenish. But it has assumed such a diversity of forms, that it is sufficiently unintelligible to answer

* As this subject has been sufficiently considered in the Lectures and elsewhere in the foregoing volumes; the particular discussion of it is here omitted.

the purpose of an argument, which is most efficacious when least understood. It would be a more simple, if not a more satisfactory mode of reasoning, to offer direct proof of the reality of contingent self-determination. — Whatever was meant by the fatalism of the ancients, it did not imply that all the changes in the world are under the guidance of *a Being of infinite wisdom and infinite goodness.* — It is urged that the fatalists refer every change to a *cause.* So do believers in self-determination; not excepting even acts of the will. — Is it fatalism to believe, that he who formed the soul of man can so touch the springs of its action as to influence the will, without interfering with the freedom of its choice? Is a chain of causes, suspended from the throne of nonentity, to be likened to the purposes and agency of the omniscient Creator? Is it fatalism to believe, that motives may have a real influence in determining volition, and that they may be presented by the providence of God; that the state of the heart has also some concern in giving direction to our acts of choice, and that this native or acquired state is not always the product of chance? — The object of our inquiry is to learn whether moral acts are determined by accident. If they are not, does it certainly follow that they must be subject to the fates of the heathen? Is there no room left for any effectual influence from infinite wisdom and be nevolence?"

"The suggestion that a denial of contingent self-determination leads to pantheism, is as indefinite in its application, as the charge of fatalism. The doctrine of pantheism, as held by Spinoza and his followers, is that the universe is God. — What has this to do with the dependence of volition on the state of the heart, and the influence of motives? — If in God we live and move and have our being, does it follow that our life is his life, our motion his motion, our existence his existence? Is it pantheism to believe that he worketh in us both to will and to do? Does such agency of his imply, that there is neither willing nor acting on our part? that there is really but one agent in the universe?" *

The duty of self-denial is sometimes thought to militate against

---

* Day on the Will, Sect. 9.

the doctrine of Edwards, and to prove that our volitions do not always follow our strongest desires, or that we do not always choose according to our strongest motive. The writer of the Essay says: "Do you not at times practise self-denial, and does this consist in choosing that which is at the time of choice the most agreeable?" Again he says: "The Bible never teaches that self-denial consists in choosing that which seems most agreeable." Now, in my opinion, the duty of self-denial does plainly exemplify the principle that we are governed by the strongest motive. When a Christian denies himself, he does indeed act against certain inclinations and desires, which operate as motives. Sometimes these are very strong. And how could they be overcome without something stronger. Why does the Christian deny these inferior desires and motives? Because he is influenced by love to Christ, which is an affection of a higher and nobler kind than any which he denies. It is his supreme motive. He is willing even to lose his life for Christ's sake. He hates his earthly relations in comparison with Christ, that is, he loves Christ above them. So the apostles acted. Love to Christ constrained them. Under its influence they chose to deny themselves in regard to all their worldly inclinations. It was the most agreeable to them, as followers of Christ, to do this. It was most gratifying to their supreme desire. If any one should deny himself, without this superior motive, it would not be *Christian* self-denial. The desires of the natural, unrenewed mind are very strong, and no one will ever subdue them, unless he has a motive of superior strength. The strong man cannot be disarmed and overcome, except by one that is "stronger than he." Luke 11: 22.

If a man half believes the doctrine of Edwards; or if he believes it under a misapprehension of what it is; or if he believes it with a true apprehension of its nature, but gives it undue importance; or if he entertains the speculative belief in a heart destitute of holiness;—in either of these cases, the consequences of his belief will probably be pernicious. And it is the same with regard to all moral and religious truth. But let a man of clear understanding, and decided piety, rightly apprehend and cordially believe this doctrine, and the consequences will be salutary. The men who speak of the bad influence of believing moral necessity, are those who do not believe it. But what intelligent, good man ever believed it, without experiencing happy effects from it? We have all along heard it alleged that the doctrine has a bad tendency. But we have never discovered such a tendency. It has been lodged in the minds of multitudes of the wisest and best men. But they have all found its influence to be favorable to morality and piety. While those who declaim against it, and say that the belief of it has a pernicious effect, are those who do not believe it. It is my full conviction that the doctrine is the doctrine of the Bible, presented in a scientific form, and arrayed against hurtful errors; that it tends to honor God, to humble man, and to promote growth in grace, and that if we should embrace the antagonist doctrine, we should suffer loss.

One point more. The author of the Essay says: "According to the doctrine of free agency, the mind of man is endowed with a constitutional desire for happiness, which is the steady, abiding feeling of the mind, and is the mainspring of all the mental activity included in volition." Is this true? *Do all our choices and voluntary actions proceed from self-love, or a desire for our own happiness?* If so, then there is clearly a "uniform, invariable" connection of volition with an antecedent motive. And this "*uniform, invariable antecedence*" would, according to the author, involve the essence of fatalism; and the fatalism would be universal, leaving no place for free moral agency. For if "the desire for happiness is the mainspring of *all* the mental activity included in volition," that is, of *all* voluntary action; then all voluntary action stands in an invariable connection with one and the same antecedent motive, and, of course, excludes what the author calls *free agency.*

I am, however, far from admitting that self-love, or the desire of our own happiness, is "the mainspring" of all voluntary action. But I must content myself with a few brief observations on the subject.

That self-love is *not* the spring of all voluntary action, is, I think, evident.

First, *there are many principles* and some of them very powerful principles in the human mind, which prove springs of that mental action which is involved in volition. Love of offspring, pity for the distressed, gratitude for favors, and other natural affections are as truly elements of our mental constitution, as the desire of our own happiness; and each one of them is as truly a spring of voluntary action, as self-love. How then can self-love be the spring of *all* voluntary action? We can say with truth, it is *one* of the springs of action. In *all* minds, it is a *powerful* spring. But is it therefore the *only* spring? In *some* minds it is the *most powerful* spring, — the *supreme* motive, — the motive, it may be, which governs almost *exclusively*. But because this is the case in *some* minds, can we conclude that it is so in *all?* Take the man, who loves God with all his heart and soul. Has he no spring of action above the desire of his own happiness? Is not his affection to God a motive distinct from self-love, and of a far higher and nobler nature? And do not those who maintain, that a desire for happiness is the spring of all voluntary action, manifestly overlook important principles, and attempt to simplify beyond nature, and in opposition to truth? They discover that self-love is a very powerful motive to action, and thence conclude that it is the *only* one. Others, who find *gratitude* to be a powerful motive to action might, with the same justice, conclude that *this* is the only motive. And others again, finding that pity for the distressed operates as a motive to exertion, might lose sight of everything else, and hold that *all* our actions result from *pity*.

As there are many motives of volition, besides self-love, so there are some motives which are of superior moral worth. Suppose you know that a man performs an action or makes a sacrifice from pure love to God, or to man, without the least reference in his thoughts or feelings to his own private good. Do you not at once pronounce it a deed of uncommon excellence? Even that benevolence which is mixed with other things, and of which we can only say, that it has more influence than self-love, is regarded as a virtue. But that benevolence which is wholly disinterested, i. e., which does not proceed from any aim, direct or indirect, to promote our own gratification, is the object of universal admiration. And how many seek that admiration by appearing to be actuated by such benevolence, though really destitute of it.

It may perhaps be said, that while we are influenced by love to God or to man, we experience *pleasure;* and from this it may be inferred, that a *desire* for this pleasure is at bottom the mainspring of all moral action, and that all our other motives are to be resolved into this. But what is there in logic, or in experience, which can justify such an inference? The fact that we are *pleased* with the accomplishment of any object, as the honor of God, or the good of man, implies that we *love* that object antecedently to the pleasure we enjoy in it. Without the existence of such love to the object, how could the promotion of it give pleasure? The pleasure results from the preëxistent affection, and not the affection from a wish to obtain pleasure.

No one can doubt, that a desire for our own happiness is often the spring of our voluntary actions. But does it follow from this, that it is always so? How can that be considered as a motive to action, which is in no way contemplated by us — which is not before the mind as an object of thought or desire, at the time of action? Look at a loving father, who, at the hazard of his own life, rushes into the water or the fire to rescue his little children. What *moves* him to do this? Is it a desire for his own gratification or pleasure? But he will tell you, he had no thought of this, and that he was urged on to do what he did, by the love and pity of his heart for his dear, suffering children. If he succeeded in preserving their life, he did indeed experience a high degree of pleasure, as a consequence. But to say that a desire for that pleasure was the *motive* of the parent's efforts, would be a contradiction to his own consciousness, and an abuse of language. And surely a devout Christian may, sometimes at least, be so influenced, so constrained, so borne on by love to Christ, that all thought of himself and all desire for his own gratification will be excluded, and his fervent, holy love become the great and only motive of action. Facts of this kind certainly occur in the history of God's people. In how many instances are Christians, at the commencement of their course, and afterwards, conscious of loving God and rejoicing in his government, without any reference in their thoughts to their own interests, temporal or eternal? And is not such pure love to God, such a rising above private interest, and such annihilation of self generally regarded as among the clearest marks of holiness, and as what may be expected to exist in proportion to the measure of sanctification? The unregenerate are "lovers of themselves." They have no moral affection of a higher character than self-love. But can it be the same with those who bear the image of Christ? Is there no object in the universe which they love, except in subserviency to their own personal welfare? Is all duty performed by saints and angels from that one principle? To suppose this seems to me as unphilosophical and untrue, as to suppose that all the operations in the *natural* world are to be traced to the power of *steam*, or to *electricity*. True philosophy leads us to account for the phenomena in the natural world by a great *variety* of principles or laws, many of which are entirely distinct from each other. And why should it not lead us to do the same in the *moral* world, and to trace the actions of intelligent, moral beings, to all that variety of principles or motives, from which they evidently result? Why should we refuse to admit what is so manifest, that a *variety* of causes or springs of action as really exist and operate in the world of *mind*, as in the world of *matter?*

REPLY TO "INQUIRER."*

THE writer, whose questions and remarks I shall now consider, conceals his name, and calls himself "Inquirer." He doubtless has sufficient reasons for writing anonymously. But what weight is there in the reasons which he suggests in his "Apology?" He thinks he may be allowed to conceal his name, because he does not come forward as a *teacher*, but as a *learner*. But why is it less proper for one, who presents himself before the public as an "Inquirer" and learner, to make known his real name, than for one who presents himself as a teacher? It is certainly very honorable for a man to "take the attitude of a learner;" especially if, in that modest attitude, he manifests high intellectual attainments, and gives his readers reason to think that he is able to *teach* as well as to *learn*.

But I have no disposition to complain of "Inquirer," for not giving his name to the public. Nor will I evade the task of answering his inquiries because he writes anonymously. As the questions are important, I will seriously attend to them, without being anxious to know from whom they come. I am very willing to converse with persons behind the curtain, whose words I hear, but whose faces I have not the pleasure to see, on condition that they treat subjects with propriety, and show by their words, that they are worthy of respect, as the two anonymous writers do, with whom I am concerned in these discussions. After all, it must seem rather singular for me, in my own name, to be publicly discussing subjects with two writers, possessed of no ordinary powers of mind, but who conceal their names. I however make no objection. Still one in my case cannot be quite certain how the thing will end. If I should commit mistakes, or if I should be unsuc-

* First published in the Am. Bib. Repos., 1840 and 1841, in reply to "Inquirer," April, 1840.

cessful in my efforts, and so expose myself to shame, I might wish I had done as others have done, and wisely availed myself of the benefit of concealment. On the other hand, if my respected, but anonymous friends find, as they may, that they have escaped the hazards of authorship, and have gained honor to themselves by their anonymous publications; it will be easy for them to prevent mistakes and to let the world know to whom the honor belongs.

It is well understood, how much more difficult it is to answer questions, than it is to ask them. And what if I should think it best, by and by, to invert the present order, and to take upon myself, as I have a right to do, the humbler and easier task of asking questions, and to transfer to "Inquirer," the more honorable and difficult task of answering them? And if a man of such obvious and eminent characteristics as he possesses, should proceed a little further in laying open his mind, and should be as free in answering as he has been in asking questions, he might perhaps make himself sufficiently known without the form of giving his name.

"Inquirer" says, he finds "difficulties in *most* of the systems of mental philosophy" which he reads. It is implied, that he does not find difficulties in *all* of them; that there is at least some one system, in which he finds no difficulties. I would then at once "take the attitude of a learner," and ask him what that system is. To me all systems of mental philosophy have had their difficulties. I have not been able to fix upon any system, however well supported by argument, against which speculative objections and difficulties could not be urged. And if I had refused to believe every truth, or system of truths, which was exposed to difficulties that I could not fully obviate, I should have believed nothing. If, however, "Inquirer" has found a system which is encumbered with no difficulties, as his expression seems to imply, he will confer a great favor on me, and on many others, by making us acquainted with it. But, for the present, I am fully convinced, that the only safe and proper way is, *to believe that which is proved by sufficient evidence, especially by Scripture evidence, whatever speculative difficulties may attend it.* If our faith in divine truth is shaken, if it in the least degree wavers, on account of insolvable difficulties, we shall suffer a loss that cannot be measured.

But what "Inquirer" says afterwards, shows that we may have mistaken his meaning, and that he did not intend to signify that he was acquainted with any system of mental philosophy which is free from difficulties. For he says, distinctly, that he has not found "terra firma extensive enough to choose his dwelling-place;" and he is looking for "new treatises," making improvements upon all the old systems. He shows a commendable zeal for the advancement of mental science, and thinks "it is time that more were said and done in relation to this great subject." With a little modification my opinion coincides with his. I would say, "it is time that *more*," or *less*, "were said and done." On this subject, especially, smattering is to be deprecated. "Drink deep, or taste not."

"Inquirer" says, he never can love dispute, until he has "a new *taste*," and speaks of this as my philosophical word. I was somewhat surprised that he should call the word *taste*, used metaphorically in relation to the mind, a *philosophical* word. For I supposed that the precision required in philosophical discourse led philosophers, as far as possible, to avoid metaphorical words. Figurative language is most freely used in poetry, eloquence and common discourse. The analogy between *taste* in the *literal* sense, and an *inclination* or *desire* of the *mind*, is very obvious; and accordingly the word has been very frequently used to express such an inclination or desire. It is a just and striking *figure*, not a *philosophical* term. But if it were a philosophical word, I know not why he should call it *mine*, as though *I* had invented it, or as though I used it more than others. The word has been familiarly used by the best English writers, and by the standard divines of New England. This I might easily show. But I shall content myself with citing a single passage from a recent and well-known writer, the Rev. Moses Stuart, my respected colleague. Speaking of infants, he says: "To enjoy the sacred pleasures of that place," (heaven,) "there must be a *positive taste* for them. If now infants are saved, (which I do hope and trust is the case,) then there must be such a *relish implanted* in their souls for the holy joys of heaven. Is there nothing, then, which Christ by his Spirit can do for them, in imparting such a *taste?* *

One word more by way of introduction. My own experience has taught me, that there are many and very stubborn difficulties hanging around the subject before us, whenever contemplated in a speculative and theoretic manner. To untie all the knots which can be untied, and to determine clearly those which cannot, is no easy task. Whoever attempts to do this — whoever undertakes to answer the hardest questions, which the most powerful intellect can propose on this hardest of all subjects, ought to have time and space given him, and to be treated with a good measure of patience and candid allowance by his readers.

The first topic which "Inquirer" introduces, relates to the sinner's inability. He refers to my question respecting one who is unregenerate. "While he remains in his natural state, can he, by the power of his will, prevent it," (i. e. the feeling of enmity,) "and call forth the affection of love, and so be subject to the law of God?" This question he rightly understands as implying that the sinner *cannot* do this. The difficulties which he suggests in relation to this subject, may be summed up in the single question, *What is the sense of the words "can" and "cannot," as here used?*

I must begin my remarks by saying, that I feel utterly unable to do anything which can be satisfactory to "Inquirer" unless he admits the distinction so often made by distinguished writers between the different senses in which the words *can* and *cannot* are used. That they are used in senses which are essentially different from each other, is manifest. If we can satisfy ourselves what these senses are, and then determine definitely which of them is to be given to the words when used in relation to the present subject, we shall have a prospect of arriving at a just conclusion.

---

* Commentary on Romans, Edit. 1832, Excursus IV. p. 549.

The distinction referred to is between *natural* and *moral* inability; — i. e. between inability used in a *natural* sense, or in relation to *natural* objects, and in a *moral* sense, or in relation to *moral* objects. In the first sense, it is, as Fuller describes it, "a want of rational faculties, bodily powers or external advantages." It is *such a want of natural powers or faculties of body or mind, or such a want of the necessary means or opportunities, as excludes obligation, and prevents blame-worthiness.* "Inquirer" doubtless knows how Edwards, Bellamy, Smalley, Fuller and other writers illustrate this kind of inability, and how clearly they show, that it excludes obligation and ill-desert; as when a man cannot see because he has no eyes; or cannot walk because his limbs are palsied; cannot understand Newton's Principia for want of sufficient strength of intellect; or cannot pay his debts, though he makes all possible efforts to do it. In all cases of this kind, the inability is of such a nature as to exclude obligation. That which hinders the performance is such, that there can be no blame.

Natural impossibility is explained in the same way; — *natural necessity* is the opposite. A thing takes place by *a natural necessity*, when it certainly results from the operation of natural causes, as the falling of a stone, or a man's going to a place when compelled against his will.

Moral inability is that which results from *moral causes*, such as the dispositions and habits of the mind. In this sense, a man is unable to do a thing, when he is effectually hindered by his own inclinations, or the state of his mind. When we say: "God *cannot* lie," we set forth that moral excellence of his character, which certainly prevents him from doing wrong. And when we say of a just judge, that he *cannot* take a bribe, and of a kind mother, that she *cannot* forget her child, we refer to a hinderance of a *moral* kind. The just judge is prevented from taking a bribe by *moral integrity*, and the mother from forgetting her child, by *maternal love.* In all cases like these, the *greater* the *inability*, in other words, the greater the hinderance in the way of doing the thing mentioned, the more praise-worthy is the person. Here moral inability results from moral excellence, or is involved in it.

Again; a person in this moral sense is unable to do *right* when he is hindered from doing it by some *wrong* disposition or habit of mind; as when we say, that a man of a malevolent, revengeful temper *cannot* love his enemy, or that a miser *cannot* give away his money, or that a man of a low, base character *cannot* do a generous, noble deed. It is this sort of inability, to which the sacred writers evidently refer, when they teach, that those who are accustomed to do evil, cannot learn to do well; that those who receive honor of men cannot believe; that those who have the carnal mind cannot please God. In all such cases, the greater the *inability* — i. e. the greater that sinful disposition or habit of mind which hinders a man from doing right — the greater is his blame-worthiness. This is plain. If any one denies it, he will soon contradict himself. It is a practical truth. Whatever is doubtful, this is certain, that, in the sight of God, and in the view of every unperverted mind, a man is criminal and ill-deserving, in proportion to the strength of that wrong disposition, affection or habit of mind which hinders him from doing his duty.

Thus it appears that the distinction between natural and moral inability is perfectly manifest, and exceedingly important. *Natural* inability excludes obligation and blame. If it is entire, it entirely excludes blame. *Moral* inability to do *wrong* implies moral excellence. If it exists in the highest degree, as it does in God, it denotes the highest degree of excellence. In man, it implies goodness and praise-worthiness in proportion to its degree. On the other hand, moral inability to do *right* implies ill-desert, and implies it in proportion to the inability. Whenever the sacred writers predicate this inability of the sinner, they do it to set forth his criminality. And were it not that our moral senses are blunted by sin, we should always so understand it. If any rational, moral being should say of himself, or if another should say of him, that he *cannot love the all-perfect, glorious God*, we should be impressed with his baseness, and should exclaim, *how desperately wicked must his heart be!*

In regard to the expression of mine, above referred to, implying that the unrenewed sinner *cannot* call forth the affection of love to God and so be subject to his law, I might at once resort to the Scriptures which make the same representation. The passages in which they familiarly do this, are well known. Now the single fact, that men, who spake as they were moved by the Holy Ghost, frequently affirmed that unrenewed sinners *cannot* believe and obey, is, by itself, sufficient to justify us in using the same language on the same subject. What better reason can we have for any doctrine, or for any mode of teaching it than that we find it in the infallible word of God? Did not the inspired writers use words *correctly?* Had they not good reason to speak as they did? And when *we* speak of the same subject, and with reference to the same aspect of the subject, have we not good reason to speak in the same manner? —The word of God does indeed need *explanation.* But does it need *mending?* This then is the stand I take. *Christ and the apostles were right. They taught the truth; and the manner of their teaching was just and unexceptionable.* And they are good examples for us. It is allowed by all that their language was intended for common people, and suited to common apprehension. So that, whatever we may say respecting the proper language of philosophy or metaphysics, we are sure, that the language of the Bible is the proper language of those who preach the gospel. I am aware that some preachers at the present day are not accustomed to use the language of Scripture on this subject. When it comes in their way, and when it would be natural for them to make use of it, they still avoid it, and substitute language which is different and opposite. In the very place, where Christ and the apostles unhesitatingly say that the unrenewed sinner *cannot* believe and obey, these preachers unhesitatingly say he *can.* Now, soberly, if I should discover anything like this in myself; if when the inspired writers are accustomed to use one mode of speaking, I should be accustomed to use the opposite; if I should detect in myself this practice of shunning the language of the Bible, and using the opposite in its place; I should think it high time for me to be alarmed at my want of reverence for the word of God, and to inquire for the cause which had turned me aside. I know, for a certainty, that Christ and the apostles had a just view of our nature and relations. They understood human obligation, and the grounds of it. They understood moral agency and the *philosophy* of moral agency. And yet they declared, that sinners *cannot* believe and obey. They affirmed this repeatedly, and without qualification. And certainly they knew, better than we do, how to teach divine truth, and how to guard against whatever would expose men to mistake. Nor do we find that they used different language at different times, sometimes saying that sinners *cannot* obey, and sometimes, that they *can*. I start back from anything either in principle or practice, which implies that the words of inspiration are not fit to be used in popular religious discourse, and which would lead us to introduce language of a different import, when speaking on the same subject, and in the same connection.

"Inquirer" refers to several instances, in which *can* is used in Scripture, and common parlance, with an implied negative, signifying that the thing spoken of is "*very difficult, very revolting or very improbable;* and then asks, *whether this is the sense in which I mean the word to be understood here.* To this I reply in the negative. And if "Inquirer" will go along with me a little in the examination, he will see the reason why I cannot admit this to be the right sense of the word.

It is an acknowledged principle, that if a definition or explanation of a word is right, that explanation may be substituted for the word without injuring the sense. Now let the correctness of the above explanation be tested by this principle. Say then that the *cannot* in the cases referred to merely signifies, as "Inquirer" expresses it, that the thing spoken of is "very difficult, revolting, or improbable;" and substitute any or all of these words in place of the Scripture word to be explained, and see how it will work. First, take the language of the prophet: "Can the Ethiopian change his skin, or the leopard his spots? Then may ye also, who are accustomed to do evil, learn to do well." The passage clearly and strongly implies, that the Ethiopian *cannot* change his skin, or the leopard his spots, and that those who are accustomed to do evil *cannot* learn to do well. Try now the explanation above proposed. Begin with the word "difficult," thus: As it is "very difficult" for the Ethiopian to change his skin, and the leopard his spots, so it is for those who are accustomed to do evil, to learn to do well. Next try "revolting:" As it is "very revolting" for the Ethiopian to change his skin — so it is for the habitual transgressor to turn from sin to holiness. Finally, try "improbable:" As it is "very *improbable*" that the Ethiopian will change his skin, so it is, that sinners, long accustomed to do evil, will learn to do well. Again; take the text, John 15: 4, in which Christ says to some: "How *can* ye believe, who receive honor one of another, and seek not the honor which cometh from God only?" signifying emphatically, that such persons *cannot* believe; and let it be explained as above. It is "very difficult" for them to believe, who receive honor one of another; or, it is "very revolting" to them; or it is "very improbable" that they will believe. Again; take that momentous declaration of Christ: "No man can come unto me, except the Father who hath sent me draw him." According to the proposed explanation, it would read thus: It is "very difficult" for any man to come to Christ, except he is drawn of the Father; or it is "very revolting" to him; or it is "very improbable" that any sinner will come to Christ, without special divine influence. Again; "Without me ye can do nothing." Explained as above: It is "very difficult" for you to do anything, or it is "very improbable" that you will do anything, without me. Take one passage more, Rom. 8: 7, 8; "The carnal mind — is not subject to the law of God, neither indeed can be." Explained: It is "very difficult and revolting" for the carnal mind to be subject to the law, and it is "very improbable" that it ever will be subject. — "So then they that are in the flesh *cannot* please God." That is to say; it is "very difficult" for the unregenerate to please God, and "very improbable" that they will please him.

Thus it appears that this first explanation proposed by "Inquirer," fails to give the true meaning of the inspired writers. And he is right in thinking it "very improbable," that I understand the word *cannot* in such a sense.

"He" proceeds to suggest another view of the subject, namely: "that the unregenerate man has actually *no power* to love God and be subject to his law," and that it is "*actually and absolutely impossible*" for him to do it. He seems to suppose that this is the view which I adopt. How easy it is for him to make out a meaning for me, and to state it in his own words, and then to urge arguments against it, as though it were really my meaning.

But on such a subject it is important to use language which is unambiguous and plain. The phrases, "*no power*" and "*actually and absolutely impossible*" are ambiguous, being used in very different senses. There is certainly a wide difference between "*no power*" or total inability in one of these senses, and in the other. Who is ignorant of the distinction, which is so obvious and so commonly recognized, between a *natural* inability and impossibility, and a *moral?* On this subject, I go with New England divines. And I do heartily, though not with an implicit, or undistinguishing faith, coincide with them in opinion. The explanations given by Edwards, Smalley, and others do, in my opinion, afford all the satisfaction which can be had, respecting this subject. A subtle and skeptical mind may embarrass this subject by endless objections and cavils. But after all, we shall find that every important truth respecting it is obvious and certain.

There is what we call a *natural inability*, consisting in the want of those powers and faculties which are essential to a moral, accountable agent, and without which there can be no obligation to obey the divine law. But no inability of this kind belongs to sinners. The fact mentioned by "Inquirer," namely, that God requires all men to obey his commands, does certainly imply that they *ought* to obey, and of course that they have no inability which interferes with the justice of such a requisition, or with their perfect obligation to comply with it. I am far from holding that sinners have "no power" of *any kind* to obey, or that it is, in *every sense*, "impossible" for them to obey. As to those powers and faculties, or that ability which makes them fit subjects of a moral law, I maintain that they possess it *perfectly*. So that they have no need of any new mental faculties, or any increase of their natural ability, in order to their actual obedience.

It follows, that when the Scriptures teach, that sinners *cannot* obey, they must refer to the other kind of inability. And here I come to the explanation which "Inquirer" calls for. The inability of sinners is their *strong disinclination* or *aversion* to *holiness;* their settled, unyielding opposition of heart to do the will of God. This sinful disinclination or aversion is such, that it is not sufficient to say, it makes it "very difficult" for sinners to obey, or "very improbable" that they will obey. It is a certain hinderance to obedience, and will be forever, unless removed by the renewing of the Holy Ghost. No motives presented to the mind, and no means whatever can overcome it without the regenerating influence of the Spirit. It is a disinclination and aversion of heart so strong and invincible, that it prevents obedience as certainly and effectually, as a *natural impossibility* could; so that the sacred writers are perfectly justified in calling it a *cannot*, and in representing a change by the divine Spirit as absolutely necessary to bring man to faith and obedience. This has been the doctrine of the Christian church in all ages; and what is more, it is the doctrine of THE BIBLE. We know there is *a sense* in which sinners *cannot* obey, because the word of God so represents it. It must be an *important* sense, or the inspired writers would not have asserted it so emphatically. And it must be an *obvious* sense, suggested by the very nature of the subject, or the inspired writers would not have asserted it so directly, and left it, without any qualification, to be apprehended by plain common sense. We are sure they had good reason to express their meaning just as they did, and to say, that unrenewed sinners *cannot* believe and obey. And as sinners are, in this respect, the same in all ages, *we* have good reason to speak of them as the sacred writers did. And when, with this moral aspect of the subject before us, we teach, in the very language of inspiration, that sinners cannot believe and obey, we no more furnish an excuse for their unbelief and disobedience, than Christ and the apostles did. Indeed, the more strongly we affirm this, in the proper connection, the more impressively do we teach the inexcusable wickedness of sinners. For the inability of sinners is of such a nature, that the higher it rises, and the more absolute it is, the more heinous is their guilt. And we may at any time make this perfectly plain, if instead of the word *cannot*, we merely employ other words, which clearly express the same meaning. Thus, if instead of saying that sinners *cannot* believe and obey, we take words of the same import, and say, they are wholly *disinclined* to do it, that they have an absolute *aversion*, an obstinate *unwillingness* to obey, which no argument can overcome; every one sees that we mean to charge them with great wickedness. To be totally *disinclined* to do right, and *inclined* to do wrong, is the very essence of sin.

This then is the answer I give to the first question of "Inquirer," and it is the best answer I can give.

But while we are, in a proper connection, to affirm that sinners cannot obey God; are we to affirm this in *all* cases, and whatever may be the drift of discourse? By no means. When it is our object to describe men as rational and accountable agents, and to show what necessarily belongs to them as the proper subjects of the divine law, we must represent them as endued with competent powers and faculties; in other words, with a *natural* ability, commensurate with the divine requirements; so that if they fail of obedience, it will not be for want of any of the requisite natural endowments. These endowments constitute the proper ground of obligation.

But there is an important sense in which they *cannot* obey. Those who have been thoroughly convinced of sin know, by their own experience, that sinners *cannot* come to Christ, unless the Father draw them, and they know too in what the *inability* consists. Now when we are speaking of men in a religious point of view; when our object is to decribe them *as sinners*, or to show what is their moral character and state, and to induce them to look to Christ for salvation; then truth requires us to use the language of the inspired writers, and to make the alarming, humbling representation, that sinners *cannot* believe, or do anything spiritually good. Unless we tell sinners this, how do we tell them the whole truth?

There is one point more to be considered, though it must be very briefly. "Inquirer" asks whether the inability of an unsanctified man is such, "as precludes the possibility of his changing his present state for a better one." And if so, then he asks, what we are to say of the command, "make you a new heart, and a new spirit." I reply: This command, which is of the same import with the command to repent, or the command to turn from sin, is obligatory upon sinners, for the same reasons that all other moral precepts are. God's commands are holy, just, and good; and they certainly do not cease to be binding upon us because we are disinclined to obey, or because our disinclination is so strong, that nothing but the renewing influence of the Spirit can remove it and bring us to cordial obedience. Now it is clear, that we are under no other *inability* or *impossibility* to comply with the command to change from a sinful to a holy state, than the inability we are under in regard to all the other commands of God. It is an inability of a *moral kind*, consisting in the *entire depravity of the heart*, or *its total and invincible opposition to holiness*. When the command comes to sinners, requiring them to love God, or to believe in Christ, the wickedness of their heart prevents. This is the *only* hinderance; but it is an *effectual* hinderance. And when the command comes to them, to repent, to turn from sin, or to make them a new heart, the same cause prevents. Tell me in what sense unregenerate sinners are unable to love God, or what *hinders* them from loving God, and you tell me, in what sense they are unable "to change their present state for a better one," or what it is which *hinders* such a change. And that depravity or wickedness of heart, which has prevented and which now prevents them from obeying this and every other divine command, will certainly, in opposition to reason, conscience and duty, continue to prevent till the day of salvation ends, unless God is pleased to have mercy upon them, and *give* them a *new heart and a right spirit.*

I now come to the *second* difficulty which "Inquirer" presents. I had said, that "unrenewed men *invariably*, have wrong affections and desires, and perfectly holy beings *invariably* have right affections and desires, in view of moral objects." This I thought would accord with the opinion of those who believe the doctrine of the total depravity of the unrenewed. That doctrine is, that men, in their natural state, are sinful without any mixture of holiness. And it is only expressing the same thing in another manner, to say, that unrenewed men *invariably* have wrong affections and desires in view of moral objects. Does "Inquirer" deny this? Does he think that unrenewed men have a mixture of right moral affections; or that perfectly holy beings have a mixture of sinful affections? I presume not. What then is the difficulty? It is this. Some of the angels, who were *once* perfectly holy, did not continue so, but became sinful; and *now*, in their sinful state, they have wrong affections and desires. The same as to our first parents, who fell from a state of holiness, and then had wrong affections. But are these facts contrary to the position, that *perfectly holy beings invariably have right affections?* Do they show that *perfectly holy beings* have *wrong* affections? In other words, do they show that perfectly holy beings are *not* perfectly holy? To predicate right affections of perfectly holy beings is to declare what *belongs* to those who *are* perfectly *holy*, not what belongs to those who are *sinful*. The wrong affections of fallen angels or fallen men are not the affections of perfectly holy beings, but of sinful beings. "Inquirer" asks, "whether our first parents, who were once sinless beings, invariably retained right affections." I answer, they retained right affections while they were perfectly holy. And this is all that my affirmation implies, and it is all that other similar affirmations imply. If I say, a perfectly righteous judge invariably conforms to the principles of justice, I declare what belongs to such a judge. And my declaration would be true, although a judge, once righteous, should become unrighteous, and should then, as unrighteous, violate the principles of justice. It does not belong to a perfectly righteous judge to violate the principles of justice. And it does not belong to a perfectly holy being to hate God. A fallen angel is not a holy being.

"Inquirer" doubts as to the meaning of the phrase — "in view of moral objects." He says, and says truly, that I have applied this *view of moral objects* both to wrong affections and to right affections. And he adds: "It would seem, then, that the same objects occasion wrong affections in one class, and right ones in the other." I reply; it not only *seems* so, but it certainly *is* so. It is a plain matter of fact, that a view of moral objects excites affections in us according to our character and state. If we are believers, it excites love; if unbelievers, hatred. The followers of Christ saw and loved both him and his Father. But he said to unbelievers: "ye have both seen and *hated* both me and my Father." The same truths are to one class of men a savor of life unto life; to another class, a savor of death unto death. "Inquirer" is familiar with this fact. But the expression that "perfectly holy beings invariably have right affections" seems to him to imply, that there can be no change from holiness to sin; that he, who is once perfectly holy, is so forever. But I had no such meaning in my mind; and I think the language would naturally convey no such meaning to the minds of others. "Inquirer" says: "If in view of moral objects perfectly holy beings *must* invariably have right affections, what possible influence could temptation have over our progenitors?" But this is not my language. I did not say perfectly holy beings *must* invariably have right affections. This might look to the future, and might imply that no change could take place. What I said was, that perfectly holy beings invariably *have* right affections; *have* them *as* holy beings, and *while* holy; not that all holy beings are immutable.

As to the apostasy of holy beings, a speculative mind may find difficulties in abundance. What then? What if we are unable to explain metaphysically the well known fact that holy beings have become sinful? Can "Inquirer" explain it? Can he solve all the difficulties respecting the introduction of sin? That we who have never known by experience what it is to change from holiness to sin, should be unable to understand the exact manner in which the change occurred, or the process of a holy mind in becoming sinful, is nothing strange. We have all the knowledge on the subject which is necessary for practical purposes, though not all which an unbridled curiosity craves. Let us be content to know the plain, important, practical truths. First. We may lay it down as an undisputed truth, that holy beings have apostatized. Secondly. We may lay it down as an undoubted truth, that the change from holiness to sin, in those who have apostatized, took place in such a manner as not to supersede or interrupt their moral agency. In the act of their apostasy, and after their apostasy, they retained all the powers and faculties of moral agents, the proper subjects of law. This is plain. Again. Those who changed from holiness to sin were altogether culpable. The sinful act was theirs. The tempter was indeed culpable for *his* conduct. But the blame-worthiness of their apostatizing or changing from holiness to sin, was wholly theirs. The design of *God* and the ordering of his providence were holy. What *he* did was perfectly right. This is unquestionable. Once more. The fact that rational and immortal beings, who were made in the image of God, and who had motives of infinite weight to love and obey him, and who had experienced the happiness of obedience, became disobedient — this should be a subject of deep sorrow, lamentation and astonishment. It was a most unreasonable and inexcusable thing. Did we not know the fact, we should regard it as next to an impossibility, that beings endued with such faculties and placed in such circumstances should sin against God. But the dreadful fact has taken place.

I might add to these plain truths, that God, according to his eternal purpose, will overrule the apostasy of man for the accomplishment of the most benevolent and glorious purposes. That he has done this, and that he will do it in a still higher degree in future time, is made clear by the teachings of his word and providence.

Now I would charge it upon myself to be content with such plain, undeniable and useful truths; and not to perplex my own mind, or the minds of others, with any of the difficulties which a subtle philosophy has thrown around the subject under consideration.

"Inquirer" says, he can make nothing more or less of my affirmations than the simple position: "once a perfectly holy being, always so; once a sinner, always so." I have said enough to show that this was not my meaning. I will add that the last part of the sentence just quoted, expresses what I apprehend would be a certain and universal fact, were it not for the interposition of divine grace in redemption. If the sinner were left entirely under the operation of mere law, the result would be, "once a sinner, always so." I doubt not "Inquirer" would fully accede to this.

He next refers to a declaration of mine, that the divine law "pre-eminently aims to control the affections and desires of the heart." He says: "this proposition seems, at *first* view, to be a very reasonable one." And I ask, does it not appear so on a *second* view, and a *third* view? Is it not so in reality? If "Inquirer" has any doubt, let him examine the law, and see if it does not relate primarily to the heart, and aim pre-eminently to direct and regulate its affections. Does not Christ expressly teach that all the law is comprehended in two precepts? And do not both these precepts aim directly to control the affections of the heart? If "Inquirer" should undertake to set forth the sum of the divine law, would he not say at once, that it requires us to love God supremely, and to love our neighbor as ourselves? And is not this the same as to say, it aims to control the affections? or, the same as to say, it aims to control *us* in *regard* to our affections?

"Inquirer" asks: "*In what respects* does the law undertake to control the affections and desires?" I answer, in *all* respects. It asserts its dominion over the whole field of our moral affections and desires. It reaches them at all times, and in all their exercises. I should be alarmed if any one should attempt to make the law less extensive than this. And what reasonable man would wish, in respect to any of his affections, to be exempt from the authoritative direction of the divine commands?

"Inquirer" quotes my remark, that "holy and sinful affections in the saint and in the sinner, arise *spontaneously* from the presence or contemplation of moral objects." And is it not so? When the saint contemplates the divine law, does he not love the holiness which it requires? Does he not love it *instantly*, as soon as he looks at it? When he thinks of God, if he is in a right state of mind, he has no occasion to *reason* with himself, and by motives drawn from other sources, to persuade himself to love God. As soon as he has a just conception of God, he loves him. To a man of an upright mind, God's own excellence is the highest motive to love; and it is motive enough. And under the influence of this supreme motive, he will love instantly and *spontaneously*, in proportion as his heart is in a holy frame. Edwards says, that at a particular period of his life, merely seeing the name of God or Christ in a book instantly filled his heart with love and joy. This evinced a purified and spiritual mind.

Why should "Inquirer" demur at the word *spontaneous* in this case? For a man to love an object *spontaneously*, is to love it of his own accord, or, as we may say of his own free will, from the impulse of his own heart, without being urged by any foreign cause; it is to love from one's own disposition, unconstrained by any influence from without. (See Johnson and Webster on the word.) It is an obvious truth, that affections which arise *spontaneously*, show the real character of the man. If any one loves you, not sua sponte, not freely, not from his own heart, but by constraint, or under some foreign influence, what value do you set upon such affection? I appeal to experience and consciousness. When divine things, in their moral excellence, are presented to the view of a holy being, does he wait for some other consideration to come in and help to excite his love? Does he go about to reason himself into the feeling of love? Or does his heart lie dormant till it is roused to put forth the affection by a command of the will? We shall find, on careful inquiry, that we always judge favorably of ourselves in proportion as our affections towards divine objects rise spontaneously and freely in our minds; and that we cannot but look upon men as sinful in proportion as their hearts rise spontaneously against God and holiness.

What shall we think of the opinion, not unfrequently advanced at the present day, that our affections and desires in view of moral objects are neither good nor bad in themselves, but only in consequence of our voluntarily cherishing and indulging them?

If the affections or feelings which a holy being spontaneously exercises towards moral objects are not *right* affections, how can he be praise-worthy for *cherishing* them? And if the spontaneous affections of the sinner towards moral objects are not in their own nature *wrong*, how can he be *culpable* for cherishing or indulging them? Can we be culpable for indulging feelings which are in themselves innocent? If we may have affections in our hearts for a short time without fault, why not for a longer time? If we may innocently begin to exercise them, why may we not innocently continue to exercise them? When a good man cherishes any affections or desires towards moral objects, does he not do it with the idea that they are *right* — *right in themselves?* And when he endeavors to suppress or eradicate any affections towards moral objects, does he not do it from the conviction that they are in their own nature *wrong?* It is evident from our Saviour's teaching, that a man is criminal for *having* a desire after forbidden objects; not only for *indulging* it and *complying* with its cravings, but for *having it in his heart.* And is not every one, who has an awakened conscience fully persuaded that it is so? It seems to me an exceedingly strange and unfounded opinion, that the divine law justifies a man for the first exercise of malice, envy, revenge or impurity, and condemns him only for *continuing* the exercise! Who can suppose such a thing as that the divine law permits a moral agent, either at the commencement of his being, or afterwards, to put forth, for a time, such affections and desires towards moral objects, as his unsanctified heart may prompt, only requiring him not to *repeat* them? Surely that law which is "perfect," and "exceedingly broad," must bind a man through the whole of his existence, as an intelligent, moral being, at one time as well as another. I am sure that any position contrary to this is false, and that the arguments urged in its support are sophistical. It is indeed true, that an unrenewed man is culpable for *gratifying*, and for *continuing* to *exercise* the moral affections which he at first exercises spontaneously. But *why* is he culpable? Because they are *wrong* affections. Were not the affections themselves contrary to the law of God, how could he be a transgressor for *having* them in his heart, or for *continuing* to have them?

I appeal to the devout and watchful Christian, who faithfully searches his own heart, and strives to be holy. His testimony is better than speculative arguments. Does not his experience exactly correspond with that of the Apostle? In direct opposition to his settled purpose, or the determination of his will, does not pride or self-esteem, or covetousness, or envy, or ill-will, or impure desire rise in his heart? He needs not to be told that every such affection is sinful. He *knows* it to be so. He confesses it, and prays to be delivered from it, and abhors himself on account of it; and from time to time he is more or less successful in subduing it. But before he is aware, and without waiting for the previous consent of his will, it comes up again. It is what our Saviour says "proceeds out of the heart." Thus he finds the words of the Apostle verified in his own experience. *The flesh lusteth against the spirit, and the spirit against the flesh; and these are contrary the one to the other, so that he cannot do the things that he would.* It is a matter of experience, not of abstract reasoning. So it was with Paul. He found a law in his members, (doubtless meaning his affections,) warring against the law of his mind. He tells us, that the good which he would, he did not, and the evil which he would not, that he did. No wonder he was distressed with this law in his members, this body of death, and cried out, "O wretched man that I am!" I say, it is a matter of experience. And I appeal to the most faithful and spiritual Christians, whether their exercises do not correspond with those of the Apostle.

"Inquirer" asks: "To what is the law addressed?" And he suggests the difficulties which arise in his mind from supposing that it is addressed to the understanding, or to conscience, or to the will, or to the affections and desires. I think, as he does, that such a supposition involves the subject in difficulties. The law, strictly and literally speaking, is not addressed to the understanding, the conscience, the will, or the affections of man, but to *man himself;* not to any faculty or susceptibility of the moral agent, but to *the moral agent himself.* What is the language of the law? It speaks to the intelligent personal being, *man.*

"*Thou* shalt love the Lord thy God." "*Thou*," *man*, "shalt love thy neighbor as thyself." "Thou shalt not steal;" and so of the rest. Where the personal pronoun is not expressed, it is implied. "Remember the Sabbath day," i. e., remember *thou*. God addresses his law to this whole person, *me*. He commands *me* to love him. He does not command my understanding to love; for my understanding is not a *person*. He does not command my conscience, or will, or affection to love; for neither of these is a person. But he commands *me* to love. His law is addressed to me as an intelligent, accountable being. A disregard of this simple and obvious principle originates many needless difficulties.

"Inquirer" refers to my remark, that *the will has no direct power, and frequently no power at all over the affections; and that a man cannot, by the power of his will, call forth the affection of love to God.* And does not "Inquirer" know this to be the case? Is he not aware that man, while unregenerate, cannot subdue the enmity of his heart, and excite holy love in its place, by an act of his will? Does he not recognize it as a solemn truth, confirmed by Scripture and experience, that a carnal mind cannot sanctify its affections by the force of its own unsanctified volitions? And how is it with the believer? Can he, at any time, by an act of his will, banish his corrupt affections, and kindle the flame of sacred love in his heart? How is it with "Inquirer," or with any other intelligent Christian? Is this the way in which the unholy feelings and desires of his heart were first expelled? Is this the way in which his love to God and divine things is now called forth? Has anything ever occurred in his own experience, which evinces that he possesses a power to control his own affections by a volition? And does an Edwards, or a Paul, or any one who discerns spiritual things in a spiritual manner, ever entertain the thought, that the want of such a power takes away his obligation or his accountability as a moral agent? I ask not *how* the want of such a power can be reconciled with perfect moral obligation. But I ask whether the enlightened Christian is not conscious of these two facts; first, that he has no direct power, and frequently no power at all, to govern his affections *by a voli-*

tion; and secondly, that he is under perfect obligation to love and obey God, and will be inexcusably guilty if he fails to do this. If "*Inquirer*" can explain *how* these two things may be reconciled, and solve all the hard questions which come forth from a speculative mind, then he is the man to undertake the work.

But if it is so that we cannot control our affections by an act of the will, many will be inclined to ask: *What then shall we do?* I am glad to have an opportunity to answer this question. For I think here is the place where we are specially taught to feel, and must feel, our entire dependence on the divine Spirit — the very place where prayer to God is to come in for our relief. We are urged to prayer by all the principles of our rational nature. But a just conviction of our sinfulness, our ruin and our helplessness, shut us up to it. It is our only resort. So the Scriptures represent it. We must have help from God, or perish in our pollution. Holy affections are the fruits of the Spirit, not the product of our own will. This view of the subject is, you perceive, directly favorable to devotion. It begets a sense of dependence on the grace of God, and leads to constant prayer. And whatever a man's speculative opinions may be, just so soon as he looks into his own heart, and forms any just conceptions of his own depravity, he will be sensible that without the help of divine grace, he can do nothing; and he will look to God, not to the power of his own will, for the sanctification of his affections. Why is it that some ministers of the gospel use language in prayer so different from what they use in metaphysical discourse? — that while in such discourse they speak much and strongly of the sufficient power or the complete ability of all men to do all that is required of them in the law and in the gospel, as soon as they engage in prayer, they acknowledge their weakness, acknowledge that without Christ they can do nothing, that they are not sufficient of themselves for any duty, and that all their help must come from God? Why this difference? It may be, because their language and their thoughts in metaphysical discourse are not adapted to serious religion and devotion. And if they find this to be the case, let them remember it. But I apprehend the reason to be more exactly this; that, in prayer, Christians are likely to think soberly and justly — likely to discern the truth, and to use the language of truth. And if you would know what is the language of truth, search the Scripture which is the word of the God of truth. Keep close to that, and you will not err. That holy book abounds in such representations as these: — that sinners are sanctified not of the will of the flesh, nor of the will of man, but of God; that holy love is shed abroad in the heart by the Holy Ghost; and that all right affections and desires are the fruits of the Spirit. Accordingly, when a Christian prays he does not say to God: I thank thee that I have full power to do all my duty without thy assistance; that I am sufficient of myself to work out my own salvation. His language is: *My help cometh from the Lord. Without thee I can do nothing. Work in me all the good pleasure of thy goodness. Make my heart pure. Strengthen me with thy strength in my soul.* What Christian does not pray in this manner? And is not the language which sincere piety prompts us to use in prayer, the language of truth?

I had advanced the following sentiment: *that holy affections arise spontaneously in the saint, and unholy affections in the sinner, from the presence or the contemplation of moral objects.* "Inquirer" undertakes to show what *consequences* would result from this sentiment. But our first question should be, whether the sentiment is *true*. Neither I nor my correspondent can be held responsible for the consequences which may follow from the truth, or from the declaration of the truth. Is then my representation conformed to fact? When a holy angel or a holy man turns his thoughts to God, and contemplates his moral excellence, is he not at once *pleased* with it? Does he not love it spontaneously, that is, freely, of his own accord, or from the disposition of his own heart? Is he not pleased with it as soon as he sees it? If, when the object is present to his view, he puts forth any other mental act before he loves, what is that act? Is it an act of reasoning, by which he endeavors to persuade himself to love? But what need of reasoning to excite a holy being to love, when he already sees the loveliness of the object? Even if he should attempt by reasoning to excite love, what would he do, but to urge upon his own mind the supreme beauty and excellence of the object before him? Or, is the act which precedes his affection to God, an act of *self-love?* When he beholds the divine character, does his heart lie still within him, till he has time to think that loving God will make him happy? And is it in reality a regard to his own happiness, which excites his love to God? Or, is the act which precedes his love an act of his *will?* That is, when a holy being has a distinct idea of God in his mind, is it true that, instead of instantly loving him, and in order to bring himself to love, he first *wills* to love? And is it true that his love is excited by such a previous volition? I am persuaded that good men will never be led, by their own experience, to view the subject in this light. That which renders God worthy of love, and which is the objective ground of love, is his moral excellence. As soon as holy beings see this they love. It is their *cordial*, *free*, *unconstrained* act. And what is more just and reasonable, than that they should love God because he is infinitely lovely? The subjective reason is their own holy disposition. In this view they love God because they have a holy, spiritual nature, a heart in unison with divine excellence. And is not the opposite of all this true of the unholy? I ask, then, are not the facts in the case as I have represented them to be? If so, it follows, that the difficulty of which "Inquirer" speaks, and which we are all apt to feel, arises, not from any misstatement of mine, but either from the very nature of the facts, or from something faulty in the state of our minds.

"Inquirer" says, if it be so, as I have represented, "then what tendency can the divine law have upon the mind of a sinner, except to increase his hatred of all that is holy, and thrust him further and further from salvation?" Here let us, for the present, pass by the word *tendency*, which may be somewhat ambiguous, and inquire what is *matter of fact*. Take the unrenewed sinner, whose carnal mind is enmity against God, just as he is in himself, exclusively of the agency of the Holy Spirit. Is it not a fact that the law and the gospel, when brought before his unsanctified mind, do excite his hatred of all that is good, and so thrust him further and further from salvation? Is not any result contrary to this owing to the grace of God? If the sinner is left to himself, is not the law, and the gospel too, a savor of death unto death? Has he not such a deceitful, wicked heart, and does he not so act out his depravity in view of divine things, that he is continually waxing worse and worse? And so far as he is given up to his own alienated heart, without the grace of the Holy Spirit, is not this the case uniformly and always?" We see then what is the *invariable fact*.

As to "tendency," I hold that the *proper* tendency of divine truth — the tendency which it *ought* to have upon a rational being, and which it *would* have, were it not for the counter-influence of sin — is to excite holy affection, and lead to holy conduct. But the sinner has an evil heart of unbelief. He has an obstinate love of sin, and dislike of holiness. And this inexcusable wickedness of his heart opposes the proper tendency of the truth, prevents the effect which it should have on the mind, and turns the law and the gospel into a means of perdition. Coming in contact with a hard, impenitent heart, it proves to be a savor of death unto death. But this is no disparagement to divine truth. Its being followed by such an effect is to be ascribed wholly to the fault of the sinner.

"Inquirer" asks: "What then can the preaching of the law do, but to aggravate the awful doom of sinners?" And I put the question to him: *What else can the preaching of the law or the gospel do, unless the grace of God interpose, and give sinners a new heart?* If they are given over to their own unsubdued wickedness, as they justly may be, does not "Inquirer" know the deplorable fact, that whatever may be their outward privileges, they will be continually treasuring up wrath against the day of wrath? This fact is so deplorable and dreadful, that it caused the Son of God to weep, and should cause us to weep. The evil of man's heart is too obvious to be denied; and it is too deep and desperate to be remedied by human power. Can "Inquirer" think it a mistake of mine to say, that man's *depraved will* has no power to change his *depraved heart?* — in other words, that he has no power to change his depraved *heart* by an act of his depraved *will?* Would he affirm the contrary? Would he tell sinners, that by an act of their unsanctified will — which is all the will they have — they can sanctify their own hearts? — that by an unholy, selfish volition they can produce in themselves that holiness, which they neither love nor desire?

The doctrine of man's depravity is mysterious and astounding. But all that is mysterious and astounding in the doctrine lies in its truth. Man is a sinner. He has destroyed himself; and he is lost. His help is in God, and nowhere else.

"Inquirer" refers to the following remark of mine: "It is a common sentiment, that the sinfulness of men is great in proportion as their passions and desires are awakened suddenly and uncontrollably in view of forbidden objects." I stated the case in which revenge, envy, covetousness and pride arise in the mind suddenly and uncontrollably in view of their appropriate objects. Now I ask "Inquirer:" Are not revenge, envy, covetousness and pride sinful? Are they not really sinful in themselves, though not developed in outward action? And is not the degree of sinfulness proportional to the strength and violence of the sinful passions and desires?

"Inquirer" says, he could assent to all this, if I had "conjoined some limitations or modifications." But what modifications are called for? Would he have me say, that ill-will, revenge, envy, covetousness and pride are sinful in some circumstances, but not in others? Does he wish me to point out the circumstances in which a man may have them in his heart for a time, and yet be guiltless? This I do not feel myself authorized to do; and I think "Inquirer" would himself start back from such a modification as this. For if I may have in my heart the feeling of ill-will, envy and revenge once, without sin; why not twice? — and if for a short time, why not for a longer time? If the beginning of these affections is not wrong, why should we regard the continuance of them as wrong? Is it true that the divine law does not forbid the *existence* of these affections in our hearts, and that its only aim is to prevent their *continuance?* Or, to give the subject another shape, is it the intention of the law to keep these affections within certain limits, and to prevent them from going too far, particularly from coming out in visible action? Are we to understand the law as saying: you may have the emotion of enmity against God or man rise in your heart, and if it is the first emotion of the kind, and if it rises spontaneously, you are guiltless. But if you have a second and third emotion, especially if it becomes strong and violent, then you are culpable. Is this the meaning of the moral law? But suppose the second and third emotion of enmity against God or man is as spontaneous as the first. Why should it not be regarded in the same light?

In compliance with the suggestion of "Inquirer," I am very ready to give "some modifications," or rather to explain and distinguish.

There are then, as I conceive, emotions, affections and desires of different kinds. Some are in their own nature morally right, i. e. conformed to the divine law; some are sinful, i. e. contrary to the law; and some indifferent, i. e. in themselves neither holy nor sinful. As to those of the first kind — the law requires and approves them. As to those of the second kind — the law forbids and condemns them. As to those which are indifferent — such as the natural appetite for food, the desire of property and of knowledge, the love of life, the love of offspring, and the affection existing between the sexes; — what the law does in regard to these is to regulate them, to guard them against excess and perversion, and direct them to their proper end. God not only permits us to have these affections and desires, but, in the proper way, to indulge them, and act under their influence. We are as much justified in repeating as in beginning the exercise of them; in acting them out in our life, as in having them in our heart. We are only required to indulge and gratify them in proper ways and proper degrees, and for a proper end, i. e. that the glory of God and the welfare of ourselves and others may be promoted. See now how plain and obvious is the difference between these emotions and desires, and those which are in themselves sinful; and how differently they are treated in the Scriptures. Does the word of God require that we should take care to *regulate* our ill-will towards our fellow-men, and our enmity against our Maker?—that we should keep them within proper bounds, and direct them to a proper end? Why, they *have* no proper bounds. There *is* no proper end at which we *can* aim in their exercise. In their own nature they are contrary to the divine law. They are disobedience. And where does the law undertake to *regulate disobedience*, and keep it within proper bounds? Instead of this, it forbids it wholly. It forbids us to have the commencement of it in our hearts. It condemns us for the first and feeblest emotion which is contrary to holiness, though never developed in action, and even though conscience should not at the time be so wakeful as to notice its turpitude.

"Inquirer" refers to a child who has inherited from his parents a strong appetite for intoxicating drinks, but has checked and refused to indulge it; and he asks, whether that child is guilty of intemperance. I answer, No. The mere bodily appetite is not intemperance. In itself it has nothing of a moral nature, any more than the extreme thirst of a man for water. We are sure of this from our own consciousness. All that the law requires of him who inherits such an appetite is, that he should refuse to gratify it, and in every proper way strive to subdue it. If he loves God he will readily do this. And if he does this, we give him special credit for his temperance. We honor him more than if he had never been subject to such an appetite, and had never practised self-denial in refraining from indulging it. This is plain; and what "Inquirer" says respecting it is obviously just.

But there is an essential difference between such a bodily appetite and those dispositions and affections of the soul, which are in their own nature morally wrong, and which cannot for a moment exist without sin. To have a malevolent, envious, or revengeful feeling in the heart, is to be a transgressor. Merely *having the emotion* shows a man to be depraved. *Jesus* never had such an emotion. He never had the least degree, not even the beginning of the feeling of ill-will, pride or envy. In his pure heart no emotion or desire contrary to holiness was ever found, no, not for a moment.

We come now to the case of a reformed debauchee. The supposition of "Inquirer" is, that although the reformed man is now a true Christian, he is "often and violently assailed with desires and passions like those of former days," i. e. impure desires; but that he steadily opposes them. The question is, how are we to regard such a man in his present state. The man himself will answer this. He regards the impure passions and desires referred to, as the sin that dwelleth in him. He confesses them to God and mourns over them. He says within himself; how bad must the tree be which bears such fruit! How evil the heart from which proceed such vile and hateful passions and desires! In short, does he not really look upon himself as the subject of an inward defilement, a spiritual evil, in proportion to the frequency and violence with which he is assaulted by the passions and desires of his former wicked life? And when he resists them, does he not do it with the full conviction that they are morally wrong, and wholly without excuse in the sight of God? But if, through the strength of religious principle, and the help of divine grace, he overcomes and eradicates these evil passions and desires, we regard it as a great and virtuous achievement, and we honor him for resisting and subduing, not what is innocent, but what is sinful.

The principle which I have endeavored to support, is evidently true in regard to holy affections and desires. Love to God and desire for his glory show the heart to be sanctified in proportion as they arise spontaneously and fervently in view of the object. When our moral state is right, nothing is necessary to excite love to God but the sight of his character. As soon as we see what he is, we love him. The affection is awakened immediately when the object is presented before the mind, whether it is presented in consequence of a previous act of the will or not. So it was with Jesus. No reasoning, no persuasion, no antecedent act of his will was necessary to elicit his love. As soon as he thought of his Father, he loved him, and desired his glory. The affection was always joined with the thought. If it is not so with us, if, when we turn our thoughts to God, our hearts slumber, or if earthly affections lodge within us, and if we find voluntary exertion and labor necessary to dislodge those earthly affections, and to prepare ourselves to love God, it is a certain proof that the law of sin is still warring against the law of holiness, and that the work of sanctification is very incomplete.

Some writers, who admit that an act of the will has no direct control over the affections, still hold that, as it is by an act of the will that we bring before our minds those objects which excite the affections, it is this previous voluntary act which gives the character of morality to the affections. The reason why they hold this opinion is, that they have already adopted the principle, that voluntary acts, and those only, are morally good or evil. In my view, this principle, as at present understood, overlooks truths of essential importance. But I shall not enter on the consideration of the subject here, except in the way of appeal to plain common sense.

According to the opinion above stated, if by an act of our will we put ourselves in a situation where divine and spiritual objects will be presented before us, and if we do it for the purpose of awakening pious affections in our minds, those affections, when thus awakened, are holy and praise-worthy; and are so, because we voluntarily put ourselves in such a situation. And if, by an act of the will, we knowingly put ourselves in a situation, where objects will come before us which will excite wrong affections, we are then blame-worthy for those affections; and we are so, merely because we voluntarily came into such a situation.

Now I acknowledge that the previous act of the will above mentioned, and the affections which followed, are, in the first case, good and praise-worthy, and in the second case, blame-worthy. But that the affections are right or wrong, and that we are worthy of praise or blame on account of them *merely* because we voluntarily placed ourselves in such a situation,—this I do not admit. For suppose that, without any previous arrangement or choice of mine, a good man comes and presents before me some striking view of the glorious character of God, which instantly excites reverence and love in my heart. Or suppose such a view of God is unexpectedly suggested to my mind by some event of divine providence, over which I have no control; and in consequence of it, I have at once the affection of reverence and love. Must I regard this affection as destitute of piety and goodness, because I exercise it in such circumstances? Do these circumstances deprive me of moral agency? Or suppose, without any intention of mine, I am brought into a situation where objects are presented before me, which suddenly excite the feeling of ill-will, envy, or revenge. Is such a feeling innocent, and am I blameless for exercising it because I exercise it in such a way? Do I cease to be a moral agent? Is it not evident that the affection is of the same nature, and that it indicates the same character of mind, whether it is exercised in consequence of a previous act of the will, or otherwise? What difference can it make in the judgment we pass upon benevolence or ill-will, love or enmity, whether the object which elicits it comes before the mind in one way or another? Is not the object the same? Is not the affection the same? And are not we the same moral, accountable beings?

Take another case. An irreligious, wicked man knows by experience, that the truths of the gospel stir up within him strong dislike and opposition of heart. He therefore wishes to avoid every person and every situation that will be likely to bring these disagreeable truths before him. But unexpectedly and contrary to his will, a Christian goes to him, and in the kindest manner presents some precious gospel truths before him, in view of which his heart at once kindles into hatred and wrath. Do you think his feelings cease to be sinful, because the object exciting them was brought before his mind without his intention, and contrary to his choice?

See what a fearful influence the theory I am opposing would have upon the divine law. Doubtless the moral law primarily and essentially requires that, and that only, which is of a moral nature. Now, according to the theory under review, the first and great command, instead of requiring love itself, requires that previous act of the will, by which we put ourselves in a situation where the object of love shall be presented before us. And our putting forth this previous act would constitute obedience, whether the affection followed or not. On the other hand, if we should really love God when his character is brought to our view unexpectedly and without our previous design, the affection, not resulting from a previous act of the will, would lose its moral nature, and would not be obedience to the first and great command; although it is the very thing which the law requires. The same as to the command, "Thou shalt not covet." If we really covet our neighbor's house or wife, we are not transgressors, unless we had a previous voluntary agency in bringing the object before us. How often soever and how strongly soever we may covet, we are not blame-worthy, if the exciting object is presented to our view without our choice. Now who of us has any right to take such liberty as this with the law of God, and to say, that it is not obeyed by that very affection which it requires, and is not disobeyed by that very affection which it forbids?

As I understand the subject, if a man spontaneously puts forth either good or bad affections in view of objects brought before him without his previous design, this very circumstance does, in some respects, exhibit the goodness or badness of his character with peculiar clearness. If a man's heart is such that, whenever moral objects are brought before him, whether by his own voluntary act or not, he is at once filled with right affections and desires, we attribute to him the character of singular excellence. And if, whenever moral objects are brought before another man, even against his intention, his heart instantly kindles into bad emotions and desires, we say, his character is stamped with uncommon depravity. In such cases there is no restraint. The heart acts itself out with freedom. "A good man, out of the good treasure of the heart, bringeth forth good things; and an evil man, out of the evil treasure, bringeth forth evil things."

I have one thing more to say. We are, without doubt, under perfect obligation to obey the first and great command, and the second, which is like unto it. Now if we love God with all the heart and soul and mind and strength, and our neighbor as ourselves, wrong affections will be excluded. There will be no place for them. In the pure and holy mind of Jesus no sinful emotions were ever found. Now it is clear, that we must be blame-worthy and inexcusable for those wrong mental acts which take place in consequence of our neglecting a great and obvious duty. If our loving God and man as we ought would keep all right in the movements of our hearts, and would effectually exclude all improper feelings; we are most certainly answerable for neglecting that primary duty, and for all those improper feelings which rush into the mind in consequence of our neglect.

"Inquirer" signifies that desires after forbidden objects, burning unawares in the minds of men, may be evidences of their "*having been* very wicked, or their having inherited a constitution greatly vitiated." But he sees not "how they can be proof of *present* wickedness, provided they are immediately resisted, and never fostered or indulged." Here it is important to keep in mind what was before said, that there are two classes of desires; — those which are of an inferior kind, belonging particularly to our animal nature, and those which are of a moral or spiritual nature.

Take as an instance of the first kind, a desire for strong drink. If a man, with the requisite information as to consequences, does anything to form the appetite, or to indulge and continue it, he becomes culpable; — culpable for doing that which he knows to be hurtful to the body and the soul. The guilt does not lie in the bodily appetite itself, or the bodily act of indulging it, but in the inclination and choice of the mind to indulge it when the consequence is known.

The other class of affections and desires are, in their own nature, *moral* or *spiritual*. They have a direct relation to moral law, and cannot exist without being praise-worthy or blame-worthy. Such is love to God, and enmity against him. If such an object as God is presented before the mind of a rational being, *loving* will be a holy and praise-worthy act, and *hating* will be sinful. As soon as the object is before his mind, and he discerns it, he has sufficient knowledge to render him accountable for the acts he puts forth towards it. Is it said, he cannot be accountable for the *first* act of love or hatred, but only for continuing it, and for fostering and indulging it? I reply; if the goodness or badness of the affection or mental act lies in its *nature*, it must belong to the *first* act as well as to the *second*. If the *first* act of love to God is not in itself right, how can the *second* be? And if the *first* act of enmity is not in itself wrong, how can the *second* be? The moral law requires love and forbids enmity. And when we put forth the first act of love, do we not as really obey the law, as when we repeat the act? If obedience does not begin with the first act of love; it must be because love is not morally good in its own nature, but only on account of the circumstance of its being *repeated*. But I ask again, how can it be praise-worthy to *repeat* an act, unless the act is right? So on the other hand, when we put forth the first act of enmity, do we not disobey the law as really as when we put forth the second act? If not, it must be because the law does not forbid the first act of enmity, but only the repetition of it. And then the question comes up, why the law forbids the *repetition* of an act, while it *allows* the act in the first instance.

As the result of our inquiries, do we not find, that one class of affections and desires are, in themselves, of a moral nature, and that he who exercises them is always praise-worthy or blame-worthy? If a man loves God and man, whether it is the first act of love or the second, and whatever the circumstances, he has holiness. But in regard to the other class of affections above mentioned, it is evident, that they are not of a moral nature in themselves, and that it is merely the consideration of *consequences*, which gives them a moral aspect?

"Inquirer" refers to the case of our Saviour's temptations, and says: "If he had no desires or emotions like our own on such occasions," (i. e. when he was tempted,) "then how was he tempted *in all points*, as we are? If he had such emotions, and these emotions are, as Dr. Woods says, sins of the deepest die, then how was he tempted, and yet remained without sin?"

It is very difficult for me to reply as I should wish, to such a statement as this, because it is difficult to speak of the feelings and character of Christ with becoming reverence. I will, however, offer a few suggestions.

The Scripture does indeed say, that Jesus was in all points *tempted* as we are. But where does it say, that he had the *same emotions and desires with us?* Saying this, would be utterly incompatible with the spotless purity and holiness of Christ.

The word *temptation* is sometimes used to denote that irregular desire of the depraved heart, which leads to actual transgression; as in James 1: 14; "Every man is *tempted*, when he is *drawn away of his own lust, and enticed.*" Jesus was never tempted in this way. This is not the kind of temptation to which he was subjected. All other men are by nature sinners; born in such a state, that they must be born again to prepare them for the kingdom of heaven. From the first, their moral affections are corrupt; their moral nature is depraved. The actings of their minds, so far as they are of a moral nature, are all sinful. And even as to those emotions and desires which do not directly relate to moral objects, and which are not, in themselves, either morally good or evil, I cannot but think they are all tainted by the moral disorder of the heart. Even the natural affections, the corporeal and social emotions, desires and instincts, which are faultless and pure when the heart is pure, even these become irregular and faulty, by dwelling in a depraved heart. The evil pervades the whole man. There is no soundness in him. "To them that are defiled, nothing is pure." How can anything in a heart that is "desperately wicked," be what it would be in a heart perfectly undefiled? In this respect, Jesus was totally unlike all other men. He had human nature; but his human nature was incorrupt. From the first he was holy, harmless, undefiled. He never needed to be born again. And he never had a single thought, emotion or desire, which varied, in the least, from the rule of righteousness. He was indeed *tempted*. But how? Not by any irregular inclination, any lust, any solicitation to sin within his own mind. He said to his disciples: "Ye are they that have followed me in my temptations." What were his temptations? Let the story of his life answer. "He suffered, being tempted." All his sufferings were temptations, or trials. The original word, rendered *tempt*, signifies *to try*, *to put to the proof*, *in order to ascertain the disposition or character of any one*. The sufferings of Christ *tried* him, as the furnace tries the gold. They showed what he was. The opposition and enmity of the Jews, the ingratitude and obduracy of those for whose benefit he came into the world, and all the evils he endured from time to time, especially in the closing scene of his life, were *temptations* or *trials*, and made it manifest that he was without sin. If men are corrupt, trials will be likely to show it. If they are holy, trials will make that manifest. Any one who carefully attends to the word of God, will be satisfied, that the *temptations* spoken of, generally refer to the *afflictions* or *sufferings* of life. In this sense Christ was *tempted or tried as we are*. He endured all that variety of *sufferings* which his people endure, so that, by his own experience, he learned how to sympathize with them. And he passed through all these trials without sin.

He was also subjected to temptation in another way. The devil *tempted* him, that is, *solicited him to commit sin*. But he found "nothing in him." He found no sinful propensity, no depraved disposition, no bias to evil, which could give effect to temptation. The solicitation to sin was from without, not from within — from the wicked one, not from the heart of Jesus.

Thus it appears, that Jesus experienced *temptations* of two kinds ; first, in the way of *solicitation to sin*, presented before his mind from without, and secondly, *temptation* in the way of *suffering*. But neither the one nor the other had any effect, except to exercise his virtue, to show that he had no sin, to manifest his unbending rectitude and perfect purity. We see then, that his being tempted as we are, did not by any means imply, that he was like us in moral feeling, or that temptation had the same effect upon him as it has upon us, or that he had "rising desires or emotions like our own on such occasions," as "Inquirer" speaks. His temptations prove the contrary. They proved that, by his perfect holiness, he was effectually shielded against those "desires and emotions" which temptations are apt to excite in our corrupt hearts. For us, the only way of safety is to flee from temptations. But Jesus had no occasion to flee. He was perfectly safe in the midst of temptations. He was like pure gold, gold unmixed with any alloy, upon which the furnace has no effect, but to make its purity manifest.

Such is my impression as to the character of Christ, his spotless purity, and the strength of holy principle in his heart. Will "Inquirer" say that this impression is incorrect, and that I think more highly of the character of Jesus than the Apostle did, when he declared him to be "holy, harmless, undefiled, separate from sinners?" How was Jesus separate from sinners, except in what constitutes moral character, that is, in the affections of his heart, and in his outward actions? Until I am otherwise informed, I must consider it altogether unjust and dishonorable to the blessed Saviour, to infer from the fact that he was tempted as we are, that temptation excited in him any "emotions and desires," like those which it generally excites in depraved minds. At one time the tempter endeavored to excite pride or ambition in his heart, and thus to draw him into sin. But no pride or ambition was found there. At another time, the tempter addressed his motive to the appetite of hunger. But Jesus was governed by a higher principle. The desire of food, however strong, had no influence upon him in opposition to duty. His natural appetites were entirely subject to the will of God. His mind and heart were filled with spiritual thoughts and spiritual affections and joys; and he had not a single rebellious desire or feeling — he had not a single movement within him, which his conscience or his God would disapprove, or which he could ever wish to have been otherwise. He had no inclination or tendency to comply with temptation. He had no selfish disposition, no depravity of heart for temptation to work upon. As to ourselves, in our fallen state, we have to resist not only solicitations to sin from *without*, but solicitations from *within*, that is, sinful inclinations. And we know too well, that it is these sinful inclinations, these corrupt desires of our hearts, that give force to outward temptation. Our warfare is within. And if we obtain a conquest, it is chiefly the conquest of indwelling sin.

But Jesus had no indwelling sin to conquer, no unholy desire to resist, no wickedness of heart to subdue. So unlike was he to us in regard to the state of his mind, and everything which constitutes character; though he was like us in regard to what are more properly called *temptations*.

I had said, that our affections and desires are really our *actions*, (i. e. our *mental* actions,) and that our mind is as much the producing cause of them, as of our *volitions*. This "Inquirer" thinks inconsistent with the position which I maintain, namely, that the presence of appropriate objects *spontaneously* awakens these desires. But how is it inconsistent? To say, that the presence of appropriate objects *spontaneously* awakens our affections and desires, is the same as to say, that we ourselves, as intelligent, moral agents, spontaneously put forth affections and desires in view of those objects; or, that we spontaneously act in the way of loving and desiring, or the contrary, when the objects are before us. Now why should it be supposed, that our mind, in any such case, is *less active* because it acts *spontaneously?* or, that our loving and desiring are not our own actions, because we love and desire *promptly*, as soon as the object comes before us? Who can suppose that the act of loving God in the spirits of just men made perfect, is any the less their act, or any the less excellent and praise-worthy, because they love *readily* and *spontaneously;* or that hating God, in the minds of wicked beings, is any the less their own act, or any the less vile and blame-worthy, because they hate God at once, whenever they think of him? Must something come between the sight of the object and our loving it, to make our loving it our own responsible act? What a strange imagination! If a man loves God and delights in him with all his heart, as soon as he thinks of him, he does nothing morally good! Why? Because he loves *spontaneously*, freely, from the impulse of his own mind! If his love did not arise so soon; if his heart was a little reluctant and slow to move, and waited to have its love excited by something besides the sight of the divine excellence — by some effort of reasoning or some urgency of will, it would deserve the name of holiness, but not as it is! And if a man is displeased with God, and his heart rises in enmity against him, as soon as the thought of his character comes to his mind, it is not sin! And why? Because the displeasure or hatred rises in his mind spontaneously! — because he hates God at once, as soon as he thinks of him.

I suppose this opinion is adopted to support a favorite metaphysical theory — the theory, that nothing is of a moral nature unless it follows an act of the will. This theory is true in regard to external bodily actions. For these we are not responsible, unless they are voluntary, that is, unless they take place in obedience to an act of the will. The actions, in themselves, are neither morally good nor evil. The same is true in regard to many acts of the *mind*. In themselves they are not of a moral nature; and we regard them as right or wrong, only as they are directed to a good or bad end.

You ask, how we can determine what acts of the mind are in themselves morally good or evil. I answer, we can do this, *first*, by the help of conscience. As to one class of mental exercises, a feeling of approbation or disapprobation accompanies them, or is consequent upon them. This is an ultimate fact, arising from the law of our nature. The same law of our nature leads us to look upon another class of mental actions as, in themselves, neither right nor wrong, and to look upon ourselves as neither praise-worthy nor blame-worthy for them, except with a view to the motives by which we are influenced.

Secondly. We can distinguish those acts of the mind which are in themselves of a moral nature from those which are not, by the moral law. That which the law requires, and *as* the law requires it, is right. The contrary is wrong. Now the law requires the affection of love, and love implies that we have complacency in the divine character, that we delight ourselves in the Lord. Without cordial complacency in God, we cannot rightly seek his glory, nor rightly determine to serve him, nor rightly choose him as our God and portion. And as the law requires love to God, we know that love, in all its forms and exercises, is morally right. Here conscience and the divine law perfectly agree. The awakened sinner, both from his conscience and from the requirement of the moral law, knows that the enmity of his heart against God, which no act of his will can remove, is, in itself, exceedingly sinful. And when, through the renewing of the Holy Spirit, he begins to feel complacency in the character and government of God, he knows that complacency to be right. But neither the divine law nor conscience has anything to do with the inquiry, whether either the good or the bad affection is exercised in consequence of a previous volition. We look directly at the affection itself, whether love or hatred, and we see it to be right or wrong. And I cannot but regard it as a mistake, to turn off our attention from the *nature* of the mental state or mental exercise, called *love*, or *enmity*, and instead of judging of it by the plain rule of conscience and the divine law, to make another rule, and judge of it by the circumstance of *its following an act of the will*.

I have thus far used the word *volition*, or act of the will, to denote that imperative or executive act of the mind, which directs something to be done, or leads to the doing of it.

But there is another sense, which is found more or less in common and in philosophical discourse, and which is favored by some passages of Scripture, and by the usage of the older class of writers. According to this usage, the *will* stands for *the whole moral faculty*, or *the moral nature* of man. All the affections and dispositions belong to the will. Love and hatred, desire and aversion, and all the feelings of the heart, are considered as properties and acts of the will. So Edwards generally uses the word, though not always.

Now it is clear, that using the word *will* in this extensive sense occasions a great difference in the mode of speaking and reasoning on the subject. And unless we are specially attentive to the meaning which different writers attach to the word, we shall be involved in confusion, and shall be unable to do justice either to them, or to the subject they treat. If the word *will* is taken in this large sense, then indeed nothing is of a moral nature but volitions, or acts of the will. To be pleased and to be displeased, to love and to hate, to desire and to feel aversion, are all acts or states of the *will.* So are all the emotions, all the feelings of the heart, especially those relating to moral objects. — If now you think proper to give the word this broad signification, and will take care uniformly to adhere to it, I will not complain, but will endeavor, as far as I can, to fall into your track, and to understand words and phrases as you do. And this may perhaps prevent some difficulties. For now you can say, we are responsible for our affections and desires, because they are *voluntary;* not *consequences* of volition, but themselves volitions, or acts of the will, and controlled by the will only as the will puts them forth. We could not however go far in this way, without finding it necessary to distinguish among these various acts of the will, and to arrange them under different classes, making some generic or immanent volitions, such as the habitual affections or dispositions of the heart; and others *specific, emanent,* or *imperative,* such as the determinations or decisions of the mind as to particular things to be done. These last are the manifestation of the former in specific actions. So be it. The name we give to a thing does not alter its nature. Whether we call love to God voluntary or involuntary, an affection or volition, it is really the same thing. Calling it voluntary does not make it holy, and calling it involuntary would not take away its holiness. Whatever epithet we apply to it, it is the sum of obedience to the moral law.

I will only request you to fix the meaning of the word voluntary, and to adhere to it uniformly. You must use the word to denote either that which is itself an *act* of the will, or that which *follows* an act of the will. Take one or the other of these senses, but *not both.*

I shall only add, that if you assert that all virtue and vice lie in the acts of the will, and if by the acts of the will you mean its imperative or executive acts, you then make virtue and vice to lie in that which really has no moral nature, except in a secondary or relative sense, i. e. as derived from the inward disposition or motive. But if when you assert that all virtue and vice, lie in the acts of the will, you mean to include in the acts of the will all the affections, dispositions, desires and emotions, as well as the volitions; it is clear that using the word in such a large sense, a sense which includes things so widely different in their nature, must be unfavorable to clearness in treatises on the philosophy of the mind.

"Inquirer" presses the question: "What is free agency?" In reply, I would describe free agency, not as a work of imagination, but as a reality, a thing which truly exists among men. I take it to be a point in which we are all agreed, that man *is* a free moral agent. Thus far controversy is excluded. And if we would know exactly what moral agency is, and how it operates, we must look upon the moral agent, man, and see what he does, and how he does it. Take any man as an example. Take Paul and begin with his unconverted state. What did he do? Why, he acquired learning; he observed the ceremonial law; and he persecuted the followers of Christ; and he did all this under the influence of a deceitful heart, and a misguided conscience. In all this, he was a free, moral agent; *free*, because he followed his own inclination and choice, and was not influenced by physical force. He was free from whatever would prevent him from choosing and acting according to his own inclinations. And Paul was a *moral* agent, because he exercised affections and performed actions which had a moral nature, and related to a moral law. Such was Paul before his conversion, and, as to moral agency, at his conversion, and after his conversion.

And as it was with Paul, so it is with every man, whether good or bad. Acting just as he does, he is free. He has no want of any power or faculty which is required in moral agency; he has no principle operating in himself, and is exposed to no foreign force, which hinders his moral agency. There is, then, no need of conjecture, or abstract reasoning, or hard and perplexed thinking on this subject. We are free, moral agents at any rate. This is settled.

Do you bring up the question, whether we are under a *necessity* of choosing as we do? My answer is, that we are under no necessity, except that which makes us rational, free, accountable beings. We *are* under this necessity; and we can never get away from it. It holds us fast; and will do so forever. We have no power to divest ourselves of our rationality, our freedom and accountability, how much soever we may desire it. The necessity which holds us to this, is perfect and uncontrollable. It is the unchangeable purpose of our almighty Creator and Preserver, that we shall forever be free, moral, accountable beings. Many things are submitted to our choice. But this is not. We can no more cease to be moral agents, than we can cease to exist. And every law or principle of action, which essentially belongs to us as moral agents, is also unalterable. It is a law of our being, that, in all our volitions and choices, we shall be influenced by motives, that is, by our inward affections and desires, and our views of outward objects; and who can prevent the operation of this law? And who would *wish* to prevent the operation of a law, which makes us *rational beings?*

In the discussion of this subject, my aim is to make the whole question respecting the powers or capabilities of a moral agent, a question of *facts*. In this way my own doubts and difficulties have been relieved; for I too, as well as "Inquirer," have had speculative difficulties in abundance on this subject. And I have thought, that the mode of investigation which has afforded relief to my own mind may do something towards relieving the minds of others. With this view I make the proposal to any who wish to examine the controverted questions respecting the powers of man, that, *instead of pushing the abstract inquiry, what it is possible for man to do, or what he has power or ability to do, we should endeavor, first of all, to determine what are the facts in the case, — the facts made known by past and present experience.* In what manner and under what influence does man as an intelligent, moral being, act? Do not inquire first how he *can* act, but how he *does* act? From what influence, and under what conditions does he put forth his volitions? Is he influenced in his choices by his predominant dispositions, affections and desires? Does even conscience govern him, except as the inclinations or desires of the heart give force to its dictates? The same as to every other case. Whenever the question as to *power* or *ability* comes up, put it thus: has man a power which has ever accomplished the thing supposed; a power which has availed, or which ever will avail? Take the question respecting the power of the unrenewed to repent and believe without the regenerating influence of the Spirit. We inquire, whether any sinner has actually repented and believed, without that influence. Whatever motives may have acted upon him, and whatever efforts he may have made in his natural state, has he ever done this? And has he power, in himself, which will prove to be sufficient in future time, so that he will, in any instance, actually obey the gospel, without special divine influence? If now it is an obvious fact, that no sinner ever did, or ever will truly repent, without the renewing of the Holy Spirit, do we not find here what may be called a *principle* or *law* of our moral nature in our fallen state? For what is a *law* in this sense, but the invariable manner in which events take place, or in which effects are produced?

"Inquirer" refers again to the fact which I had stated, "that good beings invariably have good affections in view of moral objects, and wicked beings invariably have wrong affections;" and he asks: "Does it then actually belong to the nature of free agency in *a state of probation*, to produce invariably one and only one set of emotions? Is there any example of such a uniformity in heaven or earth?"

My position is, that a being entirely good, invariably has right feelings, and a bad being invariably has wrong feelings, in view of moral objects. This, as I have said, does not imply that a good being may not become bad, nor that a bad being may not become good. But when a good being has become bad, the position that a good being uniformly has right feelings, does not apply to him; for he is not now a good being, though he was so once. And when a bad being has become good, the position that a bad being uniformly has wrong feelings, does not apply to him; as he is not now a bad being.

But I have nowhere said, that a moral agent has "uniformly

and invariably, one and only one *set* of emotions." I maintain that we have many *sets* of emotions, both holy and unholy.

"Inquirer" presses the question whether there is, in heaven or earth, any example of the uniformity or invariableness of moral affections, which I have spoken of, in those who are on probation. Undoubtedly there is. The holy angels were once in a state of probation; and during that probation, their affections were invariably right. This is an example in heaven. Jesus, as a man, was in a state of trial while on earth; and his affections were uniformly right. This is an example on earth of the most exalted kind. And all who die impenitent, are examples of the opposite character. Their moral affections are evil, only evil, and that continually.

"Inquirer" thinks, that I make "man a simple *passive recipient* in his affections and emotions." If *passive* is used to denote what is *not active*, it is far from expressing my opinion. I maintain that the mind *acts* as *really* and *powerfully*, in loving and hating and desiring, as in willing or choosing. Wax is a passive recipient of the impression made upon it. In *receiving* the impression, as we speak, it has no activity. But it is not so with the mind. It is indeed the *subject* of an influence from without; but it is an *intelligent*, *active* subject. It is not properly a *recipient of* its affections, but an *agent in* them.

I had said, "volition depends as much on motives, as the passions and feelings on their appropriate exciting objects." "Inquirer" asks, whether it depends "on motives drawn from things ab extra only?" I answer, by no means. It depends chiefly and ultimately on *inward* motives. "Inquirer" then says what deserves special notice: "Suppose that the soul from its own *nature*, *state* or *condition* wills or chooses this or that; is this to be put on par with desires necessarily and involuntarily excited in us by objects *without* the soul?" Let it be remembered, that the language in the closing part of the above quoted sentence, is not *my* language, and the thing implied in it is not according to my apprehension. But that which "Inquirer" suggests in the first part of the sentence, is, *in my* view, an important truth;

namely, that the soul wills or chooses *from its own nature, state or condition;* in other words, that volitions or choices result from the nature, state, or condition of the soul. In this I agree with "Inquirer." Whatever may be the motives presented from without, it is a well-known fact, that a man's inward disposition, or the state of his mind determines his choices, and his voluntary actions. And is not this equally true of the affections and desires? Do not the unholy affections of an unregenerate man proceed from the state of his heart? If he had a sanctified heart, would not his affections be holy? When Paul was renewed, did not the character of his soul give character to his emotions? Now if the fact that "the mind wills and chooses from its own nature, state or condition," makes our choices free, and makes us justly accountable for them; why does not the same fact concerning the affections and desires make *them* free, and make us justly accountable for them? That the affections do come from the state of the heart is clear. Christ declares that "from within, out of the heart, proceed evil thoughts, covetousness, lasciviousness, an evil eye and pride," as well as "adulteries, murders, thefts and blasphemies." The former are emotions, affections and desires, as evidently as the last are voluntary actions. And they all proceed alike from the heart in its depraved state. "Inquirer" holds this, so far as relates to volitions. But the affections and desires he regards as *necessary*, and on this account he thinks we are not accountable for them. And yet there is no more necessity in respect to the affections, than in respect to the volitions. For as "Inquirer" suggests, "the soul *wills* and *chooses* from its own nature, state or condition." And this is what I maintain in regard to the affections. They proceed out of the heart. And it is this circumstance which seems to lead "Inquirer" and many others, to think that they are not morally good or evil. The emotions and desires arise in the mind, they say, by *necessity* — which precludes freedom. But our volitions and choices take place by the same necessity; they proceed "from the nature, state and condition of the soul." So "Inquirer" thinks. How then, I ask, can we be accountable for them? And if not accountable either for our volitions, or our affections, how can we be accountable for anything?

"Inquirer" says: "If God has made *free agents*, has he not given them the power of choice, after all the motives which the nature of the case admits, are placed before them?" Certainly he has given such a power; and we exercise it every day. But in what way? Let "Inquirer" tell how *he* exercises this power of choice. In all his more important and deliberate choices, does he not carefully weigh the motives or reasons which come before him, and then decide in accordance with those which appear to him the strongest? And does he not feel that he is a free and accountable agent when he uses his power of choice in this way? In cases where our power of choosing has its most free and perfect exercise, do we ever choose in any other way? And if at any time we will and act suddenly, without deliberation, and from the impulse of some strongly excited passion; is not this very impulse of passion the motive which governs us? I predict that "Inquirer," and all other men, in the free exercise of the power of choice, will determine, will, or choose, either according to what appear to them the strongest reasons, after deliberation, or under the influence of some strongly excited passion, which leaves them no time for deliberation.

"Inquirer" says: "Dr. Woods will see, on looking over page 191, that he has made a singularly incorrect statement of the orthodox doctrine respecting the influence of Adam's sin. As the words now stand, they represent the orthodox as maintaining that native depravity and all our sinful actions and volitions, which are the invariable consequence of Adam's sin, are *fatalism*, entirely precluding free, accountable agency." One and another have said to me: *How could "Inquirer" make such a mistake?* I ascribe it not to any intention of his to misrepresent, but to his hasty attention to the paragraph referred to. In the closing part of my remarks on cause and effect, it was my object to point out the consequences of adopting the theory of the Essay. This object was pursued in the passage referred to by "Inquirer" which any one may read for himself. First, I state the orthodox doctrine as to the invariable connection between Adam's sin and the sinful volitions and actions of his posterity. Having done this, I turn to the Essay, which maintains that such an invariable connection of antecedent and consequent proves the existence of such a "producing cause," as "excludes free agency." I then show what must follow from the theory of the Essay; namely, either that the orthodox doctrine on this subject is true, and so, *according to the theory of the Essay*, that our depravity and all our sinful volitions and actions, being the invariable consequence of Adam's sin, are matters of fatalism, entirely precluding free agency; or else that there is no such connection, and that the orthodox doctrine is false. Thus, what I expressly represent as a consequence of the theory which I oppose, "Inquirer" thinks I represent as the doctrine of the orthodox.

After closing his remarks very candidly and kindly, "Inquirer" returns to the general subject in a postscript, and advances some things to which he doubtless expects me to reply. He says: "Dr. Woods makes us mere *passive recipients* in all our passions and desires." But these are *his* words, not mine. To the word *passive*, as explained by Edwards and Day, and as generally used by the older divines, I have no objection. A man is *passive* in this sense of the word, when he is the subject of an influence from another, or is acted upon by another, *how active soever he himself may be.* Thus a man is said to be both passive and active in his repentance and obedience. He is the *subject* of the divine influence, or is *acted upon* by the Spirit; and he himself *acts*, that is, repents and obeys, in consequence of that influence. God works in believers, and, in consequence, *they* work. But "Inquirer" doubtless uses the word *passive* as opposite to *active*, and *recipient* as opposite to *agent.* Now as every reader will see, I have taken great pains to show that, in this very matter, we are, in the most proper sense, *agents;* that in our affections and desires we are truly *active;* and that these mental actions are of as high an order, at least as our volitions. I everywhere oppose the idea, that, because our affections and desires are exercised spontaneously in view of appropriate objects, and are not controlled by a previous act of the will, we are not therefore free and active in them, or accountable for them. I hold that we are free, specially free in these mental acts — free, certainly, in as high a sense as in those external acts which are completely dictated and controlled by a volition.

"Inquirer" asks, how the command to love God and our neighbor is to be obeyed, and what is the nature of the obligation which lies on the sinner to exchange his enmity for love." According to the scheme which he seems to adopt, I should find it impossible to make any reply. For if the affections are not a part of our moral agency, for which we are justly responsible, I see not how they can be commanded, or what obligation can lie upon us to exercise them. But according to the view which I have taken of the matter, it is easy to say something in the way of reply. Love and hatred, and all the affections and emotions which we exercise in view of moral objects, are free, unforced, moral acts, for which we are justly accountable. God addresses his law to us as active, moral beings, and requires us to love him, and forbids our enmity. This command is right. For there is nothing more certain, than that we ought to love and obey such a being as God, and that we are blame-worthy and inexcusable for hating him. But if we take the other view of the subject, the view of those who hold that our affections and emotions are not moral acts, how can we dispose of the difficulty? How can we vindicate the law for requiring that we should exercise the affection of love, in which we are not moral agents, and for which we cannot be responsible? "Inquirer" speaks of this as a "dark, dark place." It would be very dark to me, if I should adopt the theory of my opponents. But, if I mistake not, the subject is illuminated by a light which is sufficiently clear; and nothing is necessary, but that we open our eyes to behold it. It is true at least, that we may know all which is of practical use. That we are intelligent, active, accountable beings, is an ultimate fact. The sacred writers never say a word to prove it, but always assume it as a well known fact. And they seem never to have imagined, that any one could doubt it. Whatever the laws of the mind are;

in whatever way our affections and desires are excited; under whatever influence our volitions are produced; and whatever may be found to be true in any other respect; the certainty of our moral, accountable agency is not for a moment to be questioned. It is not a subject of reasoning, but of consciousness. Treat it as a subject of speculative reasoning, and you involve it in darkness. But treat it as a fact of consciousness, and all is clear. I have said it is an *ultimate* fact. And we cannot go beyond what is *ultimate*. We cannot reach further than this, either on the right hand, or on the left. We cannot ascend to a greater height, or go down to a lower depth. This fact bounds our knowledge; except that we may look up, and see and adore the only wise God who created us. His work is perfect, and cannot be mended. With respect both to body and mind, we are fearfully and wonderfully made. As to the mode of teaching the nature and relations of man, his duty, his sin and ill-desert, and the way of recovery to holiness and happiness, we have the instructions and the example of those who spake as they were moved by the Holy Ghost. It is safe to follow their guidance. It is not safe to follow any other.

It is not well to introduce questions on the great subjects of religion, which the word of God will not help us to answer, and which must gender doubt and strife. When "Inquirer" asks *how* this and that can be; who can answer? And if I should ask *him*, in reference to one or another of his principles, *how* it can be; could he give an answer? The best and only safeguard against an unsettled, skeptical state of mind, is to avoid the habit of dwelling upon the speculative difficulties which hang about every important subject; to adhere closely and reverently to the word of God; to feed upon its precious truths, and to live in obedience to its precepts; and finally, to cherish a constant, lively sense of our weakness and danger, and a cordial reliance upon the teaching of the Holy Spirit.

I now close. I hope I shall not be severely blamed, for writing so much, or for not writing more. I have not indeed remarked on every particular point suggested by "Inquirer."

But I have not passed over anything which I supposed important. And I have not passed over anything because I thought it difficult to give an answer. Nor have I done it, because I am reluctant to tell what I think. I have frankly and unreservedly disclosed my views, and my mode of reasoning on every subject which has come under consideration; and I am willing to do so on every other subject; so that what is right may be approved, and that what is wrong may be corrected. Let those who differ from me do the same. Let us all unite in avoiding concealment, and equivocation, and every degree of undue confidence in ourselves, and of uncandid or unkind feeling towards others; endeavoring to join soundness of doctrine with the spirit of forbearance and love, and always remembering that bitterness of feeling, or the want of sincere brotherly kindness, towards any of the ministers or disciples of Christ, is one of the worst of errors.

I cannot but wish, that I had been able to think and write in a manner more worthy of the subjects which have been brought before me, and more adapted to advance the cause of truth. Still it has been my aim to do that, and only that, which will accord with the word of God, and both in asking and answering questions, to keep in mind the all-revealing day. I hope that "Inquirer" will look with favor, if not with entire satisfaction, upon what I have done. For whatever my defects or my errors in this performance may be, I have endeavored to speak the truth in love. My correspondence with my unknown friend, though not of my proposing, has been of the most pleasant kind. I thank him for the respect and candor which are apparent in his inquiries. What he and I have written is now before the public. The Lord grant, that it may so work in with the thoughts and reasonings of others, as in the end to contribute something towards illustrating and confirming the theory of divine truth.

EFFICACY OF THE WORD OF GOD.*

My present object is, to illustrate the value of the Word of God, from a consideration of *its salutary influence*.

This method of estimating the value of God's word, is evidently just, and corresponds with our practice in judging of all other things which we consider as *means*. If we would estimate the value of anything in the natural world, for example, the value of gold, or the value of food or medicine, we take into account the good effects resulting from it, and the useful purposes which it may be made to answer. It is unquestionably right to proceed in the same way, when we judge of things in the *moral* world. To take a distinguished instance, we inquire, what is the value of *Christ's death*, the most important event related in the history of the divine administration. To satisfy ourselves on this point, we take into view the benevolent ends to be accomplished by that event — the important consequences which will flow from it, in regard to the character and government of God, and the eternal condition of his people.

The efficacy belonging to the word of God, is doubtless similar, in a *general* view, to the efficacy of any other instrumental or dependent cause. That BEING, "of whom are all things," has seen fit to appoint a connection between *means* and *ends* — between *causes* and *effects*. In consequence of this divine arrangement, power to produce the effect becomes, in a dependent sense,

---

* First published in the Literary and Theological Review, Sept., 1834.

a real attribute of the cause, and efficacy to accomplish the end, *an attribute of the means*. It truly belongs to it, and so far as God's appointment goes, belongs to it invariably. In other words the means is effectual, so far as God, by his own agency, makes it effectual. Thus God is *all in all*.

The word of God, considered as an instrumental cause, has a manifest *fitness* to produce its effects; and so its effects flow from it in a manner which is obvious to those who have become properly acquainted with the nature of the subject. Considering man to be a rational and moral being, we perceive that such must be the fitness and tendency of God's word; and such must be its actual effect, unless its proper influence is prevented by some evil counteraction from without or from within. See how clearly this principle is illustrated by the parable of the sower! The seed sown has a natural tendency to vegetate and produce a crop; but, that it may actually have this effect, it must be sown in a suitable soil, and be attended with other circumstances favorable to its growth. If it be sown on stony ground, or among thorns, or by the wayside, the good effect will be prevented. In like manner, when the divine word is presented to the minds of men, their moral state may be such, and generally is such, that the proper effect will be prevented. But if there be no hinderance; if the truth meets with "an honest and good heart," its salutary effects are certain. Its own proper nature and tendency are unalterable; but in order to its *actual efficacy*, the influence of other causes must be added, and obstacles removed. This circumstance does not detract, in any degree, from the importance of the connection between divine truth and its proper effect. It only shows more clearly the *nature* and *conditions* of that connection.

But while the beneficial effects produced by the word of God are thus emphatically asserted, far be it from us to overlook the Scripture doctrine of the *special and supernatural influence of the Holy Spirit*. The very fact that the truth is the means of producing such effects, brings the divine agency directly into view. Here we *see* that agency; for *the Spirit of God produces its holy fruits in this very way*. He operates through divine truth. *The connection between the word of God and its saving effects, is as much owing to his will and agency, as the existence of the soul.* The Apostle makes a clear distinction between the mere influence of the truth and of those who preach it, and that divine influence which "gives the increase." The saving effects of divine truth would no more take place without the sanctifying Spirit, than the world would come into existence without a Creator. They result as really from his agency, as if he produced them without any means whatever. In fact, we are to consider the whole system of means, both in the natural and moral world, as designed and adapted, not to set aside or conceal the constant agency of God, but to bring it clearly into view, and so to make us acquainted with that glorious Being, on whom all causes and effects ultimately depend, and who, in a manner perfectly suited to the nature of created beings, "*worketh all in all.*"

In attempting to illustrate the happy efficacy of divine truth, I shall have recourse, both to the sacred volume, and, to the facts which occur in the experience of intelligent Christians.

The *nature* of that influence which the truth exerts, is what we learn from our own experience; it is a matter of consciousness. The efficacy of the truth takes place *in the mind*, and consists in the thoughts, apprehensions, feelings and determinations, which the mind itself has. For the truth to enlighten the mind, is for the *mind itself* so to contemplate the truth, as to have spiritual light or knowledge. For the word of God *to convert the soul*, is for the *soul itself* to turn from sin to God, in view of divine truth, and under its influence. And generally for the truth to exert a sanctifying power over the mind, is for the *mind itself* so to contemplate divine truth, as to have right thoughts and emotions, and to advance in holiness. Thus the efficacy of divine truth relates directly to *our agency*, that is, to the operations of our own minds. Or it may be still more just to say, that the influence of the truth appears in the acts which the mind itself puts forth while the truth is before it, and is to be judged of altogether by those acts.

The efficacy of God's word is conspicuous in the *conviction and conversion of sinners.* This is set forth in a very striking manner in the nineteenth Psalm. The writer here uses such strength and copiousness of style, and such reiterated expressions of the same thought, as to show that his soul waked up to ecstasy, in contemplating his subject. "The law of the Lord is perfect, converting the soul. The testimony of the Lord is sure, making wise the simple. The statutes of the Lord are right, rejoicing the heart. The commandment of the Lord is pure, enlightening the eyes." So in the New Testament. "The word of God is quick and powerful, and sharper than any two-edged sword — and is a discerner of the thoughts and intents of the heart." "Born again of the word of God, which liveth and abideth forever."

We are taught the same lesson by *experience* and *observation.* Has not every one, who is convinced of sin, a consciousness that his conviction is produced by means of the truths contained in the Scriptures? Look at the three thousand who were pricked in their hearts under Peter's preaching. It was divine truth, it was the Apostle's preaching, made up in a great measure of citations from the word of God, which awakened them, and led them to inquire what they should do to be saved. It is substantially so in all instances. Whatever event may occur that is adapted to touch the feelings of sinners; whatever may be the more remote occasion of leading them to consider their ways; no salutary conviction is produced, before the holiness and authority of God, the nature and obligations of his law, and other truths of revelation, are impressed on their hearts. Other things may excite, and agitate, and alarm. But it is *divine truth*, rendered effectual by the power of the Holy Ghost, which enlightens the conscience, convinces of sin, subdues the pride and obstinacy of the heart, and prepares the way for faith in Christ.

The general principle now stated, is one which discerning and faithful ministers of the gospel are always careful to observe. They make use of no means unauthorized by Scripture, to disturb the slumbering conscience. They employ no sounds of horror to terrify the imagination, and no images of fictitious tenderness to move the sensibilities of the heart. They hold forth *the simple word of God*, laboring clearly to explain it, and deeply to impress its truths upon the conscience and heart. In this way they always have proceeded, and always must proceed. An effect is to be produced in a moral agent; an effect of a moral nature, that is, a moral affection, or a moral state. Now acting in our province as dependent instruments, what can *we* do, except to present the proper motive, and so attempt to exert an influence, suited to the nature of man, and to the nature of the effect to be produced, that is, conviction of sin. Of what are sinners to be convinced? They are to be convinced that the divine commands are holy, just, and good; "that sin is exceedingly sinful;" that sinners deserve the penalty of the law, and must endure it, unless delivered by grace. Now, in order that they may be thus convinced, these truths must be made known to them, and inculcated upon them — must reach the inmost recesses of their souls.

The same is true as to conversion, or the actual turning of a sinner to God. This is an event which takes place in a moral agent, and in which his moral agency is directly concerned. The sinner turns from sin to holiness, from enmity to love. The rebel submits and obeys. The despiser of Christ thankfully embraces him. This is conversion. But how is this brought about? Was any one ever induced to turn from sin to holiness, without being made to see and feel, that sin is hateful and destructive, and holiness desirable and excellent? When the sinner turns, he turns with these views. These truths act upon him as rational motives, and induce him to turn. How is the sinner brought to love God? The eyes of his understanding being enlightened, and his heart renewed by the Holy Spirit, he sees that God is infinitely excellent and glorious. But this is a divine truth. And when a man really loves God, he does it under the influence of this truth. In like manner, submission, faith and obedience take place in view of different parts of divine truth. Accordingly when the ministers of Christ wish to promote the conversion of sinners, and bring them to obey the gospel, what have they to do, but to make known divine truth? This is their province — the department of labor assigned to them. By this means they seek the conversion of sinners.

The divine word equally shows its efficacy, in the progressive sanctification of believers. "Sanctify them through thy truth; thy word is truth." "That he might sanctify and cleanse the church — *by the word.*" Holiness, whether in sinners newly converted, or in Christians in the different stages of their progress, and whether it relates to God, or his law, or sin, or any other object, has an invariable relation to divine truth; so that there is no way in which we can do anything to excite holy affections in the minds of Christians, however great their progress in sanctification, but by presenting divine truth before them, and leading them clearly to understand it, and devoutly to meditate upon it. This, according to the appointment of God, is the means of promoting growth in grace. For every time divine truth is so contemplated as to excite acts of holiness, the soul is advanced in the divine life. The apostles made it their object to carry forward those who were converted to perfection. And by what means did they aim to do this? Their epistles show. They repeatedly and earnestly inculcated upon Christians the various truths of religion, for the very purpose of leading them on to higher attainments in piety. The greater part of their epistles was devoted to this object.

We are not, by any means, to regard it as necessary, that the truth which promotes spiritual growth, should be new truth. The same truth which has excited holy affection once, is suited to excite it again. If the heart is right, the more frequently any truth is contemplated, the more frequently will the corresponding affection be drawn forth. Hence the utility of our perusing the Scriptures and hearing the truths of religion publicly explained and enforced again and again. And as it is a fact, that the habit of holiness is promoted, not simply by the frequency with which holy affections are exercised, but also by the strength of the exercise; it follows, that that method of exhibiting divine truth, which produces the strongest holy affection, contributes most to sanctification. The truth as a moral cause, acting on the minds of Christians, will be efficacious to promote their sanctification in proportion to the clearness with which it is presented to view, and the intenseness of thought and feeling which it excites.

It would be easy to show, that Christians are successful in their warfare against sin, that they patiently bear trials, that they rise above discouragements, and through every difficulty press forward towards the mark, and finally gain the prize, under the influence of God's holy word. Let the word of God pass away from their minds, and they lose all their power to perform duty, or to endure trials; are carried about with every wind; are the slaves of passion, and have no means of casting off the bondage.

It is through the power of divine truth, that Christians are sustained in their last conflict. Should what the Spirit of God has taught them from the Scriptures be erased from their memories and hearts, how quickly would their joy and peace in believing, and the supports of God's presence in the valley of death, all forsake them! Their minds would be dark as midnight; and the whole moral world would be a dreary waste.

The same remarks which have been made as to the conversion and sanctification of individuals, are applicable to revivals of religion in the larger sense. A genuine revival is indeed the work of God. It is so in the highest sense; and all the glory of it is due to him. But while God's agency in this work is special and supernatural, he still makes use of divine truth. He causes a revival of religion to take place, by exerting such an influence upon the souls of men, as prepares them to believe and obey his word. One grand effect of the influence of the Spirit is, that men are made to feel the certainty and importance of the truths of revelation. Look upon any place where the Spirit of God is poured out, and where that state of things exists which constitutes a genuine *revival*, and see how all the effects produced connect themselves with the influence of divine truth. The minister of the gospel, being himself deeply affected with the truths of religion, exhibits them clearly and impressively to others. He makes this his great work. Christians are alive to divine truth, and take pains to inculcate it upon those around them. "The word of God becomes quick and powerful." It is this sacred word, which awakens multitudes from their fatal slumbers, and leads them to consider their ways. It is this, which teaches them that their character is hateful in the sight of God; that they are sinners without excuse. It is the word of God that reveals to them the abominations of their hearts, slays all their false hopes, and makes it perfectly manifest to them, that they must perish forever, unless the sovereign grace of God interpose to save them. It is the word of God, attended by the power of his Spirit, that brings men to discern the glory of the Saviour, and cordially to trust in his all-sufficient grace. And it is this blessed volume, making known the precious promises, and opening the very gate of heaven before them, that fills them with the comforts of hope, animates them in their warfare against sin, and prepares them for the crown of victory. Thus it is by the word of God, rendered effectual by the renovating power of the Spirit in the heart, that all saving religion is begun, and advanced, and finally made perfect. If, then, we would promote a revival of religion, we must plainly teach the word of God, and impress its truths upon the conscience and heart. Ministers, parents, teachers, all Christians, must do this, and must do it with sincere love and persevering diligence. Suppose the Apostle Paul were now commissioned to visit our congregations; in what way would he labor to promote the work of conversion and sanctification? He would do it, as he did in the time of his apostleship, *by declaring all the counsel of God*, and by fervent, importunate prayer for the influence of the Spirit to prepare the heart to receive the truth, and so to render the truth effectual. And if the Apostle should go to any place, and should see the people inattentive to the word of God, and indifferent to its momentous truths, he would judge them to be *far from the kingdom of heaven*. But if, in any place, he should see persons of every age, daily searching the Scriptures, especially if he should see them in their places of retirement, and their hours of solitude, devoutly reading the sacred volume, and praying that God would teach them to understand it, and then spontaneously exclaiming, *How sweet is thy word to my taste!* should he behold parents and children, thus seeking the knowledge of God's holy word, and beginning to feed their souls upon its heavenly truths; he would feel a joyful confidence that God was about to arise and build up Zion.

And the same divine word which is the means of promoting a revival of religion in particular places, is to be the means of extending salvation to all the nations of the earth. The appointment of Heaven, in this respect, is unalterable. Whatever is done for the conversion of the world, must be done by means of divine truth. The word of God will be sent forth to every land; will be preached and read in all languages; will expose the folly and wickedness of idolatry, and the evil of every kind of sin, and will make known the only living and true God, and Jesus Christ, the only Saviour. And through the power of the Holy Ghost sent down from heaven, the truth will have a saving efficacy, and the knowledge of it will be *life eternal.*

It is sometimes thought, that making so much of the efficacy of divine truth, tends to lower our conceptions of the influence of the Spirit, and to detract from the glory of God's grace.

It might be a sufficient reply to such a view of the subject, that the sacred writers, who always show the highest zeal for the glory of God, assert in the strongest terms the power of divine truth. Nor do they ever appear to have the least apprehension, that their doing so will be any dishonor to God. Indeed we find them most abundant in setting forth the influence of the truth, at the very time when their eye is evidently fixed upon the glory of God. This circumstance would naturally lead us to think that in some way the two views of the subject must be consistent, and that while the inspired writers ascribe such an influence to divine truth in the salvation of men, they mean to ascribe a still higher influence to the Spirit of God. And this we find to be the case. "I planted, Apollos watered, but *God gave the increase.*" From this, and many other passages, it appears, not only that God exercises an influence superior to the mere influence of divine truth, but that all the influence which the truth has, is owing to his special agency in the souls of men. The truth becomes effectual through the power of the Holy Ghost. So that the greater the efficacy of divine truth, the more conspicuous is that divine power from which it is derived.

Nothing can be more manifest than that God's working in this way contributes directly to his glory. If sinners were converted without the influence of divine truth, they would be converted without any *knowledge* of God, or of his law, or of any other spiritual object. Hence God could not be glorified, because he would not be known — would not be known by converted sinners, any more than by the trees of the forest. But as God operates in the moral world by means of the truth, his perfections are manifested, and he becomes the object of love and praise. When he operates thus, he operates in noon-day light, so that his hand is seen, and his name exalted and glorified. The very truth which awakens and sanctifies, is the truth which reveals his character. Why then should it ever be imagined, that the dependent influence which we attribute to divine truth as a means of sanctification, will obscure the lustre of God's glory, when that influence is but the clear light of truth kindled up in the souls of men, making his glory to be seen and his agency to be acknowledged and felt?

Behold then the immense value of the sacred volume, arising from the vast amount of good which it accomplishes; and render unceasing thanks to God for so precious a gift. The light of the knowledge of the glory of God in the face of Jesus Christ is above all price. And will you not bless God for that precious volume, which has shed this glorious, transforming light upon your souls? You thank God for your daily bread; but his holy word supplies *spiritual food* "*the bread from heaven*, which if a man eat he shall live forever." You thank God for bodily health, and for the means of preserving it, and when lost, of restoring it. But you owe him warmer gratitude for the gift of his word, which is the means of healing the diseases of the mind, and imparting spiritual health and vigor. You may remember the time when you were regardless of your eternal interests and in a state of moral slumber. From that fatal slumber the word of God roused you. Once you were enemies to God by wicked works. But the divine word, accompanied by the special agency of the Spirit, has slain your enmity, and kindled holy love. Once you were in servitude to sin. But the power of the gospel has freed you from that cruel servitude, and brought you into the liberty of the sons of God. You may call to remembrance seasons of darkness, struggles, fears and sorrows. And do you not remember, too, how many times the word of God has enlightened your minds, dissipated your sorrows and fears, strengthened you, and given you peace? When you have been in a lukewarm and backsliding state, has not the word of God been the means of reclaiming you, and rekindling your zeal? What spiritual maladies has it healed! How has it been a lamp to your feet, and a light to your path! What comfort has it afforded you in affliction! With what power has it prompted you to live to God, and to labor and suffer for the interests of his kingdom! Call to mind your deliverances from danger, your seasons of repentance, and love, and communion with God, your pious labors, your victories over sin, and your hopes of heaven. Call these to mind, and learn the efficacy of God's holy word, and the reasons you have to bless God for such a gift.

But while it is true that the word of God has mingled its healing, purifying, comforting influence with your past experience; it is also true, that it must continue to have the same influence, and must have it in an increasing degree. There is a great work of sanctification still to be accomplished. And your heavenly Advocate prayed that this might be accomplished by means of the divine word. "Sanctify them through thy truth; thy word is truth." You may still have many a dark and dreary place to pass through, many difficulties, distresses and dangers to encounter, before you arrive at your final home. And, it is this same divine word which must afford you the assistance you will need. Look then at what remains to be done before you can receive the unfading crown, and learn how precious is that word of God, by means of which it is all to be accomplished, and what everlasting thanks you owe to God for such a blessing. Look also at the display of grace which must be made in the conversion of the world. What darkness must be dissipated! From what errors and sins must the earth be purged! Oh! what a work it must be to renovate such a world as this, and to fill it with the fruits of holiness, and the joys of salvation! This difficult and glorious work the Spirit of God will accomplish through the instrumentality of his holy word. It will all be *the work of God;* but he will accomplish it through the truth. In the progress of his merciful administration, he will give his word a more efficacious and extensive influence than ever before, and so will make its value more clearly to be seen. As far as the heavens are above the earth, so far does the Bible exceed in preciousness every worldly good; and it ought to be received with higher gratitude, and with gladness of heart more pure and rapturous. May God send out his light and truth. May all the nations of the earth soon receive his life-giving word, and experience its saving efficacy, and so may they be prepared to unite in one chorus of praise to the God of love, who has bestowed such a gift, and whose sovereign and gracious influence invests it with such power to illuminate, and purify, and comfort the souls of men.

SERMONS

IN THREE SERIES.

1. FUNERAL SERMONS. 2. ORDINATION SERMONS.

3. SERMONS ON VARIOUS SUBJECTS, DOCTRINAL AND PRACTICAL.

A SERMON

DELIVERED IN ANDOVER, MAY 3, 1812, AT THE FUNERAL OF SAMUEL ABBOT, ONE OF THE FOUNDERS OF THE THEOLOGICAL SEMINARY.

Heb. 6: 12.—THAT YE BE NOT SLOTHFUL, BUT FOLLOWERS OF THEM, WHO THROUGH FAITH AND PATIENCE INHERIT THE PROMISES.

IN this passage, the Apostle directed the thoughts of the Hebrews to Abraham, Isaac, and Jacob, and other saints, who through faith in the promises and patient expectation of their accomplishment, and through meekness and fortitude under the sufferings of life, had gone beyond the reach of trouble and danger, and were in possession of the heavenly inheritance. He directed their thoughts to those ancient believers, not to excite their admiration, nor to gratify their curiosity, but *to rouse them to diligent imitation.*

It is *our* duty, brethren, as it was the duty of the Hebrews, *to imitate the example of believers.*

I would by no means intimate that the character of believers, even those most distinguished for holiness, is without fault. The best Christians on earth must not be set up as infallible guides; they must not occupy the place of Jesus Christ.

The general consideration by which I would enforce the duty of following the saints, is *the excellence of their example.* They all have the spirit of Christ, and walk in his steps. They are clothed with humility. The love of God is the governing affection of their hearts, and shows itself by obedience. The law of God is the rule of their actions. Their religion does not consist in bare profession or ostentatious zeal, but in a *good life*—life of sincere benevolence and piety. Such, in a measure, is the life of all Christians. A *Christian* without the spirit of *Christ*—a *good man* without a good life, is a palpable absurdity. If Christians had nothing but profession; if with all the respect which they occasionally show for religion, they were as covetous, selfish, false, and useless, as men of the world are; their example would mislead and destroy. But with all their lamented imperfections, they are the excellent of the earth. By the Spirit of God they have been renewed to holiness; and are comely through the comeliness which divine grace has put upon them. Now it is plainly our duty to imitate them in everything that is excellent and praiseworthy. We should imitate the faith, by which they confide in the infallible truth of the word of God; by which, especially, they receive Christ as he is offered in the gospel. We should imitate their humility, by which they are brought to take their place at the feet of Jesus, and to prefer others to themselves. We should imitate their supreme love to God and their active benevolence to men, by which they comply with the spirit of the moral law. We should imitate their patience in affliction, their forgiveness of injuries, their zeal to do good, their spiritual mindedness, and their habitual devotion. Whatsoever things are pure, whatsoever things are excellent, whatsoever things are lovely in them, we ought diligently to copy.

It is hardly necessary to remark, that *good example* more clearly shows the beauty of holiness, and is much better calculated to make a salutary impression on our minds than *mere precept*. This is true of the good example of every intelligent being, of whatever rank. But the example of believers has *peculiar* advantages, being the example of those who are possessed of the same nature, and subject to the same trials with ourselves. Are we weak and depraved, and exposed to temptations and difficulties from without and within? So were all the saints whose names are recorded in the Scriptures. Nay, in most instances, the difficulties they had to encounter were far greater, than those which exist at the present day. Their example then clearly shows that religion is attainable; that duty may be practised; that all the excellent virtues, which their life manifested, may be manifested in ours.

But the good influence of Christians is much increased if they live in our own times, in our own country, in our own circle; and above all, if we have a personal acquaintance with them. In these circumstances, we obtain clearer views of their character. We do indeed see more of their *failings*. But we also see more of their *virtues;* and we see them in their own proper light. The moral features of those who are distant from us, are liable to be misrepresented and misconceived. When you paint the character of a Christian of a distant age or place, you may set it off with all the glowing colors which the imagination can give it; and you may make it a *finished character*. But it is the character of no Christian on earth. Nor is it the character of any saint or angel in heaven; for no painter can give an exact portrait of one whom he never saw. Whom then does it resemble? No one. It is a false picture. And the impression it will make upon us, will be as slight, as the image is false. But when we fix our eyes upon a follower of Christ who is near us, and with whom we are personally acquainted; we are brought back to *realities*. We see a character which the grace of God has formed. We discern its features exactly. We want no picture; for we have the original before us. The beauties we behold are *true* and *substantial;* and unless some great fault in us prevents, the sight of them will contribute to our lasting improvement.

The example of believers is attended with greater advantages still, if, besides acquaintance with them in the common intercourse of life, *we have known their more private views, trials, and enjoyments.* In these ways, we come to a more exact discernment of their character. We learn the secret springs of their actions. They show us something of that spiritual life, which is hid with Christ in God. We see the faithfulness of their conscience, the tenderness of their heart, and their struggles with temptation. We hear their groans under the burden of remaining sin, and their sighs after deliverance.

And how peculiarly impressive does their example become, if we have access to them on the bed of languishing. Have you been conversant with a good man, when finishing his course, when near his everlasting home? Have you seen him at the threshold of heaven? Have you seen in him that faith, which overcometh the world? Have you witnessed his humble hope, his panting after God, his meekness and patience, his hatred of sin, his love of the saints, his forgiveness of enemies, his steady and earnest desire for the prosperity of the church, and his compassion for the world? Have you witnessed his submission to the will of God, and that tranquillity which bodily weakness and distress and the prospect of a speedy dissolution could not disturb? Have you seen celestial joy kindle in his soul at the thought of arriving at his journey's end, and being forever with the Lord? You must then have an undoubting conviction of the reality and excellence of his religion, and deeply feel the influence of his example. The death-bed of the saint is not a place of delusion. There, the dreams and visions of the world vanish, and things appear what they are. Infidels may dispute, and the profane world point the finger of scorn; but if you have witnessed the last end of a good man, you have evidence of the solid foundation of his hope which must be forever conclusive, and a motive, which nothing but hardness of heart can resist, to copy his example.

But, in many instances, the example of a good man exerts a salutary influence in the highest degree, in consequence of *his decease*. His example now becomes more impressive than ever, being associated with all the tender recollections excited by his departure. We now remember, with new emotions, the loveliness of his temper, his edifying conversation, his useful deeds, and every excellence of his character. Many things, little regarded and soon forgotten during his life, are now recalled. We fix our thoughts upon his whole character and life, and view it in a more consistent and affecting light than ever before. At the same time the influence of his example is increased and rendered more beneficial, by our thinking *what* and *where* he now is, and what will be his condition through everlasting ages.

This brings us to the particular consideration suggested in the text: "Be followers of them, who through faith and patience *inherit the promises.*" They were not afraid to engage in the Christian warfare, nor prevented from persevering. They fought a good fight, and overcame all their enemies. Many were the difficulties and dangers they met in their way; but they finished their course. The path which they travelled, led them to a peaceful death and a happy immortality. In the promises of God they firmly trusted; and now, far removed from sin and suffering, they inherit the promised good. Christ has said, "To him that overcometh will I grant to sit with me on my throne." The fulfilment of this promise they now experience. They have obtained the end of their faith, the salvation of their souls. Shall we not imitate a life, which has terminated so happily? Shall we not pursue a course, which has always led to glory? If the departed saints had found their labors in vain, and had, after all, fallen short of the heavenly rest; we might be discouraged. But what more animating motive can stimulate us to follow their steps, than the unfailing success of their labors, the blessed issue of their trials, and the glorious victory which has crowned their warfare?

In our feelings toward Christian friends, especially those who have entered into rest, are we not frequently chargeable with a great fault? We may have respected their character, been delighted with their conversation, applauded their benevolence, and been affected with momentary grief at their death. But is this all that we owe them? And is this all that we owe to the grace of God on their account? When we contemplate their amiable and pious character, ardent love should be kindled in our hearts. We ought to admire the power and glory of divine grace in creating them anew in Christ Jesus unto good works, and preparing them for the heavenly inheritance. Their goodness should make a deep and permanent impression upon us. And what is more, *we should diligently follow their steps.* Every other proof of affection is nothing, without this. If we truly love the saints, we shall imitate them, and labor to promote their benevolent designs. The cause of Christ, which was so dear to their hearts, will be dear to ours. All their pious wishes we shall endeavor to carry into effect. To think, *this was the desire of that dear saint, now in heaven*, will be a powerful spring to exertion. I repeat it, that *a faithful compliance with the pious wishes of departed Christians, and a careful imitation of their holy example, is the best proof we can give of sincere affection for them.* The Lord grant, that we may all give this proof of our cordial esteem and love for that dear Christian, whose lifeless body is now before us. And may all the honor which we render to his memory, ultimately redound to God, by whose power he was created; by whose Spirit he was, as we trust, renewed and guided and trained up for glory. That there has been *such a man* among us, will, we doubt not, be to the praise of the glory of God's grace.

The first thing in his character which I shall mention, was *habitual devotion*. His life furnished pleasing evidence, that he sincerely and unreservedly devoted himself to God, saying, with the Psalmist, "Lord, I am thine." Our departed friend loved the house of God. He loved the saints. He loved the Holy Scriptures. He delighted in religious contemplation and prayer and *conscientiously observed the commands of God*, and what better evidence could he give of real and habitual piety?

His devotion had no flights, and usually no raptures. But it had the marks of humility, of seriousness and tenderness, of constancy and earnestness. *He walked with God.*

His attention to duty was *universal*. He did not think of atoning for the neglect of the duties he owed to mankind, by multiplying his religious performances. Nor did he think of atoning for the neglect of religion, by punctuality in social duties. He had respect to all the divine precepts, and hated every false and sinful way.

He was remarkable for *sincerity and uprightness*. The sin of flattery he abhorred. One of his maxims was, "to praise no man in his presence, and speak evil of no one in his absence." If he had any difficulty in his mind respecting others, he considered it a sacred duty to apprize them of it. He would *not suffer sin upon his neighbor*. And his kindness, his lovely simplicity and meekness enabled him to give reproof with the greatest advantage. No one could be offended. His uprightness and veracity were so uniform and remarkable, that all who knew him, could unite in saying, "He was an Israelite indeed, in whom was no guile."

In an uncommon degree, *he had the government of his passions.* His was the happiness of ruling his own spirit. He attained to such self-command, that there is reason to doubt, whether he was angry the last twenty years of his life. The agitations and contentions of the world left his passions cool. He kept at a distance from the storm, and found a refuge in the calmness and gentleness of his own mind.

He was equally remarkable for *the government of the tongue.* The Apostle James states this as one of the best marks of real goodness. "If any man offend not in word, the same is a perfect man." Who ever heard that tongue, now silent in death, utter falsehood, reviling, or slander? That good man governed his speech by the meekness of wisdom. He had well considered the effects of an unbridled tongue, "that unruly evil, that world of iniquity, that deadly poison, that fire which sets the whole course of nature in a flame." Against these evils he watched and prayed, and employed his tongue in harmless, kind, and profitable discourse.

He was a man of *prudence.* He exercised this virtue in the management of all his concerns. No man perhaps ever had less of that rashness which flows from imagination without judgment, and from ardor without experience, and which often renders the best plans abortive. He had a deep conviction that he was liable to err. This conviction induced a habit of cautious deliberation, and, on important subjects, of being slow in forming conclusions. His prudence led him to guard against extremes in religion. He loved the obvious, sober sense of Scripture. In matters of doctrine, he chose the happy medium; in matters of practice, *the plain path, the footsteps of the flock.* In short, he had that useful wisdom, which results from an honest and teachable mind and long acquaintance with the affairs of the world. This wisdom effectually preserved him from hurtful mistakes, and enabled him successfully to execute his plans, without giving "offence either to Jew or Gentile."

He was eminently a *peace-maker*. Few Christians so fully comply with the Apostle's direction: "If it be *possible*, as much as lieth in you, live peaceably with all men." When duty permitted, he was willing to give up his own rights, and to do anything, or be anything, for the sake of peace.

He had a *quick sense of moral evil*, especially in himself. Judging of things by the word of God, he perceived many feelings and actions to be sinful, which are commonly regarded as innocent. Wandering thoughts in religious duties, the want of warmth in his affections, and of life in his devotion were his constant burden and grief, and made him long after heaven. Any impropriety or error in managing his domestic concerns was quickly perceived, and as quickly acknowledged.

He was distinguished for a *simple respect to the will of God.* He sought seriously and prayerfully, to know God's will, that he might do it. And he obtained the promised good. Rarely can a Christian be found, to whom the path of duty is generally made so plain as it was to him. In the most important transactions of his life, particularly those which related to the establishment of the THEOLOGICAL SEMINARY, his duty, as he often declared, was made as clear to his mind, as if it had been pointed out to him by a voice from heaven. This entire satisfaction respecting the path of duty, which was perhaps the most distinguishing trait in his character, resulted, not from the extent of his knowledge, nor from any enthusiastical impression, but from that habit of calm deliberation, that single regard to the will of God, and that divine teaching, which afford the safest and best guidance.

Finally, he was remarkable for his *beneficence*. He had sincere compassion for the poor, and opened his hand for their relief. With warm and steady affection, he endeavored to promote the welfare of civil society. For the instruction of children in every branch of useful knowledge, especially for their religious education, he was greatly concerned. This favored church and society know what he did for this object, and for their religious interest in other ways. Many years ago he began to give assistance to young men of talents and hopeful piety, in their preparation for the ministry. But none of his plans of doing good satisfied him — none corresponded with the extent of his benevolence, before he entertained the design of founding *an institution for the education of theological students.* This design he often declared, was first suggested to him by no man on earth; but by the Spirit of God. This he seriously and constantly believed; and this no Christian can doubt. The nature and design of the Seminary exactly agreed with his feelings. Religious beneficence had become his grand object. To this he had consecrated much of the wealth which God had given him. His strict economy and all his exertions to retain and increase his property were directed to the great design of doing good to the church of Christ. It was his own expression, "you can't tell how much pleasure I have taken in saving for this object." He did not labor to hoard up riches. He did not live to himself; but labored to be rich in good works. By his pious beneficence, or using his substance for the promotion of religion, he showed that he knew the real value and proper use of riches. The method of doing good which he adopted, was both in its nature, and in the extent of its fruits, superior to all others. He frequently mentioned it, as his end in what he had done for the Seminary, to bring thousands and millions to glory. This Institution was his favorite object; and its prosperity constituted much of his comfort in the concluding years of his life. In this centered his warmest affections. He connected it with his most solemn devotions, his purest pleasures, his best hopes of the church's prosperity. It was his deliberate and full persuasion, that he had done *well* in contributing to the establishment of such a Seminary; that so great an object called for his *utmost exertions.* We have no doubt that he thinks so still, and that the judgment day will confirm the persuasion.

I owe to the memory of my patron and friend to declare, that I have considered it one of the most precious privileges of my life, to enjoy his paternal affection, and to be near him in his feeble and languishing state. The observations, therefore, which I have made, and those which I am about to make, are not founded on vague report, but derived from the most intimate personal acquaintance.

There is reason to believe that for several of his last years, his religion, which commenced in early life, became more deep and operative, and his enjoyments more constant and spiritual. He evidently grew in grace and in the knowledge of Christ. He had an increasing conviction of the truth and importance of those evangelical doctrines, for the propagation of which he helped to found this Seminary. But his belief of those doctrines was not produced by reasoning, but was the result of childlike submission to the authority of God in his word. In this way his faith became altogether practical, and was at the same time an act of piety. But it was not on this account less rational or sure. It rested on the proper ground, and partook more of affection than of intellect. His faith in the truths of revelation was fixed and invariable. Whatever doubts he might sometimes have respecting his own piety, he had none respecting the doctrines of the gospel.

His unwavering and cordial belief of those doctrines was the foundation of his religious character, and the source of his enjoyments. I wish you could fully know what tranquillity of mind he possessed during the last six months. Confined to his house — then to his chamber, and with a very feeble and sometimes distressed bodily state, he had the peace of God which passeth all understanding. Self-righteousness he utterly renounced. He had nothing which he looked upon, as in any degree the ground of acceptance with God. All his benevolent and useful deeds he counted loss for the excellency of the knowledge of Christ. With the most lively sensations, and sometimes with weeping, he expressed his entire reliance on the mere mercy of God. He saw no other foundation. He desired no other.

He felt more and more satisfied, that in his religious charities he had been directed by the Spirit of God, and had done what he should rejoice in forever. He frequently expressed a hope, that his beloved Seminary would become far more extensively useful, than he at first conceived; that it would be the means not only of doing good to the churches in this country, but of spreading the gospel among distant heathen nations. Often, when contemplating the Institution in this light, did he turn his thoughts upon himself, and say, with every token of humility and tenderness, — "I am astonished, that God should make use of such a poor creature as I am, to do this great *work*."

In the chamber of sickness, frequent prayer was his delight and refreshment. He seemed more and more perfectly to resign himself to the will of his Father in heaven. He was tired of sin; though not tired of living in God's world; nor was he tired of laboring and suffering for God. "I desire to live," he often said, "if God has anything more for me to *do* or to *suffer*." His cheerful patience, meekness, and resignation, together with the uniform and regular exercise of his reason, rendered his sickness very edifying to his Christian friends.

When he came near to his home, he showed increasing desires after God, saying repeatedly — "there is enough in God; — I want nothing but God." Just before his speech failed, he was asked, whether he could say — "whom have I in heaven but thee? and there is none on earth I desire beside thee;" — "Yes," — he answered very feelingly — "*with all my heart, and with all my soul, and with all my mind.*" At times he felt a joy, almost too intense for his feeble body to sustain, at the thought of being forever with the Lord, and seeing him face to face.

With the mourning Widow the hearts of many most tenderly sympathize. In the midst of her grief she will not forget to thank God that, for *more than fifty years* she was blessed with a consort, who was an example of conjugal love and tenderness. May she be enabled to glorify God by pious resignation; and by continuing to walk in the steps of her inestimable friend, now sleeping in death. May her heart be cheered by the hope of meeting him in heaven. While she remains in this world of sorrow may the God of all grace and comfort grant her his presence.

This dispensation of providence imposes a sacred duty on all who are connected with this Seminary — the surviving Founders, Visitors, Trustees, Professors, and Students. We ought to humble ourselves under the mighty hand of God. We ought to praise the Giver of all good, for raising up such a benefactor, such a distinguished pattern of Christian beneficence. Above all, we ought to consider and fix in our minds, what was his object in his benefactions to this Seminary, and in what manner he has directed us to pursue that object. His death ought to be a new excitement to the faithful discharge of all our duties relative to this Sacred Institution. If we overlook his great object, disregard his directions, misapply his charity; and forget his love of union and peace, we shall be guilty of trampling his honor in the dust. If we do *this*, how can we meet him at the Judgment seat of Christ?

Beloved hearers, a *man of God* has been among you, and by divine grace shown you how to use this world, how to live, and how to die. I beseech you by his many exertions, sacrifices, and prayers for your good; by the piety and usefulness of his life; by his meekness and comfort in sickness; and by the rest, which we doubt not he now enjoys in God; — and I beseech you by the meeting you must have with him before the tribunal of Christ — by all these considerations, I earnestly beseech you, to remember the character of that godly man, to make a thankful and pious use of his bounties, and diligently walk in his steps; — and above all, to love and imitate his chosen Saviour, who was holy, harmless, undefiled, and separate from sinners.

SERMON

DELIVERED AT THE FUNERAL OF REV. SAMUEL SPRING, D. D., MARCH 9, 1819, IN NEWBURYPORT.

---

1 Thess. 5: 13.—AND TO ESTEEM THEM VERY HIGHLY IN LOVE FOR THEIR WORK'S SAKE.

THE Apostle Paul showed the highest respect for the ministers of Christ, and inculcated it, as the duty of all Christians, highly to esteem and love them. But he did not demand this peculiar regard for Christian teachers, because they were men of distinguished gifts, nor even because they were *good* men; but for their *work's* sake. It was on account of the *dignity* and *usefulness* of their *office*.

I know not, my respected hearers, how I can more effectually excite the reverence and love, which are due to that excellent minister, whose death we deplore, and give a right direction to the sorrow which fills your hearts, than by describing briefly *the usefulness of that sacred office which he sustained.* This is my particular object. Accordingly, although I am called on this occasion to honor the memory of one of the dearest friends that I ever had on earth, I shall aim to excite no veneration or love for him, except what is due on account of the holy office which he filled, and the manner in which he performed its duties.

Turn your thoughts, then, to the usefulness of a faithful minister of Christ. Consider him as a teacher of divine truth. This is the most obvious and most important view of the Christian minister's work. He publishes the word of God. He is the grand medium of communicating to the world the knowledge of the true religion. A sober examination of facts and of the nature of the case will show, that there is no way of keeping up, to any good purpose, the knowledge of divine truth in the world, but by the labor of Christ's ministers. Now it is through divine truth, that sinners are converted and saved. This is "the incorruptible seed," of which they are "born again." And it is the work of the Christian minister to make known this divine truth, to plant this incorruptible seed. And thus he becomes an active instrument in the salvation of sinners. And consider for a moment *the value of salvation.* Consider what it would be for one of you to *perish forever!* — for an immortal soul to be perpetually under the dominion of the most malignant, tormenting passions! What would it be for you, with all your faculties and sensibilities awake, to see yourself abhorred of God; to be cast away from his presence; to know by your own wretched experience, what is that indignation and wrath which he will render to his enemies, and how unspeakably precious that salvation must be, which implies deliverance from this everlasting misery! — Consider too what is the positive good implied in salvation; what it is to be adorned with divine grace; to bear the image of Christ; and after being made perfect in holiness, to dwell where Jesus is, and be forever filled with all his fulness. What would it be for you, a single child of Adam, to be delivered from all this misery, and raised to the enjoyment of all this blessedness! And how great would be the usefulness of the sacred office, if ministers should be successful in bringing all this eternal blessedness upon *you alone!* But this good is to be conferred upon thousands and millions. The kingdom of Christ will contain a great multitude which no man can number, of those who have been redeemed from among men. And the infinite good enjoyed by this kingdom of grace, is effected chiefly through the agency of ministers. Whatever is desirable and excellent in the holiness of the saints on earth or in heaven; whatever is precious in their everlasting joys, is related to the holy office of Christ's ministers, and is an illustration of its incomparable usefulness.

Thus far I have considered the sacred office in one comprehensive view. I might descend to many particulars. For in fact, Christians obey the divine precepts, grow in knowledge and grace, find strength and support in their trials, are faithful and useful, and become prepared for heaven, under the influence of those divine truths which it is the business of the ministry to inculcate. And do not Christians, who are deprived of the advantages of ministerial labor, generally exhibit symptoms of a dark, low, pining state?

The scheme of truth contained in the Bible, makes known the perfections of God and the principles of his government, vindicates his character and administration from the reproaches of a wicked world, illustrates his infinite grace in redemption, and points to a future state of retribution, where his glory will shine forth with ever-increasing splendor. Wherever this scheme of divine truth is faithfully declared, the character of God is placed in an honorable and glorious light. Where it is not declared, the divine glory is obscured. The manner, therefore, in which the character of God is likely to be regarded in the world, depends very much upon the agency of Christian ministers.

Is it important that social and civil order should be supported; that sound morality should prevail; and that mankind, delivered from violence and cruelty, should live in peace? Just so important is it, that the servants of Christ should faithfully preach the truths of revelation. For it is by the influence of those truths on the minds of men, that the violence of their passions is restrained, and those moral principles established, which are the basis of social and civil order. All that gives to Christian society superiority over the society of pagans, is owing, under God, to the influence of the teachers of religion. Only let the ambassadors of Christ cease to preach the truths of religion, and what would be the condition of the fairest part of the world one hundred years hence? What is the condition of those places in our own country, where the labor of faithful ministers has ceased, for half that period? What especially is the condition of those countries, where the voice of Christ's ministers has not been heard for ages? It is moral desolation. And this desolation would soon appear even in this land of the Puritans, if the place of Christian ministers, when removed by death, should not be supplied by other laborers. The garden of the Lord would be overrun with briars and thorns; its hedges would be broken down, and the wild beasts of the field would devour it.

I might expatiate upon the usefulness of a faithful minister of Christ, in relation to the particular church and society committed to his charge. It is by his plain and solemn addresses to Christians, and the influence of his example and his prayers, that they are excited to live unto God. It is by his wisdom, and fidelity, and persevering vigilance, that the church is built up, and its order and purity promoted. It is in a measure by his patient, affectionate labors, that the young are restrained from folly and vice, and trained up in the nurture and admonition of the Lord, and thus prepared to be useful members of the community. His friendship and pastoral visits are among the most precious blessings to every family, especially in times of trouble. How soothing to the feelings of the afflicted is the presence of a minister, who has a heart to weep with those who weep, and who knows how to make their grief tributary to their spiritual good. Ask the children of God, when they are sick and languishing, and find the time of their departure drawing near, whether any earthly good could be a compensation to them for the want of an affectionate, heavenly-minded minister. When such a one comes to their bed side, and with a sympathetic heart repeats to them the sure promises of God, converses with them of the glories of Christ and the joys of heaven, and unites with them in fervent prayer; they forget their pains, and their hearts swell with unutterable joy at the thought of being absent from the body and present with the Lord.

And how is it with dying *sinners*, who have hitherto slighted the instructions and warnings of the gospel? They send a hasty message for their minister. They long to hear his voice. For worlds they would not forego his instructions and prayers.

It would be interesting to contemplate the sacred office in relation to the Sabbath. For it is perfectly apparent, that the utility of that holy day depends essentially on Christian ministers. They must teach how that sacred rest is to be employed, so as to honor God, and profit immortal souls. Public worship, which is one of the most important duties of the Sabbath, is then only what it should be, when it is conducted by able ministers. The religious instruction which is to be given is not likely to answer the purpose, unless it comes from the ambassadors of Christ, whose work it is to study the Scriptures, and to speak in the name of God. The good which people derive from reading the Bible, depends much upon the discipline of mind which they receive from the labors of their spiritual guide. What is the Sabbath in those places where the labors of ministers have long ceased? Is it a day of spiritual rest? Or is it a day of idleness and dissipation?

But Christian ministers do not limit their useful labors to a single church or society. They stand in relation to the glorious Redeemer, and to his universal kingdom. They are his agents in the great work of promoting the welfare of that kingdom. What then is to be done for the kingdom of Christ? What are the means to be used, for the advancement of his holy cause? His ministers must be the chief agents in this work. They must open the book of prophecy, and proclaim the approach of the day, when the knowledge of the Lord shall fill the earth. By their moving addresses and their earnest cries to heaven, Christian churches and nations must be awakened to action, and must consecrate their wealth and their labors to the enlargement of the Redeemer's kingdom. Revivals of religion must take place throughout Christendom. Young men turned from their sins by the power of the Holy Ghost, must in great numbers be trained up for the service of the church. Those literary and religious institutions which are already in operation must be raised to a higher degree of prosperity; and many new ones must be added.

The gospel must be proclaimed in pagan lands. Dumb idols must be cast away, and temples of idol worship consecrated to Jehovah. All nations must be given to Christ for an inheritance. In all these movements of divine providence, the ministers of Christ must have a principal agency. The Lord of the universe has appointed them to this work, and has promised them strength to accomplish it. Let them take their place *thankfully*, for it is a place of high honor. Let them take their place *humbly*, for it is a place of self-denying labor. Let them take their place with *resolution* and *patience;* for it is a place of great *difficulty* and *suffering*. Let them march forward with steady pace, their eyes fixed on God, their hearts trusting in his strength, and panting to see the day when his kingdom shall come, and his will be done on earth as it is done in heaven.

Is it true that many, who do not bear the sacred office, are great and successful instruments in advancing the cause of Christ? These furnish no exception to the principle which I have asserted; for they all act under the influence of those moving truths, which are inculcated from the pulpit. They have heard the reign of Christ proclaimed. The preciousness of his cause, the wretched condition of a perishing world, the worth of salvation, the sure promises of God in favor of Zion, and the abundant evidence which the present day affords, that great things are soon to be done for the Redeemer's kingdom, have been impressed indelibly on their hearts by the ministry of reconciliation; and it is by these considerations, that they are excited to be diligent in business, fervent in spirit, and to abound in their labors and sacrifices for the cause of Christ.

From this brief illustration you perceive how important is the office of Christian ministers, and in how interesting a relation that office stands to all that is desirable and happy on earth. You learn the importance of this office, from all that is excellent and worthy of regard in those sacred truths which ministers explain and inculcate. You learn it from the infinite value of that salvation which is effected through their labors. When you look into the region of darkness, and into the world of glory, you learn how to regard the work of those, who are God's appointed instruments in delivering his people from the miseries of the one, and raising them to enjoy the blessedness of the other. You learn the usefulness of their office, from the growing knowledge and holiness of believers; their good works; their comfort in affliction; their peace, and hope, and triumph on the bed of death. You learn it from the salutary influence of the Sabbath, and the blessings of social and civil order. You learn it from the rising prosperity of the church; from all the mighty operations which are contributing to its increase; and from the glory with which it will shine, when all the kingdoms of the world shall bow to the sceptre of Jesus. You learn it, in a word, from all that alleviates the miseries of earth, or sheds radiance upon its gloom; and from all that lifts the eye of hope to mansions above the skies.

We are assembled brethren and friends to attend the funeral services of a venerable father in the ministry. All who are in any measure acquainted with the character of DOCTOR SPRING, and consider the usefulness to which he attained, as a minister of Christ, must respect his memory, and feel the sincerest sorrow at his decease.

I shall not attempt to give a particular recital of the events of his life, or a full description of his character. On his dying bed, when he expressed his desire that I should perform this mournful service, he left a special charge, that I should say but *little respecting him.*

For more than forty years, Doctor Spring was a minister of the gospel in this place. They, who have had the privilege of attending his ministry well know, with what ability and seriousness, with what clear discrimination and fidelity he declared the counsel of God. Few ministers have preached the word of God with greater simplicity and honesty, with greater freedom from that fear of man which bringeth a snare, or in a manner more instructive to the understanding, more awakening to conscience, or more affecting to the heart. The people of his charge will remember, and will delight to testify, with what strength of reasoning he demonstrated the great doctrines of religion, and with what earnestness and pungency of address, he enforced the obligation of its holy, self-denying duties. They will remember also, in what manner he went in and out before them, visited their families, conversed and prayed with the sick and the dying, consoled the afflicted, instructed the young, and labored for the order and purity of the church.

There is no blessing on earth, which a minister of Christ can hold dearer, than the affectionate attachment and confidence of his people. There is nothing, but the consideration of duty, which can operate as a stronger excitement to diligence; and nothing, but the presence and approbation of God, which can do more to render his labors delightful. I say this with special emphasis, respecting the esteem and love of real Christians. What are the best friendships, founded on mere natural affection, compared with the pure, spiritual love of fervent Christians toward a minister who has labored successfully for their salvation? Their love to him becomes associated with all the precious, heavenly truths which they have heard from his lips, and which the Spirit of God has rendered effectual to their sanctification. It is associated with the recollection of the solicitude he manifested for them while they were impenitent, of his labors and prayers for their conversion, and of the joy which swelled his heart, when he perceived the indications of their repentance. It is associated with the recollection of his watchful care over them, and his unceasing efforts to excite them to walk as children of light. It is associated finally, with the holy pleasures which he has helped them to enjoy, and with the precious hope which he has so often kindled in their breasts. So tender, so pure, and in its nature so permanent, is the love of Christians to their spiritual father and guide. Now in what way shall a minister secure this love and confidence of Christians, and the general attachment of those committed to his charge? The only way in which he ought to seek it, and in which he has any prospect of obtaining it, is, by being an *affectionate, faithful, devoted minister of Christ;* by preaching the truth as it is in Jesus, with the spirit of Jesus; thus commending himself to every man's conscience in the sight of God; by being willing to spend and be spent for the souls committed to his care; not seeking to please man, but God who trieth the heart; and yet, in the right sense, becoming all things to all men. Such, in a good measure, was the ministry of Doctor Spring. He gave himself to his work. He turned not aside to entangle himself with the affairs of the world. His conscience, his judgment, and his heart held him back from pursuits foreign to his office. It was in this way he gained the high place which he possessed in the respect and love of his flock. And he often lamented the mistake of ministers, who think they can obtain a lasting reputation for usefulness in any other way.

Doctor Spring had uncommon *strength* and *decision* of character. He was never disheartened by difficulties and never intimidated by dangers; and where duty was plain he was fearless of opposition and reproach. However many or great his afflictions, he was never overpowered. In pursuit of an object which conscience approved, who ever surpassed him in perseverance? He had, in fact, many attributes as a man and as a Christian, which qualified him for great undertakings. Accordingly, he did not labor and pray and live, for the interests of religion, merely in one particular place. He had too large a heart for this. In all the great operations of the present day for the promotion of the kingdom of Christ, he felt a lively interest; and in some of them he had a principal agency.

In behalf of Greenville College, in Tennessee, he exerted his influence with animating success. About the same time, the Massachusetts Missionary Society was formed. That useful Society was indebted to him as much as to any man, for its existence and prosperity.

But the highest objects which excited his affection, his zeal, and his prayers, are yet to be mentioned. Several years before anything was done in this quarter toward a Theological Institution it was with him a subject of deep thought and serious conversation. He regarded it as one of the most important branches of Christian beneficence, to *increase the number of well qualified ministers of the gospel.* No man ever felt more deeply the importance of a *learned ministry*, or pursued that object with a more steady purpose, or in a more disinterested manner. The influence with which it pleased God to favor him, in turning the attention of wealthy and benevolent individuals to such an object, and in giving existence and form to our favored Seminary, I shall not particularly mention; though the recollection of it is inexpressibly interesting to my feelings. In all the measures, which preceded the establishment of the united Institution, I was intimately conversant with him; and I am a witness of the invincible attachment to the cause of divine truth, which evidently actuated him; of the sleepless anxiety he showed, lest, in the plan of the Seminary, the great ends of revelation should be overlooked. It is with the most delightful sensations I now recollect, how often, at that interesting period, I was invited, sometimes in the stillness of midnight, to kneel down with him, to invoke the name of God, to render praise for his goodness, and to ask his guidance and blessing. I am a witness of his laborious and unceasing efforts in the cause of the Seminary from its commencement till his last sickness; of the joy and gratitude and tenderness which he often expressed, that he had lived to realize more than his highest hopes; and of the pious fervor with which he waked up, almost from the slumbers of death, to give the sacred Institution, and those connected with it, his dying benediction.

Doctor Spring was a father to the Seminary. He watched over its interests and prayed for its prosperity, with a father's heart. His visits, his conversation, and his addresses to the members of the Seminary, were expressions of paternal love. And we had reason to thank him, not only for his incessant watchfulness, but even for his *jealousy* over us; because it was a *godly jealousy*. The concern of an anxious father; — it was an apprehension, for which there was too much reason, that a spirit of literary pride should insinuate itself into the Institution, and the light of truth and holiness be obscured. But I cannot proceed. Scenes rush upon my memory, which language cannot describe. Thanks to God that such a man has been raised up to bless the church; that he was continued so long, and enabled to do so much for the Institution. But the scene is closed. Our friend sleepeth. On those occasions, when his visits have, for ten years, uniformly cheered us, and his counsels quickened us to duty, we shall see his face no more. Whenever those occasions return, we shall remember afresh the kindness of his heart, the fidelity of his counsels, and the usefulness of his labors for the Seminary.

Doctor Spring acted a most important part in originating the Foreign Mission from America. The measures which led to the organization of a public body for the promotion of that great object, were first suggested by him. And in the whole management of that benevolent and successful undertaking, he was among those who were entrusted with the principal agency.

Whoever, therefore, reviews the public life of Doctor Spring especially the last twenty years, must be satisfied, that few men have done more than he for the cause of Christ.

Were I to speak of what was peculiar in his Christian character, I should say he felt an uncommon loathing and dread of whatever had the least appearance of enthusiasm or ostentation in the concerns of religion. I should say too, that he had in an unusual degree, the habit of insisting upon the distinction between true and false religion and extraordinary caution in judging of the evidence of regeneration in himself, and in others. He professed to have only slender evidence of his own piety; and frequently said, *if he had any religion, he had it in a very low degree.* This may be thought a singular conclusion. But what Christian or minister does not adopt a similar conclusion respecting himself, who with equal honesty, searches his own heart, and with the same unsparing severity, tries his own motives and actions by the standard of God's word?

Doctor Spring was, however, a man of remarkable cheerfulness and equanimity. And though he had little enjoyment in view of his own religious character, he had unfailing enjoyment in contemplating the perfection and government of God and the truths of his word.

It would be a thing unheard of in this imperfect world, if any human character, even one possessing the most attractive virtues, should have no imperfections. Doctor Spring was not without imperfections He had himself a deep conviction of them, and made them the subject of daily confession before God. But he is gone, we believe, beyond the region of imperfection and trial. And, brethren, if our intercourse with him, while on earth, was so pleasant and profitable; Oh, what a privilege would it be, could we see and converse with him *now*, when his character, distinguished even *here* by such intellectual and moral excellences, has been freed from every clog and blemish, and displays, without mixture, the *beauties of holiness*.

The mourning widow and children are called to submit to no ordinary affliction. They have frequently known the day of adversity. But they have never before experienced the grief of losing a friend so near and so useful. What can I do for their comfort, but to remind them of those heavenly truths which he preached, of that all-sufficient Saviour whom he so often recommended to them, and whose infinite grace he always found a refuge in trouble?

What shall I say to this mourning church and society? Your beloved minister was indeed spared to you many years; he lived to a good old age. But he has finished his work and gone to receive his reward. Look back, now, upon his ministry, ye who were converted or edified by his labors. Remember the earnest exhortations he gave you to watchfulness and self-denial, to persevering diligence, fidelity and prayer. Remember what zeal he showed that you might increase in the knowledge of God and abound in good works. It is a privilege for which you ought to give thanks to God, that you have had such a minister. But now, brethren, as he is removed by death, you will be looking and praying for some man of God to supply his place.— Great Shepherd of Israel, be near to this destitute, mourning flock; preserve them from evil; keep them perfectly joined together in faith and love; and speedily provide for them a pastor after thine own heart.

Fathers and brethren in the ministry, see in that breathless body, that silent tongue, and those eyes closed in death, to what *we* are coming. It is all that remains of that minister, who was once so active, so useful and beloved. A few more Sabbaths, and it will be all that will remain of *us*. Let us then be excited to *finish our work*. If we love Christ and the souls of men, we are desirous of doing good; and we have our plans of doing good. How grievous would it be, should we be overtaken by death, before our favorite plans are accomplished! Let us then, as ministers of Christ, lay out the business of life wisely, and execute it with all diligence. And let us begin in season, to do our *last* works. We may be looking for an opportunity in some distant period, to perform those things which belong to the closing scene of life. But let us beware of trusting to this. A sudden removal, without any premonition, may await us. Or if God shall kindly exempt us from such a stroke, we may still lose the opportunity we are expecting. When our health declines, our mental vigor may also decline. He that has the strongest understanding, may then exhibit the understanding of an infant, or no understanding at all. The power of speech, the power of action, and the power of thought may fail us; and all those things which we deferred to the end of life, may be left undone forever. Let us then be doing our *last* things. Let us be saying our last words to our partners and our children. Let us be writing our last sermons, and our last letters. Let us be making our last addresses to our flocks. Let us be performing our last acts of Christian friendship toward our brethren in the ministry, and our last acts of benevolence for the promotion of the cause of Christ. And when we go into our closets, let us feel, as though we were about to search our hearts and raise our cries to our God and Saviour for the last time before the all-revealing day. O brethren, if we might be duly affected with such a sentiment as this, it would cure the vanity of our minds; it would impress the character of seriousness and piety upon our daily conduct, and would effectually constrain us to preach and live as *dying men*.

Let us learn one more lesson. However beloved and venerated the ministers of Christ may be — however elevated and useful their station — *they must die*. What then is most important to a minister when he comes to the close of life? What is it but the manner in which he has treated his Saviour and his own soul, and discharged the duties of his holy office? If he can then say, "*I know in whom I have believed; I have fought a good fight, I have finished my course, I have kept the faith; henceforth there is laid up for me a crown of righteousness, which the Lord the righteous Judge will give me at that day;*"—what more can he desire?

Finally, though *under shepherds* die, the *great Shepherd* lives. He will take care of his sheep and his lambs; not one of them shall perish. His cause is safe. And as an encouragement to diligent exertion, let us consider what a train of good effects may result from our labors. We have contemplated the distinguished usefulness of that venerable minister, whose funeral solemnities we are now attending. But we shall find, that the highest instances of his usefulness were consequent upon a few efforts of enlightened piety, which we might have thought of inconsiderable moment. Those few efforts have, through divine favor, had a leading influence to set in motion engines of good, whose operation already begins to be felt in various parts of the Christian and pagan world, and whose blessed effects, uniting with the effects of other plans of benevolence, will we doubt not, constantly spread to a wider and wider extent, and reach to the end of time, and to everlasting ages. Brethren, we live in a period highly favorable to the accomplishment of great designs. Let us be meditating good for Zion, and striving in one way and another, to promote its prosperity. Who can tell what holy enterprises, what useful institutions, and what enlargement to Christ's kingdom, may spring from our feeble efforts? Our seasons of meditation and prayer, our studies, our consultations, and our correspondence, may, through the blessing of God, give rise to a good, which eternity only can measure. Let us then be up and doing. And when God summons faithful ministers to leave their place here, and engage in the work of heaven, let us still trust in him and take courage. He is the Lord of the harvest, and will send forth other laborers. He will not leave his cause without advocates, nor his churches without pastors, nor the heathen world without missionaries.

After we are laid in our graves other ministers will rise up better than we; for a better day is at hand. The churches will shine with brighter lustre. A purer spirit will pervade the ministry; a spirit of deeper humility, of more fervent love, and more perfect harmony, a spirit of greater wisdom and zeal, a spirit of higher effort and more exalted piety. Great will be the company of those who will publish the word of the Lord, and great the success which will crown their labors. The fervent prayers offered up by our lamented father, and by the thousands now with him in glory, and the prayers of thousands on earth now panting for the conversion of the world, will be answered, in the universal reign of the Prince of Peace.

A SERMON

OCCASIONED BY THE DEATH OF THE REV. SAMUEL WORCESTER, D. D., SECRETARY OF THE AM. BOARD OF COMMISSIONERS FOR FOREIGN MISSIONS; DELIVERED IN THE TABERNACLE CHURCH, SALEM, JULY 12, 1821.

---

1 Sam. 25: 1.—AND SAMUEL DIED; AND ALL THE ISRAELITES LAMENTED HIM.

WHENEVER a good man dies, the world sustains a loss. But among good men, there is an obvious ground of distinction. God has constituted his moral kingdom, as he has the natural body. Though there is but one body, there are many members. And though the members are all necessary; some hold a place of higher importance than others, and the loss of them is more severely felt. When the Apostle touches upon this distinction among Christians, he does it for the purpose of stigmatizing a spirit of emulation and envy, and of promoting mutual love and sympathy, and a paramount regard to the good of the whole. And why should the difference, which God has made among the members of his spiritual empire, ever excite any other feelings, than these? For what is the difference, but a difference in the degree of usefulness? That man is marked with the highest distinction, who does the most good. True greatness is combined with the best interest of the world. And if we love the best interest of the world, we shall love the man who promotes it;

and we shall love him most, who promotes it in the highest degree. In the contemplation of the great object which benevolence seeks, we are raised above self-interest. We forget our individual importance; we forget all personal distinctions. Let the highest degree of good be accomplished, whether by us or by others as instruments, and we have our desire. Mere intellectual greatness, or worldly greatness is indeed an object, to which ambition looks up with impatient aspirations. But what is it in the sight of God, or in the sight of good men? It is the greatness of *Christian benevolence*, that we admire; it is the greatness, not of the man who *has* superior endowments, but of the man, whose superior endowments are devoted to the cause of Christ; the greatness of the man, who, feeling that he is not his own, presents himself a living sacrifice to God, and exists only for the welfare of his kingdom. This is the greatness that disarms hostility, that puts envy to shame, that attracts universal love, and that does not moulder in the grave.

I propose on this occasion, to inquire briefly, *by what causes and in what manner the character of true greatness is formed.*

Here I begin by ascribing to God all that constitutes excellence of character — all that fits men for distinguished usefulness. *In God's hand it is to make great.* He creates and sustains the immortal mind with all its powers. He creates and sustains the body, with all its vigor and activity. And it is by his Spirit that a man is *new-created* — "created in Christ Jesus unto good works." Everything which gives improvement to the understanding or the heart, is from God. Let it be that the powers of the mind are cultivated and strengthened by the use of various *natural means*. Who appointed those means but God? And who but God gives a heart to use them, and makes that use successful? Be it so that Christians are sanctified *through the truth.* It is God that sanctifies them in this very way. The *truth* is his instrument; and from him comes all its efficacy. When therefore you fix your eye upon a Christian, who exhibits the character of distinguished greatness; you see the *workmanship of God* — the expression of his power and his goodness.

The Christian is what he is, *by the grace of God.* To God then be all the glory of those faculties, which distinguish men from the beasts of the field; of that holiness, which distinguishes Christians from the ungodly; and of every degree of piety and usefulness, which raises one Christian above another.

I shall now endeavor to show *in what way a Christian, possessing the requisite natural endowments, and enjoying the guidance and blessing of God acquires the character of true greatness.*

In the first place, he directs the powers of his mind to *the most excellent and worthy object — the salvation of men — the good of Christ's kingdom.* If a man turns his thoughts and labors to the good of his country, his heart grows patriotic and noble. But if he exercises his thoughts and affections upon Christ and his kingdom, the effect on his character will be as much higher, as the glory of Christ and the value of his kingdom are more excellent, than any earthly object. The heart becomes assimilated to the object of its attachment. He that contemplates and loves the character of Christ, is by degrees changed into the same image. He that employs himself in so great a work as building up the kingdom of Christ, will be constantly ennobled by the nature of his employment. He will derive a greatness from the greatness of the work in which he is occupied.

But the Christian, who acquires the character of greatness, contemplates the glory of Christ, and pursues the welfare of his kingdom *with intense affection.* And it is very much in proportion to the frequency and strength of his benevolent and pious efforts, that he experiences a salutary influence upon his own mind. When a man comes to such a state, that the glory of the Redeemer and the precious interests of his church are the objects of his contemplation from day to day; when they occur spontaneously; when other things, which formerly had a place in his mind, in a great measure retire; when these divine objects get so strong a hold of his thoughts, that no pleasures, no cares or sufferings can exclude them; in short, when his attachment to the cause of Christ becomes his ruling passion; then he experiences a rapid growth in everything excellent and praise-worthy. Whatever is earthly in his nature dies away. His thoughts and affections range in a higher and brighter region. He acquires moral purity, enlargement and strength, and advances rapidly towards the elevated character of just men made perfect.

My brethren, do any of you aim at eminence in Christian piety and usefulness? See here what course you must pursue. And see here the course actually pursued by *that distinguished servant of Christ*, who has recently been taken from us. Beloved man! Wherever his name is known, not only among those who were personally attached to him, but through the Christian world, it is associated with all that is precious in the cause of the Redeemer.

Our departed brother was, in the best sense, a man of *distinguished excellence*. He possessed eminent qualifications, and attained to eminent usefulness. The qualities of his understanding and heart were such, as would have rendered him beloved and useful in any condition. Had he lived in the most retired village; the inhabitants would have been enlightened by his wisdom, and benefited by his pious example and benevolent services. Had he lived in days of persecution, and had the power of his enemies immured him in a prison; he possessed excellences of character, which would have been manifested even there. His meekness and self-government would have checked the impatience of his fellow sufferers; his affectionate counsels would have enlightened and comforted them; and the ardor of his prayers and praises would have taught them the happiness of devotion.

But his peculiar greatness arose very much from the *circumstances in which he was placed* and *the relations which he sustained.* It is indeed very obvious, that he had an original structure of mind, exactly suited to the work which God designed for him. Still it was his situation — it was his being actually called to his work, and successfully engaged in accomplishing it, which made known the value of his talents, and led to their highest improvement. In a very important sense, *a man is made by circumstances.* The time when he lives; the particular place where he acts; the dispositions and pursuits of those with whom he is most nearly connected; the nature of the duties allotted to him, and the degree of success by which his labors are animated, all conspire to impart to his character the qualities which it finally exhibits.

I have no doubt that a skilful biographer, well acquainted with the early life of Doctor Worcester, could fix upon a variety of incidents, which tended at once to unfold the peculiar properties of his mind, and to produce those habits of thought and action, which afterwards became chief ingredients in his character. God knows for what service he designs every man; and he frequently gives such a direction to the events of childhood and youth, that those peculiar properties of mind, which will be of the highest use in after-life, shall be early exercised and strengthened; and while the man himself and those around him know nothing of the matter, God is preparing him for his work; and preparing him by means, which will afterwards be seen to have been exactly suited to the end, and so will be a subject of grateful acknowledgment and admiration.

But my remarks can extend no further, than to the commencement of his public life.

He was first called to discharge the duties of a Christian minister in a situation attended with peculiar trials. And those trials were important means of qualifying him for the work which divine providence allotted to him. No man ever acquires strength and decision of character, without contending with difficulties. If all is smooth and prosperous, the mind contracts inactivity and softness. But the frequent occurrence of straits and sufferings raises a mind, happily constituted, to a high tone of resolution, and prepares it for firm and energetic action.

Our brother before his removal from his first charge, gave evidence of uncommon discretion and forethought; of patience and self-control; of great strength of understanding and integrity of heart, and a steady attachment to the interests of the church.

In the year 1803, he entered on the duties of the ministry in this place. The station was highly important; and it involved duties, which no man of ordinary qualifications would have been competent to discharge. Here he labored with wisdom and zeal, with firmness and perseverance. He kept his eye upon the spiritual interests of the church. A revival of religion, which he was permitted more than once to witness as the fruit of his labors, he regarded as the most desirable of all events. As a preacher, he exhibited soundness of faith, manly strength of intellect, a cultivated taste, and a warm heart. His preaching was always serious, affectionate, and instructive, and frequently impressive. His church and people knew — every parent and every child knew, that he loved their souls, and sought their everlasting welfare. In all cases of difficulty, which occurred in the church or congregation, he was a most judicious counsellor; in affliction, a friend, a father, a comforter. *He magnified his office.* It is a rare thing that a minister enjoys, in an equal degree with him, the affection and esteem of his people. And I wish I were not obliged to say, that it is a rare thing for a minister, in an equal degree, to love the sacred office. There was nothing more distinctly marked in his character, than the strong, permanent affection which united him to the pastoral work. He cleaved to it, as to his life. With this close adherence of his affections to the holy office, he could not but become more and more assimilated to the objects, with which that office made him conversant. The regular performance of its duties, prompted by his *heart* as well as his conscience, imparted an increasing purity and elevation to his character. If I mistake not, it was evident to his friends generally, that he became more and more a consecrated man. This, I am aware, is to be ascribed to the effectual operation of God. But God operates through means. And I cannot but think, that one of the principal means of his spiritual improvement was, the diligence, the affection, and the pleasure, with which he discharged the duties of the ministry. His employments as a minister, animated by the true spirit of his office, contributed directly and powerfully, to advance him in the exercise of every virtue, and to give him the visible impress of Christian sanctity.

But Dr. Worcester's usefulness extended beyond his particular charge. His reputation for practical wisdom, and for an acquaintance with the principles and forms of ecclesiastical proceedings in

New England, occasioned frequent applications to him for counsel and assistance. And the public sentiment respecting him was finally such, that scarcely an instance occurred of great difficulty in our churches, where his advice was not sought. The collected thought, the foresight, the decision, which he exhibited in the business of ecclesiastical councils, gave him great influence with those who agreed with him in principle, while they secured to him the honest respect of his opposers. But by nothing did he more distinguish himself in such concerns, than by his sincere love of peace, and his success in reconciling contending parties.

The frequent agency he had in the transaction of ecclesiastical business brought him into a closer connection with the ministers and churches of Christ, made him more familiarly acquainted with their circumstances, and gave him a more lively interest in their welfare, and at the same time it gained for him, in a higher and higher degree, the public confidence, and prepared the way for him to enter, with brighter prospects, into a more extensive sphere of public duty.

Dr. Worcester's feelings were averse to religious controversy; though the peculiar structure of his mind, and his habit of close, patient thinking qualified him to be a distinguished controversial writer. I shall only say on this occasion, that those who receive the common doctrines of orthodoxy, must consider it as a special favor of heaven, that they have, I will not say the *opinions*, but the *arguments* of Dr. Worcester on the grand controversy of the present day.

But I have not yet mentioned what chiefly accounts for the elevation of our dear brother's character, or chiefly constituted the usefulness of his life. I refer to *his connection with the Missionary cause;* first, with *the Massachusetts Missionary Society*, of which he was many years *Secretary*, and afterwards *President;* and then with *our Foreign Missions*. I say not that there is any office on earth, more exalted and holy, than the *Christian ministry*, or any object more important than that which the ministry is designed to promote. The fact is, the *missionary cause* is the same as that, which every minister labors to advance. It is the same cause, taken in a more extended sense. It is the cause of benevolence — the cause of Christ, in relation to the whole unevangelized world. And the office which our departed brother filled, in connection with the missionary cause, was the office of a Christian minister, in its largest sense. As to the extent of its design, it resembles the office of the apostles, who were commissioned to "go into all the world, and preach the gospel to every creature." Now if I would show you exactly what Dr. Worcester was; if I would fix your eye upon the highest distinction which marked his character; I must present him before you, as *Corresponding Secretary of the American Board of Commissioners for Foreign Missions.* It was for this office he was designated in the purpose of God. It was for this office, so important and arduous, that all his previous labors and trials contributed to prepare him. It was in this office, that his peculiar talents found room for their most appropriate exercise. *Here* he was in his proper place. And *here*, through the mercy of God, his character acquired its brightest lustre.

Can it be necessary for me, in this age of Christian knowledge and Christian effort, to produce *arguments* to prove the importance and excellence of the missionary cause? Are there any among us, who will award to our departed brother the honor of sincere and pious endeavors, and yet doubt the soundness of his judgment in directing them to the accomplishment of such an object? Are there any, who can witness the zeal, the liberality, the sacrifices and prayers, which are employed for the promotion of the missionary cause, and say, that they are all employed in a useless or doubtful enterprise — that the cause they are designed to promote is not worthy of such exertions — and that the man who devotes his life to that cause, though he may deserve our candor for his honesty, and our respect for his talents, and our love for the goodness of his heart, must have our compassion for his weakness? Gladly would I remove the doubts and misapprehensions of any who view the cause of missions in such a light. And gladly would I excite the active zeal of those who have better views.

Will you then estimate the importance of the missionary cause from *its design?* What is that design, but *the salvation of sinners perishing in the darkness of paganism?* Now are not the souls of men in heathen lands *immortal* as well as *ours?* And is not *their* immortality stamped with as great worth, as ours? If then we deem it important that *our* souls should be saved, and *our* immortal existence be made happy; it is equally important that those who are in pagan countries, should obtain the same blessings. Has not all Christendom pronounced that to be an excellent precept, which requires us *to love our neighbors as ourselves?* And can any one, who is guided by this rule, and who has any proper regard to his own eternal happiness, think lightly of the eternal happiness of his fellow-creatures? But if the salvation of the heathen is so important; no man can question the importance of those efforts, which are directed to the single purpose of furnishing them with the means of salvation, and of making them heirs of all its blessings. If, indeed, the human race were in such a moral condition, as the lax theology of the day represents; if men had no depravity to be subdued by the power of the Holy Spirit; if they had no sins to be pardoned and no pollution to be washed away by atoning blood; and if those, who have never known the name of Jesus, had as good a prospect of heaven, as any in Christian lands; we might quiet all our anxieties respecting the heathen, and indulge feelings of sincere benevolence towards them, without any efforts for their conversion. And I am very willing to concede, that for those, who deny what we believe to be the doctrines of revelation in regard to the character and prospects of man, it is every way consistent to think the missionary cause of no value, and to look with indifference on all that is done to convert the heathen world. But if all men are "by nature children of wrath;" and if there is no other name under heaven whereby they can be saved, but the name of Jesus; and if the preaching of the gospel is the appointed means of bringing men to enjoy that salvation; then it is utterly impossible to separate the exercise of *benevolence* from the cause of *missions;* and no friend of man can be content, without making every possible exertion to send the gospel to all nations. Did the Son of God deem it necessary to come down from heaven, and suffer and die, to procure salvation for sinners? And can we deem it of no consequence that they should be made acquainted with that salvation? If Christianity is of any value to us, it is certainly of as great value to the heathen. Was not the Christian religion a blessing to those who were converted by the labors of the apostles? Was it not a blessing to our forefathers in Europe, who were turned from the basest idolatry, and made members of Christ's kingdom? Think of the difference between us, and the people of those countries where pagan ignorance prevails. To what is all this difference owing, but to *the Christian religion?* And must not those labors be important, which are one day to secure to idolatrous nations all that is precious in our holy religion, and to render them as enlightened, as pious, as happy, as the best Christians here? Just imagine all the millions of Asia, Africa and America, who are now in a state of heathenism, formed into Christian churches, engaged publicly and privately in worshipping God, observing all the commands and ordinances of the gospel, and living as examples of righteousness and peace. See parents, once bowing down to dumb idols, and practising the most degrading, vices, now walking before their households in uprightness of heart, and bringing up their children in the nurture and admonition of the Lord. See children listening to the voice of Christian instruction. See angels rejoicing over sinners brought to repentance. See believers abounding in good works; in affliction, submitting to God; in death, rejoicing in hope of eternal glory. Would not such a state be infinitely better, than their present state of stupid idolatry, and of brutal ignorance and wretchedness? The friends of the missionary cause are attempting to accomplish all this; and to accomplish it, not for one generation, but for all generations, to the end of time. Where is the man, that can question the excellence of this attempt? And who, that loves his fellow-creatures, can refrain from rejoicing in the most distant hope, that the attempt will be successful? And are we forbidden to indulge this hope? Is the conversion of the heathen world impracticable? Has not God power enough and benevolence enough to convert them? Are not the provisions of the gospel sufficiently large and abundant? Is not the way that is opened to heaven sufficiently broad? Have not many actually been converted, who were once as far from righteousness as they? We indeed believe that the heathen are much more depraved and degraded, and much more disinclined to embrace the gospel, than the opposers of missions believe them to be. We see more and mightier obstacles, than they do, to the success of the missionary cause. But we find no reason for despair. Were the difficulties in the way of Christianizing the heathen far greater than they are; we should still have confident hopes of success; hopes resting, not on the natural tendencies of the heart, nor on the efficacy of human persuasion to counteract those tendencies; but on the promise of God, and on that divine grace which superabounds where sin hath abounded. The conversion of the world, though impossible for man, is an easy work for God. It required as great an effort of divine power and divine love to save *any of us*, as it would require to save stupid idolaters. And as God is the common Father of men, and is no respecter of persons; why should we suppose he will confine his special favors to a small portion of our race? Why should we form such an opinion of that Being who made the world, and whose tender mercies are over all his works, as to think, that he is not as willing to exert his power in behalf of the heathen, as in *our* behalf; or that he will not be as ready to prosper our endeavors to convert sinners in heathen lands, as in our own country?

But it is unnecessary for me to dwell on this subject. For it seems impossible, that any man who regards the Christian religion as a *blessing*, should not desire its universal diffusion, or that he should not rejoice in the exertions now made to bring the whole world under its influence. Objections against the missionary cause are consistent enough from the mouths of infidels. But for *Christians* to make them, is a shocking absurdity.

Here then we have a cause of the highest conceivable moment. Other enterprises for the welfare of man are benevolent and useful. But the *missionary* cause is superior to all others. It is more benevolent, more exalted, more glorious. It aims at nothing less, than to communicate the blessings of the everlasting gospel through the whole extent of the earth's population. And notwithstanding all the difficulties which stand in its way, and which are so apt to discourage our faint hearts, it has a certain prospect of success. The undertaking, in which the friends of missions are now engaged, is one upon which future generations will look back, as we do upon the labors of the apostles and succeeding missionaries, in Christianizing particular parts of the world. They will look back, and bless God, that he put it into the hearts of his people at this day, to begin this work of love; and they will bless God for its accomplishment. And when converted myriads shall call to mind the commencement of those efforts, which brought them to the knowledge of the truth, they will remember our lamented Worcester, and will associate his name with what was done for their salvation. In the history of the church, Christians will, from generation to generation, read the history of our honored *Secretary*, and will form a juster estimate, than we can, of the importance of the office which he filled, and of the cause which he promoted.

My hearers will not, I hope, charge me with a needless digression in what I have said, when they consider that the character of Dr. Worcester was identified with the *missionary cause.* If the missionary cause is insignificant; so must we consider the man who made an offering of himself for its advancement. But if that cause is great and excellent — if it is, in truth, the cause of human salvation, the cause of infinite love; then the character of the man, who had so distinguished an influence in promoting it, must have a corresponding greatness and excellence.

In every office which our Corresponding Secretary previously sustained, he so united talent and fidelity, as to gain an honorable place in the public esteem. But in this last office, he appeared before the world with a character of more finished excellence. Here all his talents and acquisitions, as a scholar and a minister, and all his virtues as a Christian, combined their influence to produce one grand result. And when we look at his agency in this great concern, we see what God intended by *the peculiarities* of his character. In this his peculiarities were all turned to account. They conspired with the other attributes of his mind to produce in him such a remarkable fitness for his work, that no one could doubt for what God designed him. Our beloved Secretary was as manifestly in his proper place in the kingdom of Christ, as the hand or the head is in its proper place in the natural body. In the station which he finally held, he exhibited a greater symmetry and a stronger expressiveness of character, than ever before. And now, you might as well think of doing justice to the character of Paul, without exhibiting him as the Apostle to the Gentiles, as to the character of Dr. Worcester, without exhibiting him in this highest and most arduous sphere of his labors.

Learn the manner in which he filled this office, from facts. Learn it from those Reports of the Board which he wrote, especially the two last. Learn it from his correspondence with the missionaries, should that interesting correspondence ever be made public. Learn it from the character of our missionary establishments in different parts of the world. I think it impossible that any competent judge should not perceive the superior wisdom which these establishments display. They are all adapted to permanent operation, and to permanent and increasing success. They are conducted so manifestly according to the dictates of sober, Christian judgment, that they have already done much towards silencing the objections of opposers, and will, I am confident, soon unite all candid, pious men in the cause of missions. Learn too the manner in which our brother filled his office, from the influence he had with the community, and the success which uniformly attended his earnest appeals to them, in behalf of the funds of the Board. The American people are a discerning people, and when possessed of sufficient evidence, are not prone to judge incorrectly. They would not invest a man with the highest degree of influence, unless his conduct entitled him to confidence. Had there been any material defect in the qualifications of our Secretary, or had there been anything exceptionable or suspicious in his public or private conduct; the treatment he would have had from the community would have been very different from what it was. The various plans of missionary operation, adopted by the Prudential Committee, have repeatedly involved the Board in expenses, far beyond their resources. Had the good people of our country suspected any want of wisdom in those expensive plans, or in him who had a principal agency in concerting them; they would not, at his solicitation, have so promptly increased their contributions, and so generously relieved the embarrassments of the Board.

The evidences of the distinguished character of our Secretary, which I have now suggested, are before the public. But there are other evidences, which have necessarily been concealed from the public eye; I mean the steady, long-continued intenseness of his mental labors in private, and the part sustained by him in the deliberations of the Prudential Committee. Could the friends of our Foreign Missions have seen him in those deliberations, and those intense labors of mind, they would have seen him in his strength; and would have learned something of the secret spring of those systematic movements, by which the American Board and American Christians have been aiming to enlighten and save the heathen.

It was one of the peculiar excellences of Dr. Worcester, that he had the habit of investigating a subject more patiently and thoroughly, and, in difficult cases, of suspending his judgment longer, than most other men. His mind was not indeed distinguished for that rapidity of thought, which might have helped him to decide and act with promptness as well as propriety, in ordinary concerns, but which, in business of great weight and difficulty, might have proved an essential disqualification. He had the superior advantage of that slower and more exact movement of thought, of that longer reach of intellect, and that more particular and more consummate deliberation, which qualified him to look through all the relations of a complicated subject; to foresee the distant results of the measures under consideration; to foresee dangers, and by seasonable precaution to avoid them; and to carry forward a systematic plan, involving interests of the greatest conceivable moment, to a gradual, but sure accomplishment. In these vast concerns he had nothing that savored of presumption; nothing precipitate; nothing showy, visionary, or extravagant; and nothing of transient utility. He took time to form his judgment; but when formed, it seldom needed reconsideration. I might say of him, and of the other principal agent of the American Board, what could be said of few men living, that such was the fairness and thoroughness of their investigations, and the judiciousness of their decisions, that it was scarcely necessary to *inquire* into the expediency or feasibility of any measure, which they deliberately recommended.

It must be considered as a special token of divine favor, that a man of such a character was raised up at a time, when exertions so extensive and so difficult were to be made, and that he was permitted to devote himself so long to the concerns of our Foreign missions. Gladly would I increase the public esteem and affection which generally fall to the lot of men, who become public agents in business so weighty and complicated. The cares, and labors, and anxieties, to which they are incessantly exposed, would, if fully known, excite more general sympathy.

It was one of the most valuable qualifications of Dr. Worcester, that difficulties and dangers, however various and unexpected, never disconcerted him. He could meet with many a discomfiture, without being either subdued or discouraged. In those emergencies, which agitate and overwhelm men of ordinary minds, he collected new strength and rose to higher animation and to mightier efforts. In many cases which occurred in the prosecution of his business, he could see no present means of relief. Difficulties multiplied, and put on an appalling aspect. But in him, there was no sinking, no trembling. The ultimate success of the undertaking was inseparably connected in his mind, with the almighty agency and faithfulness of God. He had confidence that great things would be done. At times his way was hedged up with difficulties. But he had no doubt the difficulties would be cleared away. Now it was a night of thick darkness. But he expected the morning would come with its cheering light. In the greatest straits, he was so entirely a stranger to that despondency which enervates the mind, that he was all the while spontaneously preparing himself for more powerful action. When others were disheartened, then was the time for him to go forward. Under every pressure, he acquired more intense ardor of feeling in favor of his object, and became more fruitful in arguments to prove its excellence, and in expedients to secure its accomplishment.

I shall mention one more property which belonged to our departed brother; namely, that in regard to the various objects of Christian benevolence, his mind was *well balanced* and his zeal *well proportioned.* I do not mean, that he gave such a portion of his own thoughts and labors to each object, as agreed exactly with its comparative importance. No intelligent being, who is not infinite, can do this. But I mean, that his judgment was not so biassed by the business which engrossed his attention, that he overlooked the importance of what other good men were striving to accomplish. He guarded in a good measure against the fault, to which every man in a public station is liable, namely, that of looking so earnestly at his own particular object, as to lose sight of others. Although he was occupied constantly with the labors of an office so public in its nature, and so extensive in its design; he never ceased to feel the importance or to love the duties of the pastoral office. Nor did his zeal for Foreign missions prevent his feeling a deep interest in missionary efforts for the benefit of our own country, or in any other works of Christian charity. It was obvious to him, and it was a sentiment which he took pleasure in cherishing and expressing, that the various objects, which Christians are now laboring to accomplish, are in the most important respects one, and are all entitled to a far more liberal and efficient patronage, than they have ever yet received.

I have now portrayed the leading features of Dr. Worcester's public character. I have represented him as a man of distinguished eminence in the church. But in what did his eminence mainly consist? He had nothing of that brilliancy of genius or eloquence, and nothing of that enchanting popularity of manners, which gains admiration and applause from the multitude. He indeed had a powerful and well cultivated mind, and a taste of no ordinary refinement. But his eminence chiefly consisted in his rightly filling an office of vast and eternal consequence — an office involving labors, burdens and anxieties, which are insupportable to mere human strength. It consisted in his pursuing the business of that office with intensity of thought; with simplicity of aim; with inextinguishable zeal, and with the perseverance and activity of a man, who knows the greatness and goodness of his undertaking, and who, relying not on the resources of his own mind, but on the help of God, and on the uncontrollable movements of his providence, resolves on its execution. It consisted, in short, in his consecrating himself and all that he had to a cause superlatively excellent, and in his studying and laboring earnestly for its advancement.

But we must come to the closing scene of a life, which was so full of great and useful actions. Unremitted labor had created or increased various bodily infirmities. Those infirmities had for some time been assuming a more and more alarming aspect. The consent of our brother to visit the establishments at Brainerd and Elliot was in part produced by his solicitude for the missionary cause in those places, and in part by a desire to repair that constitution, which his long-continued labors had almost undermined. It may seem full of mystery, that he should be removed far away from his family and friends to die in the wilderness. What could have appeared more desirable to us, than that, in his last sickness, his pains should be alleviated and his heart comforted, by the tender assiduities of his own beloved family. And what could have appeared to be more desirable, or to promise more good to the missionary cause, than for his fellow-laborers to have some seasons for free consultation with him in his last days, and to be made acquainted with the views and emotions, which must have been produced in a mind so mature and elevated as his, by the visible approach of death.

But it was the appointment of God that he should go far hence, to sicken and die. The pains he took to learn the will of God respecting his absence, and the considerations which finally convinced his hesitating judgment of the expediency of the voyage, stated particularly in a letter to the Treasurer, must have given entire satisfaction to the public. So must his subsequent reflections, as exhibited in the same letter. — "It has been," he says, "no slight satisfaction to my mind, that I came hither in obedience to God's direction, and not, as I would humbly trust, without some degree of filial submission, and confidence, and hope. What the end is to be, is not yet to be read. It may be the final exit from all earthly scenes, and the dropping of this slender tabernacle, though far away from its kindred dust, yet in the place, whether in the sea, or upon the land, appointed by sovereign goodness for its rest till the rising day. — It may be the accomplishment of something for life and immortality to the wanderers of the wilderness, or dwellers in the dark places of the earth, by an instrumentality so feeble, as to make it manifest — that the excellency of the power must have been of God." "At the age of fifty, with a family requiring a father's as well as a mother's care — a people holding his heart with a thousand ties — a study, his loved retreat, 'Fast by the oracles of God' — responsibilities the most weighty, and objects of attention and action for which only he would live and labor — one could not leave home for an absence so long and with prospects so precarious, without many reluctances and regrets, and thoughts of serious import, and movements of the inmost heart." — "But what is time, or place, or outward condition? — God is at all times, and in all places the same; and to feel that we are in him and he in us, is enough for happiness. To feel that we are where he would have us be, and doing what he would have us do, is all that for ourselves we should desire."

In the following quotation from the same letter, he expresses his mature, unwavering judgment as to the cause of missions. — "One thing is settled in my mind; and that is a full and delightful conviction, that the cause of missions has never held too high a place in my estimation, or engaged too large a share of my attention. — It immeasurably transcends the highest estimation of every created mind. And what is the sacrifice of health, what the sacrifice of life, to such a cause? Be the event what it may — recovered health, or early death — I never can regret what I have done in this work; but only that I have done so little, and with a heart so torpid."

It would be highly interesting to trace the progress of our beloved brother, amid weariness, infirmity and pain, from New Orleans to our Indian establishments. The heart of Jacob was not more fondly set on going down to Egypt and seeing Joseph before he died, than his heart was, on visiting those missionary stations. At a little distance from Elliot, he wrote the following apostolic letter to the missionaries at that place; a letter which most strikingly shows the sacred passion which ruled his heart. He says — "In various scenes and changes; in perils of the sea and perils of the wilderness; in much weakness, weariness, and painfulness, my heart has been cheered with the anticipation of being refreshed at Elliot. At present, however, it seems to be the will of our ever to be adored Lord and Master, that the anticipation, so fondly entertained, should not be realized. I bow to his sovereign pleasure, always good — infinitely good. Still my heart melts with longing and with tenderness towards that consecrated spot — towards all the members of the missionary family, both those whom I have seen, and those whom I have not seen; and towards the dear children of the forest, the objects of benevolent labor and care. May the God and Father of our Lord Jesus Christ, the Father of mercies and the God of all grace, bring you nearer and nearer to himself, and keep you more entirely in his love — grant you abundant supports and consolations — make you faithful unto death. May he bless the school, and prosper the work in the nation, and make the wilderness and solitary place to be glad for you. — And when our labors and trials on earth shall be finished, in his infinite mercy, may we meet in his presence above, and rejoice in his glory forever."

When he arrived at Brainerd, May 25, he was extremely feeble, and as it seems, looked upon the time of his departure as near. "God," he said, "is very gracious. He has sustained me, as it were by miracle, thus far, and granted me one great desire of my heart, in bringing me to Brainerd. And if it be agreeable to his holy purposes, that I should leave my poor remains here, his will be done." He was able to attend to no business, and to speak but little. In few words he addressed the members of the church, and some of the congregation. After that, though much exhausted, he expressed a particular desire that the children of the school, according to their request, should come in. "I want"—he said with tears—"I want to see all my dear children, and to take them by the hand." They were then called in, and he took each of them by the hand, as they passed by his dying bed. Having all passed round in procession, they stood and sung a hymn. He was affected to tears most of the time. He then in the most affectionate manner, addressed them while they were melted to tears. . . . . . . There, on the seventh of June in the morning, at that consecrated spot in the wilderness, dearer far to him than any city or mansion on earth, this servant of the church, worn out with fatigue, and exhausted with sickness, lifted up his eyes towards heaven, and with a delightful smile upon his countenance, fell asleep in Jesus.

The grief of the missionary family on this occasion, you shall learn from their own language. When beginning to write their Journal, the day on which their beloved counsellor and father died, they thus describe the overwhelming sorrow of their hearts. —"With reluctance we enter on the events of this day. Our thoughts recoil. Our pen stops. Tears darken our eyes. We seek where to weep. We enter into our closets and weep there. We resolve to be men, and not children. We resume the task. Our weakened hands refuse to perform their office. We look at each other, and say, who shall bear the doleful tidings? A solemn silence casts a still darker shade over the gloomy scene. Every heart is faint; every head is sick; every hand is weak."

But the missionary family at Brainerd are not alone in their grief. There is a general mourning. And this mourning will spread through various and distant parts of the world, as soon as the tidings of Dr. Worcester's death shall be heard. Our missionaries in the east, and in the west loved him and confided in him as a father, by whose mature wisdom and faithful friendship they were guided and cheered in all their labors. How will their hearts bleed, when they hear that this beloved, honored friend is no more! — I might mention the sorrow of his church and society; of the Prudential Committee and the American Board; of our Theological Seminary, in which he had been recently called to the office of a Visitor; of the Massachusetts Missionary Society, and the American Education Society, and of other religious and charitable societies with which he was connected; of the churches and ministers of Christ; of the friends of missions and the friends of man.

But it becomes us to restrain our feelings, and seriously to inquire, in what manner we should bear this visitation of providence, and what use we should make of it.

Let us then thank the God of all grace, that he has prepared a heaven of glory and blessedness for his faithful servants. O how sweet the rest of heaven, after a wearisome journey through this wilderness! How blessed to be rid of all imperfections and sins. Imperfections and sins our dear brother had, or he could not have been human. He confessed them and looked to the blood of atonement for forgiveness, or he could not have been a Christian. But from his life and death, we have the best reason to think, that he now sees his Saviour face to face, and will serve him with perfect love and perfect joy forever.

We ought to give thanks to God for raising up a man of so distinguished a character, and making him the instrument of so much good to the church. And we ought, with reverence and submission, to notice the hand of God in *the place and circumstances of his death.* The progress of the divine dispensations may soon show, and the light of eternity will certainly show, that important ends were to be answered by *his dying at a missionary station.* It seems as though God meant in this affair, to set aside the wishes of his relatives, his people and his fellow laborers here, for the sake of some great public good. The man who has here acted so conspicuous a part in the missionary cause, and who has secured the strongest attachment of the Christian community, is removed from his family and friends, and is carried away to a spot in the wilderness — a spot on which have centered so many charities, and labors, and prayers. He is carried to the place where our beloved Kingsbury, with so much ability and success, began to collect and teach the Indian children. Though a sick and dying man, he has this desire of his heart — to see the consecrated place — to see the missionary family — to see and embrace the children of the forest, now the children of a Christian school, and in words faint and few, to give his last counsel, his dying benediction. There he is, in the most tender and interesting moments of his life. There he commits his soul to his God and Saviour. There his body lies in the dust. And now, brethren, the happy consequence will be, that all the esteem and love, which Christians in America have for his character, all their gratitude for his services, all their sympathy for his sufferings, and all their grief at his death, will be associated with *that missionary establishment*, and with *the missionary cause.* The recollection that a man so great, and wise, and good, went to die on missionary ground, must excite a new interest in the public mind. The place where Dr. Worcester died, and where he sleeps in the grave, will be a *consecrated* place. And who can ever go to that place, without emotions of mingled veneration and love and tenderness, at the remembrance of the devoted minister who came there to die. In the minds of Christians, that place will be closely united with the cause which is there to be promoted. And so that precious cause will hereafter stand out to public view, as having the nearest connection with all that was great and useful in the life, and all that was solemn and peaceful in the death of this beloved servant of Christ.

And now, brethren, shall we faint under this heavy stroke? Shall the friends of missions be disheartened, and say, what can we do? — "Hast thou not known, hast thou not heard, that the everlasting God, the Lord, the Creator of the ends of the earth fainteth not, neither is weary? There is no searching of his understanding. He giveth power to the faint, and to them that have no might, he increaseth strength."—Every instance in which he raises up a great and useful man to bless his church, is a new evidence of his goodness, and of his unalterable purpose to carry forward the work of love, till all flesh shall be saved. God will multiply these evidences of his goodness. Our beloved brother said in the last hours of his life, "Though I am taken away from this delightful labor, the Lord lives, and will raise up other instruments to carry on his work." In that day of glory to the church which is drawing near, God will raise up men, who will far outshine all who have gone before them. O could you but see in clear prospect, what will quickly be seen as a present reality, how would your hearts leap for joy. Friends of Zion,—friends of the missionary cause, lift your heads, for Jesus lives. Jesus, infinitely greater than all human agents—Jesus the Saviour of the world, lives and reigns forever. AMEN.

A SERMON

ON THE DEATH OF MOSES BROWN, ONE OF THE ASSOCIATE FOUNDERS OF THE THEOLOGICAL SEMINARY, ANDOVER; DELIVERED IN NEWBURYPORT, FEB. 18, 1827.

---

1 Tim. 6: 17—19.—CHARGE THEM THAT ARE RICH IN THIS WORLD, THAT THEY BE NOT HIGH-MINDED, NOR TRUST IN UNCERTAIN RICHES, BUT IN THE LIVING GOD, WHO GIVETH US ALL THINGS RICHLY TO ENJOY; THAT THEY DO GOOD; THAT THEY BE RICH IN GOOD WORKS, READY TO DISTRIBUTE, WILLING TO COMMUNICATE; LAYING UP IN STORE FOR THEMSELVES A GOOD FOUNDATION AGAINST THE TIME TO COME, THAT THEY MAY LAY HOLD ON ETERNAL LIFE.

THE duty of those who are rich, needs to be inculcated at the present day, as much as it did in the first age of Christianity. For, although we have seen many animating proofs of increasing benevolence in the Christian community; still the public benevolence falls far below what the exigencies of the world and the spirit of our religion demand. This deficiency greatly impedes the progress of divine truth, and retards the approach of that day, when the world shall be filled with the glory of the Lord. The various consequences which flow from the want of a more general and active benevolence, we have had many reasons to deplore.

The example of that friend of man, who has lately closed his eyes in death, will furnish a happy illustration of the principle which I shall aim to establish, and render more impressive the arguments by which I shall enforce it.

My position is, that *those who are rich are under sacred obligations to devote a portion of their substance to benevolent purposes.* I here speak of benevolence in its highest sense — benevolence directed to objects peculiarly *Christian.* The cause which I plead, is the cause of *religious* charity; charity exercised to promote the spiritual and eternal interests of men.

The *first* argument I urge is, that *property is the gift of God.* So it is represented in the text, "Charge them that are rich — that they trust not in uncertain riches, but in the living God, *who giveth us all things richly to enjoy.*" How often has it been demonstrated, that no economy or foresight, no degree of skilfulness in our plans, or diligence in our efforts, can secure to us the possession of riches, or even of competence, without the blessing of God. Calamities, which no human care can prevent, frequently occur, and reduce men from wealth to poverty, or from a state of competence to embarrassment and suffering. If then you have been successful in your exertions to acquire and preserve property, you owe it to that Almighty Being, who controls the winds, and the seasons, and all the affairs of men. Be it more or less, it is all *his gift.* And no obligation can be more evident, than our obligation to use a *gift* according to the will of the *giver.* To neglect this would betray an ungrateful heart. And if the gift was bestowed upon us with the express design that we should devote it to a particular object; we could not use it in any other way without palpable unfaithfulness. These remarks introduce my

Second argument; namely; that *God has made it known to be his will, that we should use the property which he entrusts to our care, for benevolent purposes.* He indeed permits and requires us to provide for ourselves and our households. But the precepts of his word constantly urge us beyond this, and present it, as a prominent duty of all men, especially of the rich, to give of their substance for charitable uses. "To do good and communicate forget not; for with such sacrifices God is well pleased." Again. "Let us do good unto *all* men, especially to them who are of the *household of faith.*" God would have your benevolence expansive and universal; but he would have its holy ardor exercised specially in advancing the interests of his kingdom. Our Lord directs us, *to make to ourselves friends of the mammon of unrighteousness;* that is, to make such a benevolent, pious use of riches, as to secure the friendship of God and his people. Besides this, he requires us, by general precepts, to devote ourselves and all that we possess, to him, and to do all things to his glory. Whenever he affords us an opportunity to do good, we are gladly to embrace it; considering that *doing good* is our great work. When he opens the way to send the Holy Scriptures or ministers of the gospel to those who are perishing in ignorance and wickedness; it is obviously his will, that we should devote to these objects a portion of the substance which he has given us. This is required by those comprehensive precepts: "Thou shalt love thy neighbor as thyself;" and "Whatsoever ye would that others should do unto you, do ye also the same unto them." For imagine, brethren, that you yourselves were in the wretched condition of the heathen world, without the light of the gospel, and enslaved to the basest idolatry; and let your consciences and your hearts say, whether it would not be an act of benevolence highly commendable in Christians, to send you the news of salvation, and to afford you the means of being delivered from the deepest ignorance and wretchedness. And if so, how can you neglect to perform the same act of benevolence towards those, who are in that very state of ignorance and wretchedness, and who have no prospect of deliverance, except through the influence of your pious charity? I here urge the duty on the ground of that divine precept, which requires us *to love our neighbors as ourselves*, and *to do to others as we would that they should do to us.* There is no possibility of evading this obligation.

This then is my argument with every one who is rich. Who made you rich? Who entrusted such an estate to your care? And for what purpose? By putting such an estate into your hands, God has constituted you his steward. And being his steward, you will endeavor to learn his will respecting the objects to which you should devote his property. This you may do by attending to the teachings of his word and providence. A part of your estate is manifestly needed for the supply of your own personal wants. More may be needed as a comfortable and honorable provision for your household. What then is to be done with the residue? There are at this day many great objects of benevolence; objects far above the ability of men in ordinary circumstances to accomplish. Such men must exhaust their feebler charities upon smaller objects, or must be content with doing a little for objects of loftier magnitude. A great work remains, which can never be done, except by the benevolent use of riches. Literary and religious institutions must be established and supported. Thousands of pious youth must be educated for the ministry. Thousands of missionaries must be maintained among the heathen. The Bible must be printed in all languages, and spread through all nations; while the means of instruction and reformation must be furnished to millions among ourselves.

These things, taken together, constitute a work which is exceedingly arduous, and which cannot be carried forward and completed, without large contributions from large estates. This work is certainly of great importance in the judgment of God. And can you suppose he did not think of it, when he prospered your efforts, and made you rich? Suppose the Lord Jesus should now come to you, and give you a particular amount of property, and should expressly say to you;— *This property I commit to you in sacred trust, with this one direction, that you should use it to promote the cause which is dearest to my heart.* Would you not think yourself happy to be made the steward of his bounty? And could you have a thought of devoting what was thus entrusted to you by your Lord, to any use but to promote his own cause? Now the silver and the gold are the Lord's; and to every one who has more or less wealth, he has in fact virtually spoken in the very manner supposed. He has entrusted you with wealth, and has made known his will respecting the uses to which it shall be applied. And no duty can be more obvious to reason, or more touching to the heart, than the duty of using the substance which God has given you according to his will and for the promotion of his cause.

Perhaps you may say, this property is your own. So far as the laws of civil society are concerned, it is so indeed. And no man on earth can interfere with the right you have to use it according to your own pleasure. But the God who made us, and who has given us our time and our property, comes forward with an authority which no being in the universe can question, and commands us to devote ourselves and all that we possess to *him*. The proper inquiry then is — *what use of God's gifts will be most pleasing to him?* What use of them should we think best, if we loved him with all our heart and soul and mind and strength? If the Apostle, who was ready to be bound and to die at Jerusalem for the name of Jesus, were here, and possessed of this property of ours; what use of it, would *he* think best? And what would be most agreeable to *him who was rich, and who for our sakes became poor?* If men of every degree of wealth should entertain just conceptions and feelings on this momentous subject, they could never doubt their obligation to employ a portion of their property in religious charities. They would deem it sacrilege, to dispose of their estates, living or dying, without giving the cause of Christ a prominent place in their thoughts and in their arrangements. Covetousness would cease. Private affections would be made subordinate to Christian benevolence. And it would be as uncommon for a man possessed of a considerable estate, to make no large contributions or bequests to the cause of the Redeemer, as it is now for a man to make none to his own family. Then the records of benevolence would exhibit frequent donations and legacies of thousands and hundreds of thousands of dollars, for the various purposes of religious charity; and from men of smaller estates, their smaller contributions, no less acceptable to God than the larger offerings of the rich. Then no great and pious undertakings would flag, no good institutions would languish, and no portion of the human family would be left in ignorance or wickedness for want of pecuniary means.

Such as I have now represented is the duty of the rich; such the demand which the supreme Proprietor of their wealth makes upon them *as his stewards;* such and so sublime the purposes to which he requires them to devote their substance ; and so glorious the consequences of their conforming to his requisition, and fully accomplishing the objects for which he has entrusted them with wealth. O ye who are rich, and whose hearts the grace of God has inclined to do good, with what language can I describe the magnitude of that work you are destined by divine providence to effect, or the happiness you may enjoy, if you will rise above the grovelling conceptions of worldly men, and with the love of God in your hearts, present yourselves and your possessions, as a free-will offering to him! The obligation of men in respect to their worldly substance begins to be better understood than heretofore. But it will be understood and felt far more perfectly, before the happy day when the knowledge of the Lord shall fill the earth.

My *third* argument is, that *property, when devoted to benevolent objects, is greatly superior in value to what it can be, when used for other purposes.* Look at that man, who is favored with a large estate, but has no ear to hear the cry of distress, and no heart to feel for the miseries of his fellow men. He *loves his money ;* and would rather see a world perish, than diminish his hoarded treasures. Behold another, who expends his riches to gratify his ambition, or his love of fashion and splendor. Behold another still, who uses his wealth to please or aggrandize his children. What now is the value of riches in the hands of such men as these, compared with the value it acquires in the hands of the *Christian philanthropist*, who, without neglecting any private obligation, devotes his wealth chiefly to works of benevolence — to feed the hungry, to encourage the industry of the poor, to instruct the ignorant, and to save those who are perishing in sin? What is the wealth belonging to a miser, or a man of fashion, compared with that which belongs to a Thornton, a Boudinot, or an Abbot?

Look forward to the *final judgment*, when every man shall give account to God of the use he made of his substance. Then all worldly interests, and the delusion of worldly passions, will be ended, and things, always before seen through a mist, will appear in noon-day light. Two individuals, who prospered in their business in this world, and acquired riches, will then appear before the judgment seat. One of them remembered and loved the cause of Christ, and made it his first object to use his estate for the glory of the Redeemer, and the good of his kingdom. And in the final disposal he made of his property, he remembered his sacred obligations, and aimed seriously to make *such a Will*, as would be pleasing to his Saviour, and would most effectually subserve the same precious cause to which he had so often contributed before. And accordingly after providing generously for his own family, he bequeathed large sums to the most important objects of pious benevolence. Now what will be our judgment, and what will be the judgment of Christ, respecting the man who used his estate in such a manner, compared with the man who forgot the Saviour, and overlooked his cause, and devoted all that he had to private objects?

Fourthly. Using our property for purposes of benevolence affords *the most exalted and permanent pleasure.* Such is the constitution of the mind and the principles of the divine government, that our pleasure will be according to the nature of our predominant desires. Men who are governed by worldly, selfish desires, have their pleasures. But how low and worthless are they compared with what a benevolent man enjoys in doing good! I appeal to the experience of ages. I appeal to facts which are familiar to every man, who has used his substance for the welfare of others. Of all the money he has ever expended, that has yielded him the highest pleasure, which has been devoted to benevolent objects. Even a little, spent in this way, has afforded more happiness than much, spent in other ways. On the score of enjoyment, the gratification of all the animal appetites, and of all the selfish desires, and even of the domestic and social affections, falls far below the gratification of Christian benevolence.

And the pleasure of doing good, which is so much superior to other pleasures in its nature, is equally superior in *permanence.* The pleasures of sin are but for a moment. But the man of active benevolence has pleasures which end not. He has resources for time to come — for hours of solitude, and for days and years of adversity. Do you wish then, ye men of wealth, so to use your estates as to secure the most exalted and permanent pleasure? Then cherish the spirit of benevolence; *be rich in good works*. But if you will not seek happiness in this way; then I must tell you, that the poor widow, whose love to Christ prompts her to give away her two mites in charity, is far happier than you, with all your riches. Yea more. Your wealth is totally worthless. It is smitten with a curse; — and good had it been for you, if you had been doomed to poverty, or had never been born.

But to those whose hearts are benevolent the possession of wealth will secure the purest pleasure. Their own experience will verify the words of our Saviour: *It is more blessed to give than to receive*. And besides enjoying the present pleasures, they will "*lay up in store for themselves a good foundation against the time to come;*" that is, *a firm and durable happiness in the future world.*

How powerful then are the motives, by which men are urged to do good with their substance. If our hearts were right, our own *desire* for the welfare of others would seem, by itself, to be a sufficient inducement to devote our property to benevolent objects. But we are not left without other inducements. For God has connected present pleasures of the purest kind with the exercise of benevolence; and he will hereafter most graciously reward it with unalloyed and everlasting happiness in the kingdom of heaven.

Fifthly. The benevolent use of property is *the surest and best way to promote the welfare of our children*. This may seem a paradox to those who are unaccustomed to sober reflection. But it is a plain and obvious truth. For what is more important to the welfare of our children, than forming them to a right character? And what can we do that will have so powerful an influence upon them in this respect, as to exhibit a right example before them? And how can we exhibit a right example, without habitual compliance with the divine command *to do good, to be rich in good works?* Let a man by the proper use of his estate, make an impression upon his children, that he is free from covetousness, and that he aims to please God and to promote the best interests of his fellow men; and the impression must be salutary. His children will be powerfully drawn to copy his example. And if he may in this way be successful in forming his children to benevolence and piety, he will promote their happiness in the highest sense. Who that truly loves his children, would not rather see them adorned with piety, and imitators of the divine goodness, than possessed of earthly riches? Would you exert this salutary influence upon the character of your children most effectually; then let your example be invested with excellence of the highest degree. Let your benevolence stretch beyond the common measure. Rise to strong, constant, untiring effort; and so acquire a visible likeness to him, *who went about doing good.* With such an example before their eyes, your children, you may hope, will early imbibe the spirit and taste the pleasures of benevolence. And if they do this, their everlasting interests are secure.

But there is another view to be taken of this subject. Has not the experience of ages shown, that inheriting large estates is a dangerous snare to children; — much more dangerous, than the same estates would be, if obtained by their own diligent efforts? Is it not often found, that the wealth which the fond affection of a father bequeathed to his offspring, proves the occasion of their disgrace and ruin? And is it not often the case, that if a father could only rise from his grave, and witness the folly and dissipation of his children, and the pernicious purposes to which they devote the property they received from him; he would mourn over the mistake he had committed, and over the miseries he had contributed to bring upon those whom he so fondly loved? Let then every affectionate father, who is possessed of wealth cherish a wise and faithful regard to the happiness of his own offspring, and save them from the dangerous temptation to which they would be exposed, by inheriting large estates, and let him commit them to the care and mercy of God. It is indeed our duty to give our children a Christian education, to aid them in their entrance into life, and to provide for their comfortable subsistence. But is not the blessing of God better than riches? Suppose, by devoting a portion of our estate to Christ and the church, we diminish their inheritance. Do we not secure to them that divine favor, which is infinitely more precious than any earthly inheritance? Here then is a double good to be accomplished by the benevolent use of our property, good to our fellow men, to whose benefit we devote a portion of our substance; and good to our own children, by an act of benevolence and piety, which we may hope, through the mercy of God, will bring blessings upon their heads. I cannot but consider the condition of that child deplorable, rather than enviable, to whom an opulent father has bequeathed his *whole estate.* How much better would it have been for the child, if the greater part had been given to the Lord, and the residue, with the divine blessing, to him!

My *last* reason for a benevolent and pious use of our property, is, that *it will have a salutary influence upon our own hearts.* The acquisition of wealth has a tendency to strengthen our selfish and earthly passions; and so to exclude God and eternity from our minds. Now if Christians will take a part of that, which has been the nutriment of their selfish passions, and has withdrawn their hearts from God, and will devote it to his honor and the good of his church; they will directly counteract their covetousness, and will at the same time bring themselves into contact with higher and nobler objects, kindle purer affections and taste purer joys. Christians, to whom God has given large estates, seldom attain to eminent piety; and for the most part are destitute of those enjoyments in religion which are granted to others. They are sensible of this, and are frequently heard to complain, that they have so little fervor of piety, and so little spiritual comfort; that their souls cleave to the dust; that they cannot enjoy communion with God, and cannot find any satisfactory evidence of their title to heaven. Let such Christians inquire, whether there is not a cause for this low and comfortless state? Have you not too much of this world's riches; and do you not hold it with too strong a grasp? Does not the burden of your estate bear too heavily upon you? Your march to the heavenly world is all the way ascending. In this upward march you are grievously overloaded. Lay aside this oppressive weight, and you will soon make better progress. Diminish your earthly treasures. Be rich in good works. Thus the poison will be extracted from riches; the curse will be removed; and that which is so generally the occasion of mischief, will be turned into a blessing.

On the present occasion, my hearers have doubtless often turned their thoughts to our departed friend, as one who exemplified that principle of benevolence which I have endeavored to inculcate. He did indeed exemplify it, and compared with most of his contemporaries, in a remarkable degree. I well know that this community will confirm the truth of what I say. And I am persuaded, that they will not be satisfied, unless some public testimony shall be given to the benevolence, the usefulness, and the piety of that beloved man, whose death has filled so many hearts with sorrow. The name of Moses Brown cannot be pronounced, without respect and love. I might expatiate upon the many estimable traits of his character. I might say, that for more than half a century, in which he was engaged in acquiring and using his property, his reputation for integrity and honor was unsullied; that it was his uniform principle, to seek no advantage to himself, which would prove injurious to his neighbor; that he neither countenanced vice, nor neglected, on suitable occasions, to reprove it; that he was eminently a peace-maker, exercising, with singular success, the spirit of conciliation. I might speak of the sweetness of his temper; of the control he maintained over his own passions; of his sincerity as a friend; of his generous hospitality; and of the happy combination he possessed of the domestic virtues. I might say, that through a long life he manifested a lively interest in whatever concerned the welfare of society, of the church, and of the world; that while he was raised, by his wealth and the worth of his character, to hold so respectable a place in society, he was totally averse to splendor and show; that he scrupulously avoided all needless expense, and set an example of plainness and economy, which, if generally copied by the rich, would save enough to rescue ten thousand families from distress, and to send the gospel to all nations. But on these attributes of his character I cannot enlarge. I have a particular object in view, and to that I shall chiefly confine my remarks.

Moses Brown was born in Newbury, Oct. 2, 1742. By unceasing diligence, and the exercise of judgment and forethought, with the blessing of divine providence, he rose from small beginnings to the possession of a large estate. But he was not, like most other successful merchants, so immersed in his worldly business and cares, as to be neglectful of the wants and sufferings of the poor. He remembered what it was to be poor; and, through all the years of his prosperity, he cherished a generous sympathy for those who were placed in that condition from which divine providence had raised him up. Many a time did he, from the mere kindness of his heart, exercise a forbearance towards his debtors, which occasioned him the loss of what was justly his due. And many a time, especially in the latter part of his life, did he relinquish valuable claims upon individuals, because they could not pay him, without reducing themselves to straits.

It would be impossible to record the various forms and instances of his charity to families and individuals. The benevolent actions, of which I now speak, are known in part to those among whom he lived. But they are fully known to God only. And I trust, that when they are brought to view at a future day, our departed friend will recollect, with holy thanksgiving, that divine grace which excited him to perform them; and will know the happy import of what the God of mercy hath said: *Blessed is he that considereth the poor.*

But these charities to the poor did not satisfy the heart of this friend of man. He did not follow the steps of those rich men, who engage a little in more private charities, and there stop. His having devoted so much of his substance to the ordinary objects of benevolence, had an influence to enlarge his heart, and to prepare him to contribute to higher and nobler objects.

My lot, as a minister of the gospel, was cast a few miles from his residence. In compliance with a particular request, I had the pleasure of meeting with him, together with another friend, now living, and another, now I trust in heaven, to consult respecting the establishment of a Theological Seminary. It was twenty years ago. The subject of a Theological Institution was then new to us, and new to the public. The conversation of that evening will be one of the last things to fade away from my memory. But it was not conversation merely. The honored friends of whom I speak, were not men of *words*, but of *business*. And, feeling their obligations to God, who had given them their estates, they then entered on the plan of founding a Seminary for the education of pious youth for the ministry. And that generous man, who is now silent in death, freely offered his ten thousand dollars for this momentous object. Though he was a man of but ordinary education, and had been incessantly engaged, from early life, first in mechanical, and then in mercantile labors; and although he had never thought himself worthy to be numbered with the followers of Christ; he had a mind large enough to understand the importance and necessity of such an establishment, and a heart to give liberally of his honest treasures to promote it. That time appears like yesterday. Every word, and look, and tone of voice is fresh in my recollection. The readiness, the simplicity, the generous kindness, with which our departed friend offered his aid, cannot be described; though by those who knew him, it may easily be conceived. He merely said: It is a great object; I will give ten thousand dollars to begin with; and more afterwards. He redeemed his pledge; for he was always a nursing father to the Seminary; and after various smaller donations, and one of a thousand dollars, he gave, a few years since, twenty-five thousand dollars to found a new Professorship. Besides all this, he promoted, by generous contributions, the various religious charities of the day. And it was a remarkable trait of his character, distinguishing him from most others, that even after he came to be an old man, he could readily enter into any new plans of benevolence, how different soever they might be from those to which he had been accustomed. Such was the American Education Society, which he regarded from the beginning, as a worthy object of his patronage, and to which, at the commencement of his last sickness, he contributed a thousand dollars. Such too was the American Temperance Society, the formation of which he welcomed with all his heart, as it coincided perfectly with his own settled principles and habits, and the sober results of long observation. To this Society he made a donation of five hundred dollars. He previously contributed five hundred dollars for the benefit of Greeneville College, Tenn., and fifteen hundred to the town of Newburyport, when it was visited with a destructive fire. By his last Will, he bequeathed six thousand dollars to be kept as an increasing fund, till it should be adequate to the perpetual support of a public Grammar school in Newburyport; one thousand dollars to the Howard Benevolent Society; and one thousand acres of land in Brownville, Me., to the Theological Seminary in Bangor. He also gave a large amount of legacies to various individuals, who were not lawful heirs to his estate.

You perceive that our honored friend did not copy the example of some rich men, who retain their property with an iron grasp as long as life remains, and then, by Will, give away something, because they can hold it no longer themselves. He made a liberal use of his estate while he lived, while in health, while engaged in business, and while capable of enjoying the satisfaction of seeing the good resulting from his charities.

But the crowning excellence of his character was religious principle. His life gave evidence of his *humility* and *devotion.* He loved the doctrines of revelation, the strictness of evangelical truth. Never was there a man, who seemed to think less of himself; who was further from making any claims upon the divine favor, or indulging any hopes of heaven on the ground of his good works, though few men ever had more of these than he. But they were of no account with him in the affair of justification before God. In this respect, he regarded them as of no value, and looked for salvation to *the Lamb of God which taketh away the sin of the world.* His character had long been such, that

Christians would have rejoiced to welcome him to the Lord's Table. But from this he was deterred by his extreme self-distrust, and by an impression, which was probably not altogether correct, of the nature and design of the ordinance. But the heavy afflictions, with which it pleased God to visit him a few years since, in the death of his amiable partner, and his only child, were evidently the means of producing greater decision and maturity of Christian character, and preparing him for greater enjoyments. In consequence of this, he was induced to unite himself with the church of Christ by a public profession. I am free to express my wish, that he had done it long before, and my conviction, that he committed a serious mistake in neglecting it.

And now, brethren and friends, when we review the subject, and fix our eyes on the character of the beloved man, who has lately been removed from us to another world; we cannot but be impressed with the littleness and insignificance of wealth, devoted to selfish, worldly purposes. Oh! it is all nothing-worth, all-contemptible, as the judgment day will show. We honor the poor man, who cheerfully gives a few cents to promote the cause of his Saviour. But the man who possesses wealth, and who lives and dies, without giving any considerable portion of it to benevolent and pious objects, has no honor from God, and deserves none from man. He sinks his name and his riches into contempt. And though he may leave a large estate to his heirs, he leaves no blessing of God with it. But blessed are they whose hearts are warmed with divine love, who are "rich in good works, laying up in store for themselves a good foundation against the time to come, that they may lay hold on eternal life."

A SERMON

ON THE DEATH OF JEREMIAH EVARTS, CORRESPONDING SECRETARY OF THE A. B. C. F. M., DELIVERED IN ANDOVER, JULY 31, 1831.

Acts 10: 38. — "WHO WENT ABOUT DOING GOOD."

WE have assembled, brethren and friends, to show our respect to the memory of a faithful servant of Christ, and our sorrow at his death. That friend to the heathen, that benefactor of mankind, who has been taken from us, enjoyed the esteem and affection not only of his relatives, of the Prudential Committee, and of the American Board, but of all those in our country who love the cause of Christ. He was very dear also to the missionaries whom we have sent forth, and the tidings of his death will fill their hearts with sorrow. In Palestine, in India, in the wilderness of America, and in the Isles of the Pacific, there will be great mourning for our beloved Secretary.

Far be it from me to bestow unmeasured applause upon any man, especially upon the man whose death we deplore. The highest honor I would give him is to say, that he was a Christian, and that, in imitation of his Lord and Master, *he went about doing good.* Our departed friend was of a humble heart and contrite spirit. He disclaimed all personal worthiness, and was among the last to seek or to desire applause. And now that he is gone to a world of perfect holiness, he will be deaf to all praise, except that which is ascribed to God and the Lamb.

In this solemn service, I shall attempt to show *by what attributes of character, and by what arrangements of divine providence, we are to account for the eminent usefulness of our lamented brother, the late corresponding Secretary of the American Board.*

I shall *first* notice his *intellectual* character. The faculties of his mind were originally strong and active, and were improved by a thorough literary and scientific education, and a regular course of study in law. There are few men, whose acquisitions are more extensive or more solid. On all subjects to which he turned his attention, whether literary, political, or religious, he formed clear and comprehensive views; and whether he undertook to write or speak, he exhibited the riches of his mind in a diction uniformly natural, perspicuous and forcible. The extemporaneous addresses he made on public occasions were peculiarly modest and plain; but full of vivid, pertinent, and weighty thought. He was distinguished by patience and fairness in his investigations, by the clearness and force of his reasoning, and by correctness and despatch in business. In all his habits, whether of thought or action, he showed as little liability to mistake, as can be expected of any man in this state of imperfection.

Now it is upon the character of the mind, that our ability to do good in a great measure depends. If a man is in this respect superior to others, he will in all probability accomplish more good than they. The usefulness of his labors, unless prevented by special causes, will be very much in proportion to the amount of his intellectual powers and acquisitions.

This is a subject, on which young men, in different stages of their education, frequently entertain erroneous views. They look forward to their future profession with impatience, and are in haste to engage in its labors, apprehending that spending so much time in preparation will detract from the good they might accomplish. This is a great mistake. For all experience shows, that the whole of a man's usefulness is not so much according to the length of the time in which he is engaged in active service, as to the amount of his qualifications; and that if any one would be sure to rise to the highest degree of usefulness of which he is capable, he must spend more time than is common in preparation, leaving less for action.

The whole time which Mr. Evarts devoted to classical, scientific and professional study unquestionably contributed to his usefulness. Even those acquisitions, which might have been thought less necessary, proved serviceable in some part of the work assigned to him. For example; the knowledge he acquired of jurisprudence qualified him to perform that work of benevolence in behalf of the suffering Indians, which will be so lasting an honor to him in the view of all who love justice and feel for the oppressed. And if some of his previous studies did not in the same manner come into direct use in the cause to which he was devoted; they still had an influence in giving strength and elevation to the character of his mind, and in preparing him more effectually to accomplish his great object.

In the *second* place, I shall notice his *moral and religious* character.

In the strict evangelical sense, Mr. Evarts was a good man. His life afforded the most satisfactory evidence that he had experienced the renewing of the Holy Ghost; that he repented of sin, and believed in Christ as the only Saviour, and that he rendered habitual obedience to the divine commands.

Now this spirit of Christian piety contributed in the highest degree to his usefulness. It was this which gave a right direction to his intellectual powers, and led him to make a right use of his acquisitions. It was this, which constituted his great inward motive to a useful life. Had he possessed the same intellectual furniture, without piety; his influence, instead of being beneficial, might have been mischievous. He might have spent his life in spreading moral pestilence. And even if he had avoided this excess of iniquity, and devoted himself to the business of the profession which he originally chose; he might have done little more than to pursue his own private interests. The spread of the gospel and the salvation of the world would have had no power over his heart. Look at those who are possessed of richly furnished minds, but are destitute of religious principle. Their lives are spent in worldly pursuits and indulgences. Even those actions which have a show of goodness, are dictated by a more refined selfishness. Behold, then, the work which sovereign grace accomplishes! When God renews the hearts of sinners, he manifests great love, not only to them, but to the world. They who are renewed have the spirit of active benevolence, and so are led, by a motive of exhaustless energy, to seek the highest interests of man. They bear the image of him *who went about doing good.* When our beloved friend was renewed by the divine Spirit, his heart was brought under the influence of love to God and love to man. At his conversion he commenced a course of action, which was to fall in with a great system of benevolence, and to promote the salvation of untold multitudes in Christian and heathen lands.

But holy affection, in order to produce its proper effects, must not only exist, but be lively and fervent. Benevolence, when feeble and dormant, can accomplish but little. The good to be accomplished by the agency of Evarts required a mind enlightened and purified in an uncommon degree;—it required a benevolence steady, ardent and invincible. And such was the character to which, through the grace of God, he was formed. The affection which predominated in his breast, next to his supreme love to God, was compassion to the souls of men, and strong desire for the salvation of the heathen. This was the inward power which moved him. It was not a feverish heat, but the even pulsation and glow of health. What others might do from sudden excitement, he did from *principle*—principle which was uniform and enduring. The moral principle which actuated him was as permanent as the faculties of his soul, and the indwelling Spirit of God. Such a principle of action is essential to the highest degree of usefulness in any condition. Though it lies concealed in the shades of private life, and shows itself only in the little circle of domestic duties, or in the exercises of secret devotion; still it contributes to the welfare of the world.

But religious principle was specially important and necessary to the chief agent in our Foreign Missionary enterprise. In connection with others, he had to accomplish a work of uncommon magnitude, and to encounter numberless and formidable difficulties. He was called to guide the ship over a tempestuous sea, when strong counter currents were to be stemmed, sudden changes of wind and weather to be encountered, and rocks and shoals to be avoided. In such an enterprise, it was indispensable that he should possess a principle of great firmness and strength; a principle which would enable him to meet difficulties calmly, and to rise above all discouragements; and which would contain within itself an exhaustless power of excitement, when all other springs of action failed. Such a principle he had. It was *the religious affection* which the Spirit of God produced and cherished in his heart. It was an affection which brought him into an alliance with apostles and martyrs, and with Christ himself.

But there was a particular attribute of his moral character, which was of great importance to his usefulness, namely, *his scrupulous and inflexible integrity.*

This trait in his character was so manifest, that it raised him entirely above suspicion. The name of Jeremiah Evarts produced a general feeling of safety in regard to any interests which might be committed to his care. The evident simplicity and uprightness of his character freed him from the obstructions, which the suspicions of others always throw in the way of a man's usefulness, and secured to him the confidence and support not only of his particular associates, but of all those in the community who were attached to the cause of missions. And this manifest uprightness of character, which was indispensable to his success through the whole period of our Foreign Missionary operations, was so in a preëminent degree, at the commencement of those operations. To carry into effect the great design of the Board, it was necessary that large sums of money should be contributed, and sent in charity to various and distant countries — a business hardly known among us at that time, and not easily accomplished even in the most favorable circumstances. Now who can suppose that both the rich and the poor would have voluntarily united from year to year, as they actually did, in raising the requisite funds, had they indulged a suspicion of the integrity or disinterestedness of the man to whom the funds were to be intrusted, and who was, from the beginning, one of the principal agents in conducting all the concerns of the missions.

I proceed to say, *thirdly*, that our lamented brother had *a remarkable completeness and symmetry of character.*

We not unfrequently meet with men, who are distinguished for particular virtues, while in regard to others they are notoriously deficient. There are some, who are endued with ardor and boldness, and other shining qualities for public life, who yet are subject to failings in their private character. They are wanting in meekness and gentleness. Some make it manifest, that the applauses bestowed upon them have produced self-complacency and vanity, and that, in opposition to a divine precept, they *esteem themselves better than others.* Some, again, have a covetous or a suspicious temper; or they are wanting in Christian simplicity; or are subject to rashness, fickleness, or indiscretion. But it was otherwise with Evarts. Every one acquainted with his public life knows full well, that he was possessed of manly resolution, firmness, and activity. But he was possessed, in an equal degree, of humility, forbearance, and gentleness. He had as much of the amiable, as of the dignified.

This completeness of character was of the highest consequence to his usefulness. It was no small matter, that such a character was carried into that high station which was allotted to him, and was made to bear upon all the interests with which he was intrusted.

But I am to speak also of the *symmetry* of his character. He not only had the various qualities which belong to a good character, but had them in *just proportion.* How different was he from those, who seem to have an exact conscience respecting one class of obligations, but are inattentive to others; from those who manifest much regard to that which is appropriately religious, and but little to that which relates to common life — who reverence the Sabbath, and regularly attend to its public services, but are chargeable with irregularities of temper and conduct during the week. On the other hand, how different was he from those, who are exact in respect to their domestic duties, but regardless of those which are more public, or more directly religious. Let me not, however, be understood to imply that he had an excellence of character, which was free from all deficiency and all blemish. This would be to contradict his deep conviction of his own failings, his sincere confessions, and penitence, and self-abhorrence; and it would be to overlook that pure and spiritual law which no Christian on earth perfectly obeys for a single day, or a single moment of his life. But if the character of Evarts is viewed in comparison with that of good men generally, I think it must appear to great advantage in respect to completeness and symmetry. Who that knew him, ever thought that any part of what constitutes a good character was wanting in him, or that some of his intellectual or moral qualities grew to excess, while others, equally important, were below their proper measure?

The public character of Mr. Evarts exhibited the symmetry above mentioned, in one very important respect. With as much *ardor* as was necessary to the highest degree of effort, he united a *sound judgment.* Had the momentous concerns of our Foreign Missions been committed to a man of more zeal, and less discretion; the consequence might have been disastrous. There is a degree of heat, which discomposes the mind, and produces disorder. If a man's ardor goes beyond the bounds of moderation, and his zeal breaks loose from his judgment; the world will be afraid to trust him. He may have more active power, and for a time, accomplish more good, than any other man. Still it will be dangerous to confide in him; because, in one rash hour, he may expose to ruin all the interests committed to his care. The zeal of Evarts did indeed rise to a high degree of warmth; but it had no enthusiastic effervescence, no convulsive starts, no violence. It was just sufficient to put his mind into the fittest state for deliberation and effort;—just sufficient to afford the necessary excitement to his reason, his invention, and all his active powers. It was invariably associated with the most tranquil operations of a well furnished intellect; and it led him to adopt measures as extensive as existing circumstances would admit; measures which he pursued through successive years, with unfailing resolution, and with increasing evidence that they were both wise and practicable.

His excellence of character appeared in the sober and Scriptural views he entertained respecting the doctrines of Christianity. No man was more free from sectarian prejudice, and a pertinacious attachment to old opinions. And yet no man was more determined in opposition to novelties in religion, or more grieved at any departure from the simplicity of the gospel. On all questions of controversy at the present day, his habit of thinking was at once cautious and decided, and was conformed to the settled orthodoxy of our churches, and, in my apprehension, to the dictates of reason and revelation. His knowledge of theology was so extensive, and his manner of reasoning, both on polemic and practical points, was so candid and perspicuous, that his conversation was highly prized by the most intelligent Christians. It is hardly necessary to add, that the judicious opinions, which he was known to entertain on the subject of religion, procured for him a still higher place in the esteem of the community, and gave an additional influence to his efforts in the cause of missions.

I have now noticed the chief of those intellectual and moral properties which prepared our departed friend for eminent usefulness. But of what utility would all these excellent properties have been, had they not been brought into actual exercise? How little good comparatively would he have done, had he been left in the shades of private life, or had he been chiefly devoted to the acquisition of wealth? But the God who made him, and who furnished him with so many valuable qualifications, designed him for a particular work, and in due time prepared the way for him to enter upon it. It was a short time after he came to this vicinity, that the Foreign Mission from America was commenced, and the management of its interests committed to a Board of Commissioners. From the first, Mr. Evarts was employed in the executive business of the Board. Besides being Treasurer, he was intimately associated with Dr. Worcester, the Corresponding Secretary, in conducting the correspondence, and in all the concerns of our growing missions. By this course of labor for about ten years, he became well qualified for the office of Secretary, when it was vacated by the death of Dr. Worcester, and when the burden of its responsibilities and cares had been so much increased by the increase of missionary interest in our country. This was the station for which divine providence raised him up. In this station all his intellectual powers and moral principles were brought into constant and vigorous action, and his whole character experienced a sensible and rapid growth. It was by his labors in this station, that he arrived at his proper degree of usefulness.

When Mr. Evarts entered on the station assigned him, he consecrated his time and influence to the cause of missions among the heathen. Towards this object his thoughts, his studies, his exertions were all directed. To this chosen object he devoted his life, not that he disregarded any private obligations; — not that he undervalued any other object of benevolence, or lost his love for literature and science, or for anything which could adorn the mind, or promote the comfort of society. He showed, that a man in the most important station has no occasion to neglect his less important duties. He showed, that a great man has no need to have either great faults, or little faults. But to whatever other objects he occasionally turned his attention, he never lost sight of the cause of missions. He acted on the principle that if a man would accomplish the highest degree of good, he must have only one great object.

The object to which he thus devoted himself, and the efforts which he made, were of such a nature as to be followed by *durable* effects — by a *continuity* of good. It is not according to sound wisdom, that we should fill up the little space of time, and use the little power we have, in pursuit of a good which has no solid worth, and will last but a moment. If there is a good which is really excellent and durable, let us choose that. It was the appointment of Christ, that his apostles should bear much fruit, and that their fruit should *remain*. What they did, produced *permanent* effects;—it conduced to a good which was *everlasting.* Our beloved Secretary labored for the same object. He was of one heart with the apostles, who labored to save those that were lost. His efforts like theirs, were upon a large scale. Had he promoted the salvation of a single individual, he would have done a great and good work. But his efforts were directed to the welfare of communities and nations; to the salvation of the world. And if respect is had to the wisdom of the measures which were adopted, to the extensive and systematic operations, which have already been attended with animating success, and which are to lead on to other measures, far more extensive, and far more successful—if it is remembered that the missionary zeal, which he helped to kindle in the church, is to burn with a still purer and brighter flame, and that his labors were, by the appointment of heaven, closely connected with the ultimate overthrow of idolatry, and the establishment of Christ's kingdom in pagan lands; the good resulting from his agency will appear too great for human language to describe, or the human mind to comprehend.

In pursuing the object which was so dear to his heart, he was particularly aware, that he depended on the cordial assistance of the Christian community. The influence of a man in any station, especially in one that is public, and very difficult, may be increased in a degree above computation by being skilfully united with the influence of others. We are social beings, and are mutually dependent. Let human agency in any case be completely insulated, and it can have no efficiency. We must act together. What is deficient in one man, is to be supplied by others, who, though not superior to him in the general attributes of character, may be able to afford him the counsel and aid which he needs. Mr. Evarts successfully availed himself of this principle. Who was ever more unassuming; or more free from that self-sufficiency, which makes a man reluctant to acknowledge himself indebted to the judgment or foresight of others? Who ever came nearer to a full compliance with the direction of the Apostle, that, *in lowliness of mind, each should esteem others better than himself?* His truly modest and humble disposition, joined with his deep solicitude that everything should be done in the best manner, rendered him very desirous of counsel and assistance from his brethren, and heartily willing to own himself under obligation to them, even where it was evident that he himself possessed the highest degree of wisdom.

But while he looked to his fellow Christians for counsel and assistance, it conduced still more to his success, that *he sought help of God.* In a manner far removed from all extravagance, he believed in the efficacy of prayer. And his belief was grounded on the best possible reasons — the immutable promise of God, and the actual course of his providence. The devout supplications which he and his associates in office presented to God in all their meetings for business, together with the monthly, and weekly, and daily prayers of the great body of Christians in this land, and in other lands, have undoubtedly exerted a higher and more efficacious influence, than any other means, in promoting the spread of the gospel. Without the spirit of prayer, and the blessing of God which it secures, other efforts would have proved abortive. Suppose prayer had been omitted, and the time spent in this duty by the officers and members of the Board, by ministers, and all the friends of missions, had been spent in any other way; what would have been the consequence, but a total failure of the missionary enterprise? All our exertions would have effected nothing; or I might say, no proper exertions would have been made. Judging by the word of God, we cannot doubt, that sincere, fervent prayer, really does more, though by an unseen influence, towards accomplishing the great objects of benevolence, than all human endeavors beside. For what can human endeavors do, without the help of God? And how can that help be obtained, except by prayer?

Thus I have noticed those attributes of character and other circumstances, which contributed to the usefulness of the beloved and honored man, who has closed his earthly labors.

Among the many useful lessons which this subject is suited to teach, I can suggest only the following.

1. We see how Christians may *grow in grace and become eminently holy.*

Here I shall address myself particularly to those young men who are coming forward to labor in the cause of Christ. Our departed friend attained to eminent holiness; and why may not you? What advantages had he to grow in grace, which are not within *your* reach? What motives urged *him* to diligence in the service of God, which does not urge *you?* What divine assistance did he obtain, which you may not obtain in the same way, and in the same measure? As God has provided for you the same inspired volume, the same Sabbath, the same throne of grace, the same salutary discipline of his providence, and the same influences of his Spirit; why may you not attain to the same degree of holiness?

The *employment* of Mr. Evarts was unquestionably among the most powerful causes of his growth in piety. He was active in doing good — was continually consulting and laboring for the salvation of men. This brought into lively exercise all the pious affections of his heart, and so contributed to increase them. And if he was occasionally so engrossed with his great object as to forget himself; his sanctification, instead of being impeded on that account, was so much the more advanced. If a Christian wishes to grow in grace, let him engage, with all his heart, in some benevolent and pious work. As far as may be, let him choose his calling with a view to this important end. At the present day, there is a great variety of ways in which good may be done. There can be no lack of opportunity to any. Let every Christian then, be devoted to some work of benevolence. And if he aspires to improve his character in the highest degree; let him be active in such a way, as will require him to exercise zeal and fortitude, to practise self-denial and endure sufferings. This is the way, and the only way, to rise high in spiritual attainments. If then we covet the best gifts of heaven, let us use the right means to obtain them. If it is our desire to mortify sin, and to cultivate a spirit of elevated piety; let us engage with ardor in works of piety. And let us take care to pursue a course, which will not only be favorable to the good dispositions which we wish to cherish, but directly opposed to the sinful propensities and habits which we wish to overcome. Are we conscious of culpable indolence? Then let us do good in a way which will require diligent personal effort. Have we an inordinate love of money? Then let us be frequent and liberal in our contributions, and so diminish those treasures which are the idols of our hearts. And if any are exposed to feelings of vanity in consequence of their making donations, which are public and honorable; let them abound also in private charities, *not letting their left hand know what their right hand doeth.* If it has been our habit to treat ourselves softly and delicately, and to make our own gratification a special object of pursuit, and if in consequence of this, we are deficient in the more manly, noble virtues; then let us prefer services which are somewhat severe, and never start back from any hardship or danger which may meet us in the path of duty. If our hearts are prone to indulge feelings of distrust in regard to the perfections or the providence of God; it will be of particular importance to us to pursue a course, which will often compel us to give up every ground of confidence but the promise and faithfulness of God, and to rely on him alone for the supply of our wants, the relief of our distresses, and the success of our undertakings. Now it is obvious that such a work as that in which our departed friend was enlisted, is eminently fitted to promote the divine life. Any one who, from pure motives, makes a full surrender of himself to the cause of missions, and, either at home or abroad, devotes his talents and his life to the salvation of the heathen, will be under the best advantages to grow in the spirit of piety. And it will doubtless appear in the great day, when all characters, and all which has helped to form them, shall be revealed, that the holiness which eminent saints in all periods of the church have attained, was owing in no small degree, under God, to the exertions they made and the sufferings they endured for the welfare of their fellow men.

2. We here learn that *sincere devotion to God and diligence in doing good, are followed by the most happy results.* Great peace have they who love God's law. They who forsake all for Christ shall receive an hundred fold even in the present time. Our

deceased brother found this true in his own case. He enjoyed the cordial affection and confidence not only of the Prudential Committee and the American Board, but of all the friends of missions and the friends of Christ. And he had the respect of the public generally — not only those who agreed with him in opinion and feeling, but of those who differed from him; not only of those who favored the interest he sought, but of those who opposed it. In addition to all this, he had the pleasure of being continually conversant with objects which were gratifying to his benevolent and pious heart; and the pleasure of witnessing unexpected success in the missionary cause. He was also favored with a quiet mind, with the consolations of hope, and with many tokens of the divine presence and approbation. He was blessed of God in his family, and in his own soul. And when we come to the closing scene of his life, we may well exclaim — "Mark the perfect man, and behold the upright; for the end of that man is peace." The prevailing state of his mind may be learnt in some measure from the following paper, which he wrote, Feb. 27, 1831, it being the Sabbath, half past eleven, A. M. He was on board the ship Fama, in sight of Abaco, one of the Bahama Islands, twelve days after he sailed from Boston for Cuba.

"Daily, and many times a day, I have been disposed, I trust, to acknowledge the goodness of God, and to consecrate myself anew to his service. I had thought of making a formal and written consecration of myself to the Lord this forenoon; but my mind is so weighed down by my feeble body, that I can write nothing, except of the simplest kind, and cannot adequately dwell upon the amazing theme of being a servant of God, and of having Him for my portion forever."

At half past 3, P. M., he wrote thus,—"We have turned the south-west end of Abaco. I have looked at this work of God, which it is not likely I shall see again; — and have turned my thoughts many times to the great and blessed Creator of all.

"Here, in this sea, I consecrate myself to God as my chief good; — to him as my heavenly Father, infinitely kind and tender towards his children; — to him as my kind and merciful Redeemer, by whose blood and merits alone I do hope for salvation; — to him as the beneficent renewer and sanctifier of the saved. I implore the forgiveness of my numerous and aggravated transgressions; and I ask that my remaining time and strength may be employed for the glory of God, and for the good of his creatures."

"Whether I make my grave on the land, or in the ocean, I submit cheerfully to Him. It will be as He pleases; and so it should be. I pray that the circumstances of my death, be it sooner or later, may be favorable to religion; that I may not deceive myself in the great concerns of my soul; — that I may depart in peace, and be received, through infinite mercy, to the everlasting kingdom of my Lord and Saviour Jesus Christ. Amen."

In the near prospect of death he showed a most happy tranquillity. He had that peace of God which passeth all understanding. Who would not think himself rewarded for the toils and sufferings of a whole life, by what this faithful servant of Christ was permitted to enjoy just before his decease, when God caused so wonderful a light to shine upon his soul. He was at that time in a kind, Christian family in Charleston, S. C., but far removed from his beloved partner and children, whom he had just before particularly and most devoutly commended to God. Seeming to be nearly exhausted, he very tenderly expressed his affection for his Saviour. . . . . . . Soon after, he burst forth with expressions of rapture which cannot be described. "Praise him, praise him, praise him in a way which you know not of." And when it was said, "You will soon see Jesus as he is, and will then know how to praise him;" he exclaimed — "Wonderful, wonderful, wonderful glory! We cannot comprehend — wonderful glory! I will praise, I will praise him! . . . . Wonderful — glory — Jesus reigns."

This was no vision of enthusiasm — no feverish excitement of passion — no delirium of a heated brain. What man was ever better shielded, than he, against mental delusion, and all undue excitement? At that time in particular, a variety of circumstances which might be related, proved beyond any doubt, that he was perfectly rational and self-possessed. That which he experienced was doubtless like what apostles and martyrs and eminent saints have often experienced in a dying hour, when, through the special influence of the Holy Spirit, they have had clear views of the glory of their Saviour, and of their eternal inheritance, and have earnestly desired to be absent from the body, and present with the Lord. May God give me, in my last moments, what our dear brother enjoyed when that vision of glory burst upon his view, and I will gladly bid farewell to all that the world contains.

And what think you, must be the enjoyment of such a Christian in heaven, with a capacity so enlarged, with the powers of reason so active, with affections and desires so pure, what must be his enjoyment in the presence of him whom his soul loveth, in the society of angels and saints, and in the society of no small number, brought to that happy world by means of his faithful labors! Oh! what rest after wearisome labor, and toil, and conflict with sin! Oh! what quietness and ease, after so much sickness and pain! Oh! what blessedness, to be free forever from the feeling and the sight of moral pollution, to be like the Saviour, and to drink of the river of pleasure which flows through the heavenly Paradise.

To the mourning widow and children, there are unfailing sources of consolation. They have sympathizing friends; a present and merciful God; the great and precious promises of his word; and the throne of grace. They have the happiness of knowing that *Jesus reigns*, and that all things will work together for good to them who love God, and are called according to his purpose. These are the rich consolations which afflicted Christians commonly enjoy, and they are sufficient to quiet the agitated breast, and to soothe every grief. But the mourning relatives in this case have consolations which are *not* common. When a man even a good man dies, how seldom is it the fact, that he leaves a character entirely unblemished. And if his friends begin to speak of him in the language of respect and honor, they are soon checked by the recollection of something which marred his reputation. They do indeed cherish a cordial esteem and love for his amiable and virtuous qualities ; but they regret that their thoughts cannot range with delight over his whole character and life. But such was not the fact in regard to our departed friend. The sorrow which the relatives feel for the loss of one so dear to them, is not embittered by the recollection of any noticeable failings in his character, or any palpable errors in his conduct. Theirs is the happiness of knowing, that the beloved partner, parent, and friend, who has been removed from their sight, was not only adorned with a combination of excellences, but was remarkably free from blemishes. They must ever regard it as a precious blessing, that they have been so closely allied to one, whose example was so pure, and so attractive. And they must ever find the events of his private and public life, a subject of delightful and improving reflection. What a rich inheritance to his bereaved family! While they remember the great goodness of God in this respect, their hearts will overflow with gratitude, the bitterness of their grief will pass away.

To the members of the Prudential Committee and other Officers of the Board, this occasion is connected with so many subjects of intense interest, that I know not where to begin or where to end. It must, dear brethren, be a source of the sincerest satisfaction to us, that the chief agency in directing and executing the momentous business of our Foreign Missions, was committed to a man who possessed such qualifications. After twenty years intimate acquaintance with him, and after having been long associated with him in conducting the concerns of the Board, we can give our united testimony to his uprightness and fidelity, and can say of him as truly as of any man, "that in simplicity and godly sincerity, not by fleshly wisdom, but by the grace of God, he had his conversation in the world."

The death of such a man at such a time, we feel to be a very afflictive and distressing event. But though in itself so afflictive, it naturally suggests subjects, which are fitted to awaken lively gratitude to God, and to encourage us in the work of spreading the gospel. For we cannot but remember, that God in mercy gave what he has now taken away. And is it a small matter that, at the critical period when our Foreign Mission was commenced, and during the first years of its progress, divine providence raised up such men as Worcester and Evarts, to be the chief agents in the work? The services of such a man, as our late Secretary, must be important to any cause, at any time. But the work which the friends of missions undertook twenty years ago, was a work of vast magnitude and difficulty. A little temporary zeal and a few desultory efforts could accomplish nothing. There was a necessity for a system of operations, wisely planned, and ably and perseveringly executed. The undertaking called for men of large views, sound judgment and devoted piety — men trained to sober deliberation and efficient action, and not likely to fail either in concerting or in executing measures; — men of so much fire as to warm the hearts of others, and yet so cool and discreet, as to secure their confidence; — men too, who could bring weight of character to the work, instead of depending on the work for character. Now that God in his providence raised up such men as the new and arduous enterprise required, and that he continued one of them ten years, and the other twenty, as principal agents of the Board, and with a success, which has filled the Christian world with admiration and joy; — this, brethren, we must record as among the most encouraging tokens of God's special favor. Shall we then faint under the stroke of his hand? Shall we give way to distrust and fear, and abandon the cause of missions? Shall we even pursue that cause with less zeal, or less hope of success? No. It is enough for us that, although good men die, the Lord lives, and is the same yesterday, to-day, and forever. The cause to which we are devoted is his cause. And we go forward in our endeavors to promote it, with full reliance on his promised aid. We are confident, that he who has all power in heaven and earth, will be present with us in every emergency; that he will raise up men for every post of usefulness; that he will crown with success whatever is done for the enlargement of his church, and finally cause the gospel to triumph in every place.

To conclude. We have been calling to mind the piety and

usefulness of a fellow mortal, and have been considering him as a suitable pattern for our imitation. The contemplation of so excellent a character will, I hope, conduce to our improvement. But be it remembered, there is a character far more exalted. There is an excellence and glory, infinitely surpassing all that is human. It shines forth in this fair creation. It shines forth especially in the face of Jesus Christ. Now while we look with delight upon human excellence, let us not close our eyes to that which is divine. While we gaze upon a dim taper, let us not be blind to the light of day. Are we filled with admiration at the endowments of man who is of yesterday? What adoring thoughts then should we have of the *high and lofty One who inhabiteth eternity!* Before that great and glorious Being, the greatest of men, and the greatest of angels, are *as the small dust of the balance.* The brightest excellence we behold in creation is only a ray from the inexhaustible fountain of light. Have we confidence in a child of earth, because he evinces a good degree of intelligence and faithfulness? What unwavering trust then should we repose in God, whose understanding is infinite, and whose faithfulness never fails! And finally; do emotions of gratitude rise in our hearts, while we recollect the benevolent actions which a feeble, imperfect man performed during a few, fleeting years? How much warmer, nobler gratitude should glow within us towards that infinite Being, from whom cometh all the goodness and all the usefulness of his creatures, and all the happiness of earth and heaven; whose love has a length and breadth and depth and height 'passing all understanding; and who is so great in power and so excellent in working, that he can, in a moment, by a single act of his will, accomplish a good, which created beings can never comprehend. "Blessed, then, be the Lord God of Israel, who only doeth wondrous things; and blessed be his glorious name forever; and let the whole earth be filled with his glory. Amen."

A SERMON

DELIVERED AT THE FUNERAL OF REV. EBENEZER PORTER, D. D., PRESIDENT AND PROFESSOR IN THE THEOLOGICAL SEMINARY, ANDOVER, APRIL 11, 1834.

John 17: 4. — I HAVE GLORIFIED THEE ON THE EARTH; I HAVE FINISHED THE WORK WHICH THOU GAVEST ME TO DO.

THE work assigned to our Saviour was immeasurably greater and more difficult, than was ever in any other instance assigned to man. But he accomplished it perfectly. From the beginning to the close of his life, he never performed an action, never uttered a word, never had a thought or emotion, which varied from the will of God, the perfect standard of right. He unceasingly loved God with all his heart. He was chargeable with no waste of intellectual or moral faculties. There was nothing in his youth or manhood, nothing in his public or private life, nothing in the most secret movements of his heart, which was not perfectly pleasing to God. In the whole frame of his mind, he was so pure and holy, that the most powerful temptations produced no irregular thought or feeling. "The prince of this world came and found nothing in him" — no pride, no selfishness, no depravity in any form or degree. His object in coming into the world was to save that which was lost. He came to redeem sinners from the curse of the law, by being made a curse for them. And how was he straitened till this work was accomplished!

His feelings recoiled at the prospect of drinking the cup which his Father put into his hand; but his recoiling was that of a pure and holy soul, and was accompanied with an entire readiness to do and suffer what the will of God and the salvation of men required. In the garden his agony was such as to produce prostration and bloody sweat; but his heart was perfectly submissive, and in the midst of his distress he could say, "Not my will, but thine be done." Thus, through labor and suffering, he proceeded to Calvary; and there on the cross, in anguish of body and spirit, under the heavy burden of our sins, *he finished his work.*

Far be it from me to liken any man, even the most diligent and faithful, to this holy Saviour. Let any Christian on earth compare his life with the life of Jesus, and what can be the result, but shame and self-condemnation? How is it with him who stands highest among the saints on earth, as to attainments in holiness and diligence in the service of God? Has no part of his time been wasted in unlawful pursuits or indulgences? Have there been no years, or days, in which he has forgotten God and disobeyed his commands? Have even his best actions been free from sin? How does every just view of God's perfect law spoil our fancied goodness, and instead of leaving any room for self-complacency, lead us to abhor ourselves and repent in dust and ashes! Of the most eminent Christians it is true, that they have not already attained, and are not already perfect. They fall below not only the demands of God's spiritual law, but their own desires and aims. In many respects, what they would, they do not; and what they would not, that they do. And when from the bed of sickness, and from the judgment seat, they take a review of their life, they will be astonished to see how little of their proper work they accomplished, and will acknowledge that they were always, even in their best estate, monuments of the forbearance and mercy of God.

And yet Christians are in reality *followers of Jesus.* They have a degree of that holiness, which he had in perfection. They begin to love and obey that law, which he loved and obeyed constantly and entirely. And they begin to possess that moral purity, which he possessed without mixture. Thus having a real though a partial likeness to Christ, and truly following him, though at a distance and with faltering steps, they do, in their humble measure, glorify God, and accomplish the object of their existence. Through the constant aids of the Holy Spirit, they so far finish the work which God has given them to do, that they are, through Christ, accepted of him, and, as good and faithful servants, admitted to the rewards of grace. In this qualified sense, the Apostle said, when the time of his departure was at hand, "I have fought a good fight, I have finished my course, I have kept the faith;" though he had always been conscious that he was not yet perfect, and the highest point he ever reached was to forget the things which were behind, and to press forward to higher attainments, earnestly laboring after perfection in holiness. In this qualified sense, our beloved brother, whose funeral services we are now called to attend, could, we doubt not, have adopted the words of Jesus: "I have glorified thee on the earth, I have finished the work thou gavest me to do."

Dr. Porter was born at Cornwall, Conn., Oct. 8, 1772. At the age of seven he went with his father's family to Vermont, where he remained till he commenced his preparation for a public profession. He was graduated at Dartmouth College, 1792. While a member of college, and through the whole period of his childhood and youth, he was remarkable for his regular and sober habits. During the time that he spent with his father, he acquired a taste for agricultural and mechanical labor, which proved of immense benefit to his health in after life. He had impressions while young, of the importance and necessity of religion; but at what time he first gave evidence of decided piety, I have not been informed. After pursuing theological study under the direction of two distinguished ministers in Connecticut, Dr. Edwards and Dr. Smalley, he entered on the business of the gospel ministry, and was ordained as pastor of the church in Washington, Conn., in Oct., 1796. His pastoral relation to that church was dissolved in Dec., 1811, with a view to his accepting the appointment he had received to the Professorship of Sacred Rhetoric in this Seminary.

In common with other Christians, Dr. Porter stood in a variety of social relations. It is hardly necessary to say, that he sustained these relations and performed the various duties involved in them, to the satisfaction and profit of others. It ought never to be forgotten, that *a good private character*, by which I mean a kind and amiable disposition, and upright and blameless conduct in domestic and social life, is essential to prepare a man for any important public station. Accordingly, when the Apostle undertakes to describe the qualifications which should be found in a Christian minister, he insists particularly upon the importance of the domestic and social virtues. And sorrowful experience has often shown what a fruitful source of evil it is for a man to be put into the ministry, whose disposition is selfish, proud, resentful, or peevish, or who is wanting in probity, or fairness, or any of the qualities which constitute a good private character. The case of our departed brother happily illustrates the peculiar value of an upright, generous and conciliatory disposition, not only as it renders a man agreeable and useful in private, but as it combines its influence with higher attributes of character, to qualify him for usefulness in the most public station.

As a minister of the gospel, Dr. Porter had peculiar excellences. He possessed that combination of intellectual and moral qualities, which constitutes a permanently useful preacher. His understanding was lucid and discriminating; his imagination fertile and remarkably chaste; and his heart susceptible of strong and tender emotion. He was always serious and affectionate; and none who attended his ministry could doubt, that the principle which governed him was love to Christ and to the souls of men. His habit of reasoning was logical and convincing; and his taste, uncommonly pure and classical. He felt an utter repugnancy to all affected grandeur and floridness of language, to everything which savored of pomp or ostentation. His style was simple, neat, perspicuous, and dignified, suited to convey to his hearers the clear and orderly conceptions of his own cultivated mind. He was endued with an instinctive and delicate discernment of what was just and proper, whether in thought or expression. In respect both to the words and phrases he employed, and to their arrangement and sense, he always spoke in *pure English.* Where is the preacher or writer, whose style is more entirely free from everything provincial, pedantic, or ambiguous, or exhibits a more happy union of simplicity and ornament? As a speaker, he had many excellences, and few faults. His sermons were *doctrinal* and *practical.* They set forth the truths of religion in their Scriptural form, and carried them out into their practical uses. His appeals to the conscience and heart were direct and faithful, and often awakening and impressive. A good measure of success attended his ministry, both in the conversion of sinners and the advancement of believers in holiness; which last was as real an object with him as the former. He lived in a time of revivals, and had a marked agency in promoting them.

In February, 1812, he was introduced into the Bartlett Professorship of Sacred Rhetoric in this Institution, the office having been vacated by the resignation of the Rev. Dr. Griffin. Dr. Porter's previous acquaintance with the duties and trials of the pastoral office, together with his intellectual and moral qualifications, fitted him to enter, with pleasing prospects of success, on the department of labor assigned to him. In the various duties which fell to him in the Institution, he had ample use for all his talents and acquisitions; for all his accuracy, and taste, and judgment; for all his activity, patience, and skill. His usefulness was answerable to his qualifications, and to his habitual diligence. Any man who takes into view the good which he accomplished by his instructions in the Seminary, and the works which he published in relation to the business of his department, and considers the intrinsic value of those works, and the high estimation in which they are held, will see that he possessed powers and acquisitions of no ordinary character, and that his time here did not pass away without substantial results.

It was a matter of conscience with Dr. Porter to bend his

efforts, first of all, to the appropriate objects of his own department; secondarily, to the general interests of the Institution; and then to the welfare of the churches, and the success of Christianity at home and abroad. He was well aware that the permanent usefulness of this theological establishment could not be secured alone, but was essentially connected with the general prosperity of the church, and the flourishing state of our various public institutions. To these institutions he had a strong and enlightened attachment. And he not only felt an interest in them, but was always ready to aid them both by his personal services and by pecuniary contributions. He gave liberally to charitable institutions generally. But he contributed more particularly to this Seminary, and the American Education Society. In each of these he founded two scholarships, besides the very generous aid which he afforded to the Porter Rhetorical Society in the purchase of its library. To the American Education Society he also bequeathed the greater part of his property.

In every part of the business which he undertook, he evinced a remarkable degree of *practical wisdom.* His judgment on questions of importance, was seldom mistaken. And it was not uncommon for those who were associated with him to distrust their own opinion, as soon as they found it different from his.

Dr. Porter possessed the peculiar qualifications which are requisite in a *presiding officer.* He had kindness of disposition, self-control, intelligence, and decision. He exhibited politeness without affectation, dignity without pride, and strict adherence to rules of order, without pertinacity. With these qualifications, he was often called to preside on public occasions. And when the office of President was established in this Institution, he was at once selected by his colleagues, as well as by the guardians of the Institution, to fill that office. The manner in which he presided, both here and elsewhere, was always unexceptionable and satisfactory.

He united two qualities, which seldom exist together so eminently as they did in him; — ability to devise great plans of usefulness, and ability to carry forward those plans to a complete accomplishment. Some men, possessing warmth of imagination without judgment, and zeal without discretion or patience, are very fruitful in devising plans of benevolence, but are inclined to leave the labor of execution to other hands. Not so with Dr. Porter. He was the man, whose wisdom was sought in laying out plans of usefulness; and he was the man, to whom the full execution of them, however difficult, could be safely entrusted.

Dr. Porter was a man of *exemplary modesty and humility.* Who ever had reason to suppose that he thought of himself more highly than he ought to think? that in any respect he over-rated his talents, his services, or his piety? When and where did he expect an honor, which others were not ready to bestow upon him, or manifest the feeling that he was not held high enough among his brethren? It was far otherwise. He was so evidently unassuming and humble, that, although he was in all societies, among the first in point of influence, no one felt the least uneasiness that he was esteemed so highly.

At the present day, when there is so much love of preëminence, and so much strife for influence and promotion, it is a happy thing to find a man of high place in the Christian community, who is clothed with humility; a disinterested, straight-forward, and guileless man, who cares less for his own things than for the things which are Christ's; who will begin and end a great undertaking without any scheme for his own interest or honor; who will say just what he means, and do just what he says. Such was our departed brother.

Dr. Porter was a zealous promoter of *revivals of religion.* His Letters on Revivals show how deeply he was impressed with the importance of the subject, and what he considered the characteristics of a true revival, and the proper means of promoting it. On this subject he was well qualified to speak, having been associated with the most able and successful ministers in promoting the revivals which took place during the first part of the present century. The above-mentioned Letters, in which he collects and arranges facts so skilfully, and reasons from them so judiciously and conclusively, are adapted to permanent usefulness in the church.

It was one of his most remarkable characteristics, that he *gave no offence.* In all his conduct, whether in public or private, he was so free from self-importance and dogmatism, he showed so delicate a regard to the opinions and feelings of others, and when he differed from them, made known the difference with so much respect and kindness, and was always so cool and deliberate, that I know not that he ever wounded the feelings of any good man. In this attribute of character, how widely different was he from some, who are possessed of great activity, and are capable of accomplishing much good, who yet have such faults in their temper and manners, that they are sure to hurt the feelings and excite the prejudices of others, and sooner or later to destroy their own influence. The Apostle Paul, for the sake of doing good, took special care to give no offence to any class of men, especially good men. In things not affecting the great interests of religion, he was pliable and conciliatory. As far as he could without unfaithfulness to his Lord, he became "all things to all men," for the very purpose of removing stumbling blocks and winning souls to Christ. Why is it that any at the present day forget the example of the apostles and instead of doing all in their power, as he did, to avoid giving offence, and to conciliate those of an opposite party, seem rather to take pleasure in vexing them, and even to make it an object to provoke their resentment, and drive them to the bitterest hostility. When we witness such things, we are sometimes ready to exclaim, where is that love which Jesus enjoined upon his followers, and which the Apostle describes as the most excellent of all graces; that love which suffereth long and is kind; which seeketh not her own; which doth not behave itself unseemly; which thinketh no evil; which hopeth all things, and endureth all things? Where is that wisdom which is from above, which is pure, and peaceable, and gentle, and easy to be entreated? Where is the dove which rested upon the head of Jesus, as an emblem of the sweet, gentle spirit of his religion? This was a subject which lay near the heart of our departed brother. He ardently loved the *truths* of Christianity, and equally loved its *spirit.* He regarded a bitter, violent temper, though exercised professedly in defence of the gospel, as real *hostility* to the gospel. Both his judgment and heart adopted the maxim of the Apostle, that "the wrath of man worketh not the righteousness of God." He had such meekness and gentleness, as showed that he had been with Jesus. Influenced by such feelings, he gave no offence to any of the contending parties of the day. A decided and unreserved declaration of his opinion, even on the most controverted subjects, was received with candor by those who differed from him. Thus, instead of promoting alienation and strife among brethren, he used his endeavors to promote feelings of forbearance and kindness, and in this way to remove one of the chief causes of collision, and to bring about a more general harmony among the friends of Christ. In this way he conscientiously fulfilled the duty to which he was bound by his own disposition as well as by his inauguration promise — "on all occasions to consult the peace of the churches."

Dr. Porter was far removed from the spirit of a *partizan* in religion. He belonged to no sect. Properly speaking, a sect in religion is a number of persons who separate themselves from the general body of Christians, and maintain some opinion different from the prevailing opinion. We know what are and what have been the doctrines of evangelical Christians generally in this country. We know still more specifically what system of belief has prevailed for the last fifty years among the ministers and churches of New England. These ministers and churches surely are not to be regarded as a party. When, therefore, I say that Dr. Porter was no partizan, my meaning will not be misunderstood. He adhered to the views of Christian doctrine generally held among us; the views exhibited in the writings of Edwards, Bellamy, Brainerd, Smalley, and Dwight. These authors are not sectarian. And Dr. Porter, who honestly embraced and ably defended these views, and whose religious and ministerial character was formed under their influence, was as free as any man living from the spirit of sectarianism. This Institution, in which he was more than twenty years an instructor, is in no sense a sectarian institution. It was founded on the most liberal catholic principles; and in conformity with those principles, it actually received and gratuitously educated pious young men of six or seven different denominations. The creed appointed for the Professors is not a sectarian creed. It was in fact formed as a matter of compromise between men who agreed in the great doctrines of Christianity, but differed in the modes of thinking on minor points. Two sets of founders, previously unknown to each other, had devoted a part of their substance to the establishment of two Theological Seminaries; but, on becoming acquainted with each other's designs, were desirous of uniting their funds in one great Institution; and, for the sake of such a union, were willing, on each side, to do all they could, consistently with a good conscience, to meet the views of those on the other side. Influenced by these kind, Christian feelings, they found that the difficulties in the way of union gradually subsided. After a free interchange of thought, and many sincere efforts, and many fervent prayers to the Father of lights, those concerned on both sides became entirely satisfied, and unanimously adopted the creed as it stands in the *Constitution* of the Seminary,* with a special provision, that the theological opinions of the Professors should correspond with this Confession of Faith, and that if any one of them should cease to believe and teach according to this symbol, he should cease to be a Professor. Dr. Porter was a hearty believer in the doctrines contained in this creed, and all his instructions, both public and private, were in conformity with it. His theological opinions entirely corresponded with the intentions and the express requisitions of the founders. I say this advisedly, having had the most intimate acquaintance with all the facts in the case. And this my humble testimony I solemnly record; so that, as far as Dr. Porter's views of religion are known, there may never, in future times, be a doubt respecting what the founders meant by the creed, or respecting the theological character which they intended the Professors should sustain.

Dr. Porter's belief was *firm* and *uniform*. He was indeed far removed from pertinacity and bigotry, and was ready to adopt any

* See the Additional Statutes, which make a part of the Constitution.

opinion which was well supported by argument. But he had no fickleness, no fondness for what is new, and no tendency to be weary of an opinion, because it had long been held. As he did not adopt his opinions in haste, he was not in haste to change them. But the circumstance which most of all fixed him in the belief of the common doctrines of evangelical religion, was, that the influence of these doctrines was mixed with his devout exercises, and so the truth of them became a matter of personal experience, as well as of divine revelation. It was this which so wedded him to the great principles of religion, that no wind of doctrine could turn him one way or another. Amid all the fluctuations of the present times, he remained steadfast and immovable. And while he was so firmly attached to the cause of truth, he was alive to the danger of error. We well know with what concern and grief he looked upon any speculations on the subject of religion which he considered unscriptural or adventurous, especially upon anything like " removing the *land-marks*," as he often expressed it, and how painfully apprehensive he was of results which would be injurious to the interests of the church.

It has often been alleged by those who are called *liberal*, that a steady, uniform belief of a particular set of doctrines is utterly incompatible with free inquiry, and with progress in knowledge. But if the doctrines believed are true, free inquiry and progress in knowledge are not only *compatible* with a steady, uniform belief, but directly *conducive* to it. And does not the opposite opinion generally arise from the fact, that those who entertain it have been vacillating in their own creed, and have formed a skeptical habit of mind ? If a man who believes divine truth makes progress in knowledge ; will he therefore renounce the truth ? Did Paul or Peter change his belief in the doctrines of Christianity in consequence of growing in knowledge ? When we become Christians, we begin cordially to believe the doctrines of revelation. But our faith at first wants clearness, enlargement and strength. And these wants are to be supplied by increasing our knowledge. By this we clear away obscurity from our views of those doctrines which we have embraced ; we become more fully acquainted with their nature and their mutual relations, with their length and breadth and depth and height. Thus our faith grows in strength and assurance, and in its power to sanctify and comfort the soul. It was so with our departed brother. He knew the truth by experience. He knew God. He knew Jesus Christ. He knew the presence and power of the Holy Spirit. If he was mistaken here, then our preaching is vain, and our faith is vain, and all our efforts to promote experimental religion, and to train up evangelical ministers, are vain; and all the labors and prayers of the Christian world are folly and madness, and will issue in disappointment and shame. But he was not mistaken. The great principles of theology which he believed, are the principles of eternal truth. The more they are examined by honest and candid men, and the more they are opposed by the wicked, the more clearly will it be seen that they are the doctrines of God's word. If the Bible stands, they will stand. Nor will it, I think, be long before the great question at issue among disputants will be, not whether the doctrines commonly called orthodox, are contained in the Bible, but whether the Bible itself is true. Let it come to this. Let Socinians, Pelagians, Neologists and Infidels be on one side, and evangelical Christians on the other. The sooner it comes to this, the better. Then we shall know where we are, and who our antagonists are, and what is the meaning of their words. There will be no more fighting in the dark. The battle will be in full day light, on the open field — direct, fair, honorable, and heaven and earth will be witnesses of the strife and the victory.

It would be difficult to name a man of more unquestionable piety, than Dr. Porter. The evidence he gave of this was the evidence to which the sacred Scriptures attach the highest importance; that is, *a life devoted to the service of God, and regulated by the precepts of the gospel.* His pious affections had both strength and ardor, though they were remarkably sedate and rational. I know not whether he was more distant from extravagance and enthusiasm, or from coldness and indifference. His religion was a *steady, active, holy principle*, and not a *passionate excitement.* He "walked with God." His enjoyments in religion, whether in health or in sickness, were tranquil and uniform, rather than rapturous. He endured his long-continued infirmities, and the distressing diseases with which he was frequently attacked, with an equanimity and patience almost unparalleled. I never knew a man who accomplished so much and enjoyed so much, with health so often interrupted and feeble, and with sickness and pains so severe and exhausting.

He had from the beginning a deep and habitual impression of his responsibility as an officer in this Institution. For his pupils he cherished a sincere and paternal affection, and was solicitous for their improvement in all respects, especially for their growth in grace. In his conversation with his colleagues, and in his letters to them when absent, he frequently and with great earnestness expressed his conviction, that the promotion of elevated piety in the Seminary was of the first importance, and that whatever else was neglected, we ought never to intermit our labors and prayers for this. The Lord grant that all whose duty it will be to advance the welfare of this Institution, may keep in mind the paramount importance of *vital godliness*, regarding it as the life of the Seminary, of the ministry, and of the Christian church.

Brethren and friends, a man has been taken from us of rare excellence of character, both intellectual and moral; a man whose amiable disposition, pious example, and diligent, unremitting services have been and will be an inestimable blessing to this Institution, and to the cause of Christ. Our first duty, under this afflictive dispensation, is entire submission to the only wise God, whose ways are just and right. It is also our duty, to lift up our souls to him who heareth prayer, that through the help of his Spirit we may profit by this bereavement; not forgetting to render to him the warmest gratitude of our hearts, that he has been pleased to continue the life and usefulness of our dear brother for so many years. How can we look at a life so full of activity, usefulness and enjoyment, and see it brought to a close, without feeling a new motive to work while the day lasts. To postpone any duty to a sick and dying bed, is infatuation. What can a man do either for his own soul, or for the souls of his fellow men, when he is sinking under the influence of disease, and the pains of death are getting hold upon him. As to all the great purposes of life we may be *dead* long before we expire. Let us remember this; and let us each day apply ourselves in earnest to the work which God has given us to do.

In this visitation of his providence, God has come near to the bereaved and mourning widow. But she will utter no words of complaint, and will give place to no feelings of disquietude. She knows that God reigneth and doeth his will, and that his will is always wise and good. May God be present with her and give her peace.

This is a solemn and affecting scene to our respected friend, the only surviving founder of this Institution, to whom our departed brother for so many years sustained a relation of peculiar endearment. Our prayer for him shall be, that the comforts of the divine Spirit may cheer and support him under this affliction; that God may still prolong his life, and health, and usefulness, and enable him to finish his work.

As to those who have been called to part with a colleague, particularly those of us who for more than twenty years were most happily united with him in all the labors and trials which have here fallen to our lot, — words are not adequate to express what we feel on this occasion. In our sorrow we might be ready to ask; what shall we do without that long-tried and faithful friend and colleague, who has been taken from us? But we will rather say, " The Lord liveth and blessed be our rock;" and pray that *his grace may be sufficient for us.*

It is well known what a high place the lamented President of this Seminary held in the esteem and confidence of the Trustees and Visitors, of the members of the Institution, of the many hundreds, now engaged in the service of the church, who once enjoyed his instructions, and of ministers and Christians far and near. But we trust he enjoys that which is infinitely more precious than the highest esteem and affection of man, even the approbation of his Saviour. Blessed indeed is he, to whom the final Judge will say: " Well done, good and faithful servant, enter thou into the joy of thy Lord."

A SERMON

DELIVERED IN THE THEOLOGICAL SEMINARY, ANDOVER, FEB. 1, 1835, ON THE DEATH OF HENRY LYMAN, SAMUEL MUNSON, AND OTHERS.

Heb. 12: 11.—Now NO CHASTENING FOR THE PRESENT SEEMETH TO BE JOYOUS, BUT GRIEVOUS: NEVERTHELESS, AFTERWARD IT YIELDETH THE PEACEABLE FRUITS OF RIGHTEOUSNESS UNTO THEM WHO ARE EXERCISED THEREBY.

SINCE the commencement of our academic year, we have received the tidings of the death of five young ministers, who were lately members of this Institution. Three of them died of sickness in our own land, and two by the hand of violence in a foreign land.

These awakening dispensations, dear brethren and friends, are addressed particularly to us. And if under the influence of the divine Spirit, we open our ears to the monitory voice of these providences, we shall experience the blessed effects of divine chastisement.

It seems proper, first of all, to apply the subject to *the members of this Institution.* The young men, whose early death we have been called to mourn, recently lived within these consecrated walls. Here they pursued their studies. They joined with us in our morning and evening devotions, and assembled with us in the sanctuary to worship God, and to commemorate the dying love of Jesus. They had entered upon the active duties of their calling.

One of them had just preached his *first sermon*, which proved to be his *last*.

These affecting dispensations remind you, who are here preparing for the sacred office, that the time is short, and urge you to do with your might whatsoever your hand findeth to do. Could those brethren, who have so soon closed their labors on earth, speak to you now, they would exhort you to apply yourselves in earnest to every duty, to make the most intense efforts to fit yourselves for your sacred calling. They would tell you, that the greatest diligence and ardor which they ever exhibited here in pursuit of their object, instead of being excessive, fell far below the proper mark. I have no words to convey to your minds the impression which I have, of the vast importance of diligence and ardor in theological students. If you would apply yourselves to theological study with suitable zeal, casting off all indolence, keeping the powers of your minds fully awake, and watchfully guarding against all hinderances — if you would all come to this — my heart swells with joy to think what you might *be*, and what you might *do*. Your improvements in the seminary would be double, yea, fourfold, to what is common; and your usefulness afterwards might be increased in a like proportion. Even if your life should be short, like that of those who have so soon been taken away — in that short life, you might accomplish as much as is generally done in a long life. And if the major part of you should be continued in active service to the common age of ministers, who can tell the amount of good you might accomplish for the cause of Christ? What better use, then, can you make of these mournful dispensations, than to regard them as incitements to increased diligence and zeal in the appropriate occupation of theological students — diligence proportioned to the greatness of the object before you, and wisely distributed among your various duties.

These events of providence lead you to consider *what you should make your first and chief business during your residence in the Seminary?* Could the young ministers lately deceased speak to you on this subject from the eternal world, they would exhort you to make that your chief business here, which is in reality the chief business of life. And what is this, taken in a personal view, but to be renewed in the spirit of your minds, to grow in grace and in the knowledge of Jesus Christ, and to secure an inheritance among them who are sanctified ? You will by and by tell your fellow-men, that this is *their* great concern. It is equally *yours*. Amid the variety of objects which solicit your attention, you may be tempted to neglect your own souls, and to substitute something else in the place of personal piety. Place yourselves then in imagination, where you will soon be in fact, near the close of your probation, with death and the judgment just before you; and you will have the sentiment fixed deep in your hearts, that the care of the soul is the one thing needful for you, while you are members of the Seminary, and at every other period of your life; and that, if you neglect this, you neglect what is more important to you than all things else, and are guilty of a folly and a sin for which no tears or sufferings can ever atone.

The occasion also should lead you to consider, *what branches of intellectual improvement demand your chief attention?* Suppose that, within one or two years after entering on your profession, you yourself should be laid on a dying bed, and that a friend of yours, about to join a theological seminary, should ask you, what particular studies ought to command his attention; can you doubt what answer you would give ? Those studies, you would say, are most important, which are most intimately related to the great interests of religion; — those which lead most directly to the knowledge of the word of God, and which will help you most fully to understand, and most successfully to teach the essential truths of Christianity; those, in a word, which will fit you to do most towards accomplishing the grand object for which the Saviour came down from heaven, and died on the cross.

The occasion calls your attention to another point. Those five brethren, whose early death has been announced to us, know for a certainty, whether their hope of salvation was well founded. A *sincere* repentance, a *sound* conversion, prepares men to die, and to appear before God. But a spurious conversion, a superficial religion, though it may bear the test of human inspection, will be worthless in the state of retribution. Consider this subject now, while a mistake may be corrected. You are soon to go forth to the duties and trials of the ministry. And you are soon to go forth to meet your Lord and Judge. Behold, the bridegroom cometh. Arise, and trim your lamps; and take heed that you be not like the foolish virgins, who found, too late, that they had no oil in their lamps.

The present occasion suggests important instruction, *to those students whose purpose it is to engage in the missionary service.* An event of a sorrowful and appalling character has been announced to you. Two young missionaries, urged on by Christian love to seek the good of those who are perishing in ignorance and vice, have been suddenly cut off by an act of the most shocking barbarity. By this event you are carried back to primitive times, when it was nothing uncommon for missionaries to suffer martyrdom. How fondly have we been hoping that such times were forever gone by! And the feeling may have found a place in our hearts, that as there are fewer trials and dangers to be encountered now than formerly, lower qualifications will be sufficient. If so, then may not God have permitted this awful event for the very purpose of correcting this hurtful mistake, and making a more just impression on our minds as to the proper character of missionaries? You now see, perhaps in a more striking light than ever before, that as they who engage in the missionary service must die, and may die at the very commencement of their work; those who are looking forward to that service ought, by all means, to be living Christians, purified by faith, and changed into the holy image of God. And as difficulties and perils may lie in your path, you ought to be armed with invincible courage and patience and trust in God, and so be prepared for trials, however sudden and severe. Accustom yourselves to self-denial and labor. Banish forever the love of praise, the love of promotion, and a worldly spirit in every form. Let your heart be possessed with so strong an affection for the heathen, that the difficulties and trials associated with the missionary work may lose all their terror, and even become attractive. Ponder well those trials. Count the cost. Regard sacrifices and sufferings as constituting a substantial part of the life of missionaries. Be ready to follow Christ to suffering and to death. Have such faith in God, and such love to the souls of men, that what has taken place on the island of Sumatra will have no power to disquiet your minds, or turn you back from your holy enterprise. The last command of the risen Saviour is not — Go preach the gospel *so far as you can without exposing yourselves to persecution and death.* It is peremptory: "Go ye into all the world, and preach the gospel to every creature." The early propagation of the gospel cost thousands of lives. The mere profession of Christianity was in numberless instances attended with imprisonment, tortures, and death. But did the prospect of sufferings prevent ministers from preaching the gospel, or private Christians from adhering to it? Did their conscience bend or their heart grow faint under persecution? Persecution did indeed help to draw the line between true and false professors. So it would do now. Should dangers and troubles multiply, and should the powers of the world and the powers of darkness breathe out threatenings and slaughter against the preachers of the cross in every missionary field; what would be the effect upon the number of missionaries? Weigh the question well.

The events which have recently occurred, are eminently suited to *withdraw our confidence from human instruments and human efforts, and to bring us to put all our trust in God.* He could, if he pleased, work without any instruments whatever; or if he employed instruments, he might employ those of far higher qualifications, than imperfect dying men possess. Why then has God chosen to make use of imperfect, dying men, as agents in carrying on his work of grace? Is it because he stands in need of our help? Why, it seems to me, brethren, that for God to take such poor, weak things as we are, and make us in any measure fit for his service, and then sustain us in it, costs him, (if I may so speak,) costs him far more, than it would to do the work himself, without any agency of ours. Certainly the infinite God, if he pleased, could at once by a special revelation, communicate the knowledge of the gospel to the minds of the heathen, and by his Holy Spirit could effectually induce them to accept it, and so give them eternal life, without the labors of gospel ministers. Let him only speak the word, and all this would instantly be done, just as he said, "Let there be light, and there was light." — For God to take human beings, so ignorant, so sinful, so unfit for his service, and to employ them in the work of the ministry; to bear with their pride, and unfaithfulness, and all the faults of their character; to call them back from their wanderings; to watch over them and guard them every moment, and by the exertion of his own omnipotence, to render their poor services successful; — all this is surely a great work. I repeat it — for God to make use of such feeble, imperfect instruments in saving souls, requires more agency on his part, than to save them without any instruments whatever. For now, he does *himself*, by his own special agency, convert and save perishing men, and in addition to this, he takes us, who are but "dust and ashes," into his service, and by his great power and mercy helps us along, constantly working in us to prepare us to act for him, and then working in the souls of sinners by us — and that, too, when our miserable labors are frequently nothing but a hinderance to his own designs. My brethren, God does not call us into his service to supersede his own agency. He does it rather for the opposite purpose. It is the very nature of God and the pleasure of God to *act*. And to act as he does, is his *glory*. It costs him no effort, like what *we* call effort, to put forth his almighty agency. It is easy for God to create millions of worlds, and to sustain them for ages of ages. It is perfectly easy for him to do all this, and to do it forever if he pleases. Most surely then, the infinite God, in accomplishing the work of redemption, does not bring the power of men or angels into action to prevent the necessity of exercising his own power; but for the very purpose of *exercising it in the largest measure*. According to this exalted principle, so different from the narrow principle which governs man, God did not choose that plan which would require the *least* of his agency, but that which would require the *most*. The whole complicated machinery of the natural world, is such, as constantly to call forth and display the infinite power of God. He loves to exert his infinite power; and he loves to *display* it too — not for his own benefit, but for ours. Accordingly, if God is pleased to make use of instruments in saving sinners, we are not to imagine that he will choose those of the highest order — those endued with perfections nearest to divine; because, if such exalted agents should come out between God and us, the grandeur of their character, and the dazzling splendor of their operations, might fill the narrow field of our vision, and hide the glory of God from our view. We are rather to conclude, so far, at least, as the benefit of human beings is concerned, that God will choose instruments which have no overpowering grandeur of character — instruments altogether inadequate, of themselves, to accomplish the work designed — instruments so manifestly insufficient, that the whole world shall be compelled to look through them, and above them, to a divine agency, and to give glory to him "who worketh all in all."

It is nothing against these views, that the angels are "ministering spirits, sent forth to minister to the heirs of salvation." They are indeed ministering spirits. But their agency is all concealed from our view. For what reason? Why are we not permitted to behold those benevolent beings, that we may love and honor them, as we do the ministers of the gospel? May not the reason be found in the imbecility of our nature, and in our danger of being overawed by angelic appearances, and of being drawn into idolatry? Angels can behold angels without danger. They have stronger minds than we. When the most resplendent instruments come out clearly to their view, they can see God through them, and in them — and can see more of God, because the instruments he employs are so glorious. But is it not otherwise with us? Are we not in danger of looking even upon a mortal like ourselves, if distinguished by the lustre of his character, with an excessive veneration?

The principle above stated is exactly the one which the Apostle brings out, when he says, that God has committed the treasure of the gospel "to *earthen vessels*" — for this very purpose, "that the excellence of the power may be of God, and not of us." The weakness and frailty of the instruments are to turn off the eyes of all men from them to God, and to make it manifest, that he does the work, and deserves all the praise.

Such is the view which the Scriptures give of the agents that God employs, and the reasons why he employs them, in the work of saving sinners. Such also is the view inculcated upon us by the events of divine providence, particularly by those which have recently taken place. The missionaries whom we send forth are "earthen vessels;" the most healthy and vigorous of them are frail as the grass. They may be quickly wasted away by sickness, or still more quickly cut off by the violence of men. And those of them who are most conspicuous for their piety, are subject to weakness and imperfection. Let us, then, never place our reliance upon feeble human agents, but upon God, the Almighty Agent, "of whom, and through whom, and to whom, are all things."

But let not the events which have come to pass discourage the devoted friends of the missionary cause. These events are appointed as the means of improving our characters, and so of leading on to greater success in the end. There is something very animating in that principle of God's providence, which makes disappointments and sufferings, the means of bringing about great results. Enterprises of extraordinary moment are not carried forward smoothly and easily, but are invariably associated with difficulties, and often with disasters. May we not then indulge the cheering thought, that the various adverse and painful events which have met us in the missionary enterprise, are in reality expressions of the divine favor, and are clear indications, that the work in which we are engaged is one of singular greatness and is ultimately to be attended with glorious success.

The present occasion leads us to contemplate a *profound mystery of divine providence* — a mystery as unfathomable, as any of the doctrines of our religion. At the present day, almost two thousand years after Christ made propitiation for the sins of the world, and after so much has been done by apostles, and martyrs, and other servants of God, and so many prayers have been offered up for the spread of the gospel, and when we have been inclined to think that the darkness is almost past, and the universal reign of Christ near at hand — there is still on the island of Sumatra a tribe of cannibals — a million of human beings so savage and cruel, that they murder their fellow-men, even those who come to them on an errand of love, and then devour their mangled, lifeless bodies. Why is it that men are anywhere found possessed of a character so unutterably base and dreadful? But this mystery does not end with the cannibals in Sumatra, and in other parts of the earth. It extends in all its unsearchableness, to the whole heathen world. Why is it, that even at this day three fourths of the human race are left in darkness, having never known the name of the only Saviour? Why has not God caused them to hear the glad tidings, when at any time during the ages of darkness that are past, he could have raised up unnumbered ministers, and sent them forth into all lands, and could have made the gospel preached by them effectual to salvation; — or could have saved them with infinite ease, if he had seen fit, without the labor of any ministers? Why has he suffered so great a part of the world to remain a barren, frightful wilderness, when it has been in the power of his hand to make it a fruitful field?

It does not clear up the mystery at all to say, that *the Christian world has been in fault;* that if they had been as benevolent and active, and as fervent in prayer, as they ought to have been, the sound of the gospel, accompanied with the power of the Holy Ghost, would long ago have reached all nations. The question is why God has not *made* the Christian world thus benevolent, and active, and fervent in prayer, — why he has not actually raised up well qualified ministers in sufficient numbers to accomplish the work of the world's conversion. The mystery of mysteries is, that God, with his infinite power and wisdom and love, has not done this. The inspired writers do not attempt to answer the questions which may be raised respecting this subject. They teach us, what is important for us to know, that God in all these things, acts "according to the counsel of his own will," and that his will is infinitely wise and good — and there they leave the subject; — and they leave it there, that the loftiness of man may be brought low, and that God alone may be exalted.

I shall touch upon one point more, and that is *the true spirit of the Christian religion* — so widely different from the spirit of the world. A tribe of cannibals in Sumatra have inhumanly killed and devoured our beloved brethren, who went there from the purest benevolence. What now shall we do to avenge the innocent blood of these missionaries? Shall we petition our government to send forth an army to inflict signal punishment upon those monsters of cruelty, and to teach them, that American citizens cannot be injured with impunity? Or shall we pray God to send down fire from heaven to destroy them? No, brethren. The God whom we worship, is *the God of love.* And our Saviour, infinitely merciful himself, requires all his disciples to copy his example, and to cherish a benevolent, forgiving temper towards their worst enemies. And when, after his resurrection from the dead, he commissioned his apostles to go forth to preach the glad tidings of salvation, he directed them to *begin at Jerusalem,* where so many prophets had been killed — yes, he directed them to begin the work of benevolence *at Jerusalem,* in the midst of those who had shed his blood! Behold the true spirit of our religion! It is the spirit of meekness, gentleness and forgiveness. It is the spirit of love — love to enemies, persecutors and murderers. Guided by this spirit, let us meditate no return to those who have massacred our beloved missionaries, but to labor and pray for their eternal welfare. Let us take special pains to send the blessings of the gospel to Sumatra, and to the Batta territory where Lyman and Munson were slain. And let the missionary, selected for the purpose, be instructed to preach the gospel to the inhabitants of Sumatra, *beginning at Batta.* With holy confidence in God, let that missionary go forward to his work of mercy among those poor, wretched cannibals. And let him search out the very men who murdered our brethren, and begin with *them.* As they are first in guilt and wretchedness, let him first seek their good. With a heart that pities them, and longs for their salvation, let him proclaim to them the glorious gospel:—*Behold I bring you glad tidings. Jesus died for sinners, for the chief of sinners. I offer you pardon in his name.* Thus let him preach to those miserable heathen, the unsearchable riches of Christ. And if the grace of God should touch their hearts, and bring them to repentance — and if they should at length be seen at the feet of Jesus, weeping for their sins, and devoting their whole souls to him, and then going about to proclaim his abounding grace; — Oh! this would be a spectacle, at the sight of which angels would rejoice, and the report of which would fill the hearts of ten thousand believers with gladness. And could those two missionaries, now we trust in heaven, hear the blessed tidings of the repentance of their *murderers,* how would they join with the angels in their rejoicing, while with a Christ-like spirit, they would feel willing to go down again to earth, and bear again the pains of death, for the joy of beholding such precious fruits of God's Spirit, and such glorious triumphs of his grace!

A SERMON

DELIVERED AT THE FUNERAL OF THE REV. JOHN HUBBARD CHURCH, D. D., WHO DIED AT PELHAM, N. H., JUNE 12, 1840.

BRETHREN AND FRIENDS; I stand here to-day in compliance with the request of that beloved brother, who now sleeps in death. I visited him near the time of his decease. During that visit, he requested me to preach at his funeral; then taking his Bible, which he had by his pillow, and pointing to a particular passage, he said, "I wish you to preach from that text." It was the second Epistle to Timothy, 1: 18, "*The Lord grant unto him, that he may find mercy of the Lord in that day.*" He then said: "I want you to dwell particularly upon this idea, *that we depend on the mercy of the Lord for our salvation; and that ministers of the gospel, as well as others, will need that mercy at the judgment day.*" He repeated it: "What I wish you to show is, *that the salvation of ministers, as well as of all others, depends on the sovereign mercy of God; and that it is infinitely important that we obtain that mercy now and hereafter.* Dwell upon the idea, *that we shall need to find mercy of the Lord at the last day.*" He enlarged upon this sentiment in various ways; and in the whole of that interview he showed, that the doctrine of salvation by the free grace of God, through the righteousness of Jesus Christ, was the ground of his hope and the spring of his consolations on his dying bed.

Deeply impressed with the recollection of that last interview, I shall make it my object on this occasion to exhibit *the doctrine of salvation by grace, as exemplified in the life and character of our departed brother.* And permit me to say, that what I shall advance on this subject will not be a matter of conjecture; nor will it be made out from a mere general acquaintance with Dr. Church as a minister of the gospel; but will be the result of my intercourse and friendship with him for almost fifty years; an intercourse and friendship so free and intimate, that I have as true a knowledge of his mind and heart, as one man can have of the mind and heart of another in the present world. I speak too in the presence of a church and society for whom he labored in the ministry thirty-seven years, and who will judge of the correctness of my remarks.

Turn your thoughts then to *the doctrine of salvation by grace, as exemplified in our beloved brother; particularly as it was the object of his faith, the matter of his inward experience, and the spring of his pious and useful life.*

In the first place, the doctrine of salvation by grace was the object of his faith. He regarded this as the essence of the gospel — the great truth, in which all other truths of revelation centre. He believed, as the followers of Christ in all ages have believed, that the salvation of men is wholly of God; that it originated in his eternal love; that it is entirely and preëminently a work of divine grace.

The nature and the method of salvation imply, that man is an apostate being, alienated from God, totally lost, without any power to atone for his sins, and without any spring of holiness or tendency to obedience in himself. This ruined state of the human family is pre-supposed in the work of redemption. Christ came to seek and save that which was lost; so that all to whom the work of redeeming mercy can apply are depraved and lost. The posterity of Adam, according to the Scriptures, are all *sinners.* The evil which is in them is *moral* evil, and it is *their own*, for which they are justly exposed to the divine displeasure; and their condemnation is an act of God's *righteousness.* Such was the belief of our brother. He looked upon the law of God, and the plan of his government, as holy, just, and good. He believed the divine appointment, connecting the character and condition of Adam's posterity with his conduct, to have been an act not only of sovereignty, but of wisdom and righteousness. With his views of the divine character, he wanted nothing to satisfy him that the appointment, so plainly asserted in Rom. 5: 12—19, was just and right, but the simple fact that it was the appointment of God. And he wanted nothing to satisfy him that it was the appointment of God but the declaration of an inspired writer. This was the end of the matter. He considered it a doctrine not to be made out by human reason and philosophy, but to be taught by revelation — a doctrine to be shaped and determined, not by the weakness and shallowness of the human mind, but by the unsearchable and boundless wisdom of the divine mind.

Here the work of salvation by grace comes in. God so loved the world, that he gave his only begotten Son to die for them. And the Saviour actually died for them. To deliver them from the curse of the law, he was made a curse for them. By his obedience and death he made propitiation for sin, and procured forgiveness and eternal life for all believers. This was the faith of Dr. Church. He believed the finished righteousness of Christ, consisting in his perfect obedience and vicarious sufferings, to be the only ground of our forgiveness, the grand, meritorious cause of salvation; as it is written, there is no other name under heaven given among men whereby we must be saved, but the name of Jesus. And while Jesus is the only Saviour, he is also all-sufficient, able to save the chief of sinners, and to save to the uttermost; so that no one need to despair on account of the greatness of his sins. The salvation to be obtained is a free, gratuitous salvation, not resting at all on any moral worth in us, but springing wholly from the eternal love and mercy of God. Such a salvation, and such only, is adapted to those who have destroyed themselves, and have not now, and never can have, any worthiness to entitle them to the divine favor. To those who are in this condition Jesus Christ is presented as a complete Saviour; and those who are ready to perish, are invited to come to him and receive of his fulness. Thus the door of mercy is opened; a Saviour, unspeakably precious and glorious, and every way suited to our case, is revealed, and we are called upon by the voice of infinite majesty and infinite love to receive him. Oh! how many times, and with what affectionate earnestness has that tongue, which is now silent in death, proclaimed this glorious doctrine, this provision of mercy for the salvation of men! And how feelingly did he dwell upon it in that happy hour which I spent with him, just before his decease!

But it is implied in that doctrine of salvation which is taught in the Scriptures, and which our departed brother believed, that men in their natural state will not come to Christ that they may have life; that, while left to themselves, they are governed by that carnal mind which is enmity against God, and, consequently, that their recovery to holiness, as really as their forgiveness, must be of God. He calls sinners with a holy calling, not according to their works, but according to his own purpose and grace. They are born of God. The commencement and progress of their renewal to holiness is "*not of blood, nor of the will of the flesh, nor of the will of man, but of God.*" Their obedience springs not from any principle of action naturally in them, but from the divine Spirit. He works in them all the good pleasure of his goodness, and the work of faith with power. Every Christian virtue is the fruit of the Holy Spirit. The application of redemption to sinners is to be ascribed wholly to God. He gives them repentance. He works faith in them. He sheds abroad his love in their hearts by the Holy Ghost. So the apostles taught; and so our brother believed, and so he preached. Nor did he trouble himself to show how our entire dependence on the Spirit of God is to be reconciled with our free, moral agency. He knew them to be reconcilable, because he knew them both to be true. He left the actual reconciling of them to be made out where only it can be well made out, in the inward experience and consciousness of Christians.

An important part of salvation is the justification of those who believe; which is an act of God's free grace, wherein he pardons all our sins, and accepts us as righteous in his sight, not for our works, and not for any merit in our repentance or faith, but altogether on account of Christ our atoning High Priest, and on the ground of his death and intercession. The Apostle, Rom. 4: 6, speaks of God's imputing righteousness without works. The merit of Christ's obedience and sufferings, is imputed to believers — is so made over to them, so reckoned to their account, that it avails to their benefit, and they receive the blessings of it as really, as though they themselves were righteous. They are justified by faith — a faith which falls in with the scheme of grace revealed in the gospel, and receives Christ as the only Saviour and the blessings of salvation as a free gift. Thus the whole of salvation comes from God, and will be to the praise of the glory of his grace.

This work of salvation is so carried on in the souls of the redeemed, that they are secured against final apostasy, gradually delivered from the sin that dwells in them, and advanced from one degree of santification to another, till they are made perfect in holiness, and admitted to the inheritance of the saints in light. There they will receive their reward; but it is a reward, not of debt, but of grace. They will not stand upon their own merit at the bar of justice. The sentiment will be as deeply fixed in their hearts at the judgment-day, as it ever was before: " If thou, Lord, shouldst mark iniquity, O Lord, who could stand? Their entrance into the heavenly world will be as much a matter of grace, as their renewal by the Spirit, or the forgiveness of their sins when they first believed. So our dear brother regarded it, living and dying.

It was also his belief, that the Lord Jesus will, according to his promise, carry on this gracious work of salvation in the church and in the world, till all who were given him of the Father shall come to him, and the innumerable and glorious multitude of his people shall be presented, without spot, before the throne of God, and thus the work of grace be brought to its final consummation.

But this doctrine of salvation by grace is so extensive, that I can do nothing on this occasion, but give you some of its outlines. The subject can never be exhausted. It will be the theme of contemplation to the saints in heaven through everlasting ages.

When I say that this doctrine was the object of faith to our departed brother, I say nothing which distinguishes him from others. The belief of the doctrine is common to all evangelical ministers and Christians. But if Dr. Church was not distinguished from ministers and Christians generally by what he believed, he was by the manner of his believing, that is, by the strength and constancy of his faith. Many who really believe the doctrine of divine grace, believe it feebly and imperfectly. Their faith is divided, and fluctuating. But it was the happiness of our brother, that he held this essential doctrine with a strong and steady faith, a faith which rested, with full confidence, on the sure word of God. He was firmly anchored; and no violence of winds or waves could move him. Like Abraham, he was strong in faith, giving glory to God. Whether he conversed, or preached, or prayed, he showed that the things revealed in the Scriptures respecting the salvation of sinners were all realities to him. He would have doubted his own existence, or the existence of God, as soon as he would have doubted the doctrines of grace. If we believe these things doubtingly, we shall be likely to regard them as of little value, and to place them in the back ground. When the Apostle gave such prominence to the doctrine of Christ crucified, and resolved to know nothing else in comparison, he showed that he believed it with all his heart. The doctrines of grace are of such a nature that, if they are true doctrines, they are chief doctrines. We cannot heartily believe them, without regarding them as of the first consequence in the system of divine truth. It is, moreover, a fact, that the doctrine of salvation by grace, when rightly apprehended and firmly believed, reflects a clear light on all other related subjects. It helps us to detect error. For whatever interferes with this chief truth, or leads us to consider it as less important than the Apostle represented it to be, we know to be false; just as we know any opinion in philosophy or ethics to be false, which would withdraw our homage from God, or our confidence from his word. If we build upon the foundation of the apostles and prophets, *Jesus Christ himself being the chief corner stone*, our edifice will have symmetry, beauty, and strength. It was this which gave the stamp of excellence to the faith of our lamented brother, and made it like the faith of the apostles and first Christians. He made *Christ the chief corner stone.* Salvation by grace through the blood of the cross, was the grand article of his faith.

But I must proceed to my *second point.* While the doctrine of salvation by grace was the object of faith to the good man who has been taken from us, it was also the matter of his inward experience. Through the power of the Holy Spirit, his religious character was formed in correspondence with this gospel truth, and under its influence.

Forty-three years ago I began to have a more particular acquaintance and correspondence with this dear brother on the subject of religion. Soon after that, we were united together as companions and room-mates in the study of theology. Thus I had opportunity to know all that could be known by man of his religious views and exercises. On this subject I could with pleasure expatiate. But I must confine myself to the object proposed, namely, to show that the doctrine of salvation by grace was wrought into our brother's spiritual experience, and that his religious exercises and habits corresponded with this gospel truth, answering to it, as the impress on wax answers to the seal. I mean to say, it was so in a good measure. Entire conformity with divine truth in our inward views and affections, would imply a more exalted state than any one attains to in the present life. Of this, who was ever more conscious than Dr. Church? The leading point in his religious experience, was a deep and continually growing conviction of his own sinfulness and ill-desert. This conviction did not relate particularly to his outward conduct. For this had been remarkably fair and blameless from early life.

But during his last year at Harvard College, he had strong, and sometimes distressing conviction of sin. It was as certain to him as his own existence, that he was by nature a child of wrath; that he had that carnal mind which is enmity against God; and that, in his natural state, he had no spring of holy love, no element of goodness. After a long and painful struggle in his own mind, he came at length to the full persuasion, that it was not in him to renew his own heart. He was convinced by his own experience, that, whatever motives might be urged upon him, and whatever efforts he might make, he could effect nothing without the influence of the Holy Spirit. He was persuaded that it would be just in God to leave him to perish, and that, if he was saved, it must be by God's sovereign grace. In that state of mind he took the low place before God which properly belongs to the sinner; and there he was, humbled, broken-hearted, helpless; justifying the divine law, abhorring himself, expecting no relief from his own exertions — but still cleaving to the hope, that God would interpose and have mercy upon him. I well remember how strongly and tenderly he spoke of these things in conversation, and in his letters; and with what humble gratitude he set forth the work of divine grace, after He who commanded the light to shine out of darkness, shined in his heart, to give the light of the knowledge of the glory of God in the face of Jesus Christ; and after he was induced to accept the merciful invitation of the Saviour, "*come unto me, and I will give you rest.*" Jesus gave him rest. His religious exercises at that time were clear and decided, and gave his Christian friends very satisfactory evidence that he had passed from death to life. And yet he himself was so occupied with adoring views of the abounding grace of God, and with a sense of his own sinfulness and unworthiness, that he thought but little, comparatively, of his own exercises. His prevailing sentiment was not this: *I have now become a Christian, an heir of heaven! O! how happy I am; and how happy I shall be forever!* It was rather this: *How glorious is God! How wonderful his mercy in saving them that are lost! How vile and hateful is sin! How precious the Saviour! What shall I render to the Lord for all his benefits!*

And as this was the aspect of his spiritual experience at that period, so it continued to be through life. He felt more and more, that salvation is of God. All the good in man he ascribed to divine grace; and he relied upon that grace for the whole of salvation. It was the steady, permanent habit of his mind, to exalt God and to humble himself. The greater his knowledge of the holiness and grace of God, the greater was his self-abasement. These two appeared to keep pace with each other. In his letters, some of them written forty years ago, and some a short time before his death, he enlarged upon this precious truth, and seemed to cling to it as his only support, that *Christ is all in all* — our wisdom, our righteousness, our sanctification, and our redemption; that we must, by faith, receive of his fulness, and that in proportion as we do this, we are complete in him. Any magnifying of the power of self-ruined man for the great business of sanctification; anything which implied that there is any sufficiency in us for spiritual duty; anything which tended to hinder us from walking by faith on the Son of God, or to hide from us the truth, that all our sufficiency is of God, instantly excited his apprehension. He turned away from it as contrary to his experience, to his prayers, and to all the movements and impulses of his renewed nature; and, what is more, contrary to the spirit of the sacred writers. It cost him no labor of reasoning to find out an error like this. He had already detected it in his own heart. He knew it to be an error, just as he knew atheism to be an error.

But I must quit this pleasing topic and proceed to another, not less pleasing, namely, that the doctrine of salvation by grace, which was thus wrought into the inward experience of our beloved brother, was *the spring of his pious and useful life.* It was his full and unwavering belief of this gospel doctrine, and an inward affection and habit of mind corresponding with it, that was the efficacious principle of a holy life.

The mistake of many, and that which occasions a constant failure in their endeavors after holiness is, that they go to work in religion, without the vital *principle* of religion. They look for good fruit, without a good tree; for motion, without life. Conscience is not the effectual spring of right action. Self-love is not. Fear of misery is not. Speculative knowledge of the truth is not. Any or all of these may exist, and may produce a visible effect on the surface of a man's character. But they have no power to overcome the principle of evil in the heart. We must be created anew in Christ Jesus. The Spirit of God must give us spiritual life; and then we shall live unto God. We must have that faith which God works in the heart; and then good works will follow.

We have the best evidence that our brother had the indwelling of the Holy Spirit, which Christ represents as a well of living water, springing up to everlasting life. See how mightily this inward principle wrought in him! See what fruits it yielded! It prepared him to live and act right in all the relations and all the conditions of life. I might appeal to those who enjoyed his ministerial instructions in the language of Paul: "Ye are witnesses, and God also, how holily, and justly, and unblameably he behaved himself among you that believe; as ye know how he exhorted and comforted, and charged every one of you, (as a father doth his children,) that ye would walk worthy of God, who hath called you to his kingdom and glory." You are all witnesses, that he aimed faithfully and affectionately to declare unto you the whole counsel of God; that he sought not *yours*, but *you;* that he determined to know nothing among you save Jesus Christ and him crucified; and that his speech was not with enticing words of man's wisdom, but in demonstration of the Spirit and of power.

Doctor Church was a minister of the gospel more than forty years, and was known extensively in our community. And what minister or Christian did you ever know, who more uniformly exhibited the love, joy, peace, long-suffering, gentleness, goodness, faith, meekness, and temperance, which are the fruits of the Spirit, or who had more of the likeness of Christ? Who in our day gives clearer evidence that he has been born again; that he is dead to the world, and alive unto God? Who manifests a more ardent desire, for the spread of the gospel and the salvation of sinners? Who can more sincerely make his appeal to God, and say, "O how I love thy law!" Who is more evidently clothed with humility? Of whom can it be more truly said, that he walks with God, and thinks and acts in concert with the Holy Ghost? It is, my friends, a matter of solemn import to us, that such a man of God has, for so many years, been among us.

Doctor Church was an active friend of all our benevolent societies and institutions, and was always ready, to the extent of his ability, to contribute to their objects. Early in the operations of the American Tract Society, and for many years, he was a member of the Executive and Publishing Committee. For twenty years he was a Member of the Board of Commissioners for Foreign Missions, and a Trustee of Dartmouth College. For fourteen years he was a Trustee of Phillips Academy and the Theological Seminary in Andover. He was a Director and afterwards Vice-President of the New Hampshire Bible Society, and President of the New Hampshire Missionary Society. He was also Secretary of the General Association of New Hampshire from the time it was organized, A. D. 1809, till his death. In his relation to these and various other public institutions the influence of his religious principles was always manifest. While he was warmly attached to the cause of learning and to the welfare of civil society; he was sure never to forget *the essence of Christianity* — the doctrine of salvation by grace. His cordial belief of this doctrine had an elevating, sanctifying effect upon his public character. His piety was a permanent, practical principle, influencing him in all his public as well as private conduct. When did he form plans for his own worldly interest? Who ever thought that he was governed by ambition? Those who were associated with him in the work of the ministry, and in the management of our religious institutions, knew what entire confidence they could repose in him. Amid the commotions of the public mind, and the shipwreck of the faith of many, he stood firm as a rock. He was "stablished, strengthened, settled." Whatever fears we might have that others would be carried about with every wind of doctrine; we had no fears respecting him. The influence of a man possessing such excellences of character was every where felt. His faithful labors and fervent prayers brought rich blessings upon all with whom he was connected. And all who love the prosperity of the church, and the welfare of the human family, have reason to praise the Most High God, that he raised up such a man among us; that he endued him with such inward goodness, and such qualifications for usefulness, and continued his precious life so long. And whenever our eyes are permitted to behold a man and a gospel minister so moulded and guided by the Holy Spirit, and so like Christ as he was; we will bless God for the precious gift.

Will you now bear with the preacher, while he says a word for himself on this mournful occasion? I would not cease to thank God that, after death has removed far from me the greater part of those with whom I was most intimately associated in former years, there are still continued to me so many beloved brethren and fellow-laborers. But in vain do I look for one, with whom I have had such an uninterrupted and entire friendship for so many years, as I enjoyed with this excellent brother. My acquaintance with him commenced in my youth, almost half a century ago. From that time our friendship continued and increased. We rejoiced in each other's prosperity; and we passed together, with sympathizing hearts, through many scenes of trial and sorrow. About twenty-five years ago, I was called to stand in this place and minister to the consolation of my afflicted brother, then suddenly bereaved of the wife of his youth. The example of his peaceful submission on that occasion, and in other times of affliction, I cannot forget. I reckon it among the choicest blessings of my life, that I had such a friend and brother. How many times did his conversation and his prayers help to chase away the dark clouds which had gathered over my head! Whenever any burden pressed heavily upon me, and I felt myself ready to sink, a desire to see my brother Church always sprung up in my heart; and a visit from him never failed to encourage and strengthen me, and either to remove the burden, or to help me cheerfully to bear it. I never knew a man whose temper was more sweet and tranquil than his, or whose heart was more free from everything contrary to love, or whose tongue was guided more entirely by the law of kindness.

I cannot but consider it an inestimable privilege, that I was permitted to visit that good man a short time before his death. During that last happy hour which I spent with him, he conversed with perfect clearness and great freedom on a variety of most interesting subjects. Do you ask how he appeared on his dying bed? He appeared just as every one who knew him thought that he would appear. I presume there was no man acquainted with the manner of his life, who did not expect that his end would be peace. And so it was. On his dying bed, he had *a penitent heart* and *a contrite spirit.* He said, with evident tenderness, that he looked upon himself as a poor, unworthy, sinful man. But he was filled with admiration at the goodness of God. He felt then, as he had so long felt before, that he depended for salvation on God's sovereign grace; — he felt this as really as he did when he first called upon the almighty Saviour for the life of his soul. In that last scene his faith rested directly on its great object. His peace, and hope, and joy were derived, not from what he saw in himself — though he had satisfactory evidence of his piety, — but from what he saw in *Christ* — his infinite love, his inexhaustible fulness. He gave thanks to God that he had been directed of late, more than formerly, to meditate on the glory of Christ. He spoke of the precious books he had read within the last year or two, referring particularly to Owen on the Glory of Christ, Stevenson on the Offices of Christ, Good's Better Covenant, and Dickinson's Letters. He repeatedly expressed a strong desire that ministers, and those who are preparing for the ministry, might know more of the preciousness of Christ, and might more fully declare his unsearchable riches to others. He wanted Christ to be more honored. He said, in a very solemn impressive manner, that he had fears there were some ministers who had never been born again. And he wished all ministers to feel that they constantly needed the grace of Christ. He expressed a lively interest in the welfare of our Theological Seminary, and said he should be glad, if it might be the will of God, to visit it once more. He said, too, there were several things he had designed to do for the cause of Christ; but he was willing to leave it with God to determine whether he should live to do them or not. It was indeed a happy thing to be near such a servant of Christ, when he was so near to heaven. And now, whatever may be my lot in earthly things, the Lord grant unto me that I may live as that dear brother lived, and die as he died!

The bereaved children will, I trust, mingle gratitude and joy with their sorrows. Render hearty thanks to God that he manifested such kindness and grace towards your honored father, and impressed upon him so visibly the image of the meek and lowly Jesus. Thank God that you have so long enjoyed his counsels, his example, and his prayers. These are all treasured up in your minds; — a rich inheritance, far better than any earthly possession. I know how solitary that beloved home will be to you, where neither father nor mother can any more be found; and what a feeling of loneliness and sadness will steal into your minds after these funeral services are past. But the grace of God will be sufficient for you. Through the aids of his Spirit cultivate that sweet serenity of mind, that pious cheerfulness, and that diligent attention to all the branches of duty, which you have seen exemplified in your honored father. Remember that it is an act of love for the Lord Jesus to call his servants home, that they may be where he is. Your father was one of the happiest men I ever knew. He had a peculiar delight in the word of God and in the manifestations of his goodness in the present life. And if he was so peaceful and happy in this world, how exquisite must his happiness be in the presence of Him whom his soul loved. What joy swells his heart, to see Jesus face to face, to be wholly freed from sin, and to be filled with all the fulness of God!

A SERMON

DELIVERED AT THE FUNERAL OF MRS. PHEBE FARRAR, WIFE OF SAMUEL FARRAR, ESQ., ANDOVER, JAN. 26, 1848.

John 17: 24.—FATHER, I WILL THAT THEY ALSO WHOM THOU HAST GIVEN ME, BE WITH ME, WHERE I AM.

IT has been common for men everywhere to paint to themselves a heaven corresponding with their governing inclinations. The covetous, the ambitious, the sensual, all aspire after a happiness suited to gratify their predominant desires. Christians do the same. They aspire after a happiness which is rational and pure —a heaven suited to their rectified nature. Even if they had less particular instruction than the Scriptures give in regard to the happiness to be enjoyed—if they only knew and loved the unseen Saviour—and were only informed that they are hereafter to enjoy complete felicity, they would, I think, have an apprehension of the nature of that felicity, which would harmonize with the teachings of inspiration. What could they regard as complete happiness, but to enjoy that Saviour whom they supremely love? When we leave this earthly state, they would say—let us go to him who loved us and died for us. Let us *be with Jesus*. This is all our salvation and all our desire. This was the idea of the Apostle Paul. He speaks of a desire to depart, and *to be with*

Christ. He speaks of being absent from the body and *present with the Lord;* and of *seeing Christ face to face.* This was his prevailing sentiment. And this was also the sentiment of John, who represents heaven as a place where believers will *see Christ as he is.* And we have the most perfect and delightful expression of this idea from Christ himself. "Father, I will that they also whom thou hast given me, *be with me where I am.*" The apostles dwelt familiarly upon this view of the subject. And so it is with all those who have received their ideas of heaven from the sacred writers, and have imbibed the spirit of our holy religion. *To be with Christ is the heaven of Christians.* It is all the heaven they desire. It comprises everything that is necessary to constitute the perfection of celestial happiness.

In the *first* place, Christians in the presence of Christ, have *an object before them possessed of all possible excellence — an object suited to employ and gratify all their intellectual and moral faculties, and to fill the capacities of their souls.*

How happy must believers in heaven be, to see in their Saviour the highest perfection of *human* nature. They were once conversant with that nature in a fallen, degraded state, robbed of its proper excellence, and displaying itself in numberless forms of vileness and hatefulness. But now when they look upon Jesus, their elder brother, they see what humanity is capable of. They gaze with inexpressible pleasure, upon the exalted *manhood* of Jesus. And they delight in it the more, because they themselves are human, and they behold in him the exact standard to which they are to be conformed. He was always without sin — holy, harmless, undefiled. But while on earth, his character was little known. Even his disciples had but an imperfect discernment of it. But *now* his glory shines perpetually. And the saints love to behold it, and in the light of his glorified humanity they love to forget all that was low and weak and faulty in their fellow Christians and in themselves, and to fix their eyes upon one in their own nature, adorned with the perfection of beauty. This excellence and loveliness of Christ's human nature must be peculiarly attractive to the saints, and must bring them into a state of nearness to him, and fellowship with him, far above what they could otherwise enjoy.

But Christ, the object presented before the eyes of believers in heaven, is possessed not only of *human*, but of *divine* excellence. And in the contemplation of that excellence, they will be constantly attaining to higher and higher degrees of knowledge. On earth they saw through a glass darkly. But now their knowledge of the divine glory of Christ is clear and certain, and is always perfect according to the measure of their understanding. But he will be continually unfolding new glories, and they, with an intensity of thought of which no one on earth is capable, will behold those unfolding glories; in consequence of which their knowledge of his character will be more and more extensive — always perfect, and yet always increasing. Should they ever come to a stop in their growth, and find that no further advance in knowledge could be made, it would disappoint their hope and chill their joy. But there is no danger of this. Let their capacities enlarge and their knowledge grow, till they rise far above the highest angel, there would still be an infinite height and depth, upon which they might employ their minds millions of ages, and after all approach no nearer to a full comprehension of the lofty theme. Here is the intellectual blessedness of the saints above — their ever active understanding constantly and successfully reaching towards the heights and prying into the depths of the perfection of the Mediator, knowing more and more of this most excellent of beings, and knowing at every step that there is boundless excellence beyond, which will call forth their earnest and happy efforts through endless ages.

But the saints have a *moral* nature also — they have a *heart*. And the *heart* inclines to *love*. And it must have an object of supreme love. The heart pants after such an object, and would be desolate and wretched without it. This want is fully supplied to believers in the presence of Christ. In this world they begin to love him, though they see him not, and though they have but a feeble conception of his excellence. But what an object of affection will he be to them, when visibly clothed with the brightness of human and divine excellence in the world of light! *Love* feasts itself upon *loveliness*. Perfect loveliness satifies it. That perfect loveliness they behold in the person of Jesus. And it is not only perfect, but unbounded loveliness. The creation around us exhibits unnumbered objects, beautiful and excellent in a high degree. And in sanctified men and holy angels we see various forms of *moral* beauty and excellence, eliciting our admiration and love, and contributing to our enjoyment. But take the most illustrious forms of moral beauty and loveliness in heaven and earth — take all the beauty in God's vast universe, and let it be concentrated in one lovely, glorious person, with a lustre outshining the sun in the firmament, and what would all that splendor of excellence be to the beauty and loveliness which the eyes of the saints will behold in the Lord Jesus Christ, the king of glory! Let their hearts then swell with emotions of love, and let the emotions rise higher and higher. Their happiness will increase with the increase of their love, because the object is invested with incomprehensible, unbounded excellence, so that their love may grow forever, and yet never equal the infinite worthiness of the object; and I am almost ready to say, they will covet moral faculties which are infinite, that they may love their Saviour as much as he deserves.

Secondly. Believers are happy in the presence of Christ, because they see him to be *so highly honored and glorified*. On earth their hearts were frequently grieved, that their Saviour, who was worthy of universal honor and praise, was despised and rejected of men, and his name covered with infamy. But how will they rejoice to see that he is now exalted, and has a name which is above every name! What sacred gladness will fill their souls, to see every knee bow to him, and all the heavenly hosts prostrate before him! What music to their ears, to hear the holy creation breaking forth in anthems of praise, saying, "Honor and glory and thanksgiving and blessing and praise be unto him that sitteth on the throne, and unto the Lamb." Happy their ears, that hear these anthems of praise from angels and saints, to him who was dead, but is alive again, and liveth and reigneth forevermore!

How do they exult and boast themselves in the glory of their king! And how is the benevolent prayer of Jesus fulfilled, that his disciples might "be with him, and *behold his glory*."

Thirdly. The saints are happy in the presence of Christ, because they will see him to be *perfectly blessed*. Would it not detract from their happiness, if their Saviour should in any way, fall short of a blessedness equal to his boundless desires — if there should be the least pain or suffering mingled with his divine or his human blessedness? Does not the benevolence of Christians, demand the happiness of him who is the chief object of their love? My hearers well know that it is the very nature of finite benevolence, to be a partaker of the sorrows as well as the joys of others. Benevolence rejoices with them that rejoice, and weeps with them that weep. But in the presence of Jesus the saints have no occasion for weeping. They do indeed remember that, while on earth, he was a man of sorrows and acquainted with grief, and that when the burden of our guilt was laid upon him in the closing scene of his life, his "soul was exceedingly sorrowful, even unto death." And who that truly loved him then, could be joyful and happy to see the distress which he endured in the garden and on the cross? But his sorrows are ended. He dies no more, and he suffers no more. On the cross he finished the work of atonement. He is to be made a curse for us no more. He does not forget the sorrows he once felt — the scourging and the scorn, the nails and the thirst, the long agony, the forsaking of his God, and the last loud cry of distress. But he rejoices that these are all past, and that the result of them is experienced by his people in their eternal salvation. The Son of God is blessed in himself — and blessed in communion with his Father — blessed in all his works — blessed in beholding the happiness of angels, principalities and powers — blessed especially in seeing his redeemed church washed from their sins, delivered from all their tribulations and sorrows, and made perfectly happy in the enjoyment of his fulness. His blessedness is a benevolent and holy blessedness, and is commensurate with his boundless perfections. In view of this immeasurable blessedness of Christ, the saints in heaven rejoice with joy unspeakable and full of glory.

But *fourthly*, the saints above are *social beings;* and they enjoy, first of all, the society of *Jesus himself*, which is better to them than the society of all created beings. Should no saint or angel be near them, they would have a fulness of joy in Christ alone. The presence and converse of that one Friend and Brother, would be heaven to their souls. But no man can count up the holy, happy beings who are with them in the world above. A multitude which no man can number, possessing their own nature, delivered from the same depths of sin and misery, are with the saints in the presence of their common Lord. And who can tell what sweet intercourse they have with that holy company, especially those with whom they were associated on earth! With what lively emotions do they speak to each other of the events of their earthly life! How do they recall the scenes through which they passed together; the trials they encountered; the temptations and sins and dangers from which they were delivered; the errors which have been corrected; the evil tempers which have been subdued; the spiritual enemies — the roaring lion, the subtle serpent, and the ravenous wolf, that have been overcome; the mysteries of providence which have been unravelled; and the wonders of divine forbearance and grace which they experienced together during their unprofitable life! How do they look at each other, rejoicing that they are all safe in the heavenly Paradise, and full of delight and astonishment at the change which they see in themselves and in one another; change from the vileness of sin to the beauties of holiness; change from ignorance and error to the clear knowledge of truth, from weakness and suffering to strength and joy, their complaints all turned to thanksgiving and praise! They remember that they were once travelling the broad way to death, and were afterwards feeble Christians, often backsliding, often in the dark, mourning over the treachery and corruption of their hearts, reaching after perfection but never attaining to it. They give glory to him who rescued them from all those evils, and brought them to their home in the heavens. They give glory to their Redeemer, who has enriched them with his unsearchable riches, and given them the right to say, *All things are ours.* The purest pleasures of Christian friendship here below, are not worthy to be compared with the pleasures of that more endearing friendship and intercourse, which is the lot of the happy family of believers in the presence of Christ.

Fifthly. Christians are *active* beings; and *there is that in the presence of Christ, which calls all their active powers into the most pleasurable exercise.*

We are taught, that Christians in the world above rest from their wearisome toils, and repose quietly in the love and enjoyment of their Saviour. But they have employments suited to all their active powers. Cordial obedience to Christ and constant activity in his service, is perfect *rest* to the saints above, because all hinderances to easy, pleasant action — all clogs, all weakness and sickness, all deadness and heaviness are gone, and they are as the angels in heaven, who, for their readiness and swiftness to obey, are likened to the wind and the lightning.

The Lord Jesus Christ has a *mighty* empire, and its inhabitants who are ten thousand times more in number than this world could contain, all depend on the free goodness of their Sovereign, and are to be made happy and to be continued in their happy state by the constant exercise of his power and benevolence. But while he is, and will forever be seen to be, *all in all*, he makes use of his angels and saints as instruments of his benevolence. He communicates blessings to his kingdom through the agency of his servants. And no one can describe the variety, the extent, or the magnitude of the works which they will be called to accomplish in different parts of the wide universe. In these works they most cheerfully engage, because their *pious* hearts love to obey their righteous Lord, and their *benevolent* hearts love to do good to rational, immortal beings, wherever found. They love their neighbors as themselves. And they love a neighboring *world*, as they love their own. And in the high station they occupy, all worlds will appear to them to be what they really are, *one neighborhood*, one great, happy fraternity, to whose welfare they are to minister. It seems to me that the saints in heaven are as much more active than they ever were in this world, as they are more holy, and more benevolent, and endued with higher powers. They will no more cease to be active, than they will cease to love Christ and his kingdom. They will be active forever, because the Son of God will be active forever, and they are to be co-workers with him in accomplishing his benevolent designs. And this benevolent, useful service will be to them a perpetual source of the purest enjoyment.

The sum of what I have to say on this point is, that when Christians are where Jesus is, they bear his likeness; and as he is unceasingly engaged in doing good — as he constantly exercises his infinite power and wisdom and love in bestowing the richest blessings upon his vast kingdom; so those who are admitted into his presence do constantly, without weariness, and with heartfelt delight, exercise all their powers and faculties in accomplishing the same benevolent object, feeling it to be a high privilege and honor to coöperate with him, and to imitate, in their humble measure, his ever active goodness.

But if the saints are employed in works of benevolence in various and different parts of the creation, you may ask, how they can at the same time *be in the presence of Christ?* My reply is, that Christ is present everywhere, sustaining and governing the universe. But he is *specially* present with his servants. Wherever they are, he can reveal himself to them in all the gloriousness of his perfections. While they are doing his will in the most distant regions of his vast empire, he can give them the happiness to see his face, and to enjoy communion with him. Even in this lower state of being, do not faithful Christians enjoy nearness to their Lord? Are they barred from his gracious presence, because they are in India, or China, in the dark regions of Africa, or in the wilds of America? What think you of the precious promise of Christ, that he will be with his disciples, whenever and wherever they call upon him? And what think you of their united testimony, that his promise has been fulfilled, and that they have in truth enjoyed his spiritual presence, and seen his glory, in devout meditation and prayer, and at the sacramental table, and while engaged in arduous duties, and enduring severe afflictions? And in that higher and more spiritual world, where the Sun of Righteousness continually shines forth, making every part luminous with the beams of his noon-day glory, cannot that glorious *Sun* be *everywhere seen?* Cannot the Lord of heaven enlighten the eyes of his devoted servants, wherever they are, and show them his glory, and show them that he is near to them, and speak to them words of kindness, and hear the expressions of love and desire which their lips or their hearts utter? My brethren, the Lord Jesus is spiritually and graciously present throughout the holy universe — present to illuminate the souls of his servants — present to sustain and comfort them, and to hold familiar converse with them; so that in every place they are really nearer to him, than the beloved disciple was, when he leaned upon his bosom. Dismiss then every carnal idea; and know for a certainty, that the saints above are always *with Jesus where he is* — that whatever they do and wherever they go, they are never deprived of his presence, that he never hides his face from them, and that what he prayed for is now perfectly fufilled — "*he in them, and they in him.*" This is the presence of Christ which they desire, and which is life and peace to their souls.

I have only one point more. Christians desire their *own perfect holiness; and the presence of Christ will effectually contribute to this.*

The Apostle John says: "*We shall be like him, for we shall see him as he is.*" The Apostle Paul brings the same principle into view respecting Christians here: "Beholding as in a glass the glory of the Lord, we are changed into the same image from glory to glory." There is a way of beholding the glory of the Lord, even in this life, which has a transforming influence. This takes place when God shines in the hearts of his people, enabling them to know the things of the Spirit as they are spiritually discerned. Then they see the true excellence of Christ; and seeing, love; and loving, imitate. This is God's method. The transforming process begins in this world, and would be advanced far more rapidly than it is, if believers would make more of this one simple, gospel means, that is, fixing their eyes earnestly and directly upon him who is their chosen Saviour, and beholding steadily the combination of unparalleled beauties and excellences which his character displays. When Christians enter on their heavenly state, and are received into the presence of Christ, they are already free from the pollution of sin, and conformed to the image of Christ. But the principle of holiness, already wrought in them by the Spirit of God, must be preserved and developed, and made active in all the ways of love and obedience — active in a higher and higher degree. And this is effected in the presence of Christ. "They will be *like* him, *for* they shall see him as he is." They will be completely like him. If they saw any sin in themselves, any the least spot of moral defilement, they would be filled with shame and self-loathing, and would be dismayed to see the eyes of their holy Saviour upon them. But sin can find no admittance into that world of purity. There can be no darkness in that world of light. The glorious holiness of Christ will be like the clear light of the sun, which effectually diffuses itself, and instantly illuminates whatever is within its reach. The holiness of Christ is clear and bright — it is light itself, and in it is "no darkness at all." And this holy light pours light into the souls of the just, and that light is life.

I hope, Christian friends, I have not detained your thoughts too long upon this pleasant theme. My object has been to impress it deeply and permanently upon your hearts, that in the presence of Christ is fulness of joy — that at his right hand are pleasures forevermore. I have wished it to be believed and felt by all, that when Christ prayed that his disciples might be *with him where he is*, he showed the kindness of his heart, and asked for that which is the greatest possible good; that being *present with the Lord* is heaven indeed to holy souls — a heaven which will most delightfully employ all their active powers, and fill them with pure and ever increasing enjoyment — leaving no desire unsatisfied, no want unsupplied. And the end which I aim at is, that strong desires after heaven may be kindled in your breasts; that you may habitually long and pant after the blessedness of those who are *absent from the body and present with the Lord*, and may be awakened to the utmost diligence in preparing for that consummation of your joy.

The mournful event which has called us together, suggested the subject of this discourse. And my particular acquaintance with the religious views of our departed friend, and of other Christians, has suggested the train of remarks which I have made on this occasion.

A particular delineation of the life and character of the amiable and pious woman, who has been removed from this church, and from our domestic and social circle, is not to be expected on this occasion. Her numerous relatives and friends need no assistance from me in forming a just estimate of her intellectual and moral worth. And if I should begin to tell you just what I think of the leading attributes of her character, as exhibited in the various relations and conditions of life which she filled, I should at once be checked by what I know of her decided aversion to all high encomiums upon the living or the dead. I shall therefore attempt nothing but to touch briefly upon what pertained to her religious character.

The religion of our beloved friend, Mrs. Farrar, was marked with uniform seriousness and earnestness. But it had nothing enthusiastic or rapturous. Her understanding was too enlightened and discriminating to admit of this. She possessed a calm, well balanced state of mind, free from fervid excitements. Her hope of heaven, though sometimes clear and joyous, was for the most part a trembling hope, and was occasionally clouded, and mingled with doubts and fears. This fact I found to arise from her habitually and strictly searching her own heart, and from her clear discernment of indwelling sin. By comparing herself with the holy requirements of God's law, she discovered many evils in herself which no human eye could see, and which often kept her from those higher consolations, to which her uniformly pious character seemed to give her a title. She derived her best enjoyments, not from reflecting on the state of her own heart, or the actions of her life, but from the excellence and grace of that

Saviour in whom she believed, and from the distinguishing doctrines of his gospel. While she contemplated these divine objects she experienced joys which were truly Christian, and which her consciousness of imperfection and demerit could not take away.

Her conceptions of the nature and the truths of religion were derived from the word of God, and were consonant to the views of her excellent grandfather, Jonathan Edwards, who has been the boast of our country, and has justly been styled *the Prince of Divines.* It was no small privilege to be a descendant of such an eminent Christian and divine; and it was a great happiness that she early imbibed the sentiments and the spirit which pervade his writings, and which adorned his useful life. And it was very manifest, that those precious truths which she had deliberately adopted and which had been the ground of her hope and comfort for so long a time, shed a cheering light upon her during the last days and hours of her mortal life. Repeating to her select passages of Scripture, or referring to the abounding mercy of Christ, or to any gospel truth, would instantly compose her mind, and impart light and life to her soul, struggling with pain, and hastening to her happy home in the heavens.

But I have a special purpose in view in these closing observations. It has, I trust, been made to appear, that the heaven of Christians is, *to be with Christ.* Now it is evident to me that Mrs. Farrar had a *fitness for such a heaven as this.* The habits of her mind and her religious character were such, as to prepare her to be *happy in the presence of Christ.*

This preparation in a general view, consisted in her *love to the Saviour.* And if she loved the Saviour she must find it *heaven to be with him where he is.*

Our friend aspired after *knowledge;* particularly the knowledge of *Christ and the things of his kingdom.* And how happy must such a one be in the presence of Christ, *the light and glory of heaven,* where her mind will see clearly what it began to see and was earnestly reaching after here below, and will be forever acquiring clearer and clearer knowledge of that which is most worthy to be known, and which she most desired to know. How indescribably happy must she be, to behold the unveiled beauties of him, "whom having not seen" she loved, and whom she sincerely desired to love more — and whom she *now* loves "with all the heart and soul and mind and strength."

Our departed friend was desirous that Christ should be exalted and honored. And this desire prepared her to rejoice with exceeding joy in beholding his exaltation and glory in the world above, and in hearing the praises which are sung to him by the great multitude of the heavenly hosts.

The religion of our departed friend was remarkably *social.* She had a sincere and constant affection for her pious friends; and she loved all who showed themselves followers of Christ. And this benevolent affection was uniformly acted out in the various conditions which divine providence allotted to her. I cannot speak of the multitudes who enjoyed the friendship of Mrs. Farrar, and who will remember as long as memory lasts, that generous hospitality which formed so conspicuous a trait in her domestic character. This sanctified affection, which bore such precious fruits on earth, prepared her to enter with joy into the society of heaven; prepared her for a happy meeting with the many Christian friends, who had gone before her to the presence of their Saviour. What unutterable pleasure must she experience in such a lovely, peaceful, holy society — waiting a little while for other beloved Christians to come and fill up the happy family of Christ.

While here below, Mrs. Farrar began to be active in the service of Christ, and took great pleasure in the efforts she was able to make to promote the cause of truth, and the welfare of immortal souls. With the same habit of mind, improved and perfected, in the upper world, she is swift to do the will of God, and exceedingly happy in her obedience.

And finally, she mourned and was humbled on account of the weakness of her faith, and her manifold imperfections, and aspired after likeness to Christ. This prepared her to be admitted into the presence of her Lord, where she is like him, because she sees him as he is — where she beholds his glory and is changed into the same image from glory to glory.

And now may the Lord be graciously present with these mourning friends, the bereaved husband and children, and other relatives. You sorrow not as those who have no hope and no comfort. For henceforth you are to think of her who is taken from you, as *present with the Lord.* She has reached her home. She has, we trust, obtained all and more than all that her heart ever desired or conceived.

You will not forget my friends, that you have been highly favored of God in being blessed with *such a partner, such a mother, such a friend* — and in being blessed with her so long. How grateful should you be for this inestimable favor! And how heartily should you thank a merciful God, for what he was pleased to do for that dear friend of yours, who is here no more; for calling her early in life, as we trust he did, with a holy calling, according to his purpose and grace; for giving her such a measure of piety and peace; for sustaining her under her trials, and helping her in her spiritual warfare, and making her the instrument of so much temporal and eternal good to those connected with her. Let your mourning be sanctified by the mingling in of fervent thanks and praises to the God of all grace and comfort.

And now, Christian friends, ponder well the present subject and the present occasion. *God is speaking to you.* "*Arise, for this is not your rest.*" If you love Christ and enjoy his presence, you have a foretaste of heaven. But heaven is not here. Your portion is above. Jesus said to his disciples, "In my Father's house are many mansions — I go to prepare a place for you; and if I go to prepare a place for you, I will come again and receive you to myself, that where I am, there ye may be also." He says the same to you. Think then of the place prepared for you above. Look not at the things which are seen, but at the things which are not seen. Let nothing draw off your thoughts from your inheritance in the heavens. Jesus says, *behold, I come quickly*. Lift up your heads with joy, for your redemption draweth nigh. Your time to die is near at hand; and death to believers is the gate of Paradise. Away then with all vain pursuits and distracting cares. What have you to do with the things of earth? Awake, Christian, heir of heaven — arise — put your house in order — and put your heart in order; for verily I say unto you, to-morrow you shall be with Christ in Paradise.

A SERMON

DELIVERED AT THE ORDINATION OF SAMUEL NEWELL, ADONIRAM JUDSON, SAMUEL NOTT, GORDON HALL, AND LUTHER RICE, FIRST MISSIONARIES FROM AMERICA TO THE HEATHEN IN ASIA. SALEM, FEB. 6, 1812.

Psalm 67.—God be merciful unto us, and bless us; and cause his face to shine upon us. That thy way may be known upon earth, thy saving health among all nations. Let the people praise thee, O God; let all the people praise thee. Let the nations be glad and sing for joy. Let the people praise thee, O God; let all the people praise thee. God shall bless us; and all the ends of the earth shall fear him.

No intelligent Christian can be a stranger to the benevolent desires and pleasing anticipations here expressed. Every good man has a heart to feel for his fellow creatures, and endeavors to promote their temporal welfare. But, when he contemplates the value of their immortal souls, and what Jesus has done to save them from perdition, his tenderest affections are kindled; pure and heavenly love pervades and warms his heart. He longs for the eternal felicity of his kindred and friends, his country and the world. His desire and prayer is, that all human beings may forsake their evil ways and turn to the Lord. With this holy affection reigning in his heart, the devoted Christian presents himself a living sacrifice unto God; and counts it a privilege to do and to suffer anything for the advancement of his cause. He is ready to "endure all things for the elect's sake." In this state, no difficulty discourages, no danger alarms him. Stripes, imprisonment and death lose their terrors. Every degree of success attending the dispensation of the gospel yields him the purest pleasure. But this pleasure increases his pious desire. The progressive enlargement of the kingdom of Christ will constantly enlarge the benevolence of his heart. While there is a nation or tribe under heaven not subdued to Christ; the fervent Christian cannot rest. His unalterable object is, *that the knowledge of the Lord may fill the earth.*

This, brethren, is the true spirit of our religion. This is the affection which glows in every new born soul. This is the principle which governs and animates the church of Christ.

On this new and interesting occasion, my desire is to excite your benevolence, and to persuade you by suitable motives, TO MAKE THE SPREAD OF THE GOSPEL AND THE CONVERSION OF THE WORLD, THE OBJECT OF YOUR EARNEST AND CONSTANT PURSUIT.

My *first motive* is *the worth of the soul.* Man, a creature of yesterday, is made for *immortality.* The human mind will be ever active. No labor can exhaust it. No length of ages can waste its vigor. No pressure of guilt or suffering can destroy its activity. Such a mind, destined to exist and act forever, destined to the bliss of heaven, or the pains of hell, lives in every human being, in the savage as well as the citizen; in the heathen as well as the Christian; in the Hindoo, the Chinese, and the Hottentot, as well as the European or American. — In the name of him who died on Calvary, I call upon you, Christians, to labor for the salvation of beings that will never die. Of what consideration is their color, language, education, or manners? Here all distinctions vanish. Learned and ignorant, refined and rude, honorable and base, are all on a level in point of accountableness to God and immortality of soul. Rise then above all the distinctions which misguide our judgments, and seek the salvation of this great family of immortal beings.

In some favored hours of divine illumination, have you not seen and felt the ineffable preciousness of your own souls? Have you not cast away everything as dross, for eternal salvation? And has not the grace of God taught you to love your neighbor as yourselves? See the millions who dwell in darkness. Their souls are as precious as your own. The wisdom of God — the blood of the dying Saviour has so declared. Change places with them. Put yourselves in their condition, and them in yours. You are then spending your life in a land of darkness, ignorant of God, slaves to the basest superstition and most hateful vices. Moved by pity and love, they send a herald of the cross to preach salvation in your ears. He comes and speaks to you of Jehovah and his law; discloses your guilt, and points you to the judgment day. He preaches to you Jesus, the Saviour of sinners. With trembling, broken hearts you go to the Saviour, and he gives you rest. How happy your state! Would you not forever exalt the Redeemer's name? Would you not love and thank the messenger of his grace, and those who sent him? Now, if salvation would be so great a blessing to you, why not to those who are actually in the condition here supposed? And if you would love and thank those who sought your salvation, why not secure to yourselves the same love and gratitude from heathens saved by your labors?

Imagine your children, parents, brothers, sisters this moment in pagan darkness. Would not your hearts leap for joy to see these dear young ministers going to teach them the way of life? Would anything be too precious to part with in order to animate their zeal, and help them to rescue from ignorance and ruin the objects of your love? But have not the heathen souls as precious as the souls of your kindred? — Nay, they *are* your kindred; allied to you by the ties of a common nature; children of the same family. In every human being you see a brother or a sister.

The *second motive* by which I urge you to seek the conversion of all mankind is *the plenteousness of the provision which Christ has made for their salvation.* Were there anything scanty in this provision, anything circumscribed in the offers of mercy, our zeal for propagating the gospel would be suppressed; the hand of

Christian charity would be paralyzed. But the word of eternal truth has taught us that Jesus is the propitiation for our sins, and not for ours only, but also for the sins of the *whole world;* that a rich feast is prepared, and all things ready; that whosoever will may come and take of the water of life freely. This great atonement is as sufficient for Asiatics and Africans, as for us. The door of Christ's kingdom is equally open to them and to us. Unnumbered millions of our race have entered in; and yet there is room. The mercy of God is an exhaustless ocean. His benevolence is unbounded. You have, then, full scope for your pious efforts. In your labors and prayers for the salvation of men, you cannot go beyond the proper bounds. You are not straitened in God. You have no occasion to fear that in this cause your zeal and activity will exceed the abundance of divine grace. You have a warrant from God to strive for the salvation of the whole world. And wherever the preaching of the cross shall excite them that are lost to seek salvation, their salvation will be found. Persuade the whole heathen world to enter into the kingdom of Christ, and they will all be admitted. Every perishing sinner on earth would find the same welcome with yourselves. Remember then, Christians, you cannot exhaust the mercy of God. Exert yourselves to the utmost for the salvation of mankind; your exertions will fall far short of the length and breadth of redeeming love.

The *third* motive, I shall present, is *the command of our Lord;* —"*Go ye into all the world, and preach the gospel to every creature.*" This command is an expression of the heart of Jesus; a display of the vastness of his love. It would be very easy to show that the obligation of this command is limited to no age or nation. The reasons which moved the apostles to preach the gospel to every creature, remain in full force. Nations without the gospel are as wretched now as they were in the time of the apostles. Their salvation is as important, and as easily accomplished.

Will any say *this command is obligatory upon the ambassadors of Christ, and not upon private Christians?* It is indeed the duty of ambassadors of Christ to go and preach the gospel to all the world. The Messiah is given to be a light to the Gentiles. They must hear the glad tidings. "But how can they hear without a preacher? And how can they preach, except they be sent?" If ministers must go forth, the Christian world must send them. If they must devote their life to the business of evangelizing the heathen, the Christian world must support them.

Does the thought arise, that the apostles went forth without such support? They did; — for there was no Christian nation overflowing with wealth, to support them. But whatever their peculiar circumstances obliged them to do, the general maxim which they laid down was, "*that no man goeth a warfare at his own charges.*"

But I make my appeal to your generosity. Those who go to teach your brethren in pagan lands, must be maintained. But at present they cannot receive maintenance there. The heathen must be converted, and formed into Christian societies, before adequate provision for the ministers of Christ can be expected from them. Will you then see your missionaries, who have left all to preach the gospel of peace among the heathen, reduced to the necessity of abandoning their sacred office, and engaging in servile labor for their daily bread? Will you see the ambassadors of peace from America, clothed in rags, and compelled to beg or starve? And must they tell the heathen that they are thus forsaken of their Christian brethren who have enough and to spare?

It is obvious, that the Christian community at large has a deep concern in the command of Christ, "to go into all the world and preach the gospel to every creature." I urge this command of our risen Saviour, as absolutely requiring you to *seek the conversion of the world.* The command was given just before our Lord ascended into heaven. He had finished his work on earth, and was about to return to his Father and our Father, to his God and our God. He knew the ruined state of man, and the saving power of his cross. With the love and authority of the King of Zion, he gave the command, *to evangelize all nations.* And who that has the heart of a Christian can refuse obedience?

My *fourth motive* is derived from *the conduct of those who received this command, and of Christian missionaries in succeeding times.* The apostles "went forth, and preached everywhere." They travelled into various parts of the idolatrous world, calling sinners to repentance, planting and watering churches, and encountering cruel persecutions. Their invariable object was, that *God's way might be known upon earth, and his salvation to all nations.*

The same spirit appeared in primitive Christians. They assisted the apostles in their journies, and contributed in various ways to the propagation of the Christian religion.

How excellent the spirit of the apostles, and of those early converts to the Christian faith! Read the history of their self-denying labors, their deprivations and sufferings, and their inextinguishable zeal for the salvation of sinners. Read too the history of what has in later times been done in Europe, Asia, Africa, and America. While you revolve these things, do not your hearts burn within you? Do you not look with admiration upon the faithful followers of Christ? and do you not long to be partakers of their labors and sufferings, their success, and their crowns of glory?

My fifth motive is derived from *the peculiar design of Christianity, and its adaptedness to be a universal religion.* Brethren, we are not disciples of Judaism. But have we not had too much of its limited spirit? Have we not thought it enough to enjoy the Scriptures and the ministers of religion ourselves, without any care to send them to other nations? But why should we indulge feelings so adverse to the Christian dispensation, and limit that, which its divine author has left unlimited? Why should we monopolize a religion to which all nations have an equal right, and which is adapted to universal use? Why should we, who profess to believe and love Christianity, adopt principles so contrary to its celestial nature, and its diffusive, benign tendency?

My *sixth motive* is derived from *prophecy.* When we have looked upon the millions of men who are uncivilized, degraded, without God and without hope, have we not been inclined to give up their conversion as hopeless? And if it has not been the language of our lips, has it not been our feeling, that the kingdom of Christ will stop where it is, that the obstacles in the way of Christianizing the nations of the earth are too great to be surmounted; and that the most we can expect is to maintain the ground already secured. To raise you above this discouragement and indolence, I open to you *the prophetic page.* "He shall see the travail of his soul and be satisfied." "It is a light thing that thou shouldst be my servant, to raise up the tribes of Jacob, and to restore the preserved of Israel; — I will also give thee for a light to the Gentiles, that thou mayest be my salvation to the ends of the earth. Ask of me, and I will give thee the heathen for thine inheritance, and the uttermost parts of the earth for thy possession. Thus saith the Lord God; behold I will lift up my hand to the Gentiles, and set up my standard to the people. — All the ends of the earth shall see the salvation of God." These glorious predictions shall not fail of accomplishment. These unchangeable decrees of the Almighty shall not be frustrated. Heaven and earth shall pass away, but not one jot or tittle of these promises shall fail.

When we survey the idolatrous, barbarous nations of the world, our courage flags; and we ask, with desponding hearts, *can these dry bones live?* We forget the everlasting God, the Lord, the Creator of the ends of the earth, who fainteth not, neither is weary. We forget that all nations are in his hands; that he fashioneth them as he pleaseth. Because the conversion of the world is beyond our power, we think it beyond the power of God. Well may Christ say to us, "*O ye of little faith!*" Did Paul indulge such despondency when with the ardor of a young convert, and the fearless fidelity of an Apostle, he preached the word of God in Greece, in Asia, and in Rome? Did Wickliffe indulge such feelings? Did Luther? Did Swartz, Eliott, Brainerd? Away with every unbelieving thought! Is the Lord's arm shortened that it cannot save? He who died and lives again, *is not yet satisfied.* Eighteen hundred years ago he said: "And I, if I be lifted up from the earth, *will draw all men unto me.*" And he said, more than two thousand years ago: "Look unto me, and be ye saved, all the ends of the earth; for I am God, and there is none else." This word has not returned unto him void. The whole Christian world testifies, that it has been astonishingly efficacious. It will be still more efficacious. To him, with whom a thousand years are as one day, and one day as a thousand years, the things which he has foretold or determined, are as certain as though actually accomplished.

Do you still hesitate, and yield to fear? And when you hear God, by the mouth of a prophet, declaring: "From the rising of the sun even unto the going down of the same, my name shall be great among the Gentiles; and in every place incense shall be offered up unto my name and a pure offering; for my name shall be great among the heathen;" do you ask, "how can this great work be done?"

And let me ask, how the earth and all its inhabitants could be created? How could the heavens be stretched out as a curtain over your heads? What power is it that sustains the world, and causes all its motions and changes? Do you talk of *power?* The God who forms a blade of grass, and begets a drop of dew, can as easily convert a soul? And he who converts one soul, can as easily convert a nation. Every day, in the midst of heathen lands, God exerts a power that can save a universe. Who gives to the heathen life and breath, reason and conscience? Who causes their sun to shine, and their ground to yield its fruits? Say no more, then; how can the great work of converting the nations be done? *It is only for God to speak the word.* He can cause all Asia to bow to his grace, as easily as he can shake the leaves of the forest.

Finally, I point you to *the operations of divine providence at the present time.* The Lord has given the word, and great has been the company of the publishers. A large number of ministers of different denominations, moved by the love of souls, have labored in the gospel where Christ had not been named. The multiplication of Bible Societies in Great Britain and America, and the success which has crowned their operations, have exceeded the most sanguine hopes; and we are now looking forward to the time when all nations will read in their own tongues the words of eternal life. Another delightful omen is the effusion of the Holy Spirit, the revival of religion in several of our colleges, and in a great number of churches and societies, and the increased attention of Christians to the interests of the Redeemer's kingdom.

It is also a circumstance highly encouraging, that among the friends of evangelical religion greater love and harmony have begun to appear. Christians of different denominations have all been more or less disposed to attach too much importance to the points in which they differ from each other. They have had party spirit, and have often been more forward to proselyte to their own sect, than to Christ. They have had contention, and strife, and evil speaking among them. They have injured the truth by discussing the important subjects of disagreement without due meekness and candor, and by laying out too much strength on those which are unimportant. They have wanted some great object to seize their hearts, some great and common cause in which they might be purified from error, and in which the eternal truths of revelation might be maintained with unyielding firmness, and propagated with augmented zeal. The *conversion of the world* is the very object wanted, the common cause which ought to unite, and has already begun to unite the affections, prayers, and labors of the great family of Christians. This harmonizing spirit among the followers of Christ forbodes good to Zion. May it increase, and diffuse its happy influence, till Christians shall all be one.

DEAR YOUNG MISSIONARIES,

You have devoted your lives to the work of making known among the Gentiles the unsearchable riches of Christ. We know you do not leave your native land, because you have not the fairest prospect of reputation, usefulness, and comfort here. You go, we believe, because the love of God is shed abroad in your hearts by the Holy Ghost. We look upon you, as chosen vessels unto Christ, to bear his name before the Gentiles. Blessed be the Lord God of the Gentiles, that he hath put this design into your hearts.

The cause in which you have enlisted, is the cause of divine love. You have chosen the noblest and most honorable work on earth. But it is also arduous and perilous. When you have seriously contemplated the greatness of this enterprise, you have often cried out: "Lord, if thy presence go not with us, carry us not hence." I hope you will never forget, that *without Christ*, you can do nothing. Without his help you can no more advance his kingdom among idolaters, than you can scatter the darkness of midnight by a word. He that planteth is nothing, and he that watereth is nothing. The increase is wholly of God. If you should be forsaken of God, what would become of you? and what would become of your mission? Your light would go out in darkness. Shame and blushing would cover the faces of your patrons and friends; and their hearts would die within them. The bright and celestial flame, which has been kindling up among us, — how soon would it be extinguished! But if you go forth in the strength of Christ, you will be burning and shining lights in regions of darkness and death. We hope to hear good tidings of great joy from the East. Think how it will be in Asia a century or two hence. The kingdom of Christ, which you are sent to promote toward the rising of the sun, will be "like a grain of mustard seed, which, when it is sown in the earth, is less than all the seeds that be in the earth. But when it is sown it groweth up, and becometh greater than all herbs, and shooteth forth great branches, so that the fowls of the air may lodge under the shadow of it."

Dear young men, you are soon to leave your relatives and friends, and your native land; but you are not to leave your blessed Lord and Redeemer. The God whom you will worship on the plains of Hindostan, will be the same God you have worshipped here. The Saviour whom you will adore and serve *there*, will be the very Saviour, whose glory you have seen and of whose fulness you have received *here*. Go then, dear missionaries, with the partners of your life; and may God Almighty be your Preserver. Go, and "declare the glory of the Lord among the heathen, his wonders among all people." Esteem the *reproach* of Christ greater riches, than all the wealth of India. Our affections and prayers will constantly attend you. All your success, all your joys, and all your sorrows, will be ours. You will be as dear to our hearts and as near to God and to heaven in Asia, as in America. And if we are friends of God, our separation will be short. A few days hence, we hope to meet you, and those whom your labors may rescue from pagan darkness, in the presence of the Lord. With this joyful anticipation, I do now most affectionately bid you, FAREWELL.

A SERMON

DELIVERED AT HAVERHILL, MASS. ON THE DEATH OF MRS. HARRIET NEWELL, WIFE OF THE REV. SAMUEL NEWELL, MISSIONARY.*

Matt. 19: 29. — AND EVERY ONE THAT HATH FORSAKEN HOUSES, OR BRETHREN, OR SISTERS, OR FATHER, OR MOTHER, OR WIFE, OR CHILDREN, OR LANDS, FOR MY NAME'S SAKE SHALL RECEIVE AN HUNDRED FOLD; AND SHALL INHERIT EVERLASTING LIFE.

THE character which Christ here exhibits before us, is superior to the best character which was ever formed on mere worldly principles, or which can spring from man's unregenerate nature. But you may ask, where this remarkable character can be found. My reply is, that the character here set forth can be found in every place and in every condition of life, where true and consistent piety exists.

The *devout cottager*, far removed from public notice, and destined to the humblest employments and to the evils of poverty, possesses the substance of the character described in the text. He gives himself and all that he has to the Lord. He loves Christ above his cottage, his food, and every earthly object, and is ready to part with them all for *his sake*. In the sight of God, that poor man forsakes all for Christ. He who forsakes his sins,

---

* Mrs. Newell died at the Isle of France, Nov. 30, 1812.

performs a far more difficult service, than he who forsakes friends, houses, and lands. In the poor man's heart may burn as pure a flame of love and zeal, as in the heart of an apostle. It may not be visible to the world; but it is visible to him who seeth in secret. His prayers are animated by fervent affection for God and man. And when he contributes his mite for the advancement of the Redeemer's kingdom, he does it with a heart large enough to part with millions.

The character here exhibited belongs to the devoted Christian, who is possessed of *opulence*. Though he may not literally forsake houses and lands, he uses them for the glory of Christ, and is ready, when duty calls, to surrender them for the same object. To *use* riches for Christ, and to forsake them for Christ, evince the same elevation above self-interest, and the same devotedness to the cause of God. He, then, who values his estate for Christ's sake, and uses it for the advancement of his cause, has the same disposition with those, who for the same object actually suffer the loss of all things. In heart he gives his earthly all to Christ; saying with sincerity — *here Lord, I am; and here are my possessions. I will either use them, or part with them, for thy sake, as thou wilt.*

The character presented in the text belongs to *every faithful minister of the gospel*, even in the most peaceful days. Whatever may be his earthly prospects, he cheerfully resigns them for Christ's sake. The love of Christ bears him on. He declines no labor, no sacrifice, no suffering. He foregoes indulgence and ease. Worldly pursuits he abandons, and sets his affections on the kingdom of Christ.

This character is strikingly exhibited by *a devoted Christian in times of persecution*. He feels as Paul did, when his anxious friends besought him not to go to Jerusalem. "What mean ye," he said, "to weep, and to break my heart? For I am ready not to be bound only, but also to die at Jerusalem for the name of the Lord Jesus." In times of persecution and distress, the followers of Christ are led to a more serious contemplation of the heavenly inheritance, and naturally form a stronger and more operative attachment to that kingdom in which their all is contained. Accordingly, they make a more direct and unreserved surrender of everything for Christ, and become more consistent and decided in their religious character. They are less ensnared by the friendship of the world, and less awed by its frowns. The prospect of suffering, as it becomes familiar to their minds, ceases to alarm them. To give up the interests and pleasures of the world for the sake of Christ, costs them no struggle and no sigh. Yea, *they rejoice in their sufferings, and gladly fill up what is wanting of the afflictions of Christ in their flesh for his body's sake which is the Church.*

The *Christian Missionary*, whose motives correspond with his office, forsakes all for Christ in an eminent degree. Others forsake the world in affection, but enjoy it still. He renounces the enjoyment, as well as the affections. Other Christians esteem Christ above friends and possessions, and yet retain them far enough for the gratification of their natural affection. The Missionary, who has a right spirit, counteracts and mortifies natural affection, by actually abandoning its dearest objects. The distinction in short is this; other Christians have a willingness to forsake all for Christ; the Missionary *actually forsakes* all. The cause of Christ among the heathen possesses attractions above all other objects. It has the control of his heart. He forsakes father and mother, house and land, because his heart burns with the holy desire, that Christ may have the heathen for his inheritance, and the uttermost parts of the earth for his possession.

The *wife of a Missionary*, when influenced by the Christian spirit gives still more remarkable evidence of self-denial and devotion. For *her* to forsake friends and country, is an instance of greater self-denial. The tie, which binds her to her relatives and her home, is stronger. Her mind is more sensible to the tenderness of natural relations, and to the delights of domestic life. When, therefore, she forsakes all for the name of Christ, she makes a more costly sacrifice; and thus furnishes a more conspicuous proof, that her love to Christ transcends all earthly affection.

Persons of the character above described, have existed in all ages of Christianity. Indeed no other can be acknowledged, as disciples of Christ. For he himself has declared, that whosoever forsaketh not all that he hath, cannot be his disciple. And to teach us in the most forcible manner, that our affection for all other objects must fall below our affection for him, he says: — If any one come to me, and hate not his father, and mother, and wife, and children, and brethren, and sisters, yea, and his own life also, he cannot be my disciple. However severe these conditions of discipleship may seem; they have often been performed. Yea, there are multitudes who daily perform them, who have that supreme love for the Lord Jesus, which leaves little comparatively for anything else. In the very act of faith, there is an implied forsaking of all things for Christ. So that when the trial comes, and they really forsake all things on his account, they only do in open act, what they did in heart before. They made choice of Christ and his ways, Christ and his cross. Had they certainly known, when they first received Christ, that they did it at the expense of earthly good, they would not have received him with any less cordiality. Paul knew from the first, that he must part with everything for Christ; — which was only parting with trifles, to purchase a pearl of great price. "What things were gain to me, those I counted loss for Christ. Yea, doubtless, and I count all things loss for the excellency of the knowledge of Christ Jesus my Lord; for whom I have suffered the loss of all things, and do count them but dung, that I may win Christ." Such was the spirit and practice of the first Christians. They rejoice that they were counted worthy to suffer for Christ. They gladly took the spoiling of their goods, and endured persecution and death. There are those at the present day, who possess the same spirit; who willingly give up their worldly interest, that Christ may be magnified; who hold nothing so dear, that they will not cast it away for Christ's sake.

The reward of Christians is as certain, as their devotion to Christ is sincere. They receive an hundred fold in this present life. Great peace have they who love God's law. *The wicked are like the troubled sea when it cannot rest, whose waters cast up mire and dirt.* But cordial devotion to Christ imparts serenity and peace.

Devoted Christians enjoy the pleasures of *benevolence.* As this is their ruling affection, they must be happy in proportion as its object is promoted. In all that they do, and in all that others do to advance the welfare of the Redeemer's kingdom, they partake the purest pleasure. Let them see the glory of God displayed in the salvation of sinners; let them enjoy communion with Christ and see his church look forth as the morning; and they have enough. This is their treasure, the heritage which they have chosen. The eternal glory of God and the boundless good of his kingdom is an object infinitely excellent and worthy of supreme regard. The pleasure of those who are devoted to this glorious object, and see that it is perfectly secure, is a kind of divine pleasure, partaking of the nature of its divine and infinite object.

It is the uniform method of divine grace to give spiritual comfort to those, who are freed from earthly affection. The more the world is excluded from the hearts of believers, the more they are filled with all the fulness of God! What tongue can describe the happiness of the saints, when they part with all that they have for Christ, and when he fulfils his promises to them, and gives them peace. Behold the apostles, in the midst of their labors and sufferings. They speak of comfort in tribulation, of joy unspeakable and full of glory.

But all the enjoyment of Christians in this life, is only the beginning of their blessedness. The consummation of it is the everlasting life which they will inherit in the world to come, consisting in the perfect and endless enjoyment of God.

I have been led to this train of reflections by an event, which has lately arrested our attention and caused feelings of unusual interest among the friends of Christ. I refer to the lamented death of Mrs. Harriet Newell — a woman who happily exemplified the character which I have drawn. From the uniform tenor of her conduct for several years, there is reason to believe, that she truly forsook all for Christ, and received an hundred fold in this present life ; and that she now inherits everlasting blessedness in heaven.

But let God have the glory of all the moral beauty which adorned her character. If she was indeed what she appeared to be, it was by the washing of regeneration, and the renewing of the Holy Ghost.

Before she gave satisfactory evidence of spiritual renovation, she had a long season of distressing conviction, careful self-examination, and earnest prayer. Long before she thought her own salvation secure, she began to exercise an enlarged affection for the kingdom of Christ, and to be fervent in her prayers for the building up of Zion, and the salvation of the heathen. This became the prominent feature of her religion — the supreme object of her pursuits. A considerable time before a Foreign Mission from this country was contemplated, the universal diffusion of the Christian religion was the favorite subject of her meditations and prayers.

When in the course of divine providence one of those who had devoted themselves to the Foreign Mission, sought her as the companion of his labors, her great concern was to discover the will of God. As soon as she became satisfied respecting her duty, her determination was fixed. And here her character began to assume a lustre, which excited the admiration of all who shared her friendship. She consecrated herself to the establishment of the kingdom of Christ in pagan lands. To this object all her thoughts and studies, her desires and prayers tended. It was only with a view to this, that she considered her talents and acquirements of any special importance. Even her health and life seemed of little consequence to her, except in relation to this sacred object.

But this self-devotion had no tendency to blunt the sensibilities of her heart, or to extinguish her natural affections. She had these in all their vigor; but she had an affection which holds a superiority over the natural affections and makes them subservient to its purposes. Had our natural affections been designed, as the highest principles of action, the Lord Jesus would never have set up another principle above them. If there was a difference between her pious affection and that of the bulk of Christians, it consisted in this, that hers was more earnest and undivided. It is to this circumstance, that we must trace her peculiar magnanimity, and elevation of spirit. As all the powers of her soul were exerted for the attainment of one grand object, she rose to an uncommon pitch of energy, and things seemingly impossible to others, became practicable and easy to her.

In acquiring the force and decision of character which she finally exhibited, it was of great importance that the question of *duty* was fully settled in her own mind. Had not this been done, she must have been often turned aside from her object by misgivings of conscience. Her attachment to the object must have been weakened, and every step must have been taken haltingly and tremblingly. But by much deliberation, and prayer, the question of duty had been settled; after which she proceeded without wavering. Devoted, as she was, to the cause of Christ, and borne on by a strong desire of advancing it in heathen lands, she was prepared for trials. The hardships and sufferings, peculiar to the missionary life, were so closely associated in her mind with the glory of God, and the conversion of the heathen, and the contemplation of them was so continually mingled with her purest affections and joys, that instead of aversion and dread, they excited sensations of delight.

The character of Mrs. Newell had an excellence above the reach of mere human nature. Behold a tender female, when all the sensibilities of the heart are most lively — united to friends and country by a thousand ties; a female of refined education, with delightful prospects in her own country — behold her voluntarily resigning so many dear earthly objects for a distant pagan land. All these sacrifices she made calmly; with a sober deliberation; in the exercise of the most delicate sensibilities, and yet with steady, unyielding firmness, and all this not for any earthly object, but to make known among the heathen the unsearchable riches of Christ.

I should blush to offer a vindication of a character so fair and exalted as that of Harriet Newell; — a lovely saint, who has finished her course, and gone to receive an unfading crown. But if there is any one rash enough to impute extravagance and folly; I will point him to a case not wholly unlike the present. The Evangelist tells us that Mary came to Jesus as he sat at meat, with an alabaster box of very precious ointment, and poured it upon his head. Judas, and some others instigated by him, charged her with extravagance and waste. But Jesus approved her conduct, declaring that she had wrought a good work, and that it should be made known for a memorial of her, wherever the gospel should be preached.

Does any one think that "she threw herself away?" But do you not applaud the conduct of a man, who goes to the earth's end to gratify a worldly desire? And can you think it reasonable to make greater sacrifices for self-interest, than for the kingdom of Christ? — "Threw herself away!" —What! does a devoted Christian, who, for the love of Jesus, forsakes all that she has, to receive an hundred fold here, and life everlasting in heaven, throw herself away?

Do you ask what that hundred fold reward was? my appeal would be to herself — to her peace, and quietness, and joy in God. For several of the last months that she spent at home, and from the time of her leaving America till her death, her religious enjoyment was almost constant, and at times, elevated.

In her last interview with her beloved friends in America, and in the scene of final separation, the consolations of the Spirit supported her, and produced not only meekness and calmness of mind, but astonishing resolution. Her happy serenity continued through the dangers of a long voyage, and amid all the difficulties which befel her after arriving in India. Her spiritual enjoyment was not materially interrupted by the various distresses which prevented the establishment of the mission; nor by the sufferings she was subsequently called to endure; no, not even by the pangs which rent her heart, over a dear infant child, wasting away with sickness, and soon committed to a watery grave. Through all this suffering, the Lord was with her and gave her rest. During her last tedious and perilous voyage — separated by half the globe from the presence of a mother, whose presence was more than ever needed — and without a single female companion, she could thus write — "It is for Jesus, who sacrificed the joys of his father's kingdom and expired on the cross to redeem a fallen world, that thus I wander from place to place, and feel no where at home. How reviving the thought! How great the consolation it yields to my sinking heart!" "Let the severest trials and disappointments fall to my lot; guilty and weak as I am, yet I think I can rejoice in the Lord, and joy in the God of salvation."

In her last illness, which was attended with many distressing circumstances, she possessed her soul in patience and peace. God was pleased to manifest himself to her, as he does not to the world. "During her whole sickness, she talked in the most familiar manner, and with great delight, of death and the glory that was to follow." At a certain time, being advised by a physician to cast off such gloomy thoughts, "she replied, that those thoughts were cheering and joyful beyond what words could express." When it was intimated to her that she could not live through another day; "*O joyful news! she replied, I long to depart;*" and added soon after, that death appeared to her *truly welcome and glorious.*

But the simple narrative of her afflicted husband shows, better than anything which I can say, that amid all the pain and languishment of sickness, and in the near view of death, she had that enjoyment of God her Saviour, and that hope of a blessed immortality, which was an hundred fold better, than all she had forsaken.

To her widowed Mother this is an affecting scene. But in the midst of your sorrows, dear Madam, forget not what reason you have to be comforted. Remember the grace of God, which was manifested to your dear Harriet; and which, we trust, sanctified her heart. While you mourn for her early death, bless God that you do not mourn over a child, who lived without God, and died without hope. Call to remembrance her dutiful and pious temper; her resolved and peaceful mind in the parting hour; and the fortitude and resignation, which she afterwards exercised, under her various afflictions. Give thanks to God for the consolations which were afforded her throughout a languishing sickness. Divine grace was honored by her amiable and Christian conduct. Through all her sufferings, especially when her dissolution drew near, she displayed a character that was ripe for heaven.

It must afford you peculiar satisfaction to contemplate the usefulness of her life. "That life is long which answers life's great end." This was eminently the case with your beloved daughter. Had she lived in retirement, or moved in a small circle, her influence, though highly useful, must have been circumscribed. But now, her character has been exhibited on the most extensive theatre, and excited the attention and love of Christian nations. Yea, may we not hope, that her name will be remembered by the millions of Asia, whose salvation she so ardently desired, and that the savor of her piety will, by divine grace be salutary to pagan tribes yet unborn?—What comforts are these? — comforts, which many mourning parents would gladly purchase with their lives. Render thanks then to God, and magnify his name, that he has given you a daughter so lovely in her character, so useful in her life, so resigned in her sufferings, so tranquil in her death. Dwell upon these cheering thoughts, and enjoy these comforts. And may all your surviving children enjoy them too. In her example, in her writings, and in her dying counsels, she has left them a legacy, which cannot be too highly prized. Let me affectionately entreat you, beloved friends, to attend seriously to the weighty counsel which you have received from the dying lips of your sister. In her name, in the name of her bereaved husband, by whose request I now address you, and in the name of her God and Saviour, I repeat that solemn counsel. "*Tell them*, she said, *tell them from the lips of their dying sister, that there is nothing but religion worth living for. Oh, exhort them to attend immediately to the care of their immortal souls, and not to delay repentance! Let my brothers and sisters know that I love them to the end. I hope to meet them in heaven. But oh, if I should not!"* — No wonder that her tears and her sobs of grief at the thought of an eternal separation from you, prevented her saying more. "May the spirit of truth carry her dying entreaties, and tears, and sighs to your hearts;" and engage you to follow her as she followed Christ. She never repented of her undertaking, never regretted leaving her native land for the cause of Christ. And could she return and live on earth again, so far from declining any of the sacrifices she made for the advancement of the Redeemer's cause; she would repair to him earlier, give up all for him more cheerfully, and serve him with greater zeal.

In the death of Mrs. Newell her husband sustains a loss which no language can adequately describe, and no earthly good compensate. God, whose ways are unsearchable, has taken from him the wife of his youth; a companion eminently qualified to aid him in his labors, to soothe him in his sorrows, and to further the great work in which he is engaged. Had he nothing but earthly good to comfort him, a mind so quick to feel would be overwhelmed with grief. But the God of all grace, who put it into his heart to preach salvation to those who are perishing for lack of vision, will be the rock of his confidence, and a very present help in trouble. It must be a subject of delightful recollection to our afflicted brother, that he has enjoyed the privilege of being united, in the dearest of all relations, with one of so amiable a temper; of an understanding so highly improved; of benevolence and piety so eminent. He will also love to remember the favor which God conferred upon his beloved partner, in enabling her to do and suffer so much for the name of Jesus; and in carrying her so quickly to the inheritance of the saints in light.

Friends of the Missionary Cause,

Let not your hearts be troubled by adverse circumstances. Recollect the various hinderances, disappointments, and sufferings, encountered by the apostles, the first missionaries of Christ, who yet were destined to spread the triumphs of his cross through the world. The experience of ages leads us to expect that designs of great moment, especially those which relate to the advancement of Christ's kingdom, will be opposed by mighty obstacles. The adverse circumstances, therefore, which have attended the outset of our Foreign Mission, are far from presenting any discouragement. They rather afford new evidence, that this mission is to be numbered with all other enterprises, adapted to promote the honor of God and the welfare of men. These various trials, brethren, are doubtless intended not only to qualify Missionaries for greater usefulness, but also to humble and purify all who are laboring and praying for the conversion of the heathen. The cause is the cause of God, and it is vain to depend for its prosperity on human exertions. The death of Mrs. Newell, instead of overcasting our prospects, will certainly turn to the advantage of missions. The publication of her virtues will quicken and edify thousands. It will also make it apparent, that the missionary cause has attractions for the most excellent characters. Her character will be identified with that holy cause. Henceforth, every one, who remembers Harriet Newell, will remember the Foreign Mission from America. And every one who reads the history of this mission, will be sure to remember her exemplary life and triumphant death. Thus all her talents, the advantages of her education, the beauties of her mind, the amiableness of her manners, her willingness to give up all that was dear to her in her native land, her fervent love to Christ, her desires, and prayers for the advancement of his kingdom, her patience and fortitude in suffering, and the divine consolations which she enjoyed, will all redound to the honor of that sacred cause, to which she was devoted. Her life, measured by months and years, was short; but far otherwise when measured by what she achieved. She did not pray and suffer and die in vain. Other causes may miscarry, but this will certainly triumph. The Lord God of Israel has pledged his perfections for its success. The time is at hand, when the various tribes of India, and all the nations and kindreds of the earth shall bow the knee at the name of Jesus. He will see the travail of his soul, and all his benevolent desires will be satisfied. The power of God will soon accomplish a work, which, seen in distant prospect, has made thousands, now sleeping in Jesus, leap for joy. O *Sun of Righteousness*, arise ; shine upon the dark places of the earth ; fill the world with thy glorious light ! Amen.

A SERMON

DELIVERED AT THE ORDINATION OF THE REV. JOHN W. ELLINGWOOD, AT BATH, ME., NOV. 4, 1812, AND OF REV. JACOB IDE, D. D., AT MEDWAY, MASS., NOV. 2, 1814.

---

2 Tim. 2: 24, 25.—THE SERVANT OF THE LORD MUST NOT STRIVE; BUT BE GENTLE UNTO ALL MEN, APT TO TEACH, PATIENT; IN MEEKNESS INSTRUCTING THOSE THAT OPPOSE THEMSELVES.

MY principal reason for introducing this subject is, that it has been treated less frequently than most other subjects which pertain to the pastoral office, and, as I think, less frequently than its nature demands.

My single object is, to illustrate *the peculiar importance of meekness and gentleness in a minister of the gospel.*

I begin by saying, that *the spirit of meekness and gentleness is necessary to qualify a minister for the various duties of his office.*

It is necessary to prepare him for *the successful study of the Scriptures.* An Apostle directs us to "receive *with meekness* the ingrafted word." The predominance of those sinful passions which are contrary to meekness, disqualifies a minister for profitable reading and meditation. It blinds the eyes of his understanding, gives a wrong bias to his judgment, and exposes him to every kind of error. What confidence can his people have in the conclusions to which he is conducted, while under the influence of pride, anger, or any disorderly affection? But under the influence of *meekness*, he is prepared for *profitable study*. He is sensible of his own ignorance and is ready to submit unreservedly to the infallible word of God. He is willing to give up all the results of unsanctified reason, and to believe every revealed truth on the authority of inspiration. With a docile temper, he says, "Speak, Lord, for thy servant heareth." Time spent by a minister in search of divine truth with such a disposition, will not be spent in vain. The God of truth will be his teacher. "The meek will he guide in judgment, and the meek will he teach his way."

Meekness and gentleness are necessary to prepare a minister *to teach the Christian religion and perform other ministerial duties, with propriety and success.*

The Christian religion is a religion of love. It breathes peace on earth and good will to men. A minister, who possesses the virtues recommended in the text, imbibes the spirit of this religion, and is prepared rightly to teach its doctrines and duties. But if a man undertakes to preach the gospel without the spirit of meekness and gentleness, there is a manifest repugnancy between his office and his character. He calls upon others to exercise that love, which has not been shed abroad in his own heart. He inculcates upon them the meekness and gentleness of Christ, when he himself is destitute of those excellent virtues.

Meekness and gentleness are necessary to a preacher's *acceptance.* I mean not to suggest, that the best mode of exhibiting the truth would reconcile the unsanctified heart to it, or cause the offence of the cross to cease. But the preacher, who complies with the Apostle's direction now before us, has nothing offensive in his *manner;* and any opposition made against him is excited purely by the holy nature of the truth itself, and not by anything exceptionable in him, as a preacher. He will indeed love the truth, and earnestly contend for it. But in the defence of the truth he will be careful never to enlist his angry passions. His tongue will never utter invectives against others, however they differ in opinion. Nor is he transported to undue severity, either of language or feeling, against those who load him with reproaches and injuries. The only methods which he employs to bring men to the knowledge of the truth, are those which are dictated by reason, compassion, and gentleness. Let a minister preach thus, and his enemies will be able to *find no occasion against him, except concerning the law of his God.*

Meekness and gentleness are peculiarly important to a preacher's *success.* "The wrath of man worketh not the righteousness of God." Acrimonious feelings and expressions are not the instruments, by which the cause of righteousness is to be promoted. A minister is indeed engaged in a warfare; and he must contend and fight in order to his success. But what is the nature of this warfare? What is this contention, but a contention against the disorderly affections of human nature? Now with what weapons will you carry on such a warfare? Is a minister to use anger and violence, to subdue anger and violence in others? All the doctrines of the Bible are to be taught, and all errors to be opposed. The question is, *in what manner?* The Apostle answers: "The servant of the Lord must not *strive*, but be *gentle* unto *all* men, *patient*, in *meekness* instructing those that oppose themselves." A minister, who follows this direction, has the brightest prospect of success. Every one must perceive that this manner of teaching corresponds with the nature of divine truth. The incomprehensible greatness and perfect holiness of the subjects of revelation require, that they should be treated with sacred composure and meekness.—The least mixture of passion is inadmissible. Can you excite love by the language of ill will? Can you attract men to a heaven of peace, by displaying a spirit of strife? — to a heaven of kindness, by a spirit of virulence? Can you successfully inculcate condescension, forgiveness, and compassion, by displaying pride, revenge, and hardness of heart? Can you persuade your hearers to govern their passions, by showing them that you do not govern your own?

The success of a minister consists in conforming the hearts and lives of men to the character of Christ, and fitting them for the heavenly inheritance. His usefulness is to be measured by the degree, in which he promotes the fruits of the Spirit. But if he is destitute of those fruits, what reason is there to expect he will promote them among his people? He may have a burning zeal, and do much seemingly for the conversion of sinners. But who will reward him for converting men from stupidity to animosity? — for rousing them from sleep to bite and devour? A minister of a rough and violent spirit may build up his church; but the members composing it will, in all probability, be stamped with his likeness. Reposing confidence in their teacher, they will con-consider not only his doctrines, but his disposition and manners, as authorized by his religion. Thus the deformity of their character will, in a measure, be attributable to the wrong spirit of their minister.

I have now touched upon a very interesting point. To be useful a minister must be exemplary. The example of one, who possesses a right temper, is of mighty efficacy in forming the minds of Christians. They look to him as a pattern, and receive their particular cast of character from what they see in *him*. His sweet and lovely spirit diffuses itself among the followers of Christ, and promotes love, joy and peace. His example manifestly rises above the best attainments of human nature, and in the view of all beholders is a distinguished honor to divine grace.

But a minister has other duties to perform. He must visit from house to house, and converse with his people in private. He must seek access to them at all times, and administer counsel, reproof, and consolation, as their circumstances require. In the performance of all these duties, the disposition, which I have been recommending, is unspeakably important. It will allure his people to attend to his instructions. As he assumes no airs of haughty superiority; as he governs his own passions, and is always patient and kind; they will freely disclose to him all their difficulties, and with a candid, teachable temper, ask his counsel. The gentleness of his disposition will render even his reproofs acceptable. Who can take offence — whose heart is hard enough not to be affected, when a minister of the gospel goes to him, and, with meekness and tenderness, honestly tells him what he has done amiss, and announces to him, not the resentment of a man, but the displeasure of God?

A minister, adorned with a meek and quiet spirit, may be extensively useful in composing disagreements and preventing strife. He is the man to heal wounds, to calm commotions, and extinguish fires. But what can one of an opposite temper do? Can wounds be healed with his scourge? Will you send a fireband to put out a flame?

But I mean not to exalt meekness at the expense of other virtues. In fact it is not at variance with them, and never would have been thought so, had not the nature of the one or the other been misunderstood. Meekness is not only compatible with other virtues, but is their support and ornament. It is necessary even to decision of character. Where meekness is wanting you may find the stiffness of a bigot, and the surliness of a cynic; but the decision of a *Christian* you cannot find. The Apostle Paul was distinguished for meekness and gentleness. No man ever had more pliability, than he who became *all things to all men.* His passions were under such control, that no reproach or suffering could ruffle them. And yet what man ever had more *firmness?* In the Captain of our salvation, this combination of virtues was perfect. Meekness and gentleness were diffused through all his words and actions. And yet his firmness was immovable.

The same consistency appears between *meekness* and *zeal.* Meekness tempers the ardor of zeal, but never extinguishes it. Nor does meekness in the least diminish the influence of zeal; but by directing its operations, and preventing its irregularities, gives it the highest possible efficacy.

Meekness is a powerful aid to ministerial *fidelity.* Harshness of temper throws a thousand obstacles in a minister's way. It involves him in difficulties. It exposes him to perpetual war, and arms the very elements against him. From these difficulties a minister is generally preserved by the spirit of meekness and gentleness. This diminishes the number and hostility of his opposers. It clears his way of obtacles; and renders his duty practicable and easy. No minister is so likely to preach the truths of revelation with persevering fidelity, as he who preaches them in the *spirit of love and meekness.* This will make him bold to declare all the counsel of God, and to reprove wickedness, when violent men are compelled to silence.

The importance of Christian meekness appears in its *happy effects on a minister's situation and enjoyments.* Although it is sometimes considered a feeble, inactive virtue; it does really impart to a minister the highest degree of energy, and afford him absolute security against his enemies. Let them be ever so numerous, and their wrath ever so great; the victory will be his. But be it remembered, that his victory is not obtained either by force or by terror. It is the victory of wisdom over folly, of sober reason over passion, of religion over impiety. This honor belongs to every minister, who follows the meek and lowly Jesus. By governing his own spirit, by returning good for evil, and blessing for cursing, by treating his opposers with moderation and kindness, he discovers a greatness of mind, which often melts or confounds them, and is always noticed with esteem by impartial spectators. Besides this, he obtains a victory, which the world seldom beholds, but which the wise man esteems above all others —*victory over himself.*

"His warfare is within. There unfatigued,
His fervent spirit labors. There he fights,
And there obtains fresh triumphs o'er himself,
And never withering wreathes."

Meekness preserves a minister from the unhappiness of *contention.* Whatever others do, *he* will not strive. He will not participate in the agitations of the world around him. While others are suffering the wretchedness of envying and strife; he enjoys the pleasure of a serene and peaceful mind. And he often enjoys the additional pleasure of seeing serenity and joy diffused among those around him.

The value of such a temper it is impossible to describe. The world is full of disorder; and no man is exposed to see more of it, or to be more affected by it, than a minister of the gospel. He must have trials. How delightful soever his prospect at the beginning, difficulty lies before him. The day may open with a clear sky; but dark and stormy clouds will appear before night. If a minister faithfully preaches the religion of Christ, and lives accordingly, he must encounter opposition in one form or other. But amidst all his troubles, he has peace within. Others are agitated; but he is composed. Others may load him and his doctrine with ignominy. But he is gentle and patient. No resentful or envious thought corrodes his heart. The sweetness and lenity of his disposition secure to him an inward serenity, which nothing can disturb.

Allow me to say further, that ministers have real and sometimes urgent occasion for the exercise of the spirit which I have been recommending, *in their connection and intercourse with each other.* Yes, brethren, you will have occasion to exercise this Christ-like disposition towards your fellow-laborers in the sacred office. They will be called to struggle with difficulties and bear afflictions which will make an appeal to your compassion and sympathy. Therefore "put on bowels of mercy." They will need substantial acts of friendship from you. Therefore "put on kindness." They will have faults of character—faults, which may interfere with your comfort, and may excite feelings of dislike—feelings which, if allowed to lodge in your hearts, may lead on to animosity and bitterness. If you would be sure to foreclose evils so much to be dreaded, then put on meekness and forbearance towards your brethren, whatever may be their faults. You will certainly have occasion, more or less frequent, to exercise meekness, gentleness and forbearance towards your fellow-laborers in the work of the ministry. And on the other hand, your brethren may discover some faults in you, which may make it necessary for them to exercise the spirit of meekness and forbearance towards you; and thus it will be as the Apostle directs,—"forbearing *one another*, and forgiving one another."

Finally, consider the importance of the virtue enjoined in my text, as *it is necessary to assimilate ministers to the great Shep-*

herd and Bishop of souls. He is your standard. Fix your eyes then steadily upon your Lord and Master. — He was meek and lowly in heart. The spirit of the dove pervaded his whole character and life, particularly the closing scene. He was abused, insulted, reproached, and condemned. But the Lamb of God, though possessed of power to crush his enemies in a moment, bore it all with silent meekness! When they finished the work of malice and cruelty, and nailed him to the cross; no emotion of ill-will was excited in his breast; but with indescribable compassion and tenderness he said, "Father, forgive them, for they know not what they do."

My dear brother, behold your pattern! See the lovely virtue, which ought to beautify your character, and to pervade your studies, your preaching, and your pastoral labors. Cherish this excellent virtue. Grow in the meekness of wisdom; and make all your trials and sufferings subservient to this end. Banish forever that proud, irritable temper, which rises against a faithful reprover; and always consider him your best friend, who most plainly points out your failings. Complain not of injuries. — If at any time your feelings are disturbed — *look unto Jesus.* You can find no other perfect example. You can aim at no honor or happiness so great, as to bear the likeness of him who was *meek and lowly in heart.*

A SERMON

DELIVERED AT THE ORDINATION OF THE REV. JOEL HAWES, D. D., AT HARTFORD, CONN., MARCH 4, 1818.

Hebrews 13: 17.—THEY WATCH FOR YOUR SOULS AS THEY THAT MUST GIVE ACCOUNT.

A MINISTER of the gospel must give account to God, as well as the people of his charge. He describes to them the transactions which they must then witness, and in which they must bear a part. But he should remember, that it will be a day of judgment to him, as well as to them. He must stand before Christ, not to preach the gospel, but to be judged by it; not to disclose to sinners, by the light of divine truth, the secrets of their hearts, but to have the secrets of his own heart disclosed;—not to tell his flock, that Christ will come to divide them from one another, and place the saints on his right hand and sinners on his left; but to take his own place on one side or the other, according to his character.

The final account of a minister must be as strict and impartial, as that of his people. No allowance will be made in his favor, because he was solemnly ordained to be a Christian pastor, or because he went through the common labors and trials of the ministry. Nor will any favor be shown him, because he occupied an important station in the church;—nor because he preached the truth;—nor because he was held in high estimation for his talents and piety. Nor will any allowance be made in his favor, because he encountered difficulties and sufferings; — nor even because his labors were successful, and many blessed him as their spiritual father. He must be tried by the same unbending rule of righteousness with others. He must give account of all his conduct, and of the hidden things of the heart; particularly of the motives, which led him to assume the sacred office, and of the spirit which actuated his studies, his visits, and all his ministrations. If he has been a faithful shepherd, he will receive an unfading inheritance. The review of his pious labors and sufferings on earth will fill him with emotions of unspeakable delight; and the souls converted or edified under his ministry, will be his joy and his crown. But if he has neglected the duties of his calling; what can he expect but the frown of his Judge? No entreaties for mercy can then prevail. He must see at an appalling distance, those blessed mansions which were once within his reach, and which he persuaded others to secure.

This brief description of the final account which a minister of the gospel must give of himself at the last day, will help us to see what *practical influence* the expectation of that account ought to have upon him. This influence may be considered in relation to a minister's *object*, his *qualifications*, his *duties*, his *failings*, and his *trials*.

First. The practical influence, which I am to illustrate, respects a minister's *object*, or the *end* at which he ought to aim. He looks forward to the time when earthly pursuits will cease, and earthly interests disappear, and when the Lord from heaven will sit upon his throne to judge the world. What will the minister then consider to have been the most important object of his calling? Will he not see that nothing ever deserved a thought compared with the conversion of sinners, and the edification and enlargement of the church? Will he not then see, that turning aside from this great object to pursue wealth, or science, or personal promotion, was an abandonment of his sacred work? When a minister fixes his eyes upon the day of account, he must feel, that there is nothing else for him to pursue as the end of his holy office, but the glory of Christ and the advancement of his kingdom. Other things become insignificant. If he does but little for the salvation of men, he does but little of his proper business. Let him do anything that is foreign to his calling; — it is all a bubble. Those acquisitions, cares, labors, which do nothing toward saving immortal souls, will at last appear as the chaff of the summer threshing floor. Thus if a minister habitually looks forward to the day of account; the views which he knows he must then have, will obtain a present influence over him; will withdraw him from everything inconsistent with his proper work, and keep him engaged, with steady, ardent zeal, to promote the reign of Christ, as the great end of his ministry.

Secondly. This practical influence respects a minister's *qualifications*. If he judges rightly as to the proper object of the ministry, he will perceive that it calls for high qualifications; — qualifications far above what he possesses. Whatever advantages of education he may have enjoyed, and whatever length of time he may have spent in preparing for the ministry; he will fall down in the dust, when he compares his attainments, either moral or literary, with the high mark at which his office requires him to aim. His previous contemplation and study seem to have done little more, than to fix his eye upon the magnitude of the work before him, and show him how much remains to be done in obtaining the requisite qualifications. Now a proper recollection of his accountableness to God will prompt him to unwearied endeavors to obtain these qualifications; — qualifications which may be held in low estimation by the worldly mind, but are of great price in the sight of God. These qualifications he will pursue with constant assiduity. Let no idle intruder interrupt him. Let no worldly anxieties disturb him. *He is studying for the judgment day. He is making improvements for eternity.*

Thirdly. The subject is to be considered in relation to a minister's *duties*. These duties are so numerous and difficult, that, from conscious insufficiency, he is sometimes disposed to shrink back from them. And sometimes while attempting them, he is ready to be disheartened. It requires a motive of no common efficacy to carry him forward in the face of so many difficulties and discouragements, to the execution of his arduous work. One of the most powerful motives is that which we are now considering. The certain expectation of a day of reckoning, and of the endless retributions then to commence, cannot fail to elevate a pious minister above discouragement, and to inspire him with animation and perseverance equal, in some good measure, to the obligations of his office. Such an expectation adds new strength to the inward spring of holy action. Love to God rises to higher fervency, when in the anticipated light of the last day, his glorious perfections appear with new splendor. Love to souls becomes more tender and active, when a minister considers how their salvation will appear before the bar of Christ. Take into view any of the momentous duties, which devolve upon an ambassador of Christ, and see how powerful an influence the expectation of giving account to God will exert upon him.—I am now, he says, to preach the everlasting gospel; and shortly am to stand before Christ, and give account of my preaching. I am going from the pulpit to the judgment seat. Shall I not then faithfully deliver the message of Him whose I am, and to whom I must give account? Shall I not strive for the salvation of those who are put under my care, and whom I am to meet before the tribunal of justice? Shall I who am soon to stand before my Lord, spend that time for my own ends, which he commands me to spend in feeding his sheep and his lambs?

It not unfrequently happens, that ministers, who commence their public labors with a good measure of active zeal, by and by grow remiss. The business of their office loses its novelty. Avocations multiply. Domestic cares and bodily infirmities increase. Want of success disheartens them. Perhaps opposition or neglect produces alienation in their feelings. They are in danger of growing indifferent in their work—of neglecting what they can neglect, and doing what they do from an unwelcome necessity. But the habitual expectation of the final account is eminently fitted to guard a minister against these great evils. What if the business of his office does lose its novelty? Is it therefore less momentous? Are the souls for whom he is watching, less precious? And does the account he must give of his ministry, lose its importance, because it draws near? Why talk of *novelty*, when he is doing the work of Him, who is the same yesterday, to-day, and forever? What if domestic cares and burdens increase, and avocations multiply? Can these be mentioned before his Judge, as an exemption from the proper duties of his calling? If he keeps his final account in view, he will suffer no cares, or burdens or avocations to withdraw him from his great concern. Do bodily infirmities begin to invade him? This will remind him that his time is short, and the day of the Lord at hand, and so will be a new motive to all proper exertions to finish his work. And what if his labors are apparently unsuccessful, and instead of beholding sinners turning to God, he sees nothing but obstinacy in sin? What is all this to a minister who looks for the coming of his Lord, and expects to hear that voice which wakes the dead? He knows that he is not to give account of the degree of his success, but of the fidelity of his labors. These views animate him to persevering diligence; and lead him to consider even the increasing guilt and wretchedness of sinners, as a motive to still greater zeal for their conversion.

Time would fail me to recount the improprieties in the manner of inculcating the truths of Christianity, which have arisen from unsuitable feelings in the minds of preachers. Sometimes from vanity or inconsideration, they hold forth their own conjectures and dreams. Sometimes the troublesome objections urged against them, and the warmth of zeal they exercise in contending for the truth, result in irritation and bitterness. And these show themselves in language, looks, and tones of voice, that will cut and chastise opposers. Better preach nothing, than preach even the truth in such a manner as this. Prejudices are multiplied. Even Christians catch the unhallowed spirit of their teacher, and lose much of the beauty of their character. And Christianity itself is adulterated and disgraced, by being conveyed through the channel of passion.

O what a difference there is, both in manner and effect, between the preaching of one who forgets the future judgment and is governed by the corrupt passions of human nature, and of one who habitually and feelingly recollects that he must give account!

Fourthly. Every minister of the gospel is exposed, in one way or another, to faults of character, — to pride and vanity, to ambition and envy, to jealousy and evil speaking, to love of wealth and love of indulgence, or to trifling and levity. Now if ministers were, at all times, and in all companies, duly mindful that the day of the Lord is at hand, and that they must give account for all their conduct, they would watchfully guard against whatever would detract from the beauty of their character and expose them to the disapprobation of their final Judge. The seriousness and awe of such a sentiment would keep them at the greatest distance from all sinful affections and pursuits, and lead them to say, with the Apostle, " What manner of persons ought we to be in all holy conversation and godliness ? "

Fifthly. The subject has a relation to a minister's *trials*. Trials and sufferings make a part of his office. At the commencement of his work, he may see before him an enlightened, generous, united people, — and a church of active, faithful Christians. He may be surrounded by affectionate fathers and brethren in the ministry. He may behold, in every direction, a bright prospect of usefulness and comfort, and may have a glow of health and spirits, that makes brightness still more bright. But let him not be dazzled by the splendor which encompasses him. Let him wait a little, and wait in prayer. For a day of trial will come. If he preaches faithfully, and lives faithfully, some who have the form of godliness, may find themselves too heavily reproved, and begin to speak out their complaints against their reprover. Some may forsake his ministry. He may see that the followers of Christ do not grow in grace, but are immersed in business, or distracted by some unhappy strife, and so are turned off from their benevolent exertions to extend the reign of Christ. The order and discipline of the church may be neglected, and fatal errors creep in. Parents may be unmindful of their duty ; while children and youth, the hope of the church, forget their Creator, are weary of the Sabbath, and give themselves to vice and folly. In his high and holy calling he may labor from year to year, and yet see those, for whom he watches and prays, neglecting the great salvation. He may cry to Him, with whom is the residue of the Spirit, while no Spirit comes down, no rain or dew descends. And his own soul may feel the horrors of a spiritual drought.

Or if the mercy of God should preserve a minister from these afflictions, he may have to encounter others. His heart may be grieved to find the want of union and coöperation among those who sustain the sacred office, and to see, in consequence, how little can be done to check the career of iniquity and error, and promote the cause of learning and religion. Or he may have domestic affliction. It may be his sorrowful lot to see a pious partner expire, and find himself a solitary mourner; or to see children grow up in disobedience, or die in sin. Distressing pain, or lingering sickness may befall him. And he may begin to find that the vigor of his health and spirits is breaking, and the end of his usefulness drawing nigh.

Now whatever trials may be allotted to a faithful minister, it will be of great use to him, to look forward to the day of account. It will afford him no slender support, to fix his thoughts upon a time, when all his sorrows will be ended, and when he will know by experience what is that exceeding great and eternal weight of glory, which his trials have been working out for him. With such an expectation, he will regard every affliction as light and transient. Devout anticipation of the last day, and of its glorious transactions, will strengthen his heart and prompt him to diligence in duty, and diligence in duty is one of the best supports and comforts for a day of adversity. It keeps him near the God of all grace and comfort, and gives peace which the world cannot give.

Let me add, that the contemplation of a day of such solemn import, and of business so incomparably interesting to every immortal soul, and so immediately connected with an eternity of bliss or wo, must take such hold on the heart of a minister, as in a great measure to contravene the unhappy effects of adversity;

must impress on him the character of fortitude not to be subdued, and of tranquillity not to be ruffled; must preserve him from impatience and fainting in the day of trouble, and open to him sources of comfort forever inaccessible to the worldly mind.

My Dear Brother,

I have confidence in you, that through the grace of Christ, you will watch for souls as one who must give account. The day of judgment is to be solemnly remembered. Better be anything than a minister, if you forget it. The remembrance is to have an influence upon all parts of your life; upon your studies, your secret devotion, your public ministrations, and your pastoral visits. In cases of doubt and difficulty, lift up your eyes to your Lord and Saviour, just ready to come to judgment, and ask yourself, what will appear best, when reviewed before his tribunal; and how you shall dispose of your difficulties, and regulate your conduct, so that you may be prepared to give up your account.

I hope, that neither youth, nor health, nor the affection of this beloved society, nor any of the pleasing circumstances of your situation, will lead you to view the day of account as far distant. It will be present; and you will ere long look upon it as past. Your venerable predecessor could tell you, how short was the interval between the beginning and the end of his ministry. He had his day of ordination. He preached the unsearchable riches of Christ, counselled sinners, comforted believers, visited the sick and dying, endured affliction, and finished his work. You are commencing the same course, and in all probability, the days of your ministry will as soon be ended. The Lord grant that the period of your ministry may be long. But the longest is short. You will soon stand, with your fathers and brethren, before the Judge of the world, to give account of your stewardship. The event is so certain and so near, that I seem to see it already come. I see you looking up with a countenance full of joy, to behold your glorious Redeemer on the throne of judgment. You turn your thoughts back upon the scenes of your mortal state — your childhood and youth — the season of your education — the years you spent in our beloved Seminary — the day of your induction into the holy ministry — the truths inculcated and the prayers offered up on that solemn occasion. In the clear light of this day of glory, you look back upon your ministry. Say now, did you feel too seriously the magnitude of the sacred office? Did you devote yourself too exclusively to the great end of your ministry? Did you love the children of God with too much tenderness; or labor, with excessive solicitude, for the salvation of sinners? Did the cause of Christ lie too near your heart? Or did you keep your eye upon it too steadily? Did you preach too affectionately, or too faithfully? Did you pray with too much fervor? Did you make it a subject of too deep concern, how you should live, and how you should die? Did you think too much of this day of account? Has it not arrived as soon, and is not its importance as great, as you expected? And did you ever set too high a price upon the approbation of your Saviour and Judge, — or upon this redeemed, spotless church, now presented before the presence of his glory with exceeding joy?

BRETHREN AND FRIENDS OF THIS SOCIETY,

You too are going to judgment. The time is as important, and as near to you, as to your minister. And it is as important both to him and to you, as though it were now present. When you witness its transactions, and bear a part in them, eternal happiness will be as dear to you, and endless misery as dreadful, as they would be, if you were now listening to the last sentence of your Judge. Regard then, the day of God, so long desired by the saints and so dreadful to sinners, as a present reality — as actually come; and looking back from this scene of ineffable solemnity, say — did your ministers ever paint in too strong colors the evil of sin, the vanity of the world, or the dreadfulness of endless punishment? Did they ever urge you too earnestly to repent, and prepare to meet your God? Did you offer up too many prayers for your minister, or for the church? Did you strive too earnestly to enter in at the strait gate? Do you regret it now, that you forsook all for Christ, or did so much for his cause?

Where now, Oh ye children of God, where now are those worldly attachments and cares which hindered your growth in grace, and kept you poor, when all the riches of Christ were before you? Where, now, Oh sinners, are those days of mercy you once enjoyed? And where are those shadows of time, for which you turned away from the Saviour, and despised the joys of his kingdom?

A SERMON

DELIVERED IN THE SECOND BAPTIST CHURCH IN BOSTON, OCT. 28, 1821, AT THE ORDINATION OF REV. ALVA WOODS, D. D.

---

1 COR., PARTS OF CHAP. XII.—Now there are diversities of gifts, but the same Spirit.—And there are diversities of operations, but it is the same God who worketh all in all. But the manifestation of the Spirit is given to every man to profit withal. For to one man is given by the Spirit the word of wisdom;—to another, the working of miracles; to another, prophecy.—But all these worketh that one and the self-same Spirit, dividing to every man severally as he will. For as the body is one, and hath many members, and all the members of that one body, being many, are one body; so also is Christ. For by one Spirit are we all baptized into one body.—For the body is not one member, but many. If the foot shall say, Because I am not the hand, I am not of the body; is it therefore not of the body? And if the ear shall say, Because I am not the eye, I am not of the body; is it therefore not of the body?—And the eye cannot say to the hand, I have no need of thee; nor again the head to the feet I have no need of you. Nay, much more those members of the body, which seem to be more feeble, are necessary.—And whether one member suffer, all the members suffer with it; or one member be honored, all the members rejoice with it. Now ye are the body of Christ, and members in particular.

WHEREVER the author of this Epistle went, he found nothing so active in withstanding the influence of the Christian religion, or in marring its divine form, as the selfishness of the heart. Even those who professed to love God supremely, and their neighbors as themselves, showed frequently, that they were still chargeable with the spirit of pride and emulation, and needed the purifying influence of divine truth. This was particularly the case with the church in Corinth. Those very endowments, which Christ had imparted to the Corinthian believers for the confirmation of his gospel, were made an occasion of strife. In the text, the Apostle labored to remove the evils which existed among them, and to inculcate the virtues and duties which they were prone to neglect. He informed them that the diversified endowments of Christians, particularly of the ministers of religion, were all distributed by the Spirit of God, and were intended, not for the gratification of self-love, but for the welfare of the church. This he illustrated by the similitude of the human body, all the parts of which stand in an intimate relation to one another, and are necessary to the beauty, strength, and the perfection of the whole body. He showed that no Christian, especially that no public teacher should glory in his own qualifications or endowments, but should use them for the perfecting of the saints, for the edifying of the body of Christ.

Applying this interesting portion of Scripture to our own case, let us, brethren, distinctly consider *the errors against which we are here guarded, and the duties here inculcated.*

First. We are here guarded against supposing *that no difference exists and that no distinction is to be made among the members of Christ's church.* There are some who think that all Christians are on the same level; that all have the same right to preach the gospel, to be guides and teachers in the church, and to administer Christian ordinances. Now from whatever source this opinion is derived, or whatever may be the form it assumes, it is entirely contrary to the word of God. Both the Old Testament and the New make a distinction among men in regard to office, and describe the different places to be occupied, and the different duties to be discharged, by the members of God's spiritual kingdom. The text in particular guards us against every approach to the error above mentioned, by referring us to the human body, the members of which occupy different places and perform different functions, some higher and some lower, though all are essential to the perfection of the body.

The opinion that all Christians ought to hold the same rank, is contrary to *the plan of God's works*. In what part of the world can you find anything favorable to such an opinion? There is no nation or society, in which all are or could be upon a level, either as to office or influence. Where in the whole creation can you discover anything like a system of perfect equality? Even those who fill the office of the *ministry*, are not in *all respects* upon a level. I reject the idea of distinct orders among the ministers of Christ. Still we cannot but perceive that, within the compass of that one office, there are different stations to be held, and different duties to be performed, and that the variety of qualifications which ministers possess, exactly fit them for those different stations and duties. The Apostle, with his eye directly upon the public teachers of religion, repeatedly asserts that there are different qualifications and duties, and labors to show in what light those differences are to be regarded. "God hath set some in the church, first, apostles; secondarily, prophets; thirdly, teachers; after that, miracles," etc. — "dividing to every man severally as he will." And it is a fact, that whatever men's speculative opinions may be on this subject, they act agreeably to the views of the Apostle. His views are perfectly consonant to the circumstances of human beings, and to the whole scheme of God's works. In the concerns of religion, as well as in the concerns of civil society, there are places of extraordinary importance to be occupied; works of uncommon magnitude and difficulty to be accomplished. Who shall be designated for those places? Who shall be called to accomplish those works? Are all qualified alike? No. We always inquire, who possess the talents and traits of character, best suited to the particular offices to be filled. When we find this suitableness, we are satisfied, and act accordingly. A man who should act on any other principle, would be essentially wanting in Christian prudence, and would show that, however honest his heart may be, he is not fit to be trusted with the interests of religion.

Secondly. We are here guarded against the error of supposing, that God furnishes us with any talents, whether ordinary or extraordinary, merely for our own sake. It is a vain conceit, for any man to think, that the favors which God bestows upon him, are expressions of regard to him personally, and are intended for his own reputation or interest. The Apostle teaches us, that no man is made for himself; that God designs all our powers and acquisitions, for the good of the church; that the public teachers of religion, with their diverse endowments, are parts of Christ's spiritual body; just as the eyes, hands and feet are parts of the natural body, and are designed to be subservient to its security and happiness. A man's eyes are not endued with the power of vision for their own sake, but that they may be of use to the body. Nor are his feet endued with their peculiar powers for their own sake, but for the sake of sustaining and moving the body. So of all the members. A minister of the gospel, who has the views and feelings inculcated by the text, will say within himself; these intellectual and moral faculties, these acquisitions, this power of communicating instruction, this influence in society, these opportunities for useful action, were not given me for my own sake. God bestowed them as the Father of the creation, for the welfare of the whole. Let my object be correspondent with his. And let me never be guilty of devoting his gifts to any other purpose, than that for which he designed them.

Thirdly. The text guards us against ambition. The principle here inculcated is, that God divides to his ministers severally such talents and qualifications, as will fit them for the place for which he designs them; and will most effectually promote the good of the church. But ambition strives for self-promotion. It cannot be satisfied with usefulness. It cannot be satisfied with the will of God. It aspires after a distinguished name, or a distinguished office. This passion sometimes prompts a minister of the gospel to aim at a place above that for which God designed him. The foot aspires to be the head. A minister of the gospel, laboring in a retired situation, desires to preach to a larger or more cultivated congregation, to live in a more fashionable style, and enjoy the pleasures of a more refined society.

Such are the aspirings of his ambitious heart. But God may have already assigned him his proper place. In his retired, peaceful situation, he might feed the sheep and lambs of Christ's flock. His days might pass pleasantly away, filled up with the labors of love. He might enjoy the gratitude and confidence of those to whom he ministers, and witness among them the fruits of the Spirit. But his ambition seeks a higher place. Suppose he obtains a higher place; — and suppose that place proves to be above his qualifications. How deplorable the consequence! He must experience the unhappiness of one, who has been impelled by the pride of his heart, to act against the plan of divine wisdom. His ambition has totally defeated itself; for his best efforts now secure him far less respect than he had before. His whole character has been depreciated, in proportion as he has risen above his place.

But suppose that a man, who holds the sacred office in a retired station, seriously thinks himself fitted for a more important post, and that the judgment of his most judicious friends coincides with his; he ought still to guard against resorting to any measures inconsistent with uprightness, with modesty, or with Christian contentment. In regard to such a subject, there are several considerations, which ought to be made familiar to the mind of a Christian minister. The first is, that, through the influence of self-love, he is liable to mistake respecting his own qualifications, and that others are liable to mistake on the same subject, through the influence of a prepossession in his favor. God may see that his present situation is better suited to his talents, and more favorable to his usefulness and comfort, than any other. He should consider too that the situation which he contemplates, may contain trials, difficulties and sufferings, which he has not the firmness to encounter, and which, should he be actually exposed to them, would make him sigh after that place of retired labor, which he had been so ready to leave. And even if he is really qualified for a higher place, this may not be the proper time for his removal. It may be the purpose of God, in due time, to introduce him to a station of greater importance and better suited to his talents, than the one which he now has in view. Let him then remain quietly in the place which divine providence has assigned him, remembering that it is a higher honor than any man deserves, to be permitted to preach the gospel anywhere; and remembering too, that if God would have him remove to another sphere of action, he will seasonably indicate his pleasure.

But there is still another view of this subject. A man may aspire to a place for which he is well qualified, and to which, according to the arrangements of divine providence, he is soon to be introduced — he may aspire to that place for the gratification of his vanity. It is admitted to be a station of distinguished usefulness. But he fixes his eye not upon its usefulness, but its honor. Even if he resolves on the highest degree of usefulness, it is still for his own credit. It is not the glory of Christ, but his own glory that excites his zeal. In all that he does to prepare himself for an elevated place in the church, and in all his efforts to discharge its duties, he has an ultimate reference to himself. Now a minister of the gospel, who is actuated by such a motive, may conceal his baseness from man. But, in the eye of God, he is altogether selfish and vile, an enemy to the cross of Christ. And he is preëminently guilty, because he mixes his ambitious, selfish designs with the duties of a sacred and holy calling.

Fourthly. The Apostle here guards us against every degree of envy towards those who are above us. Envy is a mixture of pride, meanness, and malignity. It is a covert warfare against the wisdom of God, and misery itself to the breast where it dwells. I am ashamed to think, that this vile passion ever shows itself in ministers of the gospel. What reason, brethren, can we have to envy those, who in respect of talents, place, or reputation, are superior to us? Suppose we should become superior to them; would it be right for them to envy us? — Are there not places of various degrees of importance to be occupied? And is it not a proof of the wisdom and goodness of God to raise up men, who shall be qualified for those different places? And will you set yourself against the wisdom and goodness of God? But aside from this — what cause can we have to envy those above us? Are not men, who are called to fill stations of uncommon importance, exposed to great difficulties, hardships and sufferings? In truth, it requires benevolence, resolution, and self-denial, for men, well acquainted with the subject, to be willing to occupy such stations. Those, who have passed from more retired places to those which are more public and important, are often ready to sink under the burdens which oppress them, and often sigh after the peaceful labors and pleasures they have left.

But there is another fault, nearly connected with this, namely, a spirit of repining and discontent, because we are not distinguished. Let us never forget the severe recompense which was awarded to the indolent and repining servant, who had but one talent. That the welfare of the church may be promoted, God has seen fit to prepare men for the different places which are to be occupied, and the different works which are to be accomplished. No one has any right to say, that his talents and services are of no consequence to the church. "If the foot shall say, because I am not the hand, I am not of the body; is it therefore not of the body? And if the ear shall say, because I am not the eye, I am not of the body; is it therefore not of the body? If the whole body were an eye, where were the hearing? If the whole were hearing, where were the smelling? But now hath God set the members every one of them in the body, as it hath pleased him. And if they were all one member, where were the body?" Some men seem to lose all motive to exertion, when they find that they must act in a subordinate place. But in reality, those who possess ordinary talents, and are destined to ordinary duties in the ministry, are in some respects more necessary to the prosperity of the church, than those of distinguished talents. The good which is to be done by them is greater in the amount, and requires a larger number to accomplish it. To convert sinners and edify the church is the grand object of the ministry. By whose labors is this object to be chiefly promoted? Not by the labors of the few, but of the many. Those ministers, then, who are called to discharge the ordinary duties of the sacred office, are not to indulge a spirit of repining and discontent, as though their situation was degraded, or their employment of little value. It is far otherwise. Their employment is the same as that which engaged the attention of the apostles. It is the same as that which chiefly engaged the attention of the Lord Jesus himself, during his public ministry. Indeed, the employment of any one, who is called to preach the everlasting gospel, is important and honorable in a degree not to be measured. And ministers, however obscure their situation, who faithfully preach the gospel, do a great work, and will receive great honor at the coming of their Lord. Instead therefore of repining, it becomes them to bless God for his mercy in putting them into the ministry, and suffering them, in any circumstances, to labor in such a heavenly work; and instead of yielding to discouragement, to rouse to action all the powers they possess, and do as much as possible for the salvation of men. Let us watchfully guard our minds against the habit of making such comparisons of ourselves with others, as will lead to repining or discontent. Let us fix our thoughts upon the magnitude of the work which God has assigned to us, the vast importance of doing it faithfully, and the happiness of being approved of our Judge. And let us bear in mind how worthless all distinctions among us will appear at the last day, except that between the faithful and the unfaithful.

Fifthly. Ministers who are placed in high stations, are here guarded against *self-complacency and contempt of others.* "The eye cannot say to the hand, I have no need of thee; nor again the head to the feet, I have no need of you. Nay, much more those members of the body, which seem to be more feeble, are necessary." One who holds a superior place in the church, is as much dependent on others, as they upon him. The eye needs the hand, as much as the hand the eye. And in a perfect body, even the feebler members are necessary as well as the stronger. Why should you despise any ministers of the gospel, because their situation is less conspicuous than yours? The Lord Jesus has given them their talents, and allotted to them their situation and employment. Will you despise the benevolent appointment of Christ? — despise those whom Christ has chosen to the work of converting sinners, and training up his people for heaven? — those whose labors are as essential as your own, to the great object of redeeming love?

Further. If those who occupy subordinate stations, had been placed in your condition, their reputation and usefulness might have risen much higher than yours; and you, if placed in their condition, might have appeared to much less advantage than they. To despise them, therefore, may be to despise those, who possess an excellence of character, both intellectual and moral, superior to your own.

Let me also warn any of my brethren, against making an elevated office an occasion of *self-complacency*. Remember that your being in such an office is no evidence of the divine complacency. God often raises men up to exalted places, in whom his all-searching eye sees no real goodness. They may possess certain qualifications, which he can make subservient to the purposes of his providence. And with a view to this subserviency, he may place them in an office of distinguished importance, and lead them to perform the work allotted to them, in a useful and acceptable manner; although he knows that a day is at hand, when they will be numbered with hypocrites and unbelievers. This is a subject of tremendous import, and so far from leaving any room for self-complacency, it should fill us all with fear and trembling.

Consider further, that God may sometimes put men of inconsiderable talents in high stations, for the very purpose of exposing their folly in aspiring to distinction, and of warning others to be content with their place. And what is still more dreadful, he may sometimes punish the secret wickedness of men, by placing them in those exalted stations, where their wickedness will be disclosed, and so will involve them in merited disgrace and ruin. While they are in a lower station, some corrupt and odious passion may be indulged in their hearts, though covered from the world; and they may be acquiring a reputation and influence which they deserve not, and which would be hazardous to the interests of religion. In righteous judgment, God may raise them to a higher place, where the restraints, which they formerly felt, will be removed, and where the particular passion, which they before kept from the public eye, will acquire strength, and act itself out. But the moment it does this, their character is stigmatized, and they sink into ignominy and wretchedness.

For those who occupy high stations, to indulge feelings of self-complacency, is directly contrary to the dictates of piety. If you indulge such feelings, you do as much as to ascribe your exaltation to your own efforts or your own worthiness, like that impious king who walked in his palace, and with pride and self-exaltation, said: "Is not this great Babylon which I have built — by the might of my power, and for the glory of my majesty?" You remember how quickly God showed his abhorrence of such impiety. "While the word was in the king's mouth, there fell a voice from heaven, saying, O king Nebuchadnezzar, to thee it is spoken; the kingdom is departed from thee." If any of you, brethren, are placed in important stations, forget not to ascribe it to divine providence. It is God who raised you up; and his hand is to be devoutly acknowledged. Every circumstance of your life has been ordered by his wisdom. Let the praise of all your talents, your acquisitions, and your usefulness be attributed to him. And instead of taking any credit to yourselves on account of your station, remember how far you have failed of accomplishing the duties, to which your office binds you.

Such, brethren, are the errors of the understanding and the heart, to which the ministers of Christ are liable, and from which the passage before us is suited to guard them. Consider now briefly the peculiar duties which it enjoins.

The great duty suggested by the text, is *mutual love*. This is a duty of high importance among Christians in general. But there are special reasons why mutual love should be cherished by ministers of the gospel. They not only love the same Lord, and look for the same inheritance, but are engaged in the same employment, and are devoted to the same sacred cause; circumstances, which tend to produce the sincerest affection. Their work is so arduous, and so many are the difficulties they must encounter, that they greatly need each other's friendship. Let ministers, then, love one another with pure hearts fervently. The friendship, which binds them together should be deep and tender. It should exclude all strife, and all suspicion. It should have strength to endure trials, and to last as long as life lasts. It should burn with a flame so pure and steady, that death itself cannot extinguish it. It should be so holy in its nature and tendency, that those who are under its influence, will seize every opportunity for uniting in Christian conversation, and bending the knee together before the throne of grace.

This love would lead ministers to rejoice in each other's usefulness and honor. "If one member of the body be honored, all the members rejoice with it." If we sincerely love the church, that reputation or usefulness of our brother which promotes its welfare, will certainly give us satisfaction. Suppose that, in all valuable qualifications, he is our superior. It is just so much the better for the church. Why is it not as well for a brother of yours to do good, as to do it yourself? And if so, why is it not as well for him to possess those superior talents which qualify him to do good, as for you to possess them? And why should you not feel as real a satisfaction in his superior qualifications and usefulness, as you would in your own? Are they less valuable because they are his, and not yours? God does not regard them so. And why should you? I say, brethren, we ought not only to look without dissatisfaction on the superior talents and usefulness of others, but heartily to rejoice in them, and to bless God for them. And this we certainly shall do, if we love our brethren as ourselves, or if we feel a real attachment to the common cause. Let us banish forever that wretched, infernal temper, which is dissatisfied at the superiority of others. It is a temper which would fill the whole moral creation with misery; because all moral creatures must forever see one, who is infinitely above them, and who will receive glory which they can never attain. If we rejoice in the infinite excellence and glory of God, we shall rejoice most in that, which has the greatest resemblance to him. And surely those most resemble God, who rise the highest in intellectual and moral excellence, and do the most good. That very superiority of talents, reputation and usefulness which occasions uneasiness to the envious heart, occasions joy to the benevolent. Let us bless God for all the instances in which he gives eminent qualifications to his servants. And let us labor and pray, that the next generation of ministers may rise to far higher degrees of learning, piety, and usefulness, than any of us have attained. The Lord endue them with such intellectual and moral excellence, as will, in future ages, cast a shade over the brightest traits of our character. The Lord bring forward a time when common Christians shall rank as high, as the most distinguished ministers of the present day, and ministers as high as apostles; and when the best of the present generation shall be spoken of, as we are accustomed to speak of children in comparison with men.

Cordial sympathy with our brethren is another duty which the Apostle happily illustrates in the text. "If one member suffer, all the members suffer with it." Ministers, in common with others, must have various personal and domestic afflictions. In all these afflictions, our brethren need our sympathy, and we theirs. Ministers have various weaknesses and defects, both natural and moral, which occasion them many a painful struggle, many an hour of sadness and discouragement. Nothing on earth can afford them so much comfort and assistance, as the sympathy of their brethren. This sympathy should be free and spontaneous, like that which all parts of the body have for any member which is wounded, or suffers pain. It should be sincere and active. The hand is instantly extended to afford needed relief to any other part of the body, or to alleviate its sufferings. Fit emblem of what ought to exist in the church, and in the ministry. Our hearts should instantly be touched with the afflictions of a brother. We should hasten to his relief. And if we can do nothing more, we should give him the pleasure of seeing that we wish to relieve him. To an afflicted minister, such prompt and tender sympathy from his brethen is one of the most precious consolations. And when this sympathy cannot be expressed by personal attention, it should be done by fraternal correspondence. This mode of assisting and comforting our brethren is of much higher consequence than we are apt to think, whether they are suffering private afflictions, or contending with difficulties which result from their public station.

There is one duty suggested by the Apostle, which is not unfrequently overlooked; I mean the duty of conferring some special marks of kindness upon those whose talents and situations are less distinguished. To inculcate this duty, the Apostle, with the most delicate sensibility, reminds us, that we sometimes pay special attention to those members of the body which are wanting in gracefulness or strength; — so far are the more distinguished parts of the body from appropriating the whole of our regard. In like manner, we should sometimes give special attention to those of our brethren, who are not blessed with any of the higher traits of character. We should defend them from injury and contempt. We should cover their infirmities and weaknesses. We should assist them in everything that is good; and be sure to assign them useful and honorable employment.

Finally. The Apostle here suggests the duty of *union* and *coöperation* among the servants of Christ. All the members of the natural body act together, each one in its proper place, in promoting the welfare of the whole, and of every part. The cause of Christ is really one. His kingdom is one, and comprises all his obedient subjects. His subjects all stand in the same relation to him, and to one another. As friends and disciples of Christ, they have one common interest, one great object of affection and pursuit; that is, the honor of their Lord, the prosperity of his kingdom, and the accomplishment of his benevolent purposes.

There may be different denominations of Christians and of ministers, and each of these denominations may have something peculiar to itself, both as to the external forms of religion, and the particular methods of promoting it. In regard to these, there may be an honest difference among those who love the Lord Jesus and who endeavor to know and do his will. Among these different denominations, we are not to look for a complete coöperation. Such coöperation is not to be attempted, and may not at present be desirable. But the moment you come to anything which belongs to the substance of Christianity, anything essential to the great interest of the church, or the common duties of religion, ministers and Christians ought all to be one. Here, there should be a cordial and perfect coöperation. Here all the friends of Christ do fully agree. And they ought to show their agreement. Coöperation here is a natural and practicable duty. Should, therefore, the ministers of any denomination be full of ardor in promoting what is local, or what is peculiar to a particular part of Christ's kingdom, while they look with coldness on what relates to the common interest of the church; they would show that their hearts are misguided through the deceitfulness of sin. When the day of decision shall come; when the light of truth shall shine forth in its glory from the throne of God, and all the delusions of the understanding and the passions shall cease; we shall see, that what related to our own personal interest, or the interest of one particular denomination, in distinction from the common interest of Christ's spiritual kingdom, was worthy of little or no regard. Then every object will vanish out of sight, but the worth of the immortal soul, and the glory of Christ, and the distinction, so joyful on one side, and so tremendous on the other, between the righteous and the wicked. Oh! that Christians of every name might anticipate the views and feelings they will have, when all these clouds and shadows shall flee away, and the whole moral world be filled with the clearness and splendor of divine truth.

But here there is need of serious caution. For Christian fellowship and coöperation can properly go no further, than there is real agreement. With all who manifestly belong to the body of Christ and love his cause, we ought gladly to unite in all those duties which are common to them and us, and in every measure which is suited to advance the general prosperity of the church, whatever minor differences may at present exist. But if we would, in any way, unite with those, who do not maintain what we believe to be the essential principles of Christianity, the union must not extend to anything which involves those principles. We can safely unite with them in those things only, in which their peculiar views can have no effect on what we believe to be the vital interests of religion. In a word, while we ought to exercise the sincerest good will and kindness towards all men, towards those especially, who have in our opinion imbibed pernicious errors; we can properly maintain Christian fellowship with those only, who agree with us respecting the essential principles of our holy religion.

My Dear Nephew,

I cannot, for a moment, call to remembrance what God has done for you, and by what ways he has brought you hither, without a delightful impression of his great goodness. About eleven years ago, your honored father and I, after a long separation, had unexpectedly the pleasure of meeting at our native place. Wishing as I did to express my cordial gratitude for the pious concern he had shown for me when I was a child, I proposed that his son, whom he had very affectionately named to me, should receive a public education, and proffered all the assistance in my power in carrying such a design into effect. Many a time has his heart and mine been filled with the tenderest emotions, at the thought of the interview we then had, and of the consequences which have flowed from it. And I cannot refrain from saying, that all the solicitude which I have felt for your welfare, and the sincere, though very defective efforts I have made for your improvement, have received a four-fold reward. I say it to the glory of Him, who has been the guide of your youth — to the glory of that grace which has made you what you are.

If, my dear nephew, you look back to the time when, as we hope, God called you with an holy calling, and gave you to experience the washing of regeneration and renewing of the Holy Ghost; and then to the time when you began the arduous labor of preparing for the ministry by a regular literary and theological education; and if you call to remembrance the whole course of your life since; you must perceive, that you are indebted to the goodness of God in no ordinary degree, and that you are bound, by everlasting obligations, to devote your talents, your life, your whole being, to his holy service. You are not your own. The powers of mind which you possess; the literary acquisitions which you have gained; your skill in sacred criticism, your theological knowledge, and all your qualifications for the work of the ministry, and for the particular office you are now called to fill, are given you by the Head of the church. And for what are they given? To fill your heart with vanity and self-complacency? To excite and gratify an aspiring ambition? The Spirit of God, I trust, has taught you a very different sentiment. Just in proportion to your talents and your attainments in knowledge, are your obligations to love God and promote his cause. Your understanding, your heart, your learning, your time, health, and influence are God's. Pride, then, is impiety; it is sacrilege. Banish it forever from your heart. Or if it strives to maintain its place there, make unceasing war against it. And let the hateful thing be made to destroy itself, by occasioning deeper humility and self-abhorrence.

Study, preach, and labor from *love to Christ*, a principle of action infinitely nobler than ambition. Let that love be your ruling passion. Under its holy influence, strive in all things to excel; but with such a temper, that you will always be pleased with the superior excellence of others. Forever avoid the disposition of those who envy the height which they cannot reach, and who endeavor to stain and depress the fairest character which they see rising above them.

You are engaged, my dear nephew, in an enterprise great and arduous for any man, especially for one so young and inexperienced. But your Saviour offers you his all-sufficient grace. And there is one thing which cannot be mentioned, without bringing into view the wisdom and goodness of God; that is, that the whole course of your education has manifestly been directed by his providence with a view to the particular station for which you are designated.* Your education has been suited so exactly to prepare you for that station, that if you had from the first definitely fixed your thoughts upon it, you could not have made any desirable alteration in your plan of study. With this view of the merciful guidance which God has afforded you, and with a full reliance on his grace, take courage, and go forward in your work, always keeping a steady eye upon your great object. While laboring to discipline the minds of your pupils, and to promote the interests of learning, remember that you are a *Christian*, and a *minister of the gospel*, and that it is your duty, in both characters, to strive for the promotion of true religion, as your great object. Go forward then in the strength of God. Be faithful unto death; and your merciful Saviour will give you the crown of eternal life.

---

* *Note to the present edition of the Sermon.*

The particular situation referred to was a Professorship in Columbia College in the District of Columbia. After that, the Rev. Alva Woods, was for several years, President of the College in Lexington, Ky., and then, for a longer time, President of the College in Tuscaloosa, Alabama.

A SERMON

DELIVERED AT THE ORDINATION OF THE REV. BENJAMIN WOODBURY, AT FALMOUTH, MASS., JUNE 9, 1824.

---

1 Cor. 9: 22.—I AM MADE ALL THINGS TO ALL MEN, THAT I MIGHT BY ALL MEANS SAVE SOME.

THERE is perhaps no passage of Scripture which has been more frequently misinterpreted than this; and none which has been applied to purposes more contrary to the design of the writer. The principal abuse of it is to be found among those, whose temper inclines to indecision and timidity, and who endeavor to justify this weakness of character by the account the Apostle here gives of his own conduct. The mistake which has in this way been committed, and the injury which has resulted from it to the interests of religion, have been so palpable, that some have been led to discard altogether the principle of action asserted in the text, and thus have fallen into errors as really hurtful to religion, as those which they have labored to avoid.

It becomes then a matter of consequence, to determine what views the Apostle meant to express by the language of the text,—"I am made all things to all men." What is the import of this declaration? And what are the limitations and cautions to be observed, in a practical application of it to ministers at the present day.

Let us, in the first place, see what light we can derive from passages in the same Epistle relating to the same general subject. In the preceding chapter the Apostle introduces a question as to the lawfulness of eating things offered in sacrifice to idols. He teaches, that in those who partake of the sacrifice, there may be no violation of a good conscience; and yet that they ought scrupulously to abstain, if their partaking would be any injury to others. "Let every one of us please his neighbor for his good to edification." In other words we should consider the consciences and weaknesses of those around us, and be ready to give up our own liberty, and as far as may consist with higher obligations, our own *rights* too, for the sake of doing good. But the particular design of the Apostle in the text becomes still more apparent from the verses immediately preceding. In various forms, he asserted his right to a maintenance from those, to whom he preached. But to prevent objections which might arise against the Christian religion, and to give additional weight to his instructions, he forebore to urge this right. The mention of this instance of his benevolence led him to state more particularly in what manner he regulated his conduct in relation to such subjects as these. Though he was in the highest sense free, yet for the purpose of doing good, he made himself a servant to all. "Unto the Jews," he says, "I became as a Jew, that I might gain the Jews; to them that are under the law, as under the law, that I might gain them that are under the law; to them that are without law, as without law, (being not without law to God, but under law to Christ,) that I might gain them that are without law; to the weak became I as weak that I might gain the weak; I am made all things to all men, that I might by all means save some." In things indifferent, he conformed to the feelings and customs of those around him. In this practice of yielding, he went as far as he could, consistently with duty. He never created offence by deviating unnecessarily from the opinions or manners of those, with whom he was conversant.

But we shall be further aided in fixing the proper limitations of the Apostle's meaning, by a consideration of the object he aimed at. "I am made all things to all men, *that I might by all means save some.*" His object was the salvation of men. The means he adopted were suited to promote this object. And if so, it must be clear that, in becoming all things to all men, the Apostle could not have conformed either to the sins, or to the errors of men — as such a conformity would have had an influence directly contrary to his object. For the same reason, he could not have withheld divine truth. For he considered divine truth as the means of turning men from their sins, and training them up for heaven. To suppose that he suppressed any of the essential truths of revelation, or that he either taught or countenanced error, is to suppose that he not only forgot the end of his preaching, but put a real obstacle in the way of attaining it.

It was still of great importance, as a means of promoting his object, that he should abstain from everything in the mode of preaching that would bar the minds of men against conviction, or furnish them either with advantages to oppose religion, or with an excuse for neglecting it. The consideration of his object must also have induced him to forego any personal gratification, for the good of his fellow-creatures, and in all cases to exhibit a kind and peaceful deportment. We see what his disposition was in respect to his maintenance. He claimed it as his unquestionable right. But as there were some, who might impute wrong motives to him if he should urge his claim, and might by that means acquire an influence prejudicial to the cause of Christianity; he thought it his duty to forbear. The mention of this led him to state more fully, as in the text, that principle of condescension and self-denial, by which he sought to help forward the salvation of men. If, then, a question arise in our minds respecting the duty or propriety of any particular instance of compliance, it will conduce directly to a satisfactory answer, to inquire, whether it will have an influence favorable to the salvation of men. Will it produce or strengthen in others a disposition to listen to the truths of God's word, and attend to the duties of religion? Will it be likely to invest us with greater power over their consciences, or to open the avenues of their hearts to the doctrines we preach? Or will it diminish our influence, and render it more difficult than it would otherwise be, to make an impression upon others in favor of religion? Will the remembrance of it create embarrassment in our feelings, and hold us back from any faithful endeavors for their conversion? This reference to the end of the ministry is frequently of great moment in cases of a doubtful character.

But we may discover still more clearly what must have been the Apostle's meaning in the words of the text, by attending to *other passages found in his epistles*, and *to his own practice*. He enjoins the duty of faithfully declaring divine truth, and of contending earnestly for the faith once delivered to the saints. He exhorts Timothy to preach the word; to be instant in season, and out of season; to speak the things which become sound doctrine; and never to be ashamed of the testimony of the Lord. In his farewell address to the church at Ephesus, he says, that he had not shunned to declare all the counsel of God; that he had so faithfully preached the truth, that he was pure from the blood of all men. In another place, he speaks of himself and his fellow-apostles, as having renounced all dishonesty and craftiness; as not handling the word of God deceitfully, but by manifestation of the truth commending themselves to every man's conscience in the sight of God. "We are not," he says, "as many who corrupt the word of God, but as of sincerity, but as of God, in the sight of God, speak we in Christ." Such were his directions to Timothy; and such the account he gave of himself and his fellow-laborers. His practice was correspondent. What doctrine or duty of Christianity did he conceal? What prevalent error or sin did he not expose and reprobate? He could not however, declare all the truths of religion at once; and he was, of course, under the necessity of selecting the truths to be declared on each particular occasion. But in that selection, he was not influenced by fear of man, nor by dread of reproach and suffering, nor by desire of applause; but by that benevolence which aimed at the salvation of men, and that wisdom which chose the most suitable means to secure it. In the course of his ministry, he announced the doctrines of the gospel without any reservation, and defended them against the most artful and violent opposers. When did Paul say of this or that doctrine of religion — it is attended with so many difficulties, and liable to so many objections or abuses, that it is best to pass over it in silence? When did he, on any proper occasion, refrain from declaring the truth, because he thought it would expose him to inconvenience and suffering? Let his epistles answer. Let the history of his life answer. It was *he*, more than any other Apostle, who plainly taught those principles of Christianity, which have been an offence to the wicked world. It was *he* — pliable and condescending as he was — who boldly declared those very doctrines, which certain prudent souls of modern days think we ought never to declare. Here the Apostle made no compromise. He proclaimed and defended the truth in all its length and breadth, whether men would hear, or forbear; he did it, knowing that it would be a savor of death unto death, as well as life unto life. Had he been willing to give up a few doctrines which were specially offensive, he might have preached all the rest and yet escaped martyrdom. But he had received a commission from the Lord of heaven and earth; and he executed that commission faithfully, though fully aware it would cost him his life.

On this part of the subject, then, we are left in no doubt. Paul's being made all things to all men, implied no such conformity, as prevented him from declaring any part of divine truth, or from declaring it in such a manner, as was most likely to convey to others the very conceptions of it, which he had in his own mind. And it is an act of justice to the Apostle to add, that, notwithstanding his candor, and his disposition to conform, he was as far as possible from countenancing those, who held doctrines subversive of the Christian religion.

It is still to be remembered, that even in respect to his preaching, the spirit which the Apostle expressed in the text, had an important influence. He showed a mild, amiable temper. He preached with great humility, and with sincere affection. He warned men with tears. He manifested great unwillingness to wound the feelings of men, and never did it, except when it was required by love and faithfulness. As to those things which were aside from the object of his commission, he was ready to conform to others.

Were it necessary, I could illustrate the important principle, which governed the Apostle, by referring to *the life of Christ.* Paul had the spirit of his Lord and master. Now it is evident, that Christ conformed to his countrymen in those things, and in those things only, in which he could do it without transgressing the divine law himself, or giving countenance to transgression in others. He conformed to common usage, as to the modes of speech, and social intercourse. He conformed to the established precepts and rights of the Jewish religion. He was completely a Jew. And to cut off occasion of complaint, he did what no Jew could willingly do, that is, paid tribute to Cæsar. In these and other instances, in which Jesus practised conformity, it is clear, that there was no violation of any precept of the moral law; and that his object was to prevent needless offence, and to accomplish the benevolent work for which he came into the world. Such was the conformity of Christ, and such the end it was intended to accomplish. Doubtless the conformity of Paul, both as to its nature and object, was substantially the same.

Thus from an examination of the Epistle and chapter containing the text, from a consideration of the end which the Apostle sought, from his instructions to Timothy and others, from his own conduct, and from the life of Christ, which he made his model, it is evident, that his practice of becoming all things to all men implied no disposition to quiet the proud, rebellious heart by withholding any portion of divine truth — no disposition to refrain from a faithful annunciation of the law or its high sanctions — no disposition to refrain from declaring the guilt of man, or the evil of sin, or the only way of salvation through Jesus Christ. To these and other like subjects his conformity was never extended. It was limited either to his own personal rights and comforts, or to those opinions and customs of men, which were in their nature indifferent.

The principles which have now been exhibited, may assist us to guard against the two extremes, to which ministers are liable, in respect to the subject under consideration; the one, *excessive pliancy;* the other, *too unbending a strictness;*—the one, *a disposition to conform to others in everything;* the other, *an unwillingness to conform in anything.* To both these extremes ministers are exposed; and into both they have actually fallen, to the great injury of religion.

Shall we, then, turn our thoughts to the minister who errs on the side of an easy conformity, and consider a few moments, the peculiarities of his character, and the pleas by which he attempts to justify himself. The character he exhibits, is that of too great flexibility. To gratify his desire of pleasing, he adopts, with little discrimination the practices of others, even of the thoughtless and irreligious. When anything is proposed to him, his question is not, whether it would be agreeable to the will of God, and would help forward the interests of the soul; but whether it would be agreeable to custom; or whether it would please. You may sometimes find a minister of this sort, who is ready to fall in with any practices prevalent in the community, especially in the more respectable part of it, even so far as to join with them in their levity, their vain amusements, their disregard of the Lord's day, and their disposition to slur the doctrines and duties of religion. In his preaching, both as to matter and manner, he conforms to the wishes of his hearers, particularly of those who have the highest rank and polish. He reproves them for none of their follies or sins; or if ever he reproves them, he does it so lightly and smoothly, as to make it evident that he is much less anxious for their reformation, than for their applause. Any truths which are offensive to them, are sure to be excluded from his sermons; yea, and so pliable is his faith, from his creed too. And to justify all this conformity, he pleads the example of the Apostle, who was "made all things to all men." He forgets that the same Apostle expressly commanded Christians, "*not to be conformed to the world,*" and that another inspired writer said, "*whosoever will be a friend of the world, is the enemy of God.*" He forgets that the Apostle to whom he refers as his pattern, was of all preachers the most bold and faithful in reproving sin, in proclaiming those truths of Christianity which expose the deep-rooted wickedness of the heart, and in urging men to come out from the world and live a heavenly life. He forgets all this. He looks at only one part of the subject, and looks at that with only one eye.

But he may have other apologies. He may think that, if he should insist upon all the doctrines of the Bible, and strenuously urge men to observe all its precepts, he would create in their minds an aversion to the whole subject of religion; and that, if he should refuse to join with them in those amusements, which fashion has made essential to their happiness, he would deprive himself of the most effectual means of securing their attachment, and of bringing them to attend on his ministrations.

To this plea my reply is short. If men really possess such a temper of mind, that they are not pleased with the doctrines and precepts of the Bible, it is surely important they should know it. As these doctrines and precepts constitute the Christian religion; if we give them up, we give up Christianity. And if we give up any part of them, we give up just so great a part of Christianity. Why should we forget the example of the Apostle, who uniformly preached what was an offence to the Jews, and foolishness to the Greeks? And why should we forget the business of our calling? The Lord Jesus Christ has sent us to do a great work. The enmity of the human heart against religion, instead of being indulged and flattered, must be exposed and subdued. Instead of suppressing the doctrines and precepts of religion, we must persuade men to believe and obey them. If we fail of this we make our office a nullity. Christ has sent us to carry on a holy war against sin — against all sin, and to do it by means of divine truth. Shall we give up this holy warfare, and make peace with that mortal enemy of our Lord, which it is the great business of our office to resist and overcome?

This pliable minister thinks, that if he should refuse to join with men in those amusements, which fashion has rendered essential to their happiness, he would deprive himself of the most effectual means of securing their attachment, and bringing them to attend on his ministrations. A strange apology this! — secure the attachment of men, who are displeased with the doctrines and duties of religion, and secure it by joining with them in vain amusements! and all this, to bring them to attend on ministrations, from which the essential truths of religion are excluded!

A minister of the character above described, may proceed to say in his own justification, that religion cannot be designed to take away his enjoyments, and render him gloomy and dejected; that he has as good a right to pleasure as others, and that if he is to have any pleasure, it must be by indulgences which agree with his taste.

The very statement of this apology betrays a depravation of moral taste, utterly inconsistent with the object of a minister, and with the character of a Christian. The enjoyment which religion sanctions, is holy enjoyment, consisting in love and obedience to God, and in doing good to men. He who cannot be happy in this, has no right to the sacred office, and no right to happiness. Religion forbids the pleasures of sin; and he who chooses to enjoy them — who resorts for happiness to scenes of dissipation, instead of the duties of his office — who prefers fashionable parties to the chamber of sickness or to meetings for prayer, is no minister of the gospel, and no Christian.

After all, such a minister may think that an easy conformity to the opinions, fashions, and amusements of the world must tend to promote his object. But I ask, what object? not the object of the faithful minister, which is, to turn men from their sins, and bring them to walk by faith. If we conform to men's follies and sins, we show that we do not desire their salvation. And even if we did desire it, we could have no influence to promote it. We might publicly inculcate the obligations of repentance and holiness; but our hearers would appeal to our life, as a disproof of the sincerity of our preaching, and a full release from every duty we might enjoin. If a minister is in fact pursuing an object which he can promote by conforming to the follies and amusements of the world, he is pursuing an object entirely foreign to his office; an object, which he must forever abandon, to be a minister of the gospel, and which his people must abandon, to be Christians.

Place such a minister by the side of the Apostle. It was his object to persuade men to set their affections on things above, not on things on the earth, to practise self-denial, to shun temptation, to live as Jesus lived. His condescending and flexible temper was such, and the conduct which it prompted was such, as tended directly to promote this object. It enabled him boldly and faithfully to reprove sin, to declare the whole counsel of God, and to press the necessity of universal holiness. But the easy conformity now pleaded for, will forever prevent a minister from promoting such an exalted object. What minister, after having allowed himself to join with the thoughtless multitude in fashionable folly and vanity, would think of urging upon Christians the duty of being sober-minded, of being dead to the world, and of living in the constant expectation of the coming of their Lord?

The most common and powerful plea, used to justify a minister, who errs on the side of conformity, is, that it will conciliate the affections of others, and give him influence over them. But I question the fact. If my own observation has not led me into a mistake, the minister, who seeks popular favor by disregarding the circumspection which his religion enjoins, and by conforming more or less to the vanities of the world, will fail of obtaining his object. Corrupt as men are in their moral affections, they still possess conscience and common sense, and will generally form an opinion of the character of ministers, not far from the truth. Though the minister, who bends to compliances forbidden by the precepts of religion, may gratify the feelings of the wicked by the countenance he gives to their impiety, he forfeits their esteem, and destroys his influence over their consciences. He makes it manifest that he has no decision, no strength of character, no steady principle of action; that he is a slave to the whims of the multitude. He loses the charm of unaffected goodness. He deprives himself of that respect and confidence of men, which a dignified independence and a faithful discharge of duty always command. And in the sober judgment of the community, after all his pains to please, he is sure to stand for a weak and contemptible man.

But there is another fault, though not common at the present day, against which we ought also to guard; that is, *excessive strictness*. A minister chargeable with this fault, indulges an unyielding pertinacity in things trifling and insignificant, as well as in things of the highest moment. He insists upon having his own way, where the difference between his way and that of others is of no consideration. He knows not how to bend, even where bending would be a credit to his character, and an advantage to all the interests he is seeking. For the feelings and wishes and habits of others, whether respecting things important or unimportant, he shows no respect. He will do nothing to please, even where pleasing would be perfectly consistent with the highest demands of duty.

This is the other extreme. And we shall see what reason we have to be upon our guard against it, if we examine the *principles* from which it results, and the *consequences* to which it leads. In forming this character of stiffness and austerity, it cannot be denied that conscience may have a part. I mean, however, a mistaken conscience, arising from mistaken views of God and his law. But though conscience may do something towards forming such a character, pride unquestionably does more. It is obvious to every intelligent observer, that needless rigidness and austerity flow not so much from respect for God, or fear of sin, as from self-conceit. Were the minister now referred to, influenced by a respect for God and his law, he would exercise the spirit of gentleness and love. He would take care, as Paul directs, to "give none offence either to the Jews, or to the Gentiles, or to the church of God;" and would strive as the same Apostle did, "to please all men in all things," (that is, as far as consistent with duty,) "not seeking his own profit, but the profit of many, that they might be saved." Were he to judge of things by the standard of God's word, he would in a multitude of instances see, that the haughtiness or obstinacy, which keeps him from complying with the wishes of others, is more sinful, than the very compliances to which he is so rigidly averse.

A minister of this character *deprives religion of its most attractive beauties, and, by mixing so many of his own faults with it, renders it unamiable.* Thus, instead of conciliating the attention of the thoughtless to his instructions, he creates prejudice and aversion.

He may say that this rigidness of opinions and manners is a part of *self-denial.* But he who says this, might possibly find, if he would make the trial, that the exercise of a pliant, yielding temper would be a higher instance of self-denial — a more noble victory over himself.

He may plead, that if he should exercise that pliancy and condescension which is contended for, and should thus become all things to all men; some of the best ministers and Christians would put a wrong construction upon it, and reproach him as a time-server.

My answer is, that if the judgment or taste of Christians varies from the word of God, we ought to do all in our power to correct their mistake, not to confirm it. Excessive strictness and pertinacity is a mistake of hurtful tendency. It implies a palpable oversight as to the radical and universal principles of human nature, and the means of doing good; — an oversight, which no minister can commit, without detracting from the worth of his character, and the success of his labors. And suppose it to be the case, that by an exact conformity to the precepts and the example of Christ, we should incur the reproach of some good men, and good men of our own party too; is this any reason for neglecting a substantial duty, and violating God's holy word? May it not be as proper to suffer for Christ in this way, as in any other? Yea, if duty requires, may we not show even higher respect for Christ, and higher fortitude, by suffering reproach from good men, than from bad — from our own party, than from opposers? A minister of ordinary character, encouraged and supported by his particular friends, can well enough bear the reproach of the wicked world, and even of those good men with whom he has no connection. But for one steadily to pursue a course of conduct marked out by the word of God, when he knows it will expose him to the suspicion and censure of his friends, and his own party, requires greater firmness — requires a more powerful exercise of faith and self-denial. If a minister is ever called to this, let him stand up and meet it, relying on the strength of Christ, and looking to heaven for his reward.

I shall notice one more plea in favor of the unbending strictness above described; namely: that *it is essential to decision of character*. But of what value is that decision, which is not connected with a good disposition and a sound judgment? Unless a minister makes it apparent that his temper is benevolent, and that he has the wisdom which is profitable to direct, what power can he have to promote the great interests of religion? He may indeed possess a firmness as unyielding as the firmness of an oak; — and the firmness of an oak may be as valuable as his.

The want of a sound judgment, and of a mild, yielding temper, will continually throw difficulties in a minister's way, which will embarrass him in whatever he undertakes. The dispositions of others, the principles of human nature, the circumstances of society, and the movements of divine providence, will all be against him. Many a man, possessed of distinguished talents, and glowing zeal, and sincere piety too, and thus qualified for great things, has been totally disabled, and rendered weak as a child, by some indiscretion, some want of a mild, conciliatory manner, some aptness to mistake, or to give needless offence. While he who unites judgment with zeal, meekness with integrity, and pliableness in little things with inflexible firmness in great things, will have power to do good. Whether he aims at it, or not, he will be continually augmenting his influence. His decision has efficacy. It moves the minds of men. It moves human affairs.

But a minister wanting in goodness of temper, in soundness of judgment, or in civility of manners, may rouse all the energy he possesses in mind and in speech, and may show you how decided and fixed he is in regard to some great concern — and yet accomplish nothing at all. Other men have minds of their own, on which they place as much reliance as on his; and after witnessing the display he makes of his warmth and decision, will follow their own judgment, and leave him sovereign of himself.

The moment we appeal to facts, we see that self-will and stiffness constitute no part of real strength of character. On the other hand, we see that the greatest amiableness and pliability of temper, and a readiness, as far as is consistent, to become all things to all men, is perfectly compatible with the highest point of decision. Few men have ever exhibited greater decision than Paul. But he excelled not more in this, than in meekness and pliancy. The highest decision of character ever exhibited on earth, was in Jesus of Nazareth. And in the same blessed personage, there was the highest display ever made on earth, of kindness and gentleness and condescension.

A SERMON

DELIVERED AT THE INSTALLATION OF THE REV. NATHANIEL HEWIT, D. D., BRIDGEPORT, CONN., DEC. 1, 1830.

Eccl. 7: 1.—A GOOD NAME IS BETTER THAN PRECIOUS OINTMENT.

DESIRE for the esteem and affection of others is inseparable from our intellectual and moral constitution. But those who are conscious of a special dependence on the good opinion of others for the accomplishment of their desires respecting either their own welfare, or the welfare of their fellow men, and those too, whose moral susceptibilities are heightened and refined by cultivation, must be peculiarly alive to the approbation and esteem of their fellow men. It is accordingly found, that educated and professional men generally feel a more than ordinary interest in whatever concerns their reputation.

But on the present occasion, I shall confine my remarks to the value of a good name in respect to *a minister of the gospel.*

The subject may be considered, first, as relating to a minister's *private enjoyment.* Having, like all others, a natural desire for the esteem of his fellow men, he must be gratified when that esteem is manifested. And in consequence of his having more refined sensibilities, and a more intimate and extensive connection with others, than men commonly have, he has in an unusual degree, an aptness to be affected with whatever concerns his reputation.

The possession of an unspotted character is one of his most precious earthly comforts. It animates him in his duties, and helps to render his severest labors pleasant. It is a refreshment to him when weary and exhausted, and a precious solace in seasons of affliction. On the other hand, what calamity is there which wounds him so deeply, as a stain upon his reputation?

But if we would understand the chief value of a minister's good name, we must consider it as *the means of promoting his usefulness*. In every part of his office, the benefit resulting from his labors will be very much in proportion to the character he sustains in the view of the community. The usefulness of his labors consists in the effect he produces on the minds of those to whom he ministers; and this effect is inseparably connected with their views of his character. Say what you will as to what is desirable and proper; that which I have stated will be a fact, while human nature remains as it is.

For the correctness of this representation, I appeal to the experience of those whom I address. When you have heard a minister of blameless reputation and eminent piety preach the truths of religion; has not your reverence for the man, and your confidence in his goodness given new force to his instructions? Has not the character of the preacher been associated in your minds with the truths he has inculcated? and has it not in this way been the means of impressing those truths more deeply and permanently on your hearts, and of investing them with greater power over your actions? But if you have ever been so unhappy as to attend on the preaching of a minister whose reputation in your view was not good — especially one whose faults were palpable and glaring; has not this circumstance detracted from the benefit which might otherwise have been derived from his labors? How weighty soever the doctrines he has set forth, and how serious and eloquent soever the manner of his preaching; has not the remembrance of the improprieties of his conduct gone far towards preventing the good effect of what you have heard from his lips?

And is not the same true in regard to every other part of ministerial labor? A minister of Christ comes to you in time of affliction, and with the looks and the language of sympathy, attempts to minister to your comfort. Is not the effect produced upon your heart derived in a great measure from your views of his character? If you have confidence in his goodness; his conversation and prayers take strong hold on your feelings. Everything he says comes to your mind in close alliance with the excellence of his character. The very sight of him when he enters your house, and the thought of him when absent, infuses a kind of sacredness into the sensations of your heart. But have you ever been thus profited by the visits of a minister, for whose character you have had no cordial esteem? In such a case, has not your mind been barred against any good influence from his conversation, and even from his prayers? Have you not been conscious of a kind of involuntary resistance against the most important truths, when introduced by one, of whom you entertained so low an opinion?

You are sometimes desirous of conversing freely with your minister respecting your spiritual interests. Doubts and difficulties arise in your mind, which you wish him to solve. You have a struggle with some wrong propensity, in regard to which you need his assistance. If you esteem and love him, as a faithful minister of Christ; you can unreservedly disclose to him your inward struggles and difficulties, and in many ways derive benefit from his counsels and prayers. But if you suspect that he is not acquainted by experience with the conflicts and enjoyments of the Christian life; your intercourse with him will fail of securing to you any important benefits.

A good name is of great value to a minister, as it gives a salutary influence to his *example*. If his reputation is unblemished; his daily conduct — the whole course of his life, will have a happy effect upon the minds of his people. But only let them observe or hear anything which mars his ministerial character, and they will quickly regard with suspicion his most virtuous actions, and so even that part of his example which is right, will lose its salutary influence.

There is still another view to be taken of the subject. The Christian world is engaged in many benevolent enterprises. In most of these, ministers of the gospel have a principal agency. Their education, their office, and their influence in society qualify them to be specially useful in forwarding all the objects of Christian benevolence. But there is no way, in which they can contribute more effectually or more permanently to the promotion of these objects, than by the influence of a good name. To be espoused and advocated by one who is esteemed a wise and good man, is an advantage to any cause. The mere knowledge of this fact will make new friends to the cause, and increase the attachment and zeal of those who were friends before. If a minister has a blameless and respectable character; every argument he uses and every effort he makes in behalf of a good cause, turns to account. On the contrary, it cannot but prove a disadvantage to any cause, however excellent in itself, that a man of bad character is its advocate. All his efforts to promote it are paralyzed, or rendered hurtful, by the knowledge of his misconduct. In this way Christianity itself has suffered an injury, which human power can never repair.

Such as I have now described, is the value of a good name to a minister of the gospel, in reference to his own enjoyment, and in reference to the various ways in which he may be useful to his fellow men.

See then *in what light we are to regard those who by detraction, slander, or any of the forms of evil speaking, injure the reputation of a Christian minister.* We must regard them as guilty of a direct violation of that precept, written by the finger of God on tables of stone: *Thou shalt not bear false witness against thy neighbor.* They are guilty too of violating that comprehensive command, so often repeated in the New Testament: *Thou shalt love thy neighbor as thyself.* Who would slander himself? Who would publish his own failings for the purpose of disgracing himself?

To injure a minister's good name is to transgress that direction of Christ, which is approved by every man's conscience, and which has been pronounced by all the world to be preëminently excellent: *Whatsoever ye would that others should do unto you, do ye also the same unto them.* Now would any one of you regard it a desirable thing, that others should indulge prejudices and evil surmises against you, and by venting them in any of the ways of evil speaking, should endeavor to lower you in the public estimation? Would you wish to have your character aspersed? But if you would not be willing that others should do this to you, how can you do it to them, without transgressing this righteous precept?

The Scriptures make freedom from the guilt of backbiting and slander to be essential to the character of God's people. *Who shall abide in thy tabernacle? Who shall dwell in thy holy hill?* An important part of the reply is: *He that backbiteth not with his tongue, nor taketh up a reproach against his neighbor.* An apostle says: *If any man among you seemeth to be religious, and bridleth not his tongue, that man's religion is vain.* And another says: *Speak evil of no man.* And if you wish to know how our blessed Saviour regards evil speaking, listen to his words: "Out of the heart proceed evil thoughts, murders, adulteries, fornications, false witness, evil speakings." He puts evil speaking in company with the blackest crimes. In like manner Paul puts whisperers and backbiters by the side of fornicators, murderers, and haters of God. And when he enumerated the odious characters that should appear in the last times, he gave evil speakers a prominent place. "Men shall be lovers of themselves, covetous — evil speakers — false accusers." Such, according to God's holy word, is the guilt of backbiting and evil speaking. But this crime, always so detestable in the sight of God, is attended with peculiar aggravations, when committed against one who sustains the sacred office of ambassador of Christ, and is entrusted, in so important a sense, with the interests of the church.

Do any of my hearers wonder, that the inspired writers so emphatically forbid and reprobate evil speaking, and represent it as so heinous an offence? You will cease to wonder, if you consider from what sources it springs, and what evils follow in its train.

The sin of evil speaking, being from its very nature designed to injure others, must proceed from a malevolent disposition. It can spring from no other source. If you speak evil of another, it is because you do not love him; because you are actuated by ill will. And if any of you should endeavor, by slanderous representations, to injure the character of a *minister of Christ*, you would betray not only hatred to him, but disregard of the Master whom he serves, and of the cause which he is laboring to promote. And what can be more criminal, than disaffection, or even indifference, to the honor of Christ, and the success of his gospel?

The experience of ages confirms the truth of these remarks. For there never was a man, who was alive to the glory of his Saviour, and who cordially desired the success of his gospel, who did not at the same time feel a tender regard for the reputation of ministers.

Such then is the principle, which leads men to asperse the character of those who bear the sacred office. The heart of man, depraved as it is, is hardly capable of a disposition more contrary to goodness, or more hateful to God, than that which is exhibited by slanderers; especially those who slander the ministers of Christ.

And the evil of their conduct will be still more manifest, if you consider the consequences which naturally flow from it.

In the first place, they who slander a Christian minister, strike a heavy blow at his private interest and happiness. They rob him of that which is of more value to him than any other earthly good.

Those who injure the good name of a minister, injure his usefulness. The injury will affect every benevolent object which he aims to promote. It will affect the welfare of his church. Every follower of Christ who sits under his ministry, will suffer loss. The evil will spread as far as his influence extends; because his influence will be less salutary in proportion as he enjoys less of the esteem and confidence of his fellow-men.

Now when you take into consideration the disposition which prompts men to injure a minister's reputation, and the pernicious consequences which are likely to result from such injury, you will cease to wonder, that it is so emphatically prohibited and so severely condemned by the word of God. Your wonder will rather be, that it should prevail to so fearful an extent among those who profess to be followers of Christ.

If then there is any one in the community, who allows himself, either publicly or privately, to injure the reputation of a Christian minister — with such a one I would earnestly expostulate.

Come then, my friend, and let us reason together. Consider that a minister's character is his dearest earthly treasure ; and remember that you owe it a just respect. Rob him of his substance, and inflict wounds upon his body, rather than rob him of his good name, or wound his character. Suppress, then, those slanderous words you are about to speak, and those evil surmises you are about to utter. Though sport to you, they may be arrows and death to him.

The injury you are about to commit against the character of a minister, may also involve his domestic circle, now cheerful and happy, in sufferings not to be described.

But I wish you more particularly to consider, how far your evil surmises and slanders may go towards injuring a minister's usefulness. By aspersing his character, and destroying the confidence which the public repose in his integrity, you will do much towards rendering his best efforts abortive, and his talents and acquisitions worthless. In this way you will hinder the conversion of sinners, the sanctification of believers, and the spread of the gospel among those who are perishing.

To the man who speaks lightly of the character of gospel ministers, I must say, a heavy charge lies against you in the book of God's remembrance. You are guilty of violating God's holy law. You are guilty of doing a great injury to a fellow being, and to one who is employed in a sacred and benevolent work, and to whom a good name is preëminently important. You are guilty of committing this injury against a man who in all probability never injured you, but has cordially wished to do you good. And are you sure that you are not guilty of falsehood? I will venture to say, that at least a great part of your evil surmises and the unfavorable reports you circulate respecting gospel ministers, are utterly groundless; and that you yourself would find them so, if you should ever take pains to examine them. Have you not good reason then to fear, lest you should subject yourself to the condemnation of those who retail falsehood and calumny?

And is not your conduct stamped with cowardice and baseness? If you reproach and insult a minister to his face, though you may be guilty of impudence and rudeness, your conduct may have some appearance of courage and manhood. But to say things against him behind his back, when he can have no opportunity to defend himself; to avoid fair and open combat, and to attack him in the dark — what is this but a compound of cruelty and meanness? What but the lurking warfare of the savage, or the midnight assassin?

Such, and more than I can now set forth, is the guilt of designedly injuring the good name of a gospel minister. Such is the guilt of injuring the good name of any one who bears the sacred office. Some ministers reject the doctrines which were held sacred by the Reformers, and by the fathers of New England. But have they, on this account, forfeited their title to be spoken of with truth, and to be treated with candor and kindness? I do indeed consider a minister who rejects the doctrines commonly called evangelical, to be in a great error. But can it be proper to oppose error by slander, instead of argument? or to attempt to promote the cause of Christianity by transgressing one of its fundamental laws? These are not the weapons of our warfare. Say — if such is your belief — that a minister's opinions are erroneous, and then prove them to be so. But what right have you to load him with reproach and calumny? You may as well steal his property. Do you say, his property is his own? So is his reputation. And you have no more right to deprive him of the one, than of the other.

I have made these remarks in regard to any minister. But they must have a special emphasis in relation to one, who cordially embraces the doctrines of the gospel, who is earnestly engaged in his work, and who discharges the duties of his sacred calling with fidelity. To slander him who is truly a spiritual guide, and who desires nothing so much as the salvation of men, betrays a perverseness of disposition which is not easily described.

Possibly some one may say within himself, that he cannot submit to such restraints of his natural liberty; that his tongue is his own, and that he shall use it as he pleases. But I must tell you, my friend, that your tongue is no more your own, than your hands are; and that you have no more right to use the former as you please, than the latter. You may as well smite and wound a gospel minister with your hands, as with your tongue. To do either is disobedience to the God who made you. He claims an absolute authority over all the faculties of your mind, and all the members of your body, especially over your tongue. And to assert the right to injure the reputation of a gospel minister, is to assert the right to sin against God.

You may plead, that the minister of whom you are disposed to speak evil, has failings, of which you cannot be ignorant. And perhaps you may complain, that he has in some way given you offence.

Be it so then, that he is obviously subject to failings, and that he has in some way offended you. The Lord Jesus, by an express precept, points out the course for you to pursue. Go and tell him his fault between you and him alone. Have you complied with this just and holy command?

It is true that every minister of the gospel has failings. And, my dear friend, whom I hear complaining of the failings of a minister, have you no failings? And how would you desire that your failings should be treated? Treat his in the same manner.

But do you know with what heart-felt grief he reflects upon his failings, and how often he has confessed them and wept over them; how sincerely he abhors himself, and how deeply he is humbled before God on account of them? Have you in like manner confessed and mourned over your failings?

The pious minister, of whom you complain, has failings indeed. But with all his failings, God has put him into the ministry, and called him to engage in that most sacred work. And God, though infinitely holy, bears with his failings, and graciously forgives them. And will you reproach a penitent with those failings, which a holy and merciful God freely forgives? "It is God that justifieth; who is he that condemneth?" That Christian minister is God's servant, not yours. And the God whom he serves, and to whom he is accountable, has blotted out his sins, and will never remember them. And who art thou, that thou shouldst try to undo what the God of heaven has done? — that thou shouldst remember, and magnify, and blazon abroad those faults, which God Almighty chooses to pardon and forget?

I grant, that the minister whom you reproach, has failings and weaknesses of character even more than you have ever noticed. But does he not possess excellences also? Is there not reason to think, that he is a friend and follower of Jesus; that he cherishes a hearty concern for the salvation of men and the prosperity of the church; and that he repents and makes confession, and repairs to his heavenly advocate for pardon and cleansing? Now is it right to overlook his piety to God, his benevolence to men, his penitence, his fidelity, and usefulness — can it be right to overlook all these good qualities, and continually to dwell upon his faults, and magnify and proclaim them, as though they constituted his whole character?

But as to the particular faults which you impute to him — are you sure that they really belong to him? Is it a matter of certain knowledge with you, or is it a matter of hear-say or suspicion? Do your accusations rest on clear evidence — evidence which you are able to produce? Or do they spring from some groundless report, or some unhallowed feeling in your own breast?

To those who are disposed to treat the reputation of a minister either injuriously or lightly, I have still one word more. Remember then, that there is a God who judgeth in the earth, and that he will recompense you for the injury you do to the character of his servants. "With what measure ye mete, it shall be measured to you again!" It may not be long before your actions or motives shall be treated with unsparing severity. Your character, to which you are so alive, may be blackened by the foulest aspersions. And if you persist in the practice of evil speaking, you may by and by be subjected to general reproach, which will be the more insupportable to you, because you will feel it to be just. An attack may be made upon you, which you will be unable to resist. Public indignation may be kindled against you; infamy and contempt may overwhelm you. This may be your recompense even in the present life. And remember, that a day of final reckoning is at hand, when the Lord will judge you for all your evil surmises and hard speeches against his ministers, and in the presence of angels and men will say to you;—*inasmuch as ye did it unto one of the least of these my servants, ye did it unto me.*

Permit me to remind ministers of the gospel of the regard which they owe to *each other's* reputation. Would to God that this duty were properly attended to, and that the language of Christian ministers respecting one another were always the language of mutual forbearance, candor, and love. If it is so criminal for other men to slander ministers, it is still more criminal for ministers to slander one another, or in any way to detract from one another's reputation. It ought to be our invariable resolution, that no one who sustains the sacred office, shall ever have his character or usefulness injured by any injustice or heedlessness on our part. On the contrary, let us do all in our power, by fair and honest means, to shield the reputation and increase the usefulness of every one of our brethren; so that the world around us may have occasion to say; *behold, how these ministers love one another!*

But important as this duty is, there is one of still greater urgency; I mean the duty of taking care of our own character.

Our friends may be ever so solicitous for our reputation, and ever so watchful to shield us from calumny. But what will their solicitude avail us, unless we ourselves are awake to the subject, and carefully avoid whatever would expose our character to reproach. With an unsullied reputation, we may do much for the cause of Christ; without it, all our labors will be of little value. Let us then guard this precious treasure with unceasing vigilance.

Are we not too inattentive to the importance of this subject? The word of God makes it essential to every one who bears the ministerial office, that he should be of good report. We cannot trifle with our own reputation, we cannot neglect to guard it from injury, without neglecting a most sacred duty. For in truth, our reputation is not our own. We owe it, and all the power which it gives us to do good, to our blessed Redeemer; and we should faithfully use it, as we should every other talent intrusted to us, for the promotion of his cause. Let us then, for the sake of our usefulness, and for the credit of our holy calling, be solicitous, by all proper means, to preserve and increase our reputation. For this purpose, let us be good men, and good ministers of Christ; full of faith and good works. In the exercise of Christian discretion, let us scrupulously avoid not only what is positively sinful, but what is of a doubtful character. Be vigilant and faithful, brethren, and you may quietly trust your character with God, who will hide you in the secret of his pavilion from the strife of tongues. Never return railing for railing, or evil-speaking for evil-speaking, but contrariwise blessing. Look unto Jesus, who endured the contradiction of sinners, and copy his meekness, love, and forgiveness. And if, amid the agitation of this changing world, your reputation is sometimes obscured by a few dark clouds; those clouds will pass away. Even in this life, the righteous providence of God will generally bring to light the integrity of his ministers. And the all-revealing day is at hand, when the voice you will hear, will not be the voice of reproach from your enemies, nor of complaint from misjudging friends; but the voice of your merciful Saviour and Judge, who, will say to you, *Well done, good and faithful servant, enter thou into the joy of your Lord.* And there, in that holy, happy kingdom, which no minister can ever deserve, you will forget the reproaches and sufferings of your earthly state, and be crowned with glory, honor, and immortality.

MY BELOVED BROTHER, THE PASTOR ELECT,

The circumstances of the present occasion are peculiarly interesting to my feelings; and I am sure they must be so to yours. It is now three years since it became my duty, as a committee of the American Temperance Society, to announce to you your appointment as general Agent of that Society, and by various considerations to persuade you to undertake the arduous work of pleading the cause of Temperance before the American public. That you might be at liberty to do this, it was found necessary that you should resign the charge of a very beloved church and society. We know in some measure what a sacrifice you made, when, from a regard to the good of the community, you gave up the pastoral care of your flock. And it affords me pleasure to recal to mind the regard to the public welfare, which your people evinced, when they consented to part with a minister, who had so successfully labored for their good, and who in so high a degree enjoyed their love and confidence. — During these three years, it has been my happiness, so far as my other duties would permit, to be associated with you in consultation and in effort, for the suppression of a far-spread and destructive vice, and the promotion of a great public virtue. The benevolent enterprise, in which you and others have been engaged, has been prospered far beyond our most sanguine hopes. *Let this be wholly to the praise of God, from whom come all good designs, and all good endeavors, and all success.* And let it be a comfort to your heart, that God has made you an instrument of so much good to your fellow-men, and that this good has been accomplished in so short a time, and that you are so soon permitted to return to the office which you love above every other.

And as you have now closed the agency which you undertook,

suffer me, my brother, not only for myself, but in behalf of the American Temperance Society and its Executive Committee, in behalf of the community at large, and in behalf of the thousands who have been benefitted by your labors, sincerely to thank you for your faithful services. These services, I well know, have cost you many a sacrifice, many a season of exhaustion, and weeping, and agony of heart. But you have enjoyed that, which is among the best pleasures ever enjoyed on earth, the pleasure of laboring successfully in a great and good cause. Amidst your exhausting labors and your various exposures, your life and health have been the care of a watchful providence. And while you have been making a fearless and uncompromising attack upon the favorite indulgences and deep-rooted habits and prejudices of men in every rank of life, your character has been safe. And you are now receiving the most pleasing proofs of the gratitude and confidence of an enlightened public. Through the kindness of God, you are called to resume the pastoral office with most encouraging prospects of usefulness. I rejoice, my dear brother, that after the efforts, so wearisome to body and mind, which you have made to help forward the Temperance Reformation, you are now to resume the pastoral office with very encouraging prospects; to settle here in this united church and society, so near to your former charge, and in the midst of your beloved brethren and friends. The Lord command his blessing upon you, and upon your household; and for many happy years, give you the privilege of feeding this beloved church and society with the bread of life, and of beholding in this place, and all around you, the growing prosperity of Christ's kingdom. And when you shall have finished the work which God has given you to do, may you be a partaker of the glory that shall be revealed. Amen.

A SERMON

DELIVERED AT THE INSTALLATION OF THE REV. THOMAS MATHER SMITH, CATSKILL, N. Y., JUNE 15, 1831.

---

1 Cor. 3: 7.—So THEN NEITHER IS HE THAT PLANTETH ANYTHING, NEITHER HE THAT WATERETH; BUT GOD THAT GIVETH THE INCREASE.

As the agency of God in the concerns of his spiritual kingdom is so inexpressibly important, and is made so prominent in the instructions of his word; why are we so prone to overlook it? How comes it to pass that we make so low an estimate of the agency of God, while we assign so high a place to the agency of man?

This, I think, may be accounted for in part by the fact, that *man's* agency is *visible*, while *God's* agency is *invisible*. When a Christian minister is laboring to make known divine truth and bring sinners to repentance, the agent and the agency are both objects of our senses. But *God* is *invisible;* and so is the agency he exerts. The effects of his agency come under our observation; but the agency itself lies wholly concealed from our view. When God accomplishes the most conspicuous work, his hand is unseen, and all we can behold is the work accomplished. This circumstance, which weighs much by itself, has an increased influence, by being connected with another, namely, that in the very instances in which the invisible agency of God is specially employed, there is, for the most part a *visible human* agency. In such cases, how natural it is for us, creatures of sense as we are, to fix our eye chiefly upon the dependent, feeble agency of man, because it is *visible;* while the supreme and almighty agency of God, concerned in the same event, is comparatively unnoticed, because it is *invisible.*

I might mention it as an additional circumstance, which helps to account for the oversight above mentioned, that the *manner* of the divine agency is so different from ours. A great difference we could not but expect to find here, considering that the attributes of God are infinitely superior to ours; and that his agency is independent and almighty, while the highest agency which we can exert, is very circumscribed and wholly dependent. But is it not a general fact, that this very perfection of the divine agency turns off our attention from it? Because God has a direct and perfect access to the minds of men, and influences all their thoughts, dispositions and affections according to his own pleasure, and thus makes it manifest that his ways are not our ways, and that no one can be likened to him; we are therefore prone to disregard his agency altogether. We deny the operation of his power for the very reason which should lead us most devoutly to acknowledge it; namely, because it is infinitely superior to ours.

But there is still another reason for the mistake I have mentioned, that is, *the pride of the heart.* This naturally inclines us to make too much of our own agency, and to say, *my hand hath done this.* Just so far as we are lifted up with pride and vanity, we shall be disposed to overrate our own influence, and to withhold from God the glory which is due to him for the agency he exerts in the souls of the redeemed. He who would entertain right views on this subject, must mortify all pride and loftiness of heart, and cherish the spirit of humility and self-abasement. Such a spirit would prepare us to honor God, as the supreme cause of all good, and to say with our Apostle, "neither is he that planteth anything, nor he that watereth; but God who giveth the increase."

But my principal object on this occasion is to show, that *the doctrine of divine influence, as held forth in the text, presents the only adequate encouragement to the servants of Christ, to labor for the conversion of sinners and the prosperity of the Church.*

To convert sinners, to give success to the gospel and prosperity to the church, is a work of immense magnitude and difficulty, and far transcends the power of man. The heart of every human being is inclined to sin; deceitful above all things, and desperately wicked. This is the case even with those who are furthest removed from the contagion of vicious example, and least practised in the ways of sin.

But in addition to this general difficulty, there are various other hinderances in the way. The unrenewed not only have hearts which are naturally selfish, and alienated from God; but they are fortified against the motives to repentance by the evil customs of the world, and by the influence of invisible and malignant spirits. And when you look upon men in heathen countries, you find the case still more difficult. For their hearts are shielded against divine truth and hardened in sin, by the forms of superstition and idolatry; by despotic and persecuting governments; by the power of ignorance, and the power of caste. Satan appears to have availed himself of all the principles of our nature, even of *conscience,* in order to rivet the chains with which he has bound the souls of men, and to hinder them from casting off the miserable bondage of sin.

Now what can we expect from those who are possessed of such a character and placed in such circumstances? Have they any seeds of goodness within them, which may, by human culture, be made to bring forth fruit unto holiness? Is there any ground to hope, that good will ever spring from a will totally enslaved to sin, or a moral agency altogether misguided and perverted? Both the word of God and the history of past ages teach, that holiness can never result from any power, disposition or effort of unrenewed men.

And in regard to the conversion of sinners, what reliance can we place upon *ourselves, as ministers of the gospel?* What are *we*, that we should think ourselves sufficient for such a work? Had we the knowledge and energy of Paul, the eloquence of Apollos, the sublimity of Isaiah, and the ardor and boldness of Elijah; still what could we effect? We could not bring one sinner to repentance; we could not convert a single child. Ministers and Christians may exert all their power to make known divine truth and induce sinners to obey the gospel; but if left to themselves they will look around them, and with sorrow say, "Who hath believed our report?

It must then be evident, that if we had nothing to rely upon but our own qualifications and efforts, or the dispositions of natural men, we should be in a state of utter despondency. Looking merely at ourselves, and at unrenewed sinners, we could have no resolution to pursue our work, because we could have no prospect of success.

Here we are met by the animating doctrine of our text, that the conversion of sinners is accomplished by *the power of God.* This is the very doctrine we need. It raises us at once above discouragement. For now we become allied to a power which makes success certain. Yes, brethren, if we have faith in God, we shall take hold on his infinite strength. And then, as to all the purposes of encouragement and success, it will be as though we ourselves were almighty. For it is surely as well, that the omnipotence which is to accomplish the work should reside in *God*, as in *us*. Now if *we* had infinite power, so that we could change the hearts of sinners just when we pleased, and could cause the gospel to spread and the church to flourish just as far as we saw to be best; surely we could not feel any discouragement. For who ever felt any discouragement in regard to a work, for which he believed himself fully qualified, and which he knew he could accomplish whenever he pleased? Behold, then, that infinite power which is engaged in the work of saving sinners. True, the power is *God's*. But who can think it on that account any the less adequate to the object? The power does indeed belong to *God*. But we are to act in connection with it; and it will avail to our success, just so far as infinite wisdom sees to be best.

At a certain time, the disciples were in a ship in a violent storm. And what power had they to preserve themselves from the destruction which threatened them? Who of them could say to the winds and waves, *peace, be still?* Thinking only of themselves, they had then good reason to be filled with fear. But there was one in the ship, whom the winds and the waves obeyed. He therefore rebuked them for being of a fearful heart, because it showed their want of confidence in him. With such a friend near them, they were as safe, and they had as much reason to feel that they were safe, as if they themselves had been able to control the winds and the waves. — Brethren, the cause of God is safe; the prospect of the conversion of sinners and the enlargement of the church is certain. Omnipotence is engaged in the work, and we act in alliance with it; so that our weakness, instead of hindering the success of the gospel, will only prove the occasion of making the power of God more conspicuous. Weak and insufficient as we are, we are employed in this work; and we are employed for this very purpose, *that the excellency of the power may be of God, and not of us.*

Should we forget the power of God, and look only to ourselves; and then consider what a work is to be done for a single congregation or a single person, especially for a *world lying in wickedness;* we should be overwhelmed with a sense of insufficiency. But here we learn, that our insufficiency is no obstacle to the salvation of sinners; that they are to be converted by a power which resides in God, not in us; that, while he is pleased to appoint us as agents in this work, and even to make our faithful labors necessary to the salvation of men; the work itself is his; and his the power which accomplishes it.

However disheartening the circumstances in which we may be called to labor for the salvation of men, the doctrine of the text is suited to sustain and animate us. Suppose we should be placed where but few would coöperate with us and help forward the conversion of sinners. Suppose we should be called to a region where the whole multitude around us are enemies to the cross of Christ, and we were obliged to labor and pray alone. O! What despondency would these circumstances tend to produce! But our doctrine would afford a remedy. Only let our minds be impressed with the truth, that the power of God insures success, and that he who is with us is greater than all who are against us; and there would be no place left for despondency. An almighty and merciful Being, invisible indeed, but well known to us, would bid us go forward in our work, promising to be with us, and to give the increase, whether the laborers are many or few. In such a case the feeling of our solitariness and weakness would only lead us to trust in God alone; and such trust would cheer and animate our hearts.

Or suppose that we have labored for years and offered up many prayers for the conversion of sinners around us, but apparently with little or no success. How can we prevent the tendency of these circumstances to overcome our resolution and paralyze our efforts? Our text supplies an answer. We must consider that the success of our labors depends ultimately on God. He giveth the increase; and he giveth it when it seemeth good in his sight. And he giveth it at such a time, and in such a manner, as will make his power and grace most visible. He may suffer us to labor for a longer or shorter time without success, for the very purpose of making us feel our dependence on him, so that we may give him the glory that is due to him as the God of salvation. When he has humbled us and made us sensible that we are nothing, and that he is all in all, and when the time to favor Zion has come, he will give the increase. These views are suited to inspire unfailing resolution, and to rouse us to be diligent in business, and to abound in the work of the Lord.

Our doctrine is adapted to excite hope in regard to those who are *the most hardened in sin.* Be it so that we have often entreated them with tears, and often prayed for their salvation, while no effect has appeared but a growing insensibility to the obligations of religion. Are we to despair of ultimate success? It is indeed true, that if any of the human race — if even those who are the least contaminated with vice, and who possess the most attractive amiableness of disposition, are ever born again; it will be by no power of ours, but by the power of God. Why then should any, even the chief of sinners be despaired of? If God is pleased to send forth his new creating Spirit into the hearts of those, whom you may be ready to look upon as lost beyond recovery; what a surprising change will you soon behold! Our doctrine authorizes us to cherish the hope that such a blessed change will take place in the most hardened sinners, and to anticipate the joy we shall experience, when it actually takes place. How powerfully animating the influence of such a hope!

The doctrine of the text is obviously suited to exert a powerful and happy influence in regard to the *cause of Missions*. Here especially it is true, that mere human power can do nothing. Without the help of God, the whole body of Christians can make no advance towards bringing the heathen to the saving knowledge of Christ. Ten thousand obstacles stand in the way of their salvation, and will mock our highest efforts; and the certain, inevitable course of things will be, that crimes and miseries will continue and increase among them down to the end of time, unless the Lord of heaven and earth exert his omnipotence, and create all things new. Thus, in regard to the whole extent of the work to be accomplished for the conversion of the pagan world, we are driven away from all dependence on man. Human resources utterly fail. And unless we look to the power and wisdom and mercy of God, we can have no prospect of the world's salvation. Let us then put our trust in God. He can send forth such light and truth, and such an influence of his Spirit, that nations shall be born in a day, and every knee bow at the name of Jesus. All things are possible with God, and all things are *easy* too. If he only speak the word, the gospel will have free course and be glorified in all the earth. Shall we then be disheartened, because *our* power is not adequate to the work of saving the world? Just as well might we be disheartened in regard to the daily rising of the sun and the motion of the planets, because they are things beyond our power. Consider the precious promises of God concerning the salvation of sinners. Consider the perfect ease with which he can accomplish these promises, and the certainty that he will accomplish them. Then consider what part he has assigned to us in this work of benevolence; that although all power belongs to him, he has required us, or rather, has granted us the *privilege* to plant and water, at the same time assuring us that he will give the increase.

What more can we ask? Every other motive is weak and inefficacious compared with this. Yea, without this, every other view of the subject would leave us in a state of discouragement. There is nothing in us or in others; there is nothing in the natural tendencies of the human mind, in the state of society, or in the influence of civil or religious institutions, nothing in the lessons of wisdom taught by the experience of ages; there is nothing even in the exhibition which the Scriptures make of the mercies and the terrors of the Lord, which, separate from the influence of the Spirit, could furnish the least reason to expect, that any nation, or any individual would ever submit to the reign of Christ. We are then brought to the sovereign power and mercy of God, as the only ground of hope, the only cause of success. Here is a power that can encourage and sustain our efforts — a power that can renew sinners, and bring the world to obey the gospel, and can do it by means of our feeble services.

That the doctrine of the text possesses the influence which I have ascribed to it, has been confirmed by long experience. This doctrine has actually excited the servants of Christ, amid all sorts of difficulties and discouragements, to labor perseveringly for the conversion of sinners. Paul believed that *neither he that planteth, nor he that watereth is anything.* And whenever he did what turned to account in the cause of his Lord, he entirely disclaimed the credit of it, saying, "*not I,* but the grace of Christ that was with me." But this view of his dependence on God both for his faithfulness and his success, was accompanied with a resolution, diligence, and perseverance, which nothing could overcome. If at any time the servants of Christ forget their dependence and weakness; if they lose sight of that divine agency which renews the heart, and begin to think themselves able, by forcible argument, or by persuasive eloquence, to bring sinners to repentance;

it is then they are likely to grow remiss. But let those who are laboring to turn sinners to God, have faith in him, and keep their eye steadily fixed on his power, as the only cause of success ; and they will have a diligence and zeal, which will not only rise high, but endure to the end. New hope and new ardor will be kindled up within them ; and they will abound in the work of the Lord, knowing that their labor shall not be in vain in the Lord. Thus, while all who rely on human power shall faint and be weary, they who wait upon the Lord, shall renew their strength ; shall mount up with wings as eagles ; shall run and not be weary, and walk and not faint.

It is a fair inference from what has been said, that *the best preparation which can be made on our part for the work of divine grace in the conversion of sinners, is to become duly sensible, that we are nothing, and that God is all in all.* He who is *duly* sensible of his insufficiency and his dependence on God, is all alive to the interests of religion. He knows that sinners, whether old or young, are utterly ruined. This view of their depravity and wretchedness moves the pity of his heart. He longs for their salvation. His soul is all on fire to see the glory of God displayed in the conversion of the multitudes who are ready to perish. But with all his love and zeal, and all his fervent prayer for the salvation of those who are lost, he knows and feels, that not one of them will ever be converted without special divine influence ; that all his labor will accomplish nothing, unless it please God to interpose, and save sinners by the washing of regeneration and renewing of the Holy Ghost. Thus, while all his faculties are wakefully employed in the work which God has assigned to him, he is sensible that nothing can be done, unless God is pleased to send forth his renewing Spirit. He therefore refers it all to God's sovereign will, and fixes the eye of faith and hope on him, who *hath mercy on whom he will have mercy.*

This state of mind is highly important as a preparation for a revival of religion, because it fits us to perform the very work assigned to us. When we are in the state of mind here intended, we shall be most likely to discern clearly what our province is, and what are the particular duties which we are required to perform. All our faculties will be strongly excited, and ready for action; while our trust in God will bring us into a union with his infinite power, and so will prepare us for efforts to which our own unaided power would be wholly inadequate.

And while this state of mind will prepare us to perform the very work which God has marked out for us, it will have an important influence in preventing us from undertaking any other. If we entertain the thought that we are called to convert and can convert men by our own independent efforts, we shall be liable to adopt methods which are incompatible with the word of God. Is it not a fact, that those who have, in any period of the church, endeavored to convert men by means which they have invented, and which Christ and the apostles never used, have shown an undue confidence in themselves, and a want of reliance on the Spirit of God? If we are fully persuaded, that our success depends on the influence of the Spirit; we can have no motive to adopt any measures for the conversion of sinners, except those which manifestly accord with the dictates of the Spirit in the Holy Scriptures. Our single object will be to do the will of God as expressed in his word, and so to secure his blessing upon our labors. This makes our work plain and simple. It keeps our eye fixed upon a standard of action which is perfect and immutable, and so guards us against the restlessness of those who, instead of humbly looking for success to the blessing of God upon the faithful preaching of his word, are continually looking to some new and unauthorized measures. It makes us content to copy the example of the apostles, who used the weapons which God had furnished, and those only; who preached *his* truth in *his* way, and relied upon him to give their preaching effect.

Finally; the preparation which I have insisted upon is of great importance, because it guards us against feelings of self-complacency, and disposes us to give to God all the glory of man's salvation? Can we expect that God will work by means of our efforts, when he sees that we are inclined to arrogate to ourselves the honor which belongs to him? Pride of heart is a mighty hinderance to the work of God's grace. When this hinderance is removed, and God sees us humble and self-abased, and yet ready to do our part faithfully; then we may expect that he will revive his work.

Among our various endeavors, then, to prepare ourselves for the work of converting sinners and building up the church, this would seem to be of special importance, namely, that we take care of our own hearts, and see to it that we are rid of that pride and self-dependence, which is so exceedingly hateful in the sight of God, and that we have that lowly mind, and that reliance on his grace, which he regards as of great price. And if some of the exertions we make for more showy acquisitions, were made for the particular purpose of subduing all conceit of our own power, and cherishing deep humility and child-like dependence on God; should we not be likely to accomplish more for the salvation of sinners and the spread of the gospel? Only twelve men, and those too of moderate qualifications in a worldly view, were employed as apostles, to establish Christianity, and to propagate it through the nations. Is it not sometimes the case, that *too much human* agency is employed in our attempts to promote a revival of religion? Does not God very plainly teach us, both by his word and providence, that he sets a much higher value upon the *kind* of agency we employ, than upon its *quantity?*

And you, *my dear son*, can add your testimony to the truth of the sentiment contained in my text. Your own experience, during the short period of your ministry, has been sufficient to teach you thoroughly, what the Bible had taught you before, that a minister owes his success entirely to God. While laboring among the affectionate and beloved people whom you have lately left, you have at different times enjoyed the happiness of beholding sinners pressing into the kingdom of heaven, and large numbers added to the church. And on every conversion you have seen it written as with a sun-beam—*the work of God!* And when, in sovereign wisdom and righteousness, God has withheld the influence of his Spirit; you have found that no efforts of yours could avail anything; that in despite of the terrors of divine wrath, and the melting persuasions of divine mercy, sinners would neglect the great salvation. You have learnt by experience that men must be *born again, and born of God.* There is no other way for sinners to become heirs of heaven. For us to suppose that we can find out a new way, is all delusion. The human heart is essentially the same in all ages; and the power which renews it is the same; and that power is not the power of reason, nor the power of self-love, nor the power of human persuasion; but *the mighty power of God;* the power which raised Christ from the dead; the power which created the world. Remember this, my dear son, in the encouraging and delightful circumstances in which you are here called to labor. If any in this place have an ear to hear the messages of divine mercy; it is because God has given them an ear. If they have a heart to love the truth; it is because God has given them such a heart. If you overlook this truth; if while the work of conversion and sanctification is prospering, you and your people forget that it is *God's* work; he will withhold the tokens of his favor. No rain or dew will descend from heaven; and you will soon behold this garden of God, now beginning to cluster with the fruits of the Spirit, left to blasting and barrenness. Remember then, that salvation is of God. And begin and end the labors of your ministry here, with a deep feeling of the blessed truth, that *neither he that planteth is anything, nor he that watereth; but God that giveth the increase.*

A SERMON

DELIVERED IN THE CHAPEL OF THE THEOL. SEMINARY, ANDOVER, APRIL 8, 1840.

John 15: 5.—WITHOUT ME YE CAN DO NOTHING.

THESE words were first addressed to the apostles. But it is as true of all believers, as it was of the apostles, that they can do nothing spiritually good without Christ; that in regard to all holiness, whether in heart or in life, they are entirely dependent on him.

Dependence, in a general view, is the condition of all created beings. Their existence, their powers of action, and their means of happiness are all from God. In him they live, and move, and have their being. This condition of dependence belongs to angels in heaven, as well as to men on earth. They owe it to the will and agency of God, that they were created and are continued in a state of moral purity. And they will be indebted to him for their holiness and happiness in all future ages, as much as they were at the beginning of their existence. They will doubtless remain holy, and will grow in the strength of their intellectual and moral faculties and their spiritual affections forever. But the growing strength of their faculties and their affections will be from God. And the higher their improvement in knowledge and in holiness, just so much the more will they be indebted to the goodness of God. It is the unalterable, happy condition of the heavenly hosts, to have a growing fulness of spiritual good, and to receive it all from God.

But Christians are dependent not only in the general sense in which the angels are dependent, but in a peculiar sense, a sense appropriate to them as *redeemed sinners*. In their natural state they are children of wrath, desperately wicked. And their renewal to holiness is owing to the Spirit of God. It is by the grace of God they are what they are. And without the continuance of that grace, they would sink at once into a state of pollution, guilt and wretchedness. So that it is true in the highest sense, that without Christ they can do nothing.

I propose to show, that *the doctrine of our dependence on divine aid is taught by reason, Scripture, and experience; and that it is a doctrine in the highest degree honorable to God, and useful to man.*

In the *first* place, this doctrine is taught by *reason*. If there is anything which reason makes known with absolute certainty, it is, that all excellence and happiness in created beings is *derived*, not *self-originated;* that we are as much indebted to God for the commencement and continuance of a *virtuous character*, as for the commencement and continuance of our *being*. True virtue is far more excellent, than mere existence. And it would be very unreasonable to suppose, that we are dependent on God for that which is less excellent and yet not dependent for that which is more excellent. Certainly it would not be more contrary to reason and truth to think, that created beings originated their own existence, than that Christians of themselves originated their own holiness. And this becomes specially evident, when it is considered how many things there were without them and within them, which stood in opposition to holiness, and which it was necessary should be removed before they could be the subjects of it.

In the *second* place, the doctrine under consideration is plainly taught by the *inspired writers*. This is my chief argument. Those who spake as they were moved by the Holy Ghost, cannot mislead us. Let us then carefully consider the various ways in which the sacred writers teach us our weakness and insufficiency, and our dependence for spiritual good on divine grace.

Here we find that the *beginning* of holiness in the human heart is familiarly represented as *the work of God.* "Being born again, not of blood, nor of the will of the flesh, nor of the will of man, *but of God.*" This passage excludes all conceivable causes of regeneration, but one, that is, God. The sacred writers tell us that a saving change comes from above; that believers are renewed by the Holy Ghost.

The *continuance* of holiness is ascribed to the same cause. It is God who worketh in believers both to *will* and to *do.* They have spiritual life, because the Spirit of God dwells in them. The same God who began the good work in them, will perform it until the day of Christ. The God of peace will make them perfect in every good work, to do his will, *working* in them that which is well pleasing in his sight.

Further; the Scriptures teach that Christians are dependent on divine grace not only for holiness in a general sense, but for all the *particular forms and branches of it.* Thus if we refer to *repentance* as an important branch of holiness; we find that Christ is exalted to *give* repentance. If we refer to the *faith* of Christians; we find it is God who worketh in them the work of faith with power. And *love,* which is the principal virtue of believers, is shed abroad in their hearts by the Holy Ghost. And as to the duty of *prayer,* we are taught that Christians know not how to pray aright, and that the Holy Spirit helpeth their infirmities, and maketh intercession for them. And in regard to the saving knowledge of divine things; we find that they who have it are taught of God; that the natural man does not know and cannot know the things of the Spirit; and that it is God that causes the light to shine in the heart. The same is true of *obedience.* It is God who writes his law in the hearts of his people, and inclines them to obey. It is God that gives his people patience and firmness under trials and sufferings. Indeed the whole range of Christian virtues are the fruits of the Spirit.

The prophets and apostles teach the same truth in still another way. They *expressly disclaim all spiritual strength and sufficiency of their own, and confide in divine strength.* See how clearly their language shows the dependent posture of their minds. "Not that we are sufficient of ourselves to think anything as of ourselves; but our sufficiency is of God." "The Lord is my strength." "God is the strength of my heart." The Apostle Paul does indeed say, "I can do all things." But he at the same time shows his dependence. "I can do all things *through Christ who strengtheneth me.*"

But there is nothing which shows the feelings of good men in regard to their dependence so clearly, as their prayers. When they come to the throne of grace, their delusions vanish, and they have to do with realities. How then were prophets and apostles accustomed to pray? What thoughts and desires did they cherish, and what requests did they make? "Quicken us, and we will call upon thy name." "I will run the way of thy commandments, when thou shalt enlarge my heart." "Incline my heart unto thy testimonies." Such were the prayers of the saints under the Old Testament dispensation. And they were the same under the New Dispensation. The disciples came to Jesus, and said, "Lord, increase our faith." And Paul said to believers: "The *Lord make* you to abound in love." Again. "Now our Lord Jesus Christ and God even our Father, — *stablish* you in every good word and work." And again. "The God of all grace — make you perfect, stablish, strengthen, settle you."

Such prayers, offered up by the saints under both dispensations, imply a constant sense of their dependence on God for all spiritual good, and an earnest desire that he would bestow it upon them. Prayer to God for what we have, or for what we think we may have *of ourselves*, would be a mockery. Why should we go to God, and ask him to make us obedient and holy, while we say or think, that we are of ourselves sufficient for the work of obedience and holiness without his aid?

The texts above referred to, and many others of the same import, teach our entire dependence on God for spiritual good *very clearly* and *impressively*. They set it forth in a great variety of ways; so that, if there is any room for doubt as to the meaning of this or that text, the doubt may be removed by other texts relating to the same subject. This furthermore is not a subject which the inspired writers keep in the back ground, or which they touch upon lightly and incidentally, and to which they attach but little consequence. On the contrary, they make the subject very prominent. And finally, they never treat the doctrine of our dependence as though there was any danger of carrying it too far, or making it too important, or as though there was any danger of its interfering with any other principle of religion. They say unhesitatingly and without qualification, that believers are born of God; that he renews men, and gives them repentance. They do not say, as a matter of concession, that God must be allowed to have *some* influence in this work. But they say decidedly, that God does it. And when they pray that God would work in them all the good pleasure of his goodness and the work of faith with power; they do not pray that he would do all this by merely presenting motives before them, leaving it to their free will to comply or not. They do not say to God, we beseech thee by thy Spirit to make us obedient and holy, though we are conscious that we are perfectly able to be obedient and holy without thy Spirit. They do not say, we beseech thee, O Lord, strengthen us for duty, though we know that we have in ourselves all the strength we need without thee. They do indeed speak familiarly of their own right agency. But they speak of it as the effect of divine influence. "Quicken me, and I will keep thy word." "Work out your salvation, — for it is God that worketh in you to will and to do." — In the view of the sacred writers, holy action in us, flows from the divine operation. It is the fruit of the Spirit.

And thirdly, the same doctrine is taught and confirmed by the *experience of good men.* It is one of the first lessons which they learn in the school of Christ, that they are in themselves destitute of spiritual good; that they have no sufficiency for the performance of duty, except what they derive from divine grace; that their help is in God. This sense of dependence is essential to the character of Christians. If Christians have at any time trusted their own heart, and attempted to do the work and enjoy the comforts of religion, without Christ; how quickly have they fallen into a state of darkness and desolation! It must be the full persuasion of all consistent Christians, that if they should be separated from Christ, and should receive no further communications of spiritual strength from him, they would assuredly depart from the way of holiness, and draw back to perdition. Whatever powers of mind they may possess — and they doubtless have all the powers and faculties which are necessary to moral, accountable agents — they have no power that will preserve them from apostasy, and enable them to be faithful unto death, unless the all-sufficient grace of Christ is with them! However they may speculate about their sufficient ability for all their duty, the moment they feel and pray as Christians, their speculations vanish, and they heartily acknowledge their utter impotence and insufficiency, and their need of divine help. Their own experience teaches them more and more effectually, that they are in want of all things, and that they depend for a supply upon him in whom all fulness dwells.

I am now, in the fourth place, to show, that the doctrine under consideration is honorable to God. We honor God, when we believe and declare the general truth, that every good gift cometh down from him. But it is a truth of special importance, that God, by his Spirit, renews the depraved heart, and that he works in believers all that is pure and excellent. When we cordially receive this truth, and openly declare it, we honor the character of God. Did not Paul honor God, when he said, "by the grace of God I am what I am;" and when, after speaking of his many labors, he disclaimed the credit of them, and said, "not I, but the grace of God that was with me?" Did he not honor his Saviour when he set him forth as our wisdom, our righteousness, our sanctification, and our redemption? And do not all Christians honor him, by ascribing to him the beginning and end of their salvation? This they do even now, although they have so imperfect a knowledge of their own poverty and misery, and of their indebtedness to his grace. How much more highly will they honor him, when they come to understand the whole value of the blessings which they have received from the riches of his mercy. In the world to come, how clear and strong will be their conviction, that their holiness and blessedness were his free gift! And how joyfully will they unite in that song of praise: "Unto him that loved us, and washed us from our sins in his own blood, and made us kings and priests unto God, — unto him be glory and dominion forever and ever."

I am, in the fifth place, to illustrate *the beneficial influence* of the doctrine of our entire dependence on Christ.

The doctrine is evidently true. And is not the truth, especially such a truth as this, profitable to those who cordially receive it? What could have had a more happy influence upon the apostles, than the instruction which Jesus gave them on the subject now before us. "As the branch cannot bear fruit of itself, except it abide in the vine, no more can ye, except ye abide in me. I am the vine, ye are the branches. He that abideth in me and I in him, the same bringeth forth much fruit, for without me ye can do nothing." Was it not of great importance to them to be taught so plainly by their blessed Lord, then just about to die for them, what their real condition was, and that their growth and fruitfulness, their safety and their spiritual life depended on constant communications from him?

The doctrine is specially adapted to produce humility. One of the greatest faults to which we are liable, and which is most likely to retain its hold upon us, is *pride* or *loftiness of heart*. And the spirit of pride is the spirit of self-sufficiency of self-dependence, than which nothing can be more contrary to the nature of the Christian religion. Now the doctrine of our dependence, as taught in the text, is aimed directly against *pride* and *self-sufficiency*. For, according to this doctrine, what have we to be proud of, but our guilt, our poverty, and wretchedness? We may think we are rich, and have need of nothing. But if we truly receive the doctrine of the text, — if we are made to know and to feel, that we are in ourselves, wretched and miserable and poor and blind and naked, and that we must be so forever, unless we are delivered from our wretchedness, and our wants are supplied by our Almighty Saviour; — if we cordially believe and feel that he must work all our works for us, and that we must go forth to duty in his strength; it must have a powerful tendency to subdue the pride of our hearts. If this does not humble us, nothing can. It was the sentiment of the Stoics, that we are dependent on God for all good, *except our virtue!* How impious the pride and self-conceit, which dictated such a sentiment! And how much of this stoical spirit commonly remains in the hearts of Christians! The Apostle Paul was aware of this; and he set himself against it, and took pains to eradicate it from the minds of believers, by inculcating the doctrine of our entire dependence on the grace of Christ. "Who maketh thee to differ?" he said to the believer: "and what hast thou which thou hast not received?" He then makes use of the truth implied in his questions, to bring down the pride of the heart. With reference to that holiness which distinguishes Christians from others, he says: — "Now if thou hast received it, why dost thou glory as if thou hadst not received it?" The sacred writers hold a doctrine exceedingly different from the stoical conceit, that we are dependent on God for everything, *except* our *virtue.* *They* teach that we are dependent on God for every blessing, and most of all for our virtue; — that *all* good comes from God, *especially* that which is more excellent than any other good we possess, — our *holiness;* and so they leave us no ground of glorying, though our holiness should be superior to that of any saint on earth. How is it with the angels in heaven? They are creatures of a very high rank; and they have a thousand fold more knowledge and power and holiness, than any of us. And if the gifts of God were a just reason for pride and loftiness of heart, they might properly have a large measure of it. But those exalted beings, shining forth in the splendors of celestial holiness, and intrusted with concerns of such weight, as would crush us to the earth in a moment — those exalted beings, so superior to the wisest and the mightiest of men have no pride. They glory not in themselves, but in their Lord, and cast their crowns at his feet. They never forget that they receive all good from the fountain of being and blessedness; and especially that it is God who maketh them to differ from the apostate angels. It is perfectly known among them, that they are, and forever will be dependent on God. They desire no other condition of their immortal existence. In view of this their dependent state, they are as much more humble than any saint on earth, as they are more holy.

But the doctrine of their dependence on Christ is adapted not only to humble his followers, but also to *encourage* them, and to render them *active* in his service.

It might be supposed, that a constant conviction of our poverty and weakness would dishearten us, and sink us to *despondency*. And so it would if taken alone. Those who are wholly destitute, and have none to depend upon for a supply of their wants — who are insufficient for the work assigned to them, and without any one to aid them in that work, must be discouraged. And this would be the case with all Christians, had they not the blessed privilege of relying on the grace of Christ. Our dependence on Christ is truly an *inestimable privilege*. It must be so to all who know his name and put their trust in him. How is it, I ask again, with the angels in heaven, who are in all respects dependent on God. Unquestionably they feel their dependence on such a Being to be a most happy circumstance. It rejoices their hearts to stand and gaze upon his perfect character, and to see him continually glorified by communicating a fulness of blessings throughout his holy empire. And they are not only humble and happy in their dependent condition, but they are exceedingly resolute and active in their obedience. Whatever may be the magnitude and difficulty of the work assigned to them, they are swift as lightning to accomplish it; and they are never afraid of any failure, because God is their help, and their whole souls are pervaded with his influence and strengthened with his strength.

The dependence of believers on Christ is, I repeat it, an inestimable privilege and blessing. We are in ourselves without holiness and without spiritual strength. Our dependence did not bring this evil upon us; but the grace of Christ, on which we depend, delivers us from it. We have an almighty Saviour; and to him we may look for help in every time of need. This encourages us to undertake the most arduous duties, and inspires us with hope of success. While we are constrained to say, that without Christ we can do nothing, we are able to say also, that through Christ who strengtheneth us, we can do all things. Had you yourself the power of him by whom all things were made, you would surely be ready to engage in the most difficult work. You would feel that nothing could be above your strength. You could command every valley to be exalted and every hill to be made low. Now the power of Christ will avail you as much as if it were your own. Yes, humble believers, it is a most comforting, inspiring truth, that, if you trust in Christ, you are as well off, as though his immeasurable power were all your own. What resolution does this thought inspire! *I will go in the strength of the Lord. Through him I can overcome the world, and reach the heavenly Canaan. I am conscious of my weakness and insufficiency;— but I rise above it,— I even rejoice and glory, in it, that the power of Christ may rest upon me.* Such is the tendency of the doctrine of our dependence. And its actual results are correspondent. The noblest instances of courage and vigorous action which have ever been known on earth, have been found in those who have been most fully sensible of their own weakness, and have most cordially trusted in the all-sufficient grace of Christ.

The doctrine of our dependence on Christ, is adapted to exert *a sanctifying influence.* For, who can have a constant intercourse and communion with a holy Saviour, without being assimilated to him? Who can live near to that divine Friend and Redeemer, and receive continually the most precious gifts from him, without being powerfully drawn to imitate his spotless character? Who can daily look to him, and behold his glory, without being changed into the same image? It must also be remembered, that the spiritual influence which believers continually receive from their blessed Lord, gives purity of heart; and that everything for which they are dependent on him, and which comes to them from his fulness implies sanctification. The strength he imparts to them, is strength against sin — strength for holy action, and for a holy endurance of affliction.

Finally, the doctrine before us, conduces to the purest *enjoyment* of Christians. It is inexpressibly delightful to their hearts to enter into the deep spiritual meaning of the various passages of holy writ which represent their relation to Christ and their entire dependence upon him. Are not those the happiest hours of your life in which you have the fullest conviction of your dependence on Christ? When you can say from the heart: "His grace is sufficient for me, and his strength is made perfect in weakness;" and when you plainly see, that notwithstanding your own inconstancy and unfaithfulness, your souls are safe, resting, as you do, on the rock of ages; — when you see and feel this, are not the dark clouds, which at other times overshadow you, all chased away, and are not your hearts filled with quietness and peace?

Now if it is a plain truth, that we are in a state of complete dependence on Christ, and can do nothing without him; then why should we ever attempt it? Why should we try to do the work of Christ in that way, in which Christ himself tells us that we cannot do it? It is perfectly plain, that the branches cannot bear fruit, except they abide in the vine. How absurd and foolish then would it be, if we should entertain the thought, that the branches have in themselves the principle of life and fruitfulness, and should go about to make them live and bear fruit, when cut off from the vine!

If, brethren, you entertain any opinion respecting the power of man, which overlooks the doctrine of our entire dependence on Christ; if you give place to the idea, that you have *of yourselves* an ability, to do anything spiritually good, without the help of God's grace; — you are certainly off the line of divine truth. You have departed from the standard of God's word. Your inward thought on the subject is not like that of the inspired writers; your language is not like their language, and your feelings are not like theirs.

This I lay down as a test of the truth or falsehood of any opinion which may be maintained in regard to the subject in hand. If the opinion is such as naturally works in with what the sacred writers teach respecting our weakness and dependence; if it leads us to feel as they felt, to speak as they spake, and to pray as they prayed; then we have reason to believe the opinion is right. But if the opinion does not harmonize with the obvious teachings of the inspired writers; if it renders important parts of the Bible unwelcome and strange to us, and if its real tendency is to make us feel and speak differently from prophets and apostles; then, however plausible the opinion may be, we are sure it is untrue.

It is very clear, that we ought to endeavor to bear fruit and that we ought actually to bear fruit; but not separate from Christ. We should certainly attempt to do our duty. But we should not attempt to do it, without Christ, because in this way, we cannot do it. Such an attempt besides being unsuccessful, would be sinful. As God has pointed out the way, and the only way, in which we are to do the work that he has assigned to us; it would certainly be offensive to him if we should neglect the way which he has prescribed, and attempt to accomplish the work in another way. Such an attempt would imply an ungrateful disregard of divine goodness; a contempt of that everlasting strength which is offered to us.

Such an attempt would betray a state of mind directly contrary to our prayers. If we pray as we ought, we acknowledge our own impotence and insufficiency, and seek divine help. Now to confide in our own sufficient power, and to attempt to do the work assigned to us, without strength from above, is a virtual contradiction to our prayers. It must then be either that we do not pray with sincerity; or that we pray with one state of mind, and act with another; that we pray humbly, and act proudly; that in prayer we are sensible of our moral impotence, and then act without any sense of impotence; that we pray in faith, and act without faith; that when we pray, we are conscious that we can do nothing without Christ, and that when we act, we contradict all this, and think we can do everything without him.

Once more. Our attempting to do anything without Christ will certainly prevent the success of our labors. Christians know to their own shame, how many times their efforts have proved unsuccessful, because they have trusted in themselves, and endeavored to do their duty in their own strength. Let us then guard against pride and self-confidence, and keep steadily in mind, that we are not sufficient of ourselves for any part of the work assigned to us, and that all holiness and all blessedness, here and hereafter, must come from him in whom all fulness dwells.

A SERMON

DELIVERED IN THE CHAPEL OF THE THEOLOGICAL SEMINARY, ANDOVER, FEB. 16, 1845.

Titus 1: 15.—UNTO THE PURE ALL THINGS ARE PURE: BUT UNTO THEM THAT ARE DEFILED AND UNBELIEVING IS NOTHING PURE; BUT EVEN THEIR MIND AND CONSCIENCE IS DEFILED.

THE Apostle here suggests a general principle, namely, *that the manner in which anything affects us depends upon the state of our minds.* If our minds are pure, the things we contemplate will be pure — pure to us; that is, will produce a pure effect upon us — will excite pure thoughts and pure emotions. But if our minds are impure, then whatever comes before us will be the occasion of defilement — will excite impure thoughts and feelings. The impurity or purity is really in *ourselves;* and the influence of other things is only to give it action. The Apostle in another Epistle applies this principle to things which in their own nature are indifferent, and teaches us, that nothing of this kind is "unclean of itself," and that whatever of uncleanness or defilement there is, comes from ourselves. Our Saviour also brought this principle into view, when he reproved the Pharisees for making so much of external purity while they disregarded purity of heart, and told them to do their duty, and "all things" would be "*clean to them.*"

My object is to illustrate the *general principle* suggested by the text. And in order that you may come directly to right views of this principle, fix upon two men, one of them in a right state of mind, the other in a wrong state; one pure in heart, the other impure; and let these two men represent the two classes into which mankind are divided, the holy, and the unholy; and then contemplate the manner in which the two men are affected by the objects to which they direct their attention. It is not however to be supposed, that the different thoughts and emotions, of which I speak, belong to all the individuals of each of the two classes in the same form, or in the same degree. My position is, that the exercises of each class are of the *same nature.*

The proposed illustration will require me to touch upon several particular cases.

Begin then with those things with which we are most familiar; and consider how differently an ungodly, worldly man, and a devout Christian, are affected by *the interests and enjoyments of the present life.* The worldly man is affected by these things in a *worldly manner;* that is, he has worldly feelings. And these feelings, which are morally impure, arise from the impurity of his heart. But in view of the same interests and enjoyments, very different thoughts and feelings arise from the pure heart of the devout Christian. The worldly man and the devout Christian often engage in the same pursuits; they mingle in the same scenes, and partake of the same pleasures. But the one carries with him a selfish, worldly frame of mind; the other a spiritual frame. The one supremely loves himself, and seeks his own pleasure and honor; the other loves God, and aims to please and honor him. And as they are thus different from each other in heart, all the pursuits and interests of the world affect them in a different manner.

The principle under consideration may be illustrated by referring to cases which occur in the common course of human affairs. Go to the family of the first king of Israel, and let Saul and his son Jonathan represent the two classes of men; Saul ungodly, proud and selfish; Jonathan sincere, benevolent and pious. How differently were they affected towards David! The blameless and lovely character of the son of Jesse and his growing reputation excited the jealousy and hatred of Saul; but the same things excited complacency and joy in the heart of Jonathan. How did it happen that Saul treated David as he did? There was no fault in David. He was a faithful servant and a dutiful son-in-law. Why did Saul hate him, and try to destroy him? It was because Saul had a selfish, envious, wicked heart. He hated David for the very same reasons, for which Jonathan loved him. They both saw that he was a virtuous youth, that he was rising in influence, and had a prospect of attaining to the kingdom. This roused the bitterest feelings and the most violent and murderous designs in the heart of Saul. David was *hateful* to him, because he had an envious, malignant *heart*. But Jonathan loved David because he had a benevolent heart, the heart of a friend and brother. And he rejoiced in David's promotion, though he knew it would displace him from the kingdom.

As a still more striking illustration, take the character of Jesus, and the influence it had upon the mind of John, and upon the mind of a self-righteous, ungodly Priest. In the view of John, it was clothed with consummate beauty and excellence. In the view of the ungodly Priest, it had no form or comeliness. In the mind of the sincere disciple, it excited love and confidence. In the mind of the self-righteous Priest, it excited feelings of aversion and hostility. To the pure mind of John the character of Christ was perfectly pure. But infinite purity itself was not pure to the mind of the ungodly Priest. His heart, already defiled with selfish, worldly passions, showed its defilement more and more by coming into contact with an object, which was so uncongenial to his disposition.

The same principle is made manifest in the different thoughts and feelings of men respecting the *appetites* and *passions* which prove temptations to sin. The selfish, ungodly man says with a complaining spirit, why has God given us these strong appetites and passions, when he knew they would be the occasion of so much mischief? Why has he placed us in a condition, which clothes vice with such attractions and renders the practice of virtue so difficult? Why has he left us in such a state, that we need something above human power to make us holy and happy? *Why has God made us thus?* Such are the thoughts and feelings which are apt to arise in the selfish, carnal heart. Such are the bitter waters which flow from this bitter fountain.

How different the thoughts and feelings of the man who has a pure heart and a right spirit. *Who am I,* he says, *that I should reply against God?* "Shall the thing formed say to him that formed it why hast thou made me thus?" If such a man could himself see no goodness or justice in this divine proceeding, he would still bow submissively to the unsearchable wisdom of God, and say, "even so Father, for so it seemed good in thy sight." But, in that very constitution of man, which is so often made a matter of complaint against God, the intelligent Christian finds clear evidence of divine benevolence. For he well knows, that his natural appetites and passions, when unperverted, and regulated as they should be, are sources of pure and virtuous enjoyment; and that, if he were without them, he would be incapable of some of the best earthly pleasures, and would be wholly unfit for the present life. And suppose that the proper government of his passions costs him a *great sacrifice.* He cheerfully makes the sacrifice, for the sake of testifying his reverence and love to his Saviour and giving glory to his name. He says welcome self-denial, welcome the cross, if I may thereby honor God, and acquire a greater conformity to his holy law.

But the good man takes still another view of the subject. That his natural inclinations are so headstrong and so hard to be restrained, he considers his own fault. The passions of Jesus were not violent and ungovernable. And he knows that his own would not have been so, had he always regulated them according to the will of God, and kept himself free from the disorder of sin. Sin, and all the waywardness and turbulence of the passions which accompany it or flow from it, he ascribes not to God, but to himself.

When the selfish, worldly man looks at the evils of the present life, and reads what the Scriptures teach of the endless sufferings of the world to come; his feelings are disturbed. He asks, why there should be so dreadful a punishment for such offences. No arguments can satisfy him of the justice of God in the *evils* endured in *this* world, much less the everlasting miseries of the future state.

But this whole subject comes with a very different aspect before the mind of a humble, devout Christian. Perhaps *he* also once made objections to the present and future punishment of sin. But his objections have vanished. He has, in some measure, a just conception of the intrinsic evil and hatefulness of sin, and is fully satisfied that the punishment which God *now* inflicts, and which he threatens to inflict *hereafter*, is no more than equal to the demerit of transgressors. So far as the present life is concerned, he rather wonders that so dreadful an evil as sin is not visited with a severer retribution. And if at any time he finds that the endless misery which is to come upon the wicked has a greatness and a dreadfulness, which is incomprehensible and overwhelming, he sees also that sinning against God is an evil of incomprehensible greatness. And while he is totally unable by his own reason to measure the evil of sin, or the dreadfulness of the threatened punishment, and is of course unable to make out the exact correspondence of the one with the other; he believes they *are* correspondent; and from the infinite perfection of God, he certainly concludes that no sinner in this world or in the next ever endures a punishment which is beyond his desert, or which perfect justice and goodness do not require.

There is no subject on which different individuals have had views and feelings more at variance with each other, than the *existence of evil*, particularly *moral* evil. The unbeliever, the caviller, has objections against what is a plain matter of fact, and against the righteous government of God in regard to it. He goes back to the first human sin; and with a complaining spirit he asks why God gave so strict, and so unnecessary a prohibition to our first parents; and why he affixed a penalty so dreadful for such an offence; and why he left them exposed to so artful and powerful an enemy; and why he did not interpose for their safety?—He complains too of the fact, so clearly stated by the Apostle, and so fully confirmed by the history of the world, that the character and state of Adam's posterity were inseparably connected with his own. How is it possible, he says, to reconcile it with perfect benevolence or righteousness, that by the offence of one the whole human family should be brought into existence in such a state, that sin and ruin will certainly be the result, unless prevented by an extraordinary act of mercy? Thus the carnal mind replies against God, and finds fault with his providence;—turns away from the light of divine truth, and shrouds itself in the darkness of error and sin. To such a man, nothing in the great scheme of God's government appears right. He sees in it no marks of wisdom or goodness.

But when the Christian, in a humble, devout frame of mind, contemplates the same scheme of moral and providential government, how widely different are the exercises of his mind and heart! He is free from the darkness of error and sin, and has within him the light of the knowledge of the glory of God. In the history of our first parents, and of the whole conduct of God towards them before and after their fall, the good man sees clear evidence of divine wisdom, holiness and benevolence. As to the conduct of God relative to the *existence of moral evil*, the man who has a child-like temper and receives instruction from the word and spirit of God, has no disquietude—no want of satisfaction. The pillar of cloud, which is all gloominess and terror to others, is to him, a pillar of fire shedding a clear and brilliant light.

In the dark region of this earth, there are innumerable misty speculations and misconceptions hanging around this subject; and the carnal mind seizes upon them, and in its madness holds them fast, as though they were an invaluable possession. But the light which comes from heaven reveals precious, golden truths in relation to this subject. These truths attract the good man's eager attention. They enlighten his eyes. They quiet and comfort his heart. And what are those precious truths which so fully occupy his mind, as to banish all bewildering and restless thoughts? I will tell you what they are.

The first of these truths is, that sin, whether found in Paradise or in any other part of the earth, is to be wholly ascribed to *man*, as *his fault*. Transgression of the law is man's act entirely. All that God does in reference to sin or sinners, is pure, benevolent and wise. And for all the agency which he exercises, he is worthy to be exalted and praised. God is light, and in him is no darkness at all. God is holy, and in him is no unholiness. God is pure; and though he is so conversant with a world of sinners, and is so near to them, he is still perfectly pure. Among us, sin is contagious. *We* contract pollution from our intercourse with the polluted. But God possesses infinite and unchangeable purity. *This* is one of the good man's precious truths. His God is a God of immutable holiness. It is man that does wrong. *He* is the sinner. *His* is the criminality, the shame, the ill-desert, and the righteous punishment.

Another of the truths which the good man holds so dear, is, that God, in his wonderful working providence, will cause the wrath of man to praise him. He will make sin the occasion of good. And the good he will accomplish by means of sin is *boundless*. This begins to appear in the present world, and will appear more and more clearly forever, particularly in the work of redemption. Now the man of a right spirit rejoices that, while sin is so criminal in its nature and so pernicious in its tendency, God will overrule it for good. This good is God's work; and the man who is pure in heart rejoices in it. He contemplates with pleasure the everlasting good which will be educed from the evil of sin. Amid all the shame and sorrow which he feels on account of the prevalence of moral evil in himself and in the world, the holy government of God is light and joy to his soul.

But there is one more truth in this case, which the good man receives and binds to his heart; namely, that there is a way in which he may be delivered from the evil of sin. Instead, therefore, of wasting his time in endeavoring to solve insolvable difficulties, he gives himself to the great business of salvation; resolved that whatever may be left undone, he will incessantly apply himself to that gracious Saviour who came to redeem men from all iniquity, and will strive, through the help of the divine Spirit, to obtain deliverance from that abominable thing which God hates. This warfare against sin, and this earnest endeavor after deliverance from it becomes the business of his life, and the powers of his mind are comparatively turned off from other objects, and centered upon this. This doctrine of redemption, this opening of a new and living way of deliverance from sin, is, to the good man the crowning gospel truth which he counts worthy of all acceptation. It is a pillar of fire, a resplendent light, directing his way through the wilderness to the promised land. But to the carnal reasoner, this resplendent light is a dark, bewildering cloud. To him nothing is pure. There is nothing in the character and government of God, or in gospel salvation, which sheds light or comfort upon him, because his evil passions have blinded his eyes, and his heart is not right with God.

But other examples crowd upon us, affording clear illustrations of the same principle. Let then the two persons, before introduced, that is, the man of a proud, carnal mind, and the man of a humble, spiritual mind, contemplate the peculiar doctrines of Christianity; the doctrine that all men are naturally dead in sin, without any love to their Creator or their Redeemer; the doctrine that there is a door opened for their salvation, but that they refuse to enter in, that none will ever come to Christ, unless they are drawn of the Father; the doctrine that man must be born again, or he cannot see the kingdom of heaven; that this new birth is not of man, but of God; that God does not bestow the gift of his regenerating Spirit for any works or worthiness of ours, but according to his own purpose and grace; the doctrine that redeemed sinners are required to obey God and abound in good works not to purchase forgiveness and salvation, which are entirely of grace, but to testify their love and gratitude to their God and Saviour, and to do good to their fellow men; that those who would attain to the blessedness of heaven must all their days maintain a conflict with sin, and endure afflictions, and must forever feel and acknowledge, that the glory of their salvation belongs exclusively to God; let the two persons representing the two classes into which mankind are divided, turn their attention to these doctrines of revelation, and others allied to them; and how different will be the exercises of their minds! To the pure the whole system of divine truth will be pure; but to him that is defiled nothing will be pure.

Just glance at some of the more prominent parts of the gospel system. Present then the doctrine of redemption. Hold forth the exalted character of the Son of God, his incarnation, his instructions, his atoning blood, his spiritual kingdom, and the work of grace which he is executing in the salvation of his people. How does all this appear to the man of a carnal, self-complacent mind? How did the character and work of Christ appear to the unbelieving Jew and to the conceited Greek? To the one it was an offence; to the other, foolishness. To the ungodly man at the present day, it is often both an offence and foolishness. The whole range of gospel doctrines is unwelcome to him. It excites either his enmity or his contempt, often both. He sees no divine excellence in the character of Christ. He sees no necessity for his humiliation and death. He sees no such malignity and ill-desert in sin, as to make such a sacrifice necessary to our salvation. The doctrine of Christ crucified, which is invested with such glories to the believer, has no glory to his eyes, and no attractions to his heart. The precepts of Christ require what he is unwilling to do, and forbid what he is unwilling to forego. If this glorious gospel is urged upon him as a matter of personal obligation, calling for his faith and submission; his unsubdued heart rises against it, and utters or conceals the fatal determination, *that Christ shall not reign over him*. When the scheme of revelation is fairly presented before him, he turns away from the whole and every part of it. Pure, spiritual, holy Christianity is utterly distasteful to his impure, earthly mind.

But how different is the fact with the man, who has a *pure, spiritual mind!* To him the plan of redemption is divine beauty and excellence throughout. Nothing in the whole compass of thought can be compared with it. He looks with admiration upon the works of creation, and joins with the Psalmist in exclaiming;

"Great and marvellous are thy works." He has a relish for whatever is suited to the intellect or the taste. But the wonders of creation, and even the divine glories manifested by them, all fade away before *the higher glory of God in the face of Jesus Christ.* The very *name* of *Christ* has a sacred charm in it, and kindles the purest, sweetest emotions in his heart. Christ is all his salvation, and all his desire. He sees the necessity of Christ's being a propitiation for sinners by dying in their stead, in order that the divine character and law may be vindicated, and that God may be just, while he justifies them who believe. The grace of Christ appears to him all-sufficient, and his commands holy, just, and good. The yoke of Christ, so grievous to others, is easy to him, and his burden light. He cordially submits to Christ's authority. His pride and selfishness have been cast down from their throne, though not yet destroyed; and he takes a low place before God, and desires one still lower. He is resolved to make constant war against in-dwelling sin, till it is utterly destroyed, and to labor and strive till he attains to that complete moral purity to which he so ardently aspires.

Take another illustration from the doctrine of *divine sovereignty* in the dispensation of grace. This doctrine is exceedingly annoying to a proud, self-righteous person. There is no end to the objections which he brings against it. The distinctions which God constantly makes among men in regard to their *earthly* condition often disturbs his feelings. But that God should, in a sovereign way, choose some to salvation in distinction from others, where all are alike ill-deserving, is a doctrine which he cannot think of without dissatisfaction. But to the man who knows himself and loves God, the doctrine is full of comfort. In his view, it furnishes the only ground of hope for any of our sinful race. And he renders hearty thanks to God, who in his wonderful love has chosen him, who was by nature a child of wrath, to be an heir of eternal life.

But I cannot dilate further on this subject. The principle is plain; and it is universal. The perfections and government of God, and the character and work of Christ, his just commands, his holy doctrines, his spiritual kingdom, the work of his Spirit, the ways of divine providence, what God does, and what he does not do, — all these are repulsive to the carnal mind; but they are attractive to the spiritual mind; — all light to the one; all darkness to the other; — all harmony and beauty to the one; all jargon and deformity to the other. This fact is not always brought out clearly to view. The good man is not perfectly good. His heart is pure, but not entirely so. Divine things are presented before him, but their excellence are seen only in part, because he is purified only in part. He has not all the holy thoughts and emotions which proceed from a perfectly holy mind. And it is a fact also, that the repugnance of the unsanctified man to divine things is not always apparent, and, in this world, never perfectly so, because he is never free from checks and hinderances, and never has a perfectly clear view of divine things. But there is a time at hand, when divine objects will be seen as they are, and when the alienation and enmity of the unsanctified heart will be fully acted out. At the judgment day Christ will sit upon the throne of his glory, and all nations stand before him. Then the infinite perfections of God, the glory of Christ, the wonders of grace in redemption, the excellence of divine truth, the holiness and blessedness of heaven, — the whole range of spiritual objects will be presented in a light above the brightness of noon-day. How pure, how lovely, how glorious will the august scene be to those who are pure in heart! How will they hail the happy day! What holy raptures will the sight of those objects kindle in their souls! What a heaven will it be to them to see Christ as he is, and to be with him, and to know that they shall be with him forever. Oh! what a home will this be to those who have been strangers and pilgrims on earth! What perfect rest will they find in the bosom of God!

But what will be the condition of those who come to that great day with an unregenerate, unholy heart? In all that bright scene, there will be no bright spot to them. In all that display of divine excellence and glory, no excellence or glory will strike their eyes. A universe of spiritual beauty and loveliness is before them, and every holy heart beats high with love and delight. But they see no beauty, and feel no delight. Let them be brought to the very gate of the heavenly Jerusalem, and let them look in upon that heavenly light before which the sun is ashamed to show his face. That glorious light of heaven is all dark, dark, dark to them. They have no eyes to see the light which shines there. They have no heart to love the God who reigns there. They have no taste for the joy that fills the holy there. Let them be thrust into the heavenly Jerusalem. They would find nothing to love; nothing to enjoy. The happiness of heaven would be misery to them. They would choose to die, rather than to live. And if they *must* live, they would choose to live any-where on the earth, or under the earth, or to be carried away swiftly beyond the bounds of God's creation, rather than dwell there, amid the praises and joys of heaven, so uncongenial and painful to their feelings.

My hearers, we have now turned our thoughts upon some of the interesting objects and movements of this probationary state, and to the developments here made of the holy and the unholy heart; and we have come to the final result of the present life, a result so *happy*, and so *miserable*, that language is too poor to describe it. And now as I close, I entreat you to look seriously at two things. First, look at *sin;* and see what it *is*, and what it *does*. Men in general think sin has but little evil in it, and that it does little or no hurt. They even love it and cherish it, as though it were excellence itself. But it is immeasurably evil in itself, and is the source of all other evils. There is nothing in the universe so hateful, — nothing so pernicious. Indeed, there is nothing else, which is either hateful or pernicious. All that is vile, abominable and destructive lies in the bosom of sin. All those plagues which have come upon the world from age to age, tell you of the evil there is in sin. But they do not tell you all its evil. The miseries of hell will tell this, and will be telling it forever. Look seriously upon this hateful thing, which the Apostle tried to describe, but could do no more than to call it "*exceedingly sinful.*" This is the evil which has seized upon man, and has diffused its deadly poison through his soul. It has blinded his eyes to spiritual beauty. It has made his heart dead to holy joy. Were it not for *sin*, it would be *heaven everywhere*, because God is everywhere. But sin has changed the scene, so that the glorious presence of God causes misery instead of happiness, to the alienated heart. This is the plague, which in an evil hour entered Paradise, and which reigned from Adam to Moses, and from Moses to Christ, and from Christ to the present day; an evil which has bred all other evils; an evil so powerful in mischief, that it has required a mighty effort of omnipotence itself to restrain its malignant power, and to prevent it from destroying all the good in the universe.

Look now at one thing more. You have seen what is that evil which dwells in man; how it defiles his spiritual nature, hardens his heart, turns light into darkness, purity into impurity, and alienates the soul from God and from heaven. Now why do not all, who have this evil dwelling in them, feel the wretchedness of their condition; and why do they not inquire, with the deepest solicitude, whether there is any effectual remedy? And if there is, why do they not desire and seek it with all their heart? My hearers, a merciful God has provided a remedy, and the gospel sets it before you. It is "*the renewing of the Holy Ghost.*" He who came to save sinners, says: "*Ye must be born again.*" The regenerating work of the Spirit,—who can describe its worth? It takes away pollution, and makes the heart pure. It renders the character and the supreme dominion of God, and all the ways of his providence, welcome and joyful. It prepares man to be happy in any place, *where God is.* "Blessed are the pure in heart; for they shall see God." This will be the consummation of their blessedness. Their pure heart will be filled with all the fulness of God. Oh! the preciousness of this renewing, cleansing, sanctifying Spirit! The wealth of worlds has no value compared with it. And Christ and heaven will be no joy to us without it. Let all then, with one accord, hasten to the throne of grace, and there prostrate themselves before God in humble, earnest prayer for the precious gift of the Holy Spirit, to cleanse them from the defilement of sin, and to make them *pure in heart.*

A SERMON

DELIVERED IN THE CHAPEL OF THE THEOLOGICAL SEMINARY, ANDOVER, JUNE 21, 1846.

John 14: 28.—IF YE LOVED ME, YE WOULD REJOICE BECAUSE I SAID, I GO TO THE FATHER; FOR MY FATHER IS GREATER THAN I.

John 16: 7.—NEVERTHELESS, I TELL YOU THE TRUTH: IT IS EXPEDIENT FOR YOU THAT I GO AWAY; FOR IF I GO NOT AWAY, THE COMFORTER WILL NOT COME UNTO YOU; BUT IF I DEPART, I WILL SEND HIM UNTO YOU.

WHEN the time drew near, in which the Saviour was to finish his work on earth and return to the Father, and when he had distinctly told his disciples that he was about to go away from them; it is no wonder that sorrow filled their hearts. How grievous must have been the thought, that their Lord was soon to depart from them, and to leave them alone, poor and powerless, and exposed to dangers on every side. He apprised them of the trials and sufferings which they were to encounter. On the other hand, he took care to guard them against excessive sorrow and dejection. How encouraging and consoling were the instructions he gave them, first, in the upper room, where he instituted the sacred Supper; and then, in the garden, where he had so often met them, and where he then met them for the last time. There were *two points* which he distinctly suggested to them, for the express purpose of reconciling them to his approaching departure. In the first of these, he appealed to *their love for him;* in the second to *their regard to their own good.*

First; to reconcile his disciples to his absence, Jesus appealed to their *affection for him.* "If ye *loved* me," i. e. if ye loved me with an enlightened and consistent love, "ye would rejoice because I said, I go to the Father; for my Father is greater than I." The argument is, that Christ's going to the Father would raise him to a condition of higher glory and blessedness, than what belonged to him on earth. In coming to this world, he had divested himself of the glory which he had with the Father before the world was. His state on earth was a state of *dishonor;* for he was despised and rejected of men. It was a state of poverty. He was made poor for our sakes; — so poor that he had not where to lay his head. It was a state of suffering. Through his whole life, and especially at its close, he was a man of sorrows and acquainted with grief. Such, and more than I can describe, was the dishonor, the degradation and the suffering, to which Jesus was subjected in his earthly state. And if his disciples *loved* him as they ought, they must have sympathized with him while he endured so many sufferings, and must have rejoiced that he was soon to be delivered from them, and to be exalted to a state of unspeakable honor and blessedness at the right hand of God. The Father's being greater than the Son, seems evidently to refer to his being in that higher state, that state of *superior glory,* into which Jesus was to enter when he should leave the world and go to the Father.* The happy change which was to take place in the condition of Jesus — change from a lower to a higher state — from ignominy to glory — from pain and sorrow to celestial blessedness, must have been a matter of heart-felt joy to all his friends. How do Christians *now* rejoice when they consider that their Saviour has been delivered from all the evils he endured here below, and that he is highly exalted, and has received a name which is above every name. You cannot

* The Greek word μείζων, rendered "greater," has this meaning in some other places; and in this place such a sense of the word is required in order to give consistency and intelligible force to the passage.

forget what your Saviour suffered on earth. But you rejoice that he will suffer no more; that he has gone through the painful service which he undertook for us, and now inherits the fulness of heavenly felicity. *This* was the subject of joy which Jesus suggested to his disciples. He was then in a low suffering condition; but he was soon to go to his Father, and to partake with him of all that was exalted and glorious in the heaven of heavens. *What* could reconcile his disciples to his absence, if not such a consideration as this? And those same disciples who listened to this last discourse of Jesus, have for many happy ages, been with him in his exalted state, and know better than we can, what reason all the friends of Christ have to rejoice, that he has been delivered from his state of humiliation and enjoys the glory which he had with the Father before the world was.

The other consideration which Jesus suggested to his disciples in order to reconcile them to his absence, related to *their own spiritual interest.* "It is expedient for you that I go away." This is the point which is more particularly to occupy our attention.

In consequence of Christ's humiliation and suffering, God highly exalted him, and gave him a name which is above every name. This state of exaltation carried with it a higher and more glorious agency in accomplishing the work of saving his people, and in conducting all the affairs of his kingdom. The work which the Mediator had undertaken was a work of indescribable magnitude and importance. And he could carry forward this great work better in the courts above, than in any condition below; better on his throne, than on his footstool. The earth was the place appointed for him to humble himself, and to die for the sins of men. Heaven was the place for him to reign, and to exercise his power and mercy in the complete salvation of his people. The earth was a fit place for him to enter on the work of saving the lost. But to exercise his almighty agency as Lord of the universe, he must have a larger place and a higher position, than this earth could afford. It was then no want of love to his disciples that influenced him to leave the world and go to the Father. Far from it. His object was to exercise his benevolence in larger measures, and to promote the welfare of his people more effectually, than he could do, if he should remain on earth.

But we must attend chiefly to the particular point mentioned in the text.

At first view we might find it difficult to understand why it could be expedient for his disciples that Jesus should depart from them; that after he had been with them long enough to make them sensible of the value of his presence, and to gain their strongest affection and confidence, he should go away and leave them to mourn that they should see his face no more. You, brethren, have never enjoyed the bodily presence of Christ. But have you not often wished that you *might* have this privilege. Have not your hearts sometimes burned within you at the thought of his making a visit to you, as he often did to Lazarus and his sisters? How precious would the opportunity be! Especially when you have come to the table of your Lord, have you not sometimes spontaneously said in your hearts, O! what a privilege it would be, to behold the blessed Jesus himself — with our own eyes to see him before us, and with our own ears to hear him bless the bread and say, as he did to his disciples, *take, eat; this is my body which is broken for you; this do in remembrance of me.* One such opportunity with your blessed Lord, you may think, would be more precious to you, would excite your sorrow for sin, your faith, your hope, and your joy, and strengthen you for your spiritual warfare more effectually, than all the religious privileges you have ever enjoyed.

But Jesus assured his disciples that there was something better than all this; and their experience confirmed the truth of his declaration. They were really better off after his departure, than before. They had clearer knowledge, stronger faith, and *more fervent love.* They were more willing to labor and suffer for Christ. And they had purer joys. While Christ abode with them, they had not attained to the happy state of those to whom Peter afterwards said: "*Whom* having not seen, ye love; in whom, though now ye see him not, yet believing, *ye rejoice with joy unspeakable, and full of glory.*"

Now the ground of all this improvement in the condition of the disciples after Christ's departure, is set before us in the text. "It is expedient for you that I go away: *for if I go not away, the Comforter will not come unto you: but if I depart, I will send him unto you.*"

There are two things in particular, which are here to be considered.

First. It was the divine appointment in the economy of redemption,—that *the period following the humiliation and death of Christ*, that is, *the period of his exaltation and glory*, *should be marked with the dispensation of the Holy Spirit in a far higher degree than any period before.* God had previously given his Spirit to sanctify and guide his people. But the latter period was to be distinguished by a work of the Spirit, *far wider in extent and far higher in degree*, than was ever experienced before. This dispensation of the Spirit was so superior to what had been enjoyed under the previous dispensation, that, in the free language of the sacred writers, it is often spoken of as though it were a new thing — as though nothing of the kind had ever been experienced before. Thus also it is said, that life and immortality were brought to light by the gospel; as though they had not been known before. In all such cases, the language of Scripture is to be understood *comparatively*. The repeated declaration of Christ to his disciples, that he would send the Holy Spirit as their advocate and comforter, is unquestionably to be taken in this sense. He would send the Spirit in more *abundant measures.* Many texts represent the gift of the Spirit as peculiar to the new dispensation, as the great blessing of the Christian church; and some texts speak of it as though it were the blessing of the Christian church *only*. But all these texts are to be taken in the sense above suggested. The Holy Spirit was really given to enlighten and sanctify men during the life of Christ. It was however given only in small measures. Few comparatively were sanctified, and the faith and love of those few were less in degree than afterwards. Look at the day of Pentecost. The peculiar promises respecting that more abundant influence of the Spirit began then to be fulfilled, as the Apostle Peter set forth at the time. Now when during the life of Christ, or in any previous period, was there such a work of divine grace? When were three thousand sinners turned to God in a day? And when and where did anything take place under the former economy, like the spread of the gospel and the renewal of men to holiness, at Corinth, at Ephesus, and in a multitude of other places? I might point you also to the conversion of sinners and the spread of the gospel in modern times. What was the most successful work of proselyting Gentiles to the Jewish religion, compared with the work of the Spirit since Christ was glorified?

Thus Christ did indeed send the Holy Spirit *after his departure*, as he had never done before; and this superior dispensation of the Spirit has been the distinguishing mark of the state of the church since the Redeemer was exalted to his throne in the heavens.

Secondly; this more abundant influence of the Spirit, is of far *higher value to Christians, than the bodily presence of Christ*, so that it is *really expedient that he should be absent from them, that he might send them that richer gift.*

Followers of Jesus, I tell you the truth. A higher privilege is granted you, than the *personal presence* of your Saviour. For after all, what did such presence of Jesus really *do* for his disciples? Did it make them holy, to see his face, and hear his voice, and touch him with their hands? Did his visible presence and his free intercourse with them subdue their pride and unbelief, and make them meek and lowly in heart? Were they as constant in their adherence to him, and as ready to do and to suffer in his cause, and were they as spiritually minded and happy, as they were *after* the more abundant effusion of the Spirit? And how would it be with Christians now? You may imagine that, if you could have Jesus personally present, and enjoy his society, you should quickly overcome sin and live a heavenly life. But had you his bodily presence and nothing more, you would continue to be as unlike him, as you ever have been. Reliance upon this desired privilege would be sure to end in disappointment, just as your reliance upon outward privileges always has done. Consider then the subject in the light of truth. Through the mercy of God, you are placed under an economy which is marked by a more free and abundant influence of the Holy Spirit. The promised Guide and Comforter has come. When you retire for meditation and prayer, how great the privilege of Christ's bodily presence would be. But you have a greater privilege. And for the sake of this greater privilege, it is expedient for you to be without the other. — When called to difficult duties and trials, you may think, how great the favor would be, if you could see Jesus and converse with him, and seek of him the favors which you need. And a great favor it might indeed be. But you have a greater. — When you come to the sacred Supper, you may think, how unspeakable would be the favor, if you might see Jesus himself there, and might with your own eyes look upon him, and hear his voice, and might receive the bread and the wine from his own hands. And a great privilege this might indeed be. But my brethren, you have a privilege still greater. The illuminating, purifying, consoling influence of the Spirit, is of even more worth, than the visible presence of Jesus. Without that Spirit, the personal presence of Christ would avail nothing, and you would be as poor and miserable and wretched, as if there was no Saviour. But if that Spirit may be given you and dwell in you, you will be rich and happy, though your Redeemer reigns above the skies, where your "weak senses reach him not." You will love an unseen Saviour, you will see his glory, you will taste that he is good, and your joy will be full.

And if you do truly seek and receive that more full and powerful influence of the Holy Spirit, which belongs to the dispensation under which you live, you will really have the *presence of Jesus*. He will truly be with you in your retirement, and in the house of prayer, and on all other occasions, not indeed in a bodily sense, but in a higher and more scriptural *sense*, that is, *spiritually.** The eyes of your understanding will be opened, and you will see the transcendent excellence of your ascended Redeemer, and you will rejoice that he is gone from his suffering state on earth, and dwells on his throne on high. In the clear light which the Spirit will cause to shine within you, that high throne and he who sits upon it will be brought near you. The Son of God, the divine, Almighty Saviour will be present in reality and in truth; — present in the very sense which is most of all to be desired. You will have true spiritual converse with him. Your *heart* and your lips will speak to him, and you will know that he hears you. And he will hold converse with you, his very heart so full of love and sympathy, will speak to you, and his words will be life and peace. Oh! how blessed is the communion of believers with the present but unseen Saviour! Now thanks be to God that we live under this dispensation of the Holy Spirit, and that amidst the thousand precious blessings we enjoy, we may behold the glory of the Son of God, and have fellowship with him, and may so receive of his fulness, that we shall have no desire unsatisfied, no want unsupplied.

And, now, brethren, it is very important for us to inquire, what duty is incumbent on us in regard to the dispensation of the Spirit under which we are placed. This dispensation is certainly attended with greater advantages, than that which was enjoyed before the advent of Christ, or even during his abode on earth. It is therefore perfectly manifest, that it was expedient not only that the whole ritual service of the Mosaic economy should cease, but that Christ himself should leave the world and be exalted to his throne on high, thus making way, according to the unsearchable wisdom of God, for the Holy Spirit to come in his more abundant influences, and dwell with the followers of Christ. The important question for us is this: *how shall we secure to ourselves the peculiar benefits of the reign of Christ in heaven and the more abundant effusion of the Spirit under the present dispensation.*

---

* See Ephesians 3: 17. 1 John 3: 24. John 6: 56. 14: 21, 23. 17: 23. Rom. 8: 11. Col. 1: 27. Gal. 2: 20.

This dispensation is one of unparalleled mercy; and the blessings it brings are above all price. *By what means shall we secure those inestimable blessings to ourselves?*

On this point we may obtain some valuable information from the *recorded experience* of those who have, in a good measure, profitted by the present dispensation. See then in what way, the apostles and primitive Christians became partakers of the precious fruits of the Spirit; and how they and other eminent believers in after-times attained to that peculiar excellence of character and life which is the proper result of the dispensation of the Spirit.

On this point there has been a general agreement among eminent Christians. They have all had a deep conviction of the sinfulness and pollution of their hearts, which is the great evil to be remedied by the dispensation of the Spirit. They have been sensible of the necessity and the preciousness of this sanctifying work of the Spirit, and have earnestly prayed for it; and they have watchfully avoided all hinderances to it in their own hearts.

If then you would obtain the peculiar benefits of the present dispensation of the Holy Spirit, you must have a *deep conviction of your sinfulness and pollution*. *Sin* is the evil which it is the special work of the Spirit to remedy. It is primarily the disorder of the heart, though it shows itself in outward transgressions. When you entered on the life of piety, you began to know your sinfulness. But if you would arrive at an advanced state of piety, and would in any good degree be complete in all the will of God, you must have a growing conviction of the deceitfulness and desperate wickedness of your heart, so that you may abhor yourselves, and cry out, *Oh! wretched man that I am, who shall deliver me from the body of this death!* The low attainments of Christians generally are owing not a little to their defective views of the evil of their hearts. They who are the most holy, have the strongest conviction of the depth and malignity of the evil within them.

You must also be sensible how much you need the work of the Holy Spirit, and how precious that work is. Do you ask how much you must feel your need of this? I answer; you will never come to the right state, so long as you have any idea left that you can cure the evil in your heart by your own exertions. Here, Christians are frequently involved in a hurtful mistake. They are sensible of various sinful dispositions. But they have a secret feeling, that they are sufficient of themselves, to subdue them. They resolve to be rid of their sins; and their inward thought is, that their resolution will be effectual; and that they can put off their evil habits at *will*. This is a great mistake. It is a certain truth, and you must know it, that there is no power that can subdue your sins and cleanse your heart, but the power of the Holy Spirit.

You must be sensible of the great *value* of the work of the Spirit. You look at faith, love, humility, meekness, and all the other Christian graces, and you see their beauty and importance, and you say, how precious they are! You are drawn towards them. You long and pant for them as the hart panteth for the water brook.

And then, as a consequence of this earnest desire, you will engage in prayer for the Holy Spirit. You will go to God and ask for the gift of the Spirit, with a feeling that you cannot live without it. You will beg and plead for it as for the life of your soul. And if your petition is not granted at once, as is often the case, you will ask again; you will seek and knock, and will become more and more importunate, till you attain the blessing. Prayer is appointed, as the special means of securing the presence of the Holy Spirit, and of becoming partakers of all its fruits. And it will generally be successful in proportion to the strength and fervor of the desire which you feel for the blessing. If you pray for the Holy Spirit with groanings which cannot be uttered; if you desire it, as the covetous man desires wealth, and the ambitious man honor; you will not pray in vain. Such prayer availeth much. When children ask bread, a kind father will not give them a stone. And when they ask a fish, he will not give them a scorpion. And if an imperfect earthly father knows how to give good gifts to his children; how much more will your Father who is in heaven, and who is infinite in goodness, give his Holy Spirit to them that ask him. If your heart is truly set upon obtaining the indwelling of the Spirit; if you cry to God with unceasing earnestness, that he would bestow this invaluable blessing upon you; you will not fail of success. There never was a child of God, who turned his thoughts distinctly upon Christian love, joy, and peace, and the other fruits of the Spirit, and who desired them above all earthly good, and who looked to God for them with persevering importunity, —never was one who pursued this course, without obtaining the blessing desired. This is the way in which Christians have been gradually freed from the common faults and blemishes of character, and have been adorned with whatsoever things are true, honest, just, pure, lovely and of good report. The way is perfectly plain, in which not a few ministers and private Christians in every age, have become bright and shining lights. Christians of an *ordinary* character live in the same society; have the same Scriptures, and the same opportunities for prayer, and the same offer of God's abounding grace. Why then do they linger so far behind? Why remain with so little of the subduing, elevating, comforting influence of the Spirit? Verily, they are not straitened in God, but in themselves. They receive not, because they ask not. Their low attainments, their deficiencies and blemishes must be charged to their own sinful negligence. They might have been as holy, and they might have been as manifestly sealed for heaven by the Holy Spirit, as the apostles and martyrs were. God has said to them, Ask and it shall be given you. Open your mouth wide, and I will fill it.

But there is still another thing, which is as necessary as fervent desire and prayer; that is, that you should *watchfully avoid everything which would prove a hinderance to the work of the Spirit in your hearts.* The humble, contrite heart is the proper abode of the Spirit. But if you regard iniquity in your heart, if you allow yourself in known sin, either in your life or in your affections, you will grieve the Spirit, and hinder his sanctifying work. Here is the strange inconsistency which is often found among Christians.

They pray God to *purify* their hearts by his Spirit, and then they cherish *impure desires*. They pray that the Holy Ghost may dwell in them and make them *spiritually minded*, and they soon give place to the *carnal mind*. Now whatever is contrary to the nature and object of the Holy Spirit, whether in thought, word or deed, is a direct hinderance to his operation in the soul. How do you find it to be in your garden or field? *Weeds* which spring up and grow spontaneously, hinder the growth of the useful plant. Suppose the rain and the sun-shine come upon the plant. They come also upon the weeds which surround it. And if the weeds remain, they will grow faster than the useful plant, and will choke it, so that it will come to nothing. If you would have fruit you must clear away the weeds; not once, but constantly. So in the Christian life. Sinful thoughts and desires, and sinful words and actions, which are the natural product of the human heart, are direct hinderances to the sanctifying operation of the Spirit, and the growth of grace. Against all these you must watchfully guard, if you would have the work of the Holy Spirit advanced within you. You must labor to exclude them. You must overcome them. You pray for the sanctifying influence of the Spirit. But you might as well not pray, as to pray, and then do that which will prevent an answer to your prayer. Dear brethren, servants of the holy Jesus, let me beseech you to shun all the ways of sin, and to do the whole will of God. There is nothing else that you need to shun. There is nothing but sin, showing itself in your life, or lurking in your heart, that can be a hinderance to the increasing work of the Holy Spirit. There is nothing but sin that can offend and grieve the Spirit. That benignant Spirit can bear with your weakness, and with your innocent infirmities — yea, with infirmities which are not innocent, if you mourn for them and are humbled under them. The Spirit will not forsake you, because your natural affections and your attachment to things in themselves useful or harmless, are somewhat excessive, if you strive against that excess, He will not forsake you, because your heart has some remains of pride, or selfishness, or worldliness, or impurity, if you resist the evil, and loathe yourselves on account of it. He will not forsake you, because there is a law in your members warring against the law of your mind, and often bringing you into captivity — if you heartily condemn it, and cry for deliverance from it. But there is one thing and only one, which will cause the Spirit to depart from you, and that is, *allowed sin — living in sin.* If you open your heart to that hateful thing — if you embrace it — if you are content that it should remain, and wage no war against it; then, I forewarn you that the Spirit of God will be grieved, and his blessed influence will be quenched. That heavenly Visitant, will not be an inmate in a heart that loves sin. He will not afford his favorable presence with those whose settled habit it is to disobey the holy commands of the gospel. This it is, which will cause the heavenly Agent to depart. And if you do not find the Spirit dwelling in you, as his temple, and adding grace to grace, and comfort to comfort; then look for the cause in some abominable thing which his searching eye has seen you cherishing in your bosom. And if you have, in time past, lived in some good measure unto God, and have had evidence, from your growth in grace, that the Holy Spirit has not only come to you, but has made his merciful abode with you, working in you both to will and to do; and if after all this you now begin to be negligent of your spiritual concerns, and to comply with temptation, and to yield yourselves servants to unrighteousness; then, you may expect that want of life, that dreadful insensibility, darkness and desolation of soul, which are the certain consequences of the departure of the Holy Spirit. But how happy are they, who watchfully avoid whatever would grieve the Spirit and impede his work in sanctifying the heart. Only put away the hateful thing which resists his gracious sway within you; only remove the obstacles to his transforming influence; let the light from heaven shine upon you, and the dew and the rain from heaven water you; and how will all the humble and gentle virtues, and all the sublime and godlike virtues flourish! They are all the fruits of the Spirit; and they will grow and thrive in proportion as the Spirit blesses you with his presence. And with what pleasure will that Holy Spirit look upon that beauty which his own grace has put upon you. Brethren, if you "*walk in* the Spirit," you will find it easy to mortify the flesh with its affections and lusts — easy to let your light shine before men, that they may see your good works, and glorify your Father who is in heaven; — easy, in short, to be what those ought to be, who are so favored as to live under this higher and more glorious dispensation of the divine Spirit.

And now what remains but that we render constant thanks to God, that the day of gospel mercy is ours; that we hear these welcome truths, and behold these glorious objects. Jesus, who once visited this world on an errand of love, has gone to his celestial throne. But his departure was prompted by infinite benevolence, and secures to his followers the precious gift of the Holy Spirit in larger measures than had been enjoyed before. Under this higher influence of the Spirit, far more is done for the enlargement and prosperity of the church and the sanctification of individual believers, than had been done at any time before the ascension of Christ. And it is through this more powerful influence of the Spirit, that we behold the glory of our invisible Saviour. Though he has gone away from us in his bodily state, we truly enjoy his presence. He is indeed in heaven; but he is none the less here. We not only call to mind the wonderful events which took place during his humiliation, but we follow him to the courts above. In the exercise of a sanctified imagination and a believing heart, we behold him on his throne in the heavens. Through the influence of the indwelling Spirit his throne becomes the throne of grace to us; and we draw near to it, and find our Saviour there; and then we enjoy his presence. We want no images, no pictures, no wooden cross. Enlightened by the Spirit, we know and see the blessed Jesus without any such help as these. We are better without them. They are all too mean to set forth the excellence of our exalted Saviour. They obscure his glory. We prefer the substance to the shadow. We prefer the bright noon-day sun to the clouds that hide him from our view. Jesus promised to be with his disciples always to the end of the world. We deem it our happiness to enjoy his promised presence here, till we go to enjoy it more perfectly in the world above.

Thanks then to God, who gave his Son to die for us, and the Holy Spirit to guide and comfort us and make us partakers of his fulness. Thanks be to God for these unspeakable gifts.

A SERMON

DELIVERED IN THE CHAPEL OF THE THEOLOGICAL SEMINARY, ANDOVER, JULY 15, 1832.

Gal. 6: 14.—BUT GOD FORBID THAT I SHOULD GLORY, SAVE IN THE CROSS OF OUR LORD JESUS CHRIST, BY WHOM (BY WHICH) THE WORLD IS CRUCIFIED TO ME, AND I UNTO THE WORLD.

THE effect of the cross of Christ upon the believer is here set forth in very impressive figurative language. "The world is crucified to me." It is like one who is crucified and dead. It has lost its attractions. I have set my affections supremely on Christ; and, comparatively, I feel no interest in worldly things. The same idea is expressed, when it is said, the believer is *dead to the world*. The opposite is always implied, namely, that he is *alive unto God*. — The Apostle says also, "I am crucified to the world." That is, the world has lost its interest in me as a follower of Christ. It turns away from me as though I were a dead man. Thus the deadness is mutual. The world is crucified and dead to me, and I unto the world.

Here then we see what is the great fact in the gospel scheme, and what is its practical effect upon the followers of Christ. It is by means of the cross, that their hearts are withdrawn from the world and set upon spiritual and divine things.

But we must always keep in mind, that whatever efficacy is attributed to anything as a means or instrument, flows ultimately and entirely from the appointment and agency of God. It is he that worketh all in all. The influence of any truth is so far from superseding the work of the Holy Spirit, that it includes it, and depends upon it.

Let it also be kept in mind, that it is not the cross of Christ, considered literally and alone, which possesses the efficacy here mentioned. To obtain any just conception of this efficacy, we must consider the crucifixion of Christ in its high moral relations. We must consider it as a measure of the divine government; as related to God's holy law, and his spiritual empire. We must consider what displays the cross made of the holiness, the justice, and the grace of God; what aspect it had upon his righteous administration; what representation it made of the sin and ruin of man and the worth of the soul, and what character Christ himself exhibited, and in what relation he stood to sinners, when he endured the pains of crucifixion. When we view the cross of Christ in such lights as these, we attain to some just conceptions of the mighty efficacy ascribed to it in the text.

Here, brethren, we are taught the grand secret of the Christian life, that life which is hid with Christ in God. Here we have the principal means, by which believers subdue their sins, and obtain a conformity with God's perfect law. We have here the *principal* means, and, in an important sense, the *only* means of this. Other means in abundance have been invented and relied upon in pagan countries, and even in Christendom; but they have all proved to be in vain. And we are brought by the experience of ages, as well as by our own experience, and the word of God, to this conclusion, that the reformation of man's character and heart is to be effected chiefly by the cross of Christ. We can rely upon nothing separate from this. But the doctrine of the cross, accompanied with the divine blessing, has an unfailing efficacy. If there is anything which is really valuable in other means employed for the renovation of man; it is all found here. And as to the other means which God has appointed — it is their connection with the cross, and their being exhibited in this connection, that gives them their saving efficacy. Their efficacy is all comprised in the cross of Christ. Everything which has the nature of a motive, and everything which renders motives efficacious — everything which manifests the goodness and the authority of God — the excellence of his law — the evil of sin and the beauty of holiness — the value of eternal blessedness and the dreadfulness of eternal misery; in short, everything which can lead the sinner to repentance, and move the heart to gratitude and love, is found in the cross of Christ. And its being found here is the circumstance which gives it a true and saving efficacy. — Take the very same thing as exhibited in other ways; take, for example, the benevolence of God. Prove it, as you may, by general reasoning. Produce the evidence of it from the works of nature and providence. Unrenewed men may feel the weight of your arguments, and may be convinced that God is benevolent, and the conviction may excite their imagination to a pleasant activity. But their hearts are not subdued, and their love is not kindled. But when in the exercise of faith they look at the cross of Christ and see the benevolence of God displayed there; conscience is roused, love and gratitude are kindled, and the character is transformed.

Take another example, *the evil of sin.* From various considerations with which the science of ethics is familiar, you may clearly prove that sin is wrong in itself, and pernicious in its effects; — a disorder in the moral system — a perversion of our nature, and contrary to the purity and goodness of the Creator. But all this, presented merely in this light and proved in this manner, plays only upon the surface of the mind. It leaves the sinner coldly convinced, not savingly converted.

But let a man in the exercise of a lively faith, look to calvary; and learn the evil of sin *there.* Let him learn from the sufferings of the cross, how sin is regarded by a just and righteous God. Let him see what it brought upon the holy Saviour, and what it would have brought upon a world of sinners, had not he died in their stead. Let him judge of the evil of sin from the precious blood which was shed to atone for it. Now he is awakened from his lethargy. Now he finds, that all which the Scriptures declared, and all which the most terrible judgments of God declare, is a reality — that sin is indeed "*exceedingly* sinful." And placing himself by the side of the cross, he is ashamed and blushes to lift up his eyes to heaven, and with a broken heart cries, *God be merciful to me a sinner.*

Such are the effects produced by the doctrine of the cross, when apprehended by faith; and such the inefficacy of moral truth, contemplated in other ways.

The mere philosopher may reason correctly about abstract, speculative truth, and may please his imagination and his intellect with its harmony and sublimity; but he lives and dies under the bondage of sin. — The Christian contemplates the doctrine of Christ crucified, and the simple truths comprised in it, and contemplates them in the exercise of faith; — and behold! his fetters are loosened; he casts off the bondage of his corruptions, and enjoys the liberty of the sons of God.

How was it with the Apostle Paul? What did he do to bring men to repentance and obedience? He preached Christ crucified. That was the burden of his instructions. And he always referred to the death of Christ, when he would most powerfully enforce any moral precept. He regarded the doctrine of the cross as the substance and glory of divine truth; *the great motive*, the main-spring of action in the kingdom of grace. The Apostle had been a very learned reasoner in the science of morals and divinity before his conversion. A thousand moral and religious truths had passed before his mind, and had been made familiar to his thoughts; but they all left him an enemy to God. It was the sovereign efficacy of Christ crucified, which at last produced the renovation of his character; — it was this that turned him from pride and malice to humility and love — from persecution and murder, to a pious zeal for the glory of God, and a willingness to endure all things for the elect's safe.

The Apostle Paul was sent forth to convert the Gentile world, to turn them from their sins to serve the living God. In this great work, what means did he use? He used the very means which had been effectual in his own case. "He determined to know nothing, save Jesus Christ and him crucified;" — and his experience everywhere taught him, that *the preaching of the cross*, was made the power of God to salvation.

Now, brethren, I am happy to say to you, that the cross of Christ has lost none of its heavenly virtue. It can produce the same effects upon us, as it did upon the Apostle, and upon those to whom he preached. It is invested with a sanctifying power, which can never be exhausted. — This, I am sure, must be a welcome, precious truth to the humble and contrite in heart; — precious to all who mourn for sin, and pant after deliverance from it; to all who are burdened with remaining corruptions, and are looking for some almighty efficacy to subdue them. Hear then, and rejoice, ye humble souls, while I declare to you *the healing power*. Indulge no feelings of despondency as to your success in overcoming sin. Despondency *here* is utterly groundless and inexcusable. Suppose that you have a thousand times resolved against this and that sin, and all sin, and a thousand times endeavored to guard against it, but without success. Suppose you have been long and earnestly laboring, in various ways, to be rid of your spiritual diseases, but laboring in vain. What then? Was it not so with her, in the gospel, who tried many ways to be cured of her disorder, and spent all her living upon physicians, and yet grew nothing better, but rather worse? And how was she cured? She was cured, by applying to Jesus. And how has it been with multitudes, who have tried a variety of fruitless means to subdue sin and obtain purity of heart, but who have at last, in the simplest, easiest way, obtained success. And how have they obtained success? By looking to Jesus, — by believing in Jesus. This way is open to all. Let your hearts then swell with gratitude and joy, while I tell you, that there is a sovereign remedy for all the evils under which you labor. There is not a single spiritual disease, however inveterate — no, not one, which may not be cured — and which might not have been cured long ago, had you used the gospel remedy. Your spiritual maladies may be such as to baffle the skill of all other physicians, and may bid defiance to the highest human power. But there *is* a power, that can subdue them. There is a remedy, that always proves sure. Come then, ye who labor and are heavy laden — come to Calvary — come to the cross — come with humble confidence to Christ crucified, and he will give you rest.

The cross of Christ — I repeat the momentous truth — the cross of Christ, apprehended by faith, is the great and effectual means of subduing the power of sin, of overcoming the world, and growing in grace. It is the secret spring of a spiritual, holy, and useful life. And this, brethren, is sufficient by itself. It operates best alone. All means devised by the wisdom of man, are here unnecessary, and out of place. If there is any evil to be removed, by the cross of Christ, you may remove it. If there is any moral excellence to be obtained, by the cross you may obtain it. The humble, confiding Christian, who makes use of this simple, gospel means, is successful above others in resisting sin and in striving after sanctification. If then you should at any time be ready to yield to temptation and commit sin; I would not go about to dissuade you by arguments suggested by the wisdom of the world. I would point you to something of more certain efficacy. — *Look to the cross of Christ.* There see the holiness, the justice, and the mercy of God, the excellence of his law, and the exceeding sinfulness of transgression. There see the love of Christ, the atonement made by his precious blood, the worth of the soul, the necessity of obedience, and the holy nature of salvation. There see in blazing light, everything that can subdue and purify the heart — everything that can make sin in all its forms an object of perfect detestation. Could you but look with strong and habitual faith, to Christ crucified, the great work would be done. You would become dead to "all that is in the world," "the lust of the flesh, the lust of the eye, and the pride of life." Temptation would lose its power. And so awake would your conscience be, so pure and holy the frame of your mind, that you would rather be nailed to the cross, than to sin against God. — O Christians, could we but have that faith, which would make the cross of Christ a present reality, and keep us near it, and show us its glorious meaning and design; — could we but have that faith which would bring us as it were to live on Calvary, and to take up our abode at the foot of the cross; what blessed effects should we experience! *Love to Christ* would become our *ruling passion*, and would constrain us to live, and to labor, and suffer for his sake. And this sacred passion reigning within us, would be a strong bond of union among us; so that we should be of one mind and one heart; and all our intercourse with each other would be marked with forbearance and kindness. We should lay aside all malice, and guile, and envy, and evil speaking, and love one another with pure hearts fervently. Our supreme attachment to Christ crucified would withdraw us from all the pursuits and interests of worldly men. It would make us lowly in heart, circumspect, watchful, obedient. It would excite us to fear and avoid the very appearance of evil, to be diligent in doing good, to be holy, harmless, undefiled. And thus it would become manifest, that by living near to Christ crucified and beholding his glory, we had been changed into the same image.

We have seen, brethren, what Christianity was in the view of the great Apostle. We have seen what it was in its influence on *his* character, and on the character of those who received it from him. And thus we have seen what it is *to be Christians.* For Christ crucified is the same yesterday, to-day, and forever. And his religion is the same; and whenever it is received by faith, its influence is the same. It is not a subject which we may begin and end in mere speculation or mere belief. It is a subject which relates to feeling and to practice. It comes directly to the heart, and accomplishes its chief work there. — And if its transforming power has not in some measure reached our hearts, then we are ignorant of its real nature; and it is of no more use to us, than to those who never heard of it.

Let us bring this subject home to ourselves. Christianity is a subject of a practical nature. The doctrine of the cross, which is the sum of the gospel, is a practical doctrine. It is designed and adapted to subdue sin; to make us dead to the world; to fill our hearts with all good affections, and our lives with all good actions. How then is it with us? Let us examine ourselves by this test. The cross of Christ may have been a subject of much inquiry and discussion with us. We may have investigated its design, and noticed its influence, and may have been filled with admiration at its visible effects. But has it had a sanctifying influence upon *ourselves*. If this is in any good measure the case, then we are indeed Christians—such as Paul describes—crucified with Christ, dead to the world, and alive unto God. But if, after all our contemplations on the nature of Christianity, and all our means of understanding its doctrines, and enjoying its blessings, it has had no transforming effect upon our hearts; and if when we have turned our eyes upon Paul and others, and have seen the full influence of the cross upon them, we find an entire want of this influence in ourselves; the voice of eternal truth will declare to us, *that we are not Christians*, and that if we would ever enjoy the blessings of the gospel, we must cast away, as dross, all we have hitherto done in religion, and must become new creatures in Christ Jesus.

A SERMON

DELIVERED IN THE CHAPEL OF THE THEOL. SEMINARY, ANDOVER, JAN. 8, 1843.

---

1 John 4:16.—GOD IS LOVE.

It has been justly said, that this short expression of the Apostle John gives us more knowledge of the character of God, than all which has been written by heathen moralists and philosophers. The views which they have entertained of the Supreme Being have resulted more or less from their depraved dispositions. They have formed a god like to themselves — a god selfish, impure, false, proud, and revengeful. Now you may ask, would it not be better for us to have no object of worship, than to worship a god of such a character? It is, I acknowledge, very difficult to make a just comparison between two evils, which are both so indescribably dreadful. Think for a moment — if you can — *what would be our condition, if there were no God.* How wretched should we be, with capacities which could never be filled; with strong desires which could never be satisfied; with moral disorders which would admit of no cure; all our pursuits, all our aspirings, all our hopes, ending in total disappointment, the light of the soul extinguished, and the blackness of darkness spread all around us. The heart craves an object which it can love supremely and unchangeably. But on the supposition just made, there would be no such object. We want a friend in whom we can repose perfect confidence. But there would be no such friend. We want a benefactor, possessed of resources sufficient to supply all our need. But no such benefactor could be found. Should we ascend up into the heavens, there would be no God there. Should we descend into the abyss, there would be no God there. Should we fly to the uttermost parts of the earth — should we go and search the sun, moon, and stars, and the whole extent of the universe, we could find no God. And if no God, then no light, no resting place, no hope. And what value could we set upon our own existence, when no good end of existence could ever be attained. Take away God, and we should choose *not to exist.* Gloomy and dreadful as would be annihilation; we should pant after it, as a relief from the more gloomy and dreadful evil of existing without a God. We should wish to put an end to our own immortal being, rendered so unwelcome and intolerable; and, finding our wishes and efforts unavailing, we should anxiously look about to find some one of superior power who would do that favor for us, which we could not do for ourselves. Where — we should ask — where is one in heaven or earth, that has power to rid us of an everlasting existence, so burdensome and hateful now, though otherwise so precious?

My hearers, I bring forward no fiction. You know that an atheist considers the present life, which in his view is the whole of existence, as of little worth; and, when pressed with trouble, has no hesitation to put an end to his life, and thus, as he thinks, to plunge into a state of annihilation.

But there is no deliverance from the evils of atheism, by the worship of any other than the true God. All the gods of the heathen, and all the false gods of Christian lands are destitute of divine perfection, and have the failings and vices which are found in wicked men. Now how pernicious must be the effect of worshipping such imaginary gods! Everything faulty and vicious in them will tend to countenance and increase what is faulty and vicious in their worshippers. If the object of our worship is malevolent and revengeful, it will inflame the malice and revenge of our own hearts. If our god is impure, it will increase and perpetuate impurity in us. Among all that worship a malicious revengeful god, where can you find one that is free from malice and revenge? And who that does homage to a god of an impure, licentious character, avoids impurity and licentiousness himself? We see then if we direct our worship to a god that is the subject of depraved dispositions like ourselves, we are in double bondage to depravity; bondage from our own hearts, and from the influence of a corrupt object of worship. In such a case, repentance cannot take place. In this respect, idolaters seem to be in a worse condition, than atheists. Atheists are under the unchecked influence of their *own* vicious passions. But idolaters add to all this, the influence of vice in the gods they serve.

Consider also the *unhappiness* of those who worship a false god. In the object of their worship, they can have no complacency, no confidence. The attributes of his character inspire them with terror, or disgust, and their hearts are strangers to peace.

And how can we escape this unhappy condition so long as the object of our worship has anything short of infinite perfection — perfection truly divine? Suppose we have *any* god, except the God of Israel — *any* god, even the best we can imagine, who is wanting in any of the perfections of Jehovah. Suppose that he has power adequate to the work of creating the heavens and the earth; and also that he is benevolent; but that he is wanting in the requisite *intelligence;* that his knowledge is limited. Now if his knowledge is limited, he is liable to very great and pernicious mistakes in managing concerns of such magnitude. Can we feel confidence in such a god? Can we feel safe under his government? Can we rejoice that he reigneth? How can we know that he has contrived the plan of the creation right? What assurance can we have, that the great machine of the universe will work as he wishes? One part may interfere with another; and there may be dreadful disorder and desolation. There may be some mistake in the formation of the *mind*, which required higher skill than the formation of the material world. The mind may not be endued with a sufficient number of powers and faculties; or it may have too many; or they may be put together in wrong proportions. And after some more experience, the Creator may discover some lamentable fault in his workmanship, and may think it best to re-make the intelligent world, or to set aside the minds which he has created, as unfit for use, and to create a new set of minds on an improved plan. Or if this could not be done, it might be a subject of everlasting regret to us, and to him who created us, that a mistake, now incapable of being corrected, was made in the first formation of so important a part of the universe. Besides, if the God that *governs* the world, is destitute of infinite knowledge; how can we be sure that he will *govern wisely*, and will order things in the natural and moral world so as to answer the purposes of infinite benevolence? My brethren, what peace could we enjoy if the God that made us, and that reigns over us, though almighty and benevolent, possessed only imperfect, limited knowledge.

Suppose then that we had a god possessed of infinite knowledge, as well as goodness, but deficient in *power*. Such a god knows what is best, and chooses what is best, but is not able to accomplish it. He really preferred a different system of things in the natural, and especially in the *moral* world; but that preferable system was beyond his power; and he was obliged to take a system of inferior excellence, because he had not power to adopt the one he preferred. And who can tell in how many instances he has failed and will hereafter fail of *governing* the world aright, not because he is ignorant of what is right, or is not disposed to do it; but because he is wanting in power. We can *love* such a god; but how can we trust him? We can have complacency in his goodness; but we cannot regard him as qualified to govern — we cannot feel that our interests and the interests of the universe are safe in his hands. It is in his heart to do right. But to sustain such mighty responsibilities and manage properly such vast concerns, transcends the measure of his ability.

But there is another supposition, and one which relates more immediately to our subject. Suppose — if it is lawful to make such a supposition — suppose God to be *infinitely intelligent* and *powerful*, but wanting in *goodness*. Such a God knows all things, and his power is equal to his knowledge; but his power and knowledge are both under the direction of *malevolence.* He has a perfect discernment of that plan of creation and providence, which would result in the highest happiness of intelligent beings; and he is perfectly able to adopt it, and to carry it into full effect. But he has no disposition to do it. It is the best plan for a moral universe. But the best plan has no attractions for him. He has no kindness in his heart. He takes no delight in what delights others. If he should see his creatures happy, it would not please him. If they are unhappy, he has no compassion for them. He could fill a universe with blessedness, if he *willed* it; but he *does not will* it. Nothing gratifies him so much as the miseries of his creatures; — and the more miserable they are, the more is he gratified. — Such is the God I have wished you for a few moments to consider; — a God of infinite knowledge and power, but without benevolence. And being destitute of benevolence, he is destitute of every moral excellence. He has no justice, he has no righteousness, he has no regard to truth. There is nothing lovely in his character.

Now what should we do, and what would our condition be, if the God that made and governs the world were such a being as this? We should have a god; but we should be wholly unable to love him; and our inability to love would be in proportion as we were reasonable and virtuous. If we are benevolent, we cannot love one who is malevolent. If we are *just*, we cannot love injustice. If we are benignant and kind, we cannot love what is malignant and cruel. We should indeed have a god; but it would be a god that we ought to abhor. And we should abhor him, in proportion to our knowledge of his character. He might command us to love him; but the command would be unjust; and it would be perfectly right for us to refuse obedience. To love such a god would be totally wrong; and if we should love him, we should condemn ourselves for it; for we should have the unalterable persuasion, that we ought to hate him. But our hatred would not be a quiet, peaceful hatred — as it might be if the god we had in view were weak, as well as malignant. That malignant being would be clothed with omnipotence. He would be almighty in malice and cruelty. He would therefore be an object not only of hatred, but of terror. Yes, every thought of such a deity would fill our minds and all minds with hatred, fear, and terror. Intolerable distress and horror and misery would spread through the world, and through all worlds, under the reign of such a god. There could be no peace, day or night, no *moment* of repose through the wide creation, because there would be no possibility of escaping from the presence of that almighty, malignant being — that cruel, hateful deity.

Think, brethren, (if you can let the horrible thought pass through your mind without impiety,) — what if the eternal God were such a being as I have described? What if we were subjected to the ceaseless terror and wretchedness of being chained to the throne of such a tyrant, without any possibility of relief? — There is no misery on earth, and I know not that there is any in hell, that could be compared with the misery which we should be fated to endure in such a state.

But oh! what glorious light breaks forth upon us out of this thick darkness! What peace, what joy pervades our souls, while we lay hold of the truth, the certain, blessed truth, that *God is love!* — The only supreme and eternal Being, the God whom we adore, is *infinitely* and *unchangeably good.* He has omnipotence; but it is the omnipotence of love. He has infinite knowledge; but his knowledge is inseparably united with benevolence. He is eternal and immutable. But his eternity is the eternity of goodness; and his immutability is the immutability of goodness. He is a just God. But his justice is always in perfect harmony with his love. He hates sin; but he hates it because it is hateful; and his hatred of it comes from a heart that is infinitely benevolent. Whatever attributes he possesses, are in perfect agreement with goodness. And all that he does shows that he is love.

Such a God is the proper object of our affection. And as he is supremely good, he is the proper object of supreme affection. Our whole heart and soul should cleave to him, and rest in his everlasting kindness. We have the happiness to know—it is not a conjecture—it is not a probability—we *know* that God is love. We know that he looks upon his creatures with the purest, tenderest affection, and delights to do them good. There is love, sincere love in human hearts. But the sincerest, purest, warmest love ever found in the heart of any man, or in the hearts of all men, is not worthy to be mentioned in comparison with the love of God. Human love is not always active. Even in the hearts of the most affectionate parents, it has interruptions. But God's love is uninterrupted. It always exists in the highest activity. And it adapts itself to all conditions and circumstances. If God's people are needy—as they always are—his love acts in the way of a seasonable supply. If they are obedient, it acts in the way of approbation and complacency. If they are in a state of suffering, it pities. If they offend, it forgives. If they are defiled with sin, it purifies.

Human love may be sincere and ardent; but it is always attended with weakness, and is unable to accomplish its kind wishes. It aims and strives to make its objects completely happy; but it has not power to do it, and frequently it is compelled to witness great suffering in place of the happiness which it would confer. If the affectionate father had power equal to his love, how uniformly and entirely happy would his children be! But the love of our divine Friend is associated with omnipotence; and no obstacles can hinder its operations. God has power as well as disposition, to supply all our need, and to do exceeding abundantly for us above all we can ask or think.

Having thus considered the benevolence of God as an essential doctrine of revelation, I shall now consider it as a matter of *Christian experience.*

Men in their natural state have no true spiritual discernment of the transcendent love of God. Sin has blinded their eyes, and made them insensible of the real nature and excellence of this divine attribute. So that the experimental, saving knowledge which believers have of the love of God, is a matter of *discovery*

— discovery on their part, but spiritual *revelation* on God's part. I propose to consider this revelation and discovery in three periods; *first*, in its *commencement; secondly*, in its *subsequent progress through life*; and *thirdly*, in its *perfection in the world above.*

First, its *commencement*. It is a truth often taught in Scripture, that unconverted men know not God. Whatever may be their speculative ideas, they are ignorant of the true moral *excellence* of the Supreme Being. They have no eyes to see his glory, especially the glory of his love. Although they may, in different ways, obtain a rational belief that God is benevolent; still they do not see his benevolence to be infinitely glorious. They do not discern it *spiritually*. Accordingly when they find that the apostles were full of admiration in view of the height and depth, and length and breadth of God's love, they cannot understand the reason of such admiration.

And besides this want of actual *discernment* of the goodness of God, there is much which seems to unbelievers to be inconsistent with it. They find it difficult to reconcile some of the doctrines of Scripture, with infinite benevolence. That God has suffered the human race to come into such a depraved, wretched state; that he still suffers so great a part of the world to be ignorant of the gospel and to perish for lack of vision; that even in Christian lands he saves only a small part; that he requires so pure and perfect a service, even of sinful men, and threatens so dreadful a punishment for disobedience; these things, and others things of like kind, obscure, in their view, the lustre of divine goodness. They find difficulty also in many of the dispensations of God's providence towards themselves. And on account of these ways of God's providence and these doctrines of his word, they frequently murmur against God, as wanting in benevolence.

Such is the condition of men in their unrenewed state. Sin hath blinded their eyes to the glory of God's infinite love, and hardened their hearts against its attractions. What a precious discovery then do they make, when God, who commanded the light to shine out of darkness, shines in their hearts, to give the light of the knowledge of his glory,— the glory of all his perfections, especially the glory of his redeeming love! I speak of it as a *discovery;* and so it is. For although they may have had some speculative knowledge of divine benevolence, the evidence of which is everywhere visible; yet they have never seen it as they now see it. They have seen it in some of its outward manifestations; but now, under divine teaching, they look through these outward manifestations of the love of God, and see it in its own nature. They see its divine beauty — its boundless extent. They now *see God.* Before they only looked at his common visible operations, at the instances of good in his works. Now *God himself* is the object of their vision. They have before heard of him by the hearing of the ear. But now their eyes see him. And they see that he is glorious in goodness. They see that God is love. And this new view, this discovery of the perfect, absolute love of God, extends itself to all the doctrines of his word, and all the ways of his providence. Now, as I may say, they begin *at God*, and descend from him to the declarations of his word, to his law, to his gospel, to his government, his sovereignty, his dispensations. They see *God* to be infinitely good. And then, in the light of his own infinite goodness, they see the stamp of his goodness on all his operations. Formerly they saw not the goodness of his *law*. It appeared to them to require too much. Why? Because they had no heart to perceive, the perfect, glorious goodness of God himself. But as soon as men are divinely enlightened, and the blinding influence of sin is removed, so that they have a true spiritual discernment; they at once see that the law is good. As they see God to be infinitely lovely, they see the perfect justice of that law which requires them to *love him. Surely*, they say, *that is a just and good law, which commands us to love a Being who is supremely good.* And they become satisfied in the same way respecting all the commands of God, and all his proceedings. Having a cordial conviction of the perfect goodness of God, and a clear apprehension of the infinite kindness that dwells in his heart, they see and feel, that all his commands must be right, and that they ought most cheerfully to obey him, even when they can see no other reason to obey but this, that it is *God* who commands.

And when they fix their thoughts on God, and see that his character is invested with the glory of infinite love, they become satisfied with all his dispensations and all the doctrines of his word. In their illuminated minds, the glory of benevolence as it beams forth from the character of God, is spread over all the truths which he has revealed and all the acts of his providence and grace. Those doctrines which once appeared to them the most unjust and objectionable, now appear just and right, because they view them in their connection with the perfect character of God, in the light of his transcendent goodness. They rejoice that God reigns, and will do all his pleasure in heaven and earth, because they see that he is worthy to reign, and that all the ways of his government are but the expressions of his boundless love. Their persuasion of the righteousness and goodness of God's word and dispensations is not the result of reasoning. It is not produced by logical arguments. Or if there is any reasoning about it, the reasoning is very short. The premises are in close and inseparable contact with the inference. It is a divine logic. It is the reasoning of spiritual sight. Those who have this unction of the Holy Spirit, clearly behold God in the glory of his love; they hear him speak; they see him act. And as it is *such a God* that speaks, whether in the way of doctrine or precept, they know that he speaks *right*. As it is *such a God* that acts, whatever he does, they are sure he does right. It cannot be otherwise. The conclusion is not a probability but a certainty. And this full persuasion, this *knowledge* extends to all matters relating to God's ways, and the teachings of his word. It is the Lord; let him do what he pleases. It is *God;* it is *Love;* for *God* is *Love*—let him teach what he pleases—it must be true. Let him command and let him do what he pleases, it must be just and right. They do not say, if God does so and so, it will be unjust and contrary to benevolence. They take quite a different position. —*Let us search the word and notice the acts of God, and thus learn what he actually says and does;* and what he says and does we know to be right. Thus the discovery of God's infinite goodness removes all objections and complaints, and gives rest to the soul.

But the discovery has its highest value in regard to Christ. It relates specially and preëminently to the gift of a Saviour. See how the Apostle treats the subject in the context. He says, v. 8th, *God is love.* He then adds: "In *this* was manifested the love of God towards us, because God sent his only begotten Son into the world that we might live through him. *Herein is love*, not that we loved God, but that he loved us, and sent his Son to be the propitiation for our sins." This was love in its most glorious display. Those who are savingly enlightened, are fully persuaded of all this. Their inward, cordial conviction corresponds with the teaching of the Apostle. The glory of God in the face of Jesus Christ, is the glory of all his perfections, especially of his *love.* Formerly, when the sacred preacher or the inspired writer set forth, in glowing language, the love and grace of God manifested in the gift of his Son, they knew not how to understand it. It was all dark and unintelligible to them. Now this instance of love strikes them as exceedingly glorious. When they consider that they and their fellow creatures are all sinners, and that God so loved them as to send his Son to die for them — they are filled with astonishment, and are constrained to say, verily, *God is love.* And when they see this great design of divine love carried into effect in the salvation of those that are lost; especially when they look upon the depth of their own guilt and misery, and humbly hope that God has washed and justified and sanctified them, and that, with all their ill deserts, they are made heirs of everlasting life; they have no words to express the emotions of their hearts, and they can only say, O! the depth of the riches of divine love! It now appears strange to them, that they were ever regardless of such goodness, and unable to see its greatness and glory. And they look with grief upon the multitude of sinners around them, whose minds are blinded and whose hearts are hardened, so that they cannot see and cannot feel as John did when he said, "*herein is love*," or as Paul did, when he spoke of knowing the love of God *which passeth knowledge.* Their views and feelings harmonize with those of the apostles. The truth of what the Scriptures teach on this subject stands before them in a clear light.

The sentiment of their hearts is, O that we had words to set forth the riches of God's love! And sometimes they are constrained to cry out, "glory to God in the highest;" glory to the God of love!

I have now spoken of the first spiritual discovery which redeemed sinners make of the infinite goodness of God. I have spoken of the time when the Holy Spirit begins to illuminate their minds, when he first removes the inward cause of all their mistakes and murmurings, and makes it manifest to them, that the God, against whom they have sinned, and against whom their hearts have so often raised objections, is infinitely benevolent; makes them understand and feel, that *God is love.*

We now come to the second period referred to. The discovery which is made at conversion, is a growing discovery. It is the commencement of a light, which shines brighter and brighter in after life. There is evident need of such increasing illumination. Christians are indeed all taught of God in regard to the present subject, from the commencement of their piety. At their conversion God begins to teach them, and they begin to learn. But they have remaining obscurity and error. Their spiritual vision falls short of perfect clearness. They need to be more clearly instructed in regard to the love of God. And by his word and providence, accompanied with the influence of his Spirit, he is pleased to give them the needed instruction. This he does on different occasions and in different ways.

Christians frequently obtain juster views of the goodness of God as *the result of afflictions.* Whom the Lord loveth he chasteneth. And he brings them to know experimentally that he does indeed chasten them in love. The fruit of their afflictions is, to subdue earthly affections, to take away sin, and to promote spiritual mindedness. Nothing is more certain to the mind of enlightened Christians, than the goodness of God in their trials. They know that they need chastisement. And such from time to time is the effect of the trials which God appoints for them, that they can say with the Psalmist, "I know, O God, that thy judgments are right, and that thou in faithfulness hast afflicted me." And seeing what is the design of God in their afflictions, and what happy effects result from them, they reckon them among their choicest mercies. And they render hearty thanks to their heavenly Father, that he does not forget to chasten them. The most painful dispensations of his providence, which once appeared so inconsistent with his goodness, and which sometimes have occasioned perplexities, and hard thoughts — those very dispensations, in the end, stand before their minds as expressions of God's infinite love. And when this is the case, how gladly do they yield themselves to the divine disposal, saying from the heart, *it is the Lord — the God of love; let him do what seemeth good in his sight.* And so they count it all joy when they fall into divers trials. They love God more for his chastisements. They have more experience of his paternal kindness. They cleave to him and rest in his love with more confidence and delight. Their communion with him is more intimate and happy. And they become so conversant in their thoughts and affections with the unchangeable love of God, and so satisfied with him as their portion, that they care less and less for other things. If they may but continually taste and see that the Lord is gracious, and may truly enjoy his love they ask no more.

But it is not merely by means of afflictions, that Christians obtain an increasing knowledge of the love of God. They do this in their *devotional* exercises. Sometimes they are favored with the Spirit of adoption. They come near to God; they behold his abounding goodness and grace; they thank and praise him, and make known to him the desires of their hearts. Truly, at such times, their fellowship is with the Father, and with his Son Jesus Christ. Then nothing is dark and perplexing in his character and government. All the objects presented before them in the spiritual world are invested with light and beauty. In the house of God, in their retirements, and in the silence of the midnight hour, they think upon God, and he causes his great goodness to pass before them. He proclaims his name to them, and shows them his glory; and they gaze upon it; and they rejoice that he is, and that he is what he is, a God of boundless love. Christians sometimes have this clearer illumination and make this higher discovery respecting the goodness of God, in seasons devoted specially to fasting and prayer; and not unfrequently when they come near to the close of life. From time to time, and in different ways, God so reveals himself to their minds, and so manifests his glory, that they are ashamed that they ever lost sight of it; and they are disposed to call upon all around to join with them in exalting the name of God, and in celebrating his eternal love.

Think for a moment how dark and how wretched are the minds of ungodly men; to how many sufferings they are subjected, and how their sufferings are made insupportable by their hard thoughts of God, and their want of a peaceful confidence in his faithfulness and love. Go where you will in heathen lands and in Christian lands, and you will find that the world lieth in darkness. Unsanctified men know not God. They see no glory in his character. And when they survey the measures of his sovereign providence; when they think of themselves and of their Creator and Judge, how far are they from feeling, that *God is love.* This blessed truth does not lodge within them. Amid the various calamities of life, they have no refuge. They have no divine friend, to whom they can reveal their sorrows, and in whose sympathy and love their hearts can repose. They have no God;—or if they have a God, he is not like our God, the God of love.

But how happy are we, if we have been savingly taught of God; if in the midst of all the evils which prevail in the world, and which occasion so much distress and so much murmuring in the minds of men, we may have such clear, overpowering evidence of his perfect, unbounded goodness, as shall at once solve all our doubts and difficulties, and reconcile all seeming inconsistencies. Men are prone to go into curious inquiries respecting the evils which exist, and to ask, *how* can they be consistent with the moral perfection of God? How can the universal sinfulness of man, how can the doctrine of sovereign election, the limited spread of the gospel, the long delay of the conversion of the world, and the final ruin of so great a part, and various other inscrutable things in divine providence; how can they be reconciled with the infinite benevolence of God? They speculate on these matters; but their speculations are in vain. There is a depth and a height which their reason cannot reach. If any man thinks he is able to solve these difficult questions by mere reasoning, he will find his mistake.

Brethren, there is a more excellent way. We want a state of mind — a light from above shining within us, which will supersede the necessity of these speculative inquiries, and will settle it at once as a primary truth, a precious reality, that *God is love*, and that amid all the evils which exist, his love and wisdom reign; that he means the most lamentable events for good, and will in the end make them subservient to good. Happy, thrice happy are they who have this inward teaching of the Spirit, opening their eyes to behold the unchangeable love of God, and to see with wonder and joy the displays which he continually makes of it in all that they enjoy, and in all that they suffer, and in all the good and all the evil that takes place in the world. Happy they who have made this blessed discovery, and who make it more and more clearly and fully as they advance in the divine life, and who anticipate the time when the discovery will be perfect.

This brings me to the *third* period of spiritual illumination. The highest knowledge of the love of God which we attain in the present life, is imperfect. We see through a glass darkly. But there is a time at hand, when we shall see God face to face. How clear will be the light which will shine around us and within us in the heavenly world! In that celestial light it will be made evident, that the complaints and objections of sinful men were all groundless, and that the war they had been waging against God, was a war of wickedness against *infinite goodness.* The wicked themselves will see this, and they will stand guilty and self-condemned before God. But this celestial light will bring joy unspeakable and full of glory to the saints. In the world below they began to discover the love of God; they began to experience the fruits of that love, and hoped they should experience them in larger measures, in the world above. Now they realize their most exalted hopes. They remember that they began in the world below to taste and see that the Lord is good; and they bless God that he opened their eyes to see his goodness; and they wonder they did not see it more clearly. When they cast their thoughts back over the scenes they passed through in their probationary state, they see that their path from the beginning to the end of life, was strewed with the fruits of God's love. They see, as they never saw before, the forbearance and goodness of God towards them, while they lived in sin. They now see far more clearly than they ever saw in the world below, the glory of God's eternal and sovereign love, which provided a Saviour for them, and inclined their hearts to receive him; that love which watched over them through their whole course; which strengthened them in their weakness; which delivered them from the power of their enemies; which guarded them against the ruinous effects of a deceitful and wicked heart; which restored their wandering feet; which sustained and comforted them in all their trials, and made them conquerors and more than conquerors. When they look towards the pit of destruction, with a full consciousness, that it is their merited portion, and yet find that they are saved from it, and that an abundant entrance has been ministered to them into the kingdom of heaven, and that they are brought there, not by works of righteousness which they have done, but by the abounding grace of God; oh! what a clear view, what a vivid impression they will have of the immeasurable love of their God and Saviour! and with what wonder and delight will they dwell upon it. Their conception of divine love is so much superior to anything attained to before, that it seems to be a new discovery. It is indeed a new discovery; for they not only see with greater clearness what they saw in part before, but they see much that was concealed from them, even in their most favored state on earth. They began to discover the goodness of God when they were first enlightened. That was their childhood, the first period of discovery. The second period followed the period of youth; and through that period their knowledge of the God of love was increasing in clearness. Now they have come to the period of complete manhood in the world above; that world which needs not our inferior lights — because God himself is the Sun that shines perpetually there, and the splendor of his character fills the minds of all the inhabitants with perfect light. And yet their knowledge of God will constantly increase, because their capacity will increase; and their continual experience of the blessedness which comes from the inexhaustible treasures of divine love will make constant additions to their knowledge. This is the heaven of the saints; to be forever with God, to behold his glory, forever to love him, and forever to enjoy his love. This is the life eternal promised to believers. This is the fulness of joy, and pleasure forevermore.

TWO SERMONS

DELIVERED IN THE CHAPEL OF THE THEOLOGICAL SEMINARY, ANDOVER, APRIL 21, 1844.

SERMON I.

Isaiah 55: 8, 9.—LET THE WICKED FORSAKE HIS WAY, AND THE UNRIGHTEOUS MAN HIS THOUGHTS, AND LET HIM RETURN UNTO THE LORD, AND HE WILL HAVE MERCY UPON HIM, AND TO OUR GOD, FOR HE WILL ABUNDANTLY PARDON. FOR MY THOUGHTS ARE NOT YOUR THOUGHTS, NEITHER ARE YOUR WAYS MY WAYS, SAITH THE LORD. FOR AS THE HEAVENS ARE HIGHER THAN THE EARTH; SO ARE MY WAYS HIGHER THAN YOUR WAYS, AND MY THOUGHTS THAN YOUR THOUGHTS.

THE prophet here speaks in the name of God, and says: "Let the wicked forsake his way, and the unrighteous man his thoughts, and let him return to the Lord, and he will have mercy upon him, and to our God, for he will *abundantly pardon*, or, as it is in the original, he will *multiply* pardons, and then he adds, "*for* my thoughts are not your thoughts, neither are your ways my ways, saith the Lord; for as the heavens are higher than the earth; so are my ways higher than your ways, and my thoughts than your thoughts." The Lord will *abundantly* pardon—*for* his thoughts and ways are inconceivably higher than ours. This then is the sentiment of the text; *that the mercy which God exercises in the forgiveness of sin is exceedingly above that which is found in the heart of man.* This sentiment we are now particularly to consider. And may God grant that our contemplations on this subject may inspire us with devout admiration of the height and depth of divine mercy.

Turn then your thoughts to this theme in which we are all so deeply concerned, and consider in what respects the mercy which God exercises in forgiveness, exceeds that which is found in man.

First. The mercy of God in forgiveness is far above that which is found in man, in respect to *the number of the offences which he forgives*. The prophet says, he will *multiply* pardons. And the Apostle says: " the free gift is of *many offences* to justification." In this respect, God's thoughts and ways are far superior to ours. The spirit of forgiveness is contrary to our natural disposition. Unrenewed man, when insulted or injured, is resentful, and meditates revenge. And even Christians find it hard to forgive, especially if the offences committed against them are multiplied. There is no part of the Christian character in which we are commonly more deficient. When anything is done to lower our reputation, or to interfere with our worldly interests; how quick are our resentful passions to kindle! And if, through divine grace, we attain to a feeling of forgiveness towards a person, who injures us once, or in a few instances; how are our kind feelings overcome, and our resentment excited, if his injuries are many times repeated. What a long struggle would most of us have with our own hearts, before we could come to a feeling of real forgiveness and kindness towards one who had, in numberless instances, been acting the part of an enemy, and had plotted and labored, to injure us. Even if he should *repent*, still how difficult it would be to forgive and forget so many offences. Such is man. How feeble and scanty is the feeling of forgiveness in our hearts! And to how few offences does it reach.

Think now of the *mercy of God*. How high does it rise above what is found in man! The sins which we have committed against God, are more than can be numbered. We multiply our offences. But God can multiply pardons still more. Our transgressions abound; but his forgiving mercy superabounds.

Secondly. The same appears in regard to *the number of of-*

fenders whom God forgives. If we should get our hearts so softened with kind feeling, that we should be disposed to forget all the offenecs of a single individual; yet what could we do, if all around us should become our enemies? What could we do, if all the world should combine their efforts to vex and injure us? Who of us would have a principle of love and forgiveness powerful enough, to meet half way such a killing emergency as this? How would the flow of affection within us cease, and our spirits wither away, if only a small number of men, especially those who have been the objects of our love, should prove treacherous and hostile? Who would venture to predict that his benignant feelings would hold out, and his heart be prompt to forgive in such circumstances as these?

Behold now *the transcendent love of God!* His forgiving mercy is large enough to reach to a whole world of rebels; and it does actually reach to all believers — a multitude which no man can number. God forgives a thousand, and ten thousand offenders as readily as he forgives a single individual. He is never weary of forgiving. After he has pardoned millions of sinners, he is just as ready to pardon millions more. Verily this is not after the manner of men.

Thirdly. God's thoughts and ways are far above ours in *forgiving offences which have been long continued.*

As to *ourselves;* — though we may have a heart to forgive a man who injures us for a few days; our forgiving temper is almost sure to fail, if his injuries are long continued. For a time, we may indulge the hope that he will soon be sensible of his error, and become our friend. But if we have long experienced his injuries, and have long been impressed with the perverseness of his disposition; our feelings are very apt to be disturbed, and our meekness and kindness to give way to anger and ill will.

See now how different it is with the mercy of God. The whole race of mankind have been sinning against him thousands of years; and yet he continues to look upon them with a perfect readiness to forgive. So it is in regard to every generation of men; and so in regard to individuals. Let them sin ever so long, even to old age; he is still ready to have mercy upon them. And if they are disposed to seek forgiveness in the appointed way, he will freely forgive them. And if not, he will have the same merciful heart, as though he did actually forgive.—I lately knew a man, who had been an enemy to God and religion up to the age of eighty-three years. Through divine grace, he then thought on his ways, and said,—"I will arise and go to my Father, and will say, Father, I have sinned."—The God of mercy met that penitent, broken-hearted old man, and embraced him as kindly as though he had sinned but a day. He rejoiced over him, now returned from his wanderings, and welcomed him to his house; saying, "This my son was dead, and is alive again; he was lost, and is found." Such is the long suffering and mercy of God! And it appears, if possible, still more wonderful towards his own children, who continue their offences, in one way or another, as long as they live, and he still forgives.

Fourthly. God shows that his thoughts and ways are far above ours, in forgiving offences which are attended with *high aggravations*.

We may be able to overlook *small*, *trivial* offences, even a large number of them, and continued for a long time. But suppose a man commits offences of great criminality. Suppose he aims a fatal blow at our reputation and our happiness. Suppose that, with infernal malice, he is continually plotting our ruin; that wherever we go and whatever we do, we are forced to encounter the effects of his enmity. What feelings of impatience and resentment are likely to get possession of our hearts; and most of all, if that enemy is one whom we have often relieved in difficulty, and always treated with kindness. How could we bear with his enmity in these circumstances, and still cherish towards him a forgiving spirit.

See here how highly God is exalted above man! He is "the Lord God, merciful and gracious, slow to anger, forgiving iniquity, and transgression, and sin;"—forgiving all kinds and all degrees of sin—offences the most aggravated. Look at the Corinthian believers. They had been idolaters, fornicators, adulterers, thieves, covetous, drunkards, revilers, extortioners. And yet God was ready to forgive even them, and did actually forgive large numbers of them. They were washed, they were justified, they were sanctified in the name of the Lord Jesus and by the Spirit of their God. Look at the enemies and murderers of Christ at Jerusalem. Whose guilt could be greater than theirs? And yet forgiveness was to be offered first of all to *them*. Jesus directed the apostles to go forth with the proclamation of pardon, "*beginning at Jerusalem;*" — beginning *there* among those who hated, and crucified him. He regarded their extraordinary guilt, as furnishing an occasion for the exercise of extraordinary mercy in their forgiveness. So it was with Saul of Tarsus, who was a blasphemer, a persecutor, and a murderer — yea, a murderer of God's own children, and one of the chief of sinners. Yet God had mercy on him, and forgave him all the wrong he had done. And Paul is now exhibited before us, not as a solitary case, but as a public example of God's wonderful mercy, a witness to all after ages, that God abounds in forgiveness. You see, brethren, what mercy dwells in the heart of God. Human sin rises very high; but his forgiving mercy rises higher. Let the wicked, however wicked he may be, forsake his wicked ways, and the unrighteous man his thoughts, and let him return to the Lord, and he will have mercy upon him, and to our God, for he will abundantly pardon. For his thoughts and ways are infinitely higher than ours.

In the *fifth* place; God is distinguished above us by the perfect *freeness* with which he forgives. As we have but little benevolence and much selfishness; we generally want some gift, some special favor to help us in the exercise of forgiveness towards those who have injured us. If any one wishes us to forgive him, it is our way to say: *Pay what thou owest; repair the injury done.*

But *God's* forgiveness is *perfectly free*, "without money and without price." He requires nothing to be done by us to *purchase* a pardon. God has no selfishness to consult; no unkind, resentful feelings like ours, to be pacified. He does indeed require us to comply with certain conditions in order to forgiveness.

But he requires it for *our good*, not as a favor to himself. He desires no favor; he needs none; he can receive none. From the very nature of the case, the conditions proposed are indispensable to our enjoying the blessing of forgiveness. Forgiveness would not *be* forgiveness to us, unless we complied with the conditions prescribed. So that his insisting upon the conditions, instead of detracting from the freeness of his pardoning mercy, is only the method he pursues to make us partakers of that precious blessing. Every pardoned sinner will say, that the act of God in forgiving him was perfectly unmerited and free. Indeed, the way pointed out in the gospel, is the only conceivable way, in which the blessing of forgiveness can be enjoyed. And surely a gift is *free*, when all that is required of us is, that we should be *heartily willing to receive it.*

Sixthly. Another thing which shows that God is highly exalted above us, is the *completeness* of the pardon which he grants.

It is seldom the case with us, that we entirely forgive a person who offends us. We may say, we forgive him; and from a sense of duty, or a regard to our reputation or interest, we may treat him with common respect and kindness. But do we from the heart *completely* forgive him? Is there no bitterness of feeling left? Or if no bitterness, is there no want of kindness? Is there the sweetness of hearty love? Men sometimes say, they can *forgive*, but cannot *forget;* — which is much the same as saying, they can forgive so far as outward appearances go, but not from the heart; partially but not entirely. We seldom so completely pass by an offence, especially a great offence, that the remembrance of it does not occasionally disturb our feelings. It would be a remarkable instance of goodness in us, if we should completely bury an injury, which had been wounding to our feelings; — if we should so completely bury it, that it should no longer cause disquiet to our minds. Should we thus entirely forgive a few acts, or even one act of manifest unkindness and hostility; it would be more than is commonly done; — shall I say, more than is commonly done even by Christians? How then could such poor, selfish hearts as ours, entirely forgive a great multitude of unprovoked offences, committed for a long time, by a large number of unreasonable and wicked men — so entirely forgive them, as to blot them out from our remembrance!

But O! the height and the depth of the mercy of God! He sees all the sins which the whole multitude of his people have committed — sins more in number than the sands on the sea-shore, and like mountains for greatness; — sins ten thousand times beyond what ever have been or can be committed against man. God sees them in all their aggravations, and their long continuance — sins of crimson color — sins so gross and horrible as to make the earth to quake and to cover the face of the heavens with blackness. The eye of God sees them all; — and yet he *forgives*, completely forgives. As far as the east is from the west, so far he removes the transgressions of his people from them. He blots them out from his book. He will never remember them. He has cast them into the depths of the sea. He has so completely pardoned his believing people, that he will not suffer the least accusation to be brought against them. He will not suffer any one even to mention their transgressions. It is with this exalted view of God's mercy, in the complete forgiveness of his people, that the Apostle so exultingly exclaims: "Who shall lay anything to the charge of God's elect? It is God that justifieth; who is he that condemneth?" Who would think of reversing the sentence even of an *earthly* king, and of condemning those whom *he* had seen fit to pardon? Who then shall take upon him to reverse the sentence of the *king of kings*, and to condemn those whom he has pardoned? Who shall lay anything to the charge of those, against whom the Lord of all brings no charge, and against whom he says, that no charge shall ever be brought by any one in heaven or earth? Behold here, *the reign of grace*. God *abundantly* pardons, and *completely* pardons; and he looks upon his people and loads them with benefits, as though they had never offended.

This leads me to say, in the *seventh* place, that God's ways are above our ways in respect to *the blessings he bestows on those whom he forgives, and in token of his forgiveness.*

Where is the man, who will not only forgive from the heart

those who have done him the greatest possible injury, but will enrich them with precious gifts, and make them heirs to his estate, in common with his own children? Where is the man that would do this? Where is the king that would take a rebel that he had thought proper to pardon, and give him a place not only in his house, but on his *throne?* Where is the king, who would do anything like this? Men, even good men, are apt to be very sparing in their favors to those whom they forgive. Their forgiveness is a scanty forgiveness, and is followed by few or no acts of generous friendship.

But O! how different it is with a pardoning God! He not only forgives his people, in the limited sense; that is, he not only exempts them from the punishment they deserve, but grants them favors of infinite worth. He adopts them as his children; and has laid up for them what eye hath not seen, nor ear heard, nor the heart conceived. He has made them heirs to an unfading inheritance, yes, heirs to his own eternal kingdom. And by and by, when the work of his redeeming grace is carried into full effect, they, who were by nature children of wrath, and who know that they deserve everlasting punishment, will find themselves sitting with Christ on his throne in the heavens. They will not only have the happiness of serving their blessed Lord, and enjoying his presence, but will *reign* with him. So glorious is the mercy of God in pardoning and justifying those who believe.

I shall notice but one thing more, in which God's thoughts and ways are so far above ours; and that is, the *work he has done to prepare the way for forgiveness.*

When a man commits an offence against *us*, we expect that whatever is necessary to be done to prepare the way for his forgiveness, will be done by *himself.* If any one is to be employed to intercede for him, and to help forward a reconciliation; we feel that it belongs to *him*, not to *us*, to provide such an intercessor. Or if a sum of money is to be paid, or some special service to be performed, to prepare the way for the forgiveness of an offence; it is not according to *our* ideas of propriety, that the party *offended* should pay the money, or do the requisite service. We expect that the offender *himself* will see to that. Whatever is necessary to open the door for us to forgive one who has injured us, we stand up and say, it is not for us to stoop so low as to do that necessary thing. We say, *that* is the business of him who has injured us, if he wishes to be forgiven. If any stooping is called for, *he* must be the one to stoop. This is the manner of men.

But O! how far otherwise it is in regard to the mercy which God exercises in forgiveness. Mankind are the offenders. But they are neither able nor disposed to do anything to bring about a reconciliation. This apostate world never took a single step, never lifted a finger, towards securing forgiveness, or preparing the way for it. The conduct of Adam and Eve after their fall, shows what is natural to man. They did not hasten into the presence of God, and prostrate themselves before him, entreating him to pardon them. They did not do anything, they did not so much as *think* of doing anything, to procure forgiveness. All they did was to attempt to hide themselves from the eye of God. And this is all that a world of sinners would ever do, if left to the promptings of their own guilty souls. They would try to get away from the presence of God — to hide themselves from the face of their righteous judge. It comes then to this; that God, the offended party, must not only forgive the offenders, but must himself take all the measures which are necessary to pre pare the way for forgiveness. Whatever is to be done to open the door for the pardon of rebels, must be done on his part. If a sacrifice is called for; God himself must provide it. If a mighty work is to be done to vindicate the authority of the law and the honor of the Lawgiver; the Lawgiver himself must propose it, and see that it is accomplished — not indeed by sinners, but by one whom he appoints to act *for* sinners. Thus the business of forgiveness in all its parts must be undertaken and carried forward by God himself, or the whole world will fall under the penalty of the violated law, and perish forever. The God of heaven *has* undertaken it. And all that was necessary to prepare the way for the pardon of offenders, the Being offended has himself provided. And he has made all that provision, while it was neither sought nor desired by sinners; and while they were all the while rebelling against him more and more. This, I say, is not after the manner of men.

But, my brethren, what *was* necessary to be done, and what has God actually done to bring about the forgiveness of sin?—Let heaven and earth be astonished at this work of a merciful, pardoning God. Here is the wonder of wonders! The world is lost forever, unless the Son of God, more excellent, and more dear to the Father, than all the creation — unless he is made the sacrifice. Without the shedding of blood there is no remission. It is not possible that sin should be forgiven in any other way. You may as well say, it is possible that sin should not be sin, or that God should not be God, as that he can pardon sin without this sacrifice. Herein is love, infinitely above the highest love that is found in the heart of man. For did you ever hear of a man, did you ever hear of any man, however good, that would give up his own beloved and only son to die in the place of his enemies. Herein is love truly divine.— See what took place on that dark and doleful night, when Jesus was betrayed; and what took place the next day on mount Calvary. There to procure our forgiveness, the Son of God is nailed to the cross. And on that cross he hangs in agony which cannot be described, from hour to hour, exhausted and faint with extreme anguish, cruelly insulted and abused by his enemies — forsaken of his friends — and forsaken of his *God*— till he has drunk the cup of wrath to the very dregs. This is the astonishing method, which God takes to prepare the way for divine mercy to flow forth in the forgiveness of our sins. We see, then, to-day, and we hope to see more clearly and to acknowledge more devoutly in ages to come, that the love of God passeth all understanding; that as the heavens are higher than the earth, so is the mercy of God in the forgiveness of sin higher than any mercy ever exercised or conceived by the heart of man.

SERMON II.

ISAIAH 55: 8, 9.

This passage, taken together, brings out this sentiment, namely; that *in respect to the mercy which God exercises in the forgiveness of sin, his thoughts and ways are as far above ours, as the heavens are above the earth.*

In my attempt to illustrate this sentiment in the former discourse, I noticed the following particulars; namely; the number of offences which God forgives; the number of offenders he forgives; the long continuance and the aggravations of the offences; the freeness and the completeness of the pardon he grants; the precious blessings which he bestows on those who are pardoned; and finally, the measures he adopts to prepare the way for our forgiveness. In all these respects, we have seen, that God is exalted far above man.

I cannot be willing to dismiss a subject of such consequence as this, without calling your attention to some of its *practical uses.*

First. The *transcendent mercy which God shows in the forgiveness of our sins, should be an effectual motive with us to the exercise of forgiveness towards our offending fellow creatures.* "Be ye kind," says an Apostle, "tender hearted, *forgiving one another even as God*, for Christ's sake, *hath forgiven you.*"

The duty of forgiving and loving those who injure us, is as I have already remarked, a duty quite uncongenial to our natural disposition. We may be convinced of our obligation to forgive. It may be made perfectly plain to our understanding, that God enjoins this duty, and that our present peace of mind and our future well being require it of us. But when any one injures us it often becomes a serious question, how we can bring our proud, selfish, resentful hearts to forgive. Now, so far as motives are concerned, there is nothing which possesses such power, as the mercy which God exercises through Christ in forgiving our sins. Let us then look at the facts in the case just as they are. Let us take a view of ourselves as sinners. Let us call to mind how many and how long continued have been the offences which we have committed against God. Let it be impressed on our minds how tremendous is the amount of our guilt. Let us see and feel that we deserve nothing less than everlasting banishment from the kingdom of heaven. Let us cease to murmur against the justice of God, and become silent before him; — or if we speak, let it be only to say: "If thou Lord shouldst mark iniquity, O Lord, who could stand?" While viewing ourselves in this light, and feeling, that we deserve to suffer the penalty of the law, let us humbly and thankfully lift up our eyes to the God of mercy — to God on a throne of grace, who has freely forgiven all our sins, and delivered us from eternal death. Let us do this, brethren, and what will be the effect upon us in regard to the offences of our fellow-men? Why, their offences and injuries will appear too small to be noticed. They will all vanish out of sight, in comparison with the sins we have committed against God. And our hearts will be so softened and melted by his wonderful kindness and grace in forgiving our sins, that it will be very easy to forgive the few offences committed against us. The greatest injuries we have ever received from our fellow creatures, even from our bitterest enemies — what are they, compared with what we have done against God? When we think of this, and look into the heart of God, and see that he has mercy enough to pass by all our offences, and to make us eternally blessed in his kingdom; how can we resent any injury, or feel the smallest degree of hardness or unkindness towards any person on earth?

Or, if we should ever find this view of the subject insufficient to produce the desired effect, and our proud, resentful hearts should need an influence still more powerful; then let us think of the astonishing means, by which our forgiveness was procured. Let us look to Jesus, suffering and dying for our sins. Let us place ourselves on Calvary near the cross, and there behold the

Son of God enduring the pains of crucifixion, that the heinous sins which we have committed against him and against his Father, might all be pardoned. Such a view of Christ crucified humbles the pride of the heart; it melts the hardness of the heart; and according to the beautiful language of the Apostle, it helps us, as the elect of God, to put on bowels of mercy, long suffering, gentleness, and *forgiveness.* It helps us to feel — oh! that we could feel — as the blessed Jesus felt when he died for us; and as he now feels, when, in view of all we have done, he says, "thy sins are forgiven thee."

Dear brethren, let us remember this. Offences and injuries are to be expected from our fellow-men, and even from Christians; and, in one way or another, *we* shall doubtless offend *them.* And there will be constant occasion, as long as we live in such a world as this, for the exercise of a forbearing, forgiving disposition. And it will often be a very serious inquiry with us, what we shall do to cherish and increase such a disposition in our own hearts. Now there are many ways, in which we may do something towards accomplishing this object. But nothing will be likely to prove effectual, if we neglect the great motive which I have suggested. Worldly wisdom and philosophy will not avail us here. We must go to the cross. We must have the power of faith. We must repose on the bosom of Jesus, our kind, forgiving Saviour. — Let us then form the habit of looking at our own aggravated offences, and at that astonishing mercy of God which pardons and saves. And let us form the habit of looking unto Jesus, and dwelling in our meditations upon what he did and suffered to procure our deliverance from the wrath to come. Whenever our hearts grow resentful and hard, as they are so apt to do, towards those who injure us, *let us go immediately to God,* and deal with him respecting the numberless sins which we have committed against him. Let us renew before him our broken-hearted confessions, and our repentance, and our faith in the Lamb of God that taketh away the sin of the world. Let us renew our gratitude to God for the blessings of forgiveness. And let us earnestly beseech him to work in us all the good pleasure of his goodness, and to make our hearts forgiving and kind like the heart of Jesus. If we do this as we ought, we shall gradually overcome the selfish, revengeful feelings of our hearts; and shall, by and by, be prepared to pray, as Jesus taught us to pray; "Forgive us *our* trespasses, *as* we forgive those who trespass against *us*." We are often *afraid* to pray in this manner, lest it should bring down a curse upon us, instead of a blessing. How happy shall we be, if we may but entertain such views and feelings, and attain to such a state of mind, that we can consistently and safely pray: "forgive us *our* sins, *as* we forgive those who sin against us!"

Again. The doctrine that God is so merciful — that he so abounds in forgiveness, *should excite our fervent gratitude*, and should encourage us *in all circumstances, to repair to him, and trust in him, as a merciful, pardoning God.*

We can never get any just conceptions of the greatness of divine mercy in the forgiveness of sin, or feel due gratitude to God for that mercy, unless we have some just conceptions of the amount of sin to be forgiven. Here we find the reason why men in general, from youth to old age, entertain such low thoughts of the pardoning mercy of God. It is because they have no proper conviction of sin; no just views of the greatness of their guilt, and of the evils they deserve, as transgressors. This is the reason why they treat the gospel message with such indifference, and why the death of Christ and all the wonders of redemption pass by them as trivial concerns. For what great importance can they attach to the forgiveness of guilt *so small as theirs?* Why should they be anxious for a reconciliation with a God, against whom they have committed *only a few trifling offences?* What occasion can there be for such a wonderful stir about the salvation of men? What occasion for such deep counsels in the courts above, such strange movements in the divine government, such loud voices in heaven and earth, proclaiming glory to God in the highest, and pardon to the guilty? What occasion especially for the Son of God to come down from heaven and endure the pains of crucifixion, to purchase forgiveness — while it appears to them that there is nothing in their case calling for this, and that the sin found in them is so small that it might be easily overlooked. This all comes to pass, because, although they really owe a fearful debt — a debt of ten thousand talents, it seems to them, according to *their* way of reckoning, that they owe but a few farthings.

But as soon as sinners, under the teaching of the Spirit, have their consciences awakened from their slumbers; as soon as they are truly convinced of sin, and have any just conceptions of the holiness and justice of God, and of the retributions they are to expect from him a few days hence; oh! then, what fear and anguish take hold upon them! And how astonished are they at the quietness and security they have felt, while the wrath of God has all the time been abiding on them, and the abyss of endless ruin has been open before them! To persons in such a state, the doctrine of forgiveness is quite another matter, and to *believe* in it is quite another matter. If with this view of the justice of God, and their own ill-desert, they do truly receive the gospel message of forgiveness; and if they repose such confidence in that message of heavenly mercy, as to overcome all the decisions of natural conscience, and all their inward terrors and fears; and if they see the excellence and glory of the plan of divine grace, and cordially embrace it; and if God is then pleased, in his own way, to give them some tokens of pardoned sin, and they plainly see that they are delivered from wrath — that God is their friend, and heaven their eternal portion; how will such persons feel, and what will they say? "Wonder and joy will fill their hearts, and praise employ their tongues." "Come," they will say, "all ye that fear the Lord, and I will tell you what he hath done for my soul." They will call upon heaven and earth, upon angels and men, upon sun, moon, and stars, and trees, and mountains to join with them in praising God, who has so mercifully interposed to pardon their sins, and to save them from eternal death; and they will indulge the glad hope, that they shall render him purer, higher praise, when they arrive at heaven.

But here not unfrequently comes in a danger to persons under deep and distressing convictions of sin. When they clearly apprehend the greatness of their guilt, and the terrors of the judgment to come, they are often inclined to think that there can be no forgiveness for them; that their sins are so many and so aggravated, and their depravity so deep and dreadful, that divine mercy cannot reach them. While they are in this state, discouraging, desponding apprehensions rush into their guilty minds; and although they have so often heard, that God is merciful, and ready to forgive, they still think that their case is desperate; that for sinners like them, there is no hope. This is the natural decision of an awakened conscience, which fixes merely upon the evil of sin, the penalty of the law, and the demands of divine justice, while the gospel message of forgiveness is not duly entertained.

And not only awakened sinners, under deep convictions, but Christians also, when they become duly sensible of their exceeding criminality in backsliding from God, and in violating their obligations to redeeming grace, or when they discover, more fully than before, the unsubdued wickedness of their own hearts, and the indescribable evils of their condition — such persons are all liable, more or less, to fall in with the suggestions of a guilty conscience and an unbelieving heart; — suggestions which are exceedingly dishonorable to the boundless mercy of God, and hazardous to the interests of the soul.

Now in regard to persons in such a state — it is important not only to proclaim to them the great mercy of God, but to take pains to lift them up out of their despondency, and to induce them, in view of the unbounded goodness of God, to press through all discouragements to his mercy seat, and, with penitent hearts, to sue for pardon.

If there are any persons present, who are involved in these difficulties, or exposed to them; — any who have such an impression of the numberless evils of their hearts and lives, that they are ready to give way to discouragement, and to think that sinners like them cannot be forgiven; — to such persons I beg leave to offer a few remarks.

I would ask you, then, whether your desponding views and

feelings are derived from the word of God. The Bible is a holy book, and reveals a just and holy God. But does it shut the door of mercy against convinced and broken-hearted sinners? Does it tell them that their condition is desperate? — When God proclaims his name, and declares that he is merciful and gracious, forgiving iniquity, and transgression, and sin; does he set limits to his forgiveness, and say, it can go so far, and no farther? When God says: "Though your sins be like scarlet, they shall be white as snow; though they be red like crimson, they shall be as wool;" does he point to sins which are more than scarlet and crimson, and which cannot be forgiven? When the Prophet declares that God will *multiply* pardons; does he say, he will extend his pardoning mercy to so many sins, and then stop? When he pardoned Saul of Tarsus, and others among the chief of sinners; did he signify, that there were any, who rose so much *above* the *chief* of sinners, that they could not be pardoned?

Tell me, distressed and desponding soul, does not God know his own heart? When he plainly tells you that he is rich in mercy, and delights to forgive; does he say it to mock your miseries? When he promises pardon to all who truly seek it; have you any reason to doubt the truth of his promises? Do you despair of Divine mercy, because any sinner, even the most guilty, ever sought mercy in vain? Are there not multitudes now in heaven, who were once as guilty and wretched and helpless as you are? And is the mercy of God exhausted, so that he cannot pardon and save as he did in days that are past?

What more shall I say? Do you not know, that in this world of mercy, where atoning blood has been shed, despairing thoughts are very dishonorable to God? Can you think that you treat your heavenly Father as you ought, when you doubt whether he is powerful enough, or merciful enough to do what he has promised? Remember my friends, that the God with whom you have to do, is a great God — great in power and wisdom and holiness, and great in goodness. He has riches of grace; he has unfathomable depths of mercy, an *ocean* of love. You may very properly ask, who among the children of men, could forgive offences like yours? But you may look to God for compassion and grace which is infinitely higher than any in the heart of man. There is nothing more displeasing to God, than to call in question the greatness of his mercy, or its sufficiency for your salvation. Better doubt the omnipotence of God — better doubt his eternity, or his infinite knowledge, than to doubt the riches of his grace. The work of pardoning and saving sinners through the blood of Christ, is a work on which God has specially set his heart. In this work he intends to do such wonders of mercy as will fill the universe with astonishment and joy. And if you who are so sinful and wretched, will go to the throne of grace, and in your humble confessions present before God a depth of guilt which the human mind can never fathom, and will heartily pray the prayer of the publican — "God be merciful to me, a sinner;" he will say to you, "be of good cheer; thy sins which are many, are forgiven thee." He will certainly do this; and it will be to the praise of the glory of his grace.

But my dear friends, whether you will hear, or whether you will forbear; whether you will believe the gospel, or die in your sins; — it shall be known to you and to the world, that God abounds in goodness; that his mercy is higher than the heavens; and that whosoever cometh to him, he will in no wise cast out. And if at the last day — at the winding up of the present scene of things — the Lord grant it may not be so — but if at the last day, any of us or all of us, shall fall short of heaven; it will be known to the universe, that it was our own fault, and was not owing to any want of mercy in God.

TWO SERMONS

DELIVERED IN THE CHAPEL OF THE THEOLOGICAL SEMINARY, ANDOVER, FEB. 9, 1845.

SERMON I.

THE CONVERSION WHICH IS OF MAN.

Jeremiah 31: 18.—TURN THOU ME, AND I SHALL BE TURNED; FOR THOU ART THE LORD MY GOD.

THE Prophet here speaks in behalf of the Israelites. He acknowledges that they have been rebellious and refractory under divine chastisements; and he is aware that they have a pride and stubbornness of heart, which cannot be subdued, except by a power above that of man. With this view of their guilty state, and feeling a deep concern for them as the people of his charge, he offers up the following prayer in the name of each individual among them: "Turn *thou* me, and I shall be turned; for thou art the Lord my God." Turn *thou* me, and then I shall be *effectually* turned.

This prayer expresses a sentiment, which is fully confirmed by the current representations of God's word, and by the experience of those who are effectually enlightened by his Spirit. The sentiment is, that *true, saving conversion is the special work of God; and as such the servants of God are to seek it in fervent prayer for sinners.*

There is evidently an implied contrast between that turning or conversion which is the work of man and which is to be traced to his agency, and that which is God's work, and is to be traced to *his* agency. I propose to consider these distinctly, in the two following sermons.

First; there is a turning or conversion which is man's work — a conversion which is accomplished by man's agency, without the sanctifying influence of the divine Spirit. Such a change in sinners is frequently mentioned in the Scriptures. Multitudes heard Christ gladly, and did many things which seemed to be right, who remained unregenerate. In the parable of the sower, a large class of persons are represented by the seed which fell on stony ground, and that which fell among thorns. A remarkable effect is produced. There is an apparent turning from sin. But the change is not permanent and saving. The Apostle Peter speaks expressly of those, who have, in some sense, escaped the pollutions of the world through the knowledge of Christ, but are again entangled therein and overcome; and what he afterwards says implies, that notwithstanding their apparent conversion, they were unchanged in their moral nature. There are spurious conversions at the present time also — conversions which are altogether the work of man. There is much seeming piety, which has its origin in the will and affections of unsanctified sinners. There is an abundance of religion without holiness.

My object is to show, that that conversion which is the mere product of the powers and dispositions of unsanctified man falls short of holiness, and that true, saving conversion does not spring from this source. I shall endeavor to set forth in its true light, the religion, the very best religion which is *not of God*, and shall thus endeavor to take away the hope which sinners are so prone to indulge, that they can attain to repentance, faith and obedience of themselves, without the renewing of the Holy Ghost — a hope which is all delusion, and leads to certain disappointment and ruin.

It may assist our contemplations to consider a little what *man is;* not what he was *originally*, nor what he *should* be, nor what those finally *will* be who are renewed by the divine Spirit; but what man is *by nature*—what he is in his degenerate, unsanctified state.

It is too evident to need proof, that man is a moral, accountable being. He has a *rational* mind. But his mind is perverted and depraved. In other words, *man himself*, is depraved; he is without holiness, and inclined to sin. He has conscience, understanding and will. Sinning cannot destroy these faculties. Man's will may be corrupt, and it is so; his reason and understanding may be, and are, under a wrong influence; they are misguided and perverted. But they can never be destroyed. Man has various dispositions and affections. He has self-love; and he has the relative and the social affections. He has desires after natural good. He has hope and fear, love and hatred, joy and sorrow. He is susceptible of the feeling of reverence in view of what is *great*, of gratitude for kindness, and of respect and admiration for distinguished justice and magnanimity. He is capable of discerning the natural beauty and fitness of virtue, and the deformity of vice, and of feeling approbation of the one, and disapprobation of the other. Such is man. He is a rational, accountable, immortal being, without holiness, and without any disposition to holiness;—with a conscience which approves what is right, and disapproves what is wrong, but with a heart which rejects the right, and cleaves to the wrong; with mental powers of wonderful activity in regard to natural things; and wonderful activity also in regard to things which are moral and spiritual; though his activity is wholly under the influence of a wrong principle, and directed to a wrong end.

Now the single inquiry to which I invite your attention is this; what has man accomplished in his present fallen state, when in different circumstances, he has attempted by his own powers of mind, to turn from sin, and to form himself to piety and goodness, *without the special influence of the Holy Spirit?* It is a question of fact. To what sort of *conversion* and to what sort of *religious character* has man actually attained, and to what will he ever attain in this way?

My general answer is, that man, in the most diligent exercise of his own faculties, *without special divine influence*, never has attained and never will attain to real holiness. If the Bible is true, and if all experience is true, real holiness, whether in the form of repentance, faith, worship, or obedience, cannot spring from man's unregenerate mind. "The carnal mind" — which is all the mind that unrenewed man has — "is enmity against God, and is not subject to his law, neither indeed can be." On this account it is, that man must be born again; and this new birth must be *of God*. If we could attain to a holy character without this supernatural change, how would the change be necessary? All who are holy, will be saved. And if we could be holy without being born of the Spirit, we could be saved without it. And then the words of Christ would not hold, that "except a man be born again, he cannot see the kingdom of God."

Look into the mind of man, just as it is in its natural state. Can such a mind of *itself* originate holiness? Can you expect a being totally destitute of holiness, and opposed to it, will, *of himself*, become holy? Is there anything in unregenerate man — any power or faculty of his mind, or any disposition of his heart, from which true holiness can spring? Look at *conscience*. This is a most important faculty. It is God's vicegerent in the soul. It speaks in God's name, and with God's authority. When roused from its slumbers it speaks with a voice of thunder, as God did from Sinai. But the same corrupt and stubborn heart, which refuses to hear the voice of God from *without*, refuses to hear his voice *within*. The voice of God uttered in the soul, by an awakened conscience, and uttered with the highest authority, has no more authority — it has no more power to command obedience, than the voice of God uttered in his word, and in his providence, and in the awful thunders of Sinai.

How was it in fact with the children of Israel, who stood trembling on the extensive plain before Mount Sinai? They had conscience, and their conscience was powerfully stirred within them. But the same corrupt and obstinate heart, which was deaf to the voice of God from Sinai, was deaf to the voice of conscience. So it was with Judas after his base and criminal deed. His conscience was roused, and he saw the wickedness of what he had done, and his obligations to the Saviour. But his selfish, stubborn heart no more yielded to the power of conscience, than it had before yielded to the power of Christ's instructions and example. It is a well known fact, that conscience, when roused to the highest degree of faithfulness, has no power to change the heart from enmity to love. This inefficacy of conscience is a matter of common experience. But it comes out with special clearness in the history of awakened sinners. Such sinners may at first place much reliance upon their convictions of conscience, and may think it will be easy for them to do what they now so clearly see to be their first and highest duty. But they soon learn their mistake. Their own experience teaches them the utter insufficiency of conscience to overcome the strength of corrupt inclinations. Their desperately wicked heart stands against conscience, and refuses to obey its dictates. While they *know* the will of God they *do* it not. And the longer they continue under the power of an awakened conscience, with an unregenerate heart, the more clearly does it appear that they can never be fitted for heaven, unless they have "*the renewing of the Holy Ghost.*"

Inquire then whether *reason* can turn the heart from sin to holiness. Here we shall find that reason, in its most improved state, fails of accomplishing the necessary work, in the same way that conscience does. Man's reason may attain to the knowledge of the most important truths, and these truths apprehended by reason, would at once excite affections corresponding with their nature, *if the heart were right.* But the heart is not right. It does not fall in with these spiritual truths. They are not congenial with it. And let them be ever so clearly and fully apprehended, even as clearly as they will be at the judgment day, and let the obligations involved in them be ever so strongly impressed upon the mind ; the consequence will be, that the opposition between them and the unrenewed, carnal heart, will become more and more apparent, and impatience and dislike of the heart be more and more excited. So it has been in fact. Men of the highest intelligence, men who have had the clearest speculative knowledge of divine truth, without the renewing of the Spirit, have made no approximation to a holy character; but on the contrary by the habit of contemplating the truth, without yielding to its claims, have grown more and more hardened against its salutary influence. These are the men that our Saviour calls "the *wise* and *prudent*,"— who yet have no saving knowledge. Their hard and selfish hearts, resist the light. This deplorable fact is strikingly set forth in the words of Christ to the unbelieving Jews: "Ye have both *seen* and *hated* both me and my Father." Jesus had lived among them. They had heard his instructions and witnessed his miracles. They had *seen* him — and in seeing *him* they had seen the *Father* also. But their hearts were not won. And the unrenewed carnal heart never was and never will be won to love and obedience by the most correct and powerful actings of the faculty of reason.

But may not the sinner be effectually turned from his wicked ways by the power of *self-love?* May not a desire of happiness, together with a conviction that happiness is to be obtained only in the service of God, induce a rational being, such as man is, to engage in the service of God? This principle of self-love, is indeed a very powerful principle; and it would verily appear, at first view, that one, in whom a supreme desire of happiness is excited, and who knows that real permanent happiness can be obtained in no other way than by turning from sin and obeying the gospel, must at once turn and obey, for *the sake of obtaining that happiness which he supremely desires.* Now why is not this a just conclusion? Why may not the sinner put away this and that sin, and all sin, for the sake of obtaining that happiness which he *supremely* loves?

My first answer is, that the inefficacy of self-love has been clearly and thoroughly proved, as *a matter of fact.* In all sinners, self-love is known to be the ruling principle. Now thousands of sinners have been seriously convinced that the way, and the only way to secure their own eternal happiness, is to repent and believe in Christ — who yet have not repented and believed.

Self-love however strongly excited, has never *in fact* had an influence to induce men to turn from sin. It has not prevailed to their conversion. It is very common for sinners to imagine, that this motive is sufficient; that a serious regard to their own happi ness is all that will be necessary to bring about their conversion. But experience teaches otherwise. Clear evidence of this inefficacy of self-love arises from the case of sinners generally, who have enjoyed religious instruction. I ask such a person — do you not desire your own happiness? And are you not convinced, that the way and the only way, to obtain real happiness, is to repent and follow Christ? Why then do you not repent and follow Christ? It is clear that the motive, which seems so powerful, does not produce the desired effect. Whatever may be the reason of this, it is a plain fact, that self-love, as *it exists in unrenewed men*, has no efficacy to produce a saving conversion. This is my first answer.

I answer again, that self-love, *as it exists in the depraved mind*, is not *suited* to produce an effectual turning from sin. It is not adapted to this end. That self-love which exists in holy beings, is a *holy principle*. They love themselves *truly* and *impartially*. And they love one another *as* they love themselves. But in corrupt minds, *self-love* is corrupt. It is not a pure fountain. And the stream flowing from a fountain cannot be purer than the fountain — and it cannot rise higher than the fountain. An impure fountain or spring is not *adapted* to send forth pure water. Self-love in unregenerate man, has no tendency, no leaning to holiness. It is not of such a nature, that holiness can flow from it. The sinner, in the exercise of self-love, does indeed desire *happiness*. But what *kind* of happiness does he desire? Does he desire a *holy happiness* — consisting in the enjoyment of God? Can he *desire* a happiness, which he does not *love?* And can he love a happiness which consists in being near to *God*, without *loving God?* The happiness which any one desires is always conformed to his governing disposition or taste. The covetous, the sensual, the ambitious, all desire *happiness* — that is, they desire *gratification*. But it is a happiness suited to their inclinations; it is the gratification of such passions as exist within them. No one ever truly loves and desires any happiness, except that which agrees with his inclinations. The happiness which the impenitent desire and seek, and that which holy persons desire and seek, are as different as their inclinations. The unrenewed are just as far from truly desiring the *enjoyment of God*, which is the only true happiness, as they are from *loving* God.

It is evidently *absurd* to suppose that self-love, *as it is in fallen man*, will ever turn the heart to the love of God. For self-love in the unrenewed is *supreme* self-love. And to suppose that supreme love of self will lead to the supreme love of God, is to suppose that self-love will, by its own act, dethrone *itself*, and give the supremacy to another affection which is opposite, and to which the heart is a stranger.

And if the sinner's desire of happiness has no power to turn the heart to God, certainly *fear of punishment* cannot do it. *Fear* also is a powerful principle, and when excited has a wonderful influence over the conduct of men. When united with holy *love*, it is an effectual motive to obedience. But fear in the heart of a sinner, is as different from fear in the heart of a Christian, as any other affection is. And when it exists without love, it has no power to *beget* love. A wicked man may *fear punishment* from a ruler and a law that he hates, and that selfish fear may hold him back from various crimes which would endanger his life; but it can never turn his heart from hatred to love.

Some suppose that *free-will* is sufficient to turn a man from sin to holiness. But you will see in a moment that this is a groundless supposition. For man's *will* is as much perverted as any other faculty. It is indeed free from everything like *compulsion* or *force*. But it is not free from *corruption*. It is not free from a *wrong bias*. It is altogether prone to evil. So that you can never expect anything spiritually good to result from man's *will*, unless it is *itself* first renewed, and thus delivered from its evil bias, and from the dominion of corrupt passions.

But there is no need of further argument. The word of God decides this once for all, declaring expressly, that the requisite change in sinners is "not of *the will of man*, but of God."

But cannot a saving conversion result from the combined action of all these natural powers? I answer no;—because they are all, as truly as any one of them, under the dominion of sin, they all lead the wrong way, and so far as they are of a moral nature, they are all hostile to holiness. And what efficacy can the combined action of hostile powers have to subdue enmity and produce love? The active principles of the mind are indeed possessed of a mighty power, and if under right direction, would accomplish wonders of good. But under the direction of a wicked heart their efficacy turns only to evil. And so it would be if their power was increased to omnipotence, being still under the direction of a selfish, wicked heart.

But principles of the human mind, corrupt as they are, may produce and do produce astonishing effects. The conscience of the sinner may be so awakened, his understanding so illuminated, his desire of happiness and fear of misery so excited, that he will abandon many beloved vices, submit to many sacrifices, and assume the appearance and make the profession of a converted sinner. The powers and passions of men may be so wrought upon and their habits so moulded by a religious education and other favorable influences, that they will exhibit to their own eye and the eye of others all the characteristics of a fervent piety, and will go through all the *external* duties of a Christian life, and still remain under the dominion of sin. What transformations of outward character and what changes of feeling are often produced by impressive and inflammatory preaching, or by affecting events of providence! And how great is the power of the *machinery*, or the religious manoeuvres which have often been used in our country, to wake up the passions and to kindle what appears to be feelings of devotion, *without any change of heart*. Multitudes have been strangely affected in this way. Their minds, and sometimes their bodies too, have been mightily agitated. And hundreds have been converted in a day,—converted in man's way, and by man's power, and soon converted back again to open ungodliness. And not less wonderful is the effect which may be produced upon the minds of unregenerate men by the awe-inspiring grandeur of a magnificent cathedral — by its dim light, its burning candles, its affecting pictures, its solemn music, and its various imposing rights. In such circumstances, the feelings of a whole congregation of ungodly men may be so excited, that they will at once kneel or fall prostrate in worship, and will to all appearance at the time be as devout as apostles and martyrs — and still retain their carnal mind, and go away and sin the more.

You see how it is with all that ever has been or ever can be done by the powers and efforts of unrenewed man. Sinners may indeed be *converted*, as thousands are, by their own power, or the power of others. They may turn from this or that particular way of sinning, and yet not turn from *sin*; — as a covetous man may give up dishonest means of getting money, and make use of honest means, and still be as covetous as before. The kingdom of Satan extends over a very large territory; and those who belong to that kingdom may often change their place, and may change their dress, and their modes of living; — they may go to a great distance from where they once were, and their whole appearance may be altered, and they may put on the costume of the saints; — and yet after all continue in the empire of sin. They may even have "*another heart*," as king Saul had, and yet not have a *new* heart. All this and more may come from your natural powers and inclinations, impelled to action by natural causes, while the principle of sin still reigns within you. You may have the best conversion, the fairest form of godliness which can result from what is in man without supernatural grace, and yet be without holiness. Let conscience, let reason, let self-love, let hope and fear, let the passions, let enthusiasm and superstition, let birth and blood and education, let means and measures, rites and ceremonies, let the will of the flesh and the will of man — let any or all of these do what they can, without the grace of God, to turn the sinner from the error of his ways to the wisdom of the just, and though the sinner thus wrought upon, may be called a *convert*, and may have a name to live and may shine in the world's view, he is still dead in trespasses and sins and will fall short of heaven.

SERMON II.

THE CONVERSION WHICH IS OF GOD.

JEREMIAH 31 : 18.

In the former discourse I undertook to describe that kind of conversion which is the work of unregenerate man, and is to be traced to the principles of action naturally in his heart, *without the special influence of the Holy Spirit.* I endeavored to show that man in his unrenewed state, may be, and often is, brought under such influences from without, and within, that he is actually converted, or does actually turn, *in a certain way;* that he experiences a manifest change not only in his outward conduct, but, in some respects, in the views and feelings and purposes of his own mind; — but that the change to which he attains in this way does not reach his great, governing principle — does not go to the bottom of his heart; and that it leaves him still destitute of holiness, and unfit for the kingdom of heaven. Such is the very best conversion, which is merely the work of man, and which results from the operation of the powers and principles of his own mind and heart, without the renewing of the Holy Spirit. It is like the house which was built on the sand; and the rain descended and the floods came and the winds blew, and beat upon that house; and it fell. Such is the nature and the end of the conversion and the piety, which is of man, in contradistinction to that which is of God. And such will be our end unless we have a religion above the highest and best attainments of unregenerate man.

I shall now endeavor to set before you *some* of the marks or characteristics of that conversion, which is *of God.*

I begin by saying, that the work which God accomplishes in a saving conversion has an *intrinsic excellence*, which clearly shows who is its author. God always works in a manner worthy of himself. But when he undertakes any work of extraordinary magnitude and importance, and one which in human view is attended with great difficulty, he takes special care, by the work itself, and his manner of doing it, that his hand may be clearly seen, and that all may know that the work is his. The saving conversion of a sinner, is a work of such excellence, that it redounds preëminently to the glory of God. The wonderful works which God did in Egypt, in the wilderness, and in Canaan, made it manifest, that he was Jehovah, the Almighty, and righteous, and merciful God. And he is now constantly showing by his works and dispensations, that he is God. But what work of God has such excellence as the spiritual change which he accomplishes in the sinner? *Creation* was truly a great and wonderful work. When God made the sun — when he said, let there be light, and there was light, he acted like a God. But methinks the creation of a thousand suns has not an excellence and glory like the turning of a sinner from enmity to love, from the slavery of sin to the liberty of the son's of God. Angels rendered praise to God, when they witnessed the work of creation. But at the work of redemption, and the conversion of a sinner they cry, *glory to God in the highest.* They rejoice over every sinner that repents. And all the followers of Christ see now, and will see more clearly in eternity, that the conversion of a sinner is to the glory of God's grace.

That conversion, which is the work of the divine Spirit, has nothing deceptive in it, like the conversion which results from the workings of the natural man. The religion which is of God is not an appearance but a reality; not a shadow but a substance. It is not superficial or hollow, like that which is of man. It is solid excellence. Conversions which are the mere product of man's natural powers and dispositions, are to be seen everywhere.

But when rightly understood, they have no real beauty or excellence. They are not worthy to be called the work of God. They are rather like the works of the magicians in Egypt, which were imitations, though contemptible imitations of the miracles wrought by Moses; — but they were the best that the magicians could do with all their enchantments and juggling arts, and with the help of the wicked one. Still they were all counterfeits, ending in the confusion of those who wrought them. But when you look at the works of God, wrought by the hand of Moses, you see *real miracles*, works *truly wonderful*. You see the finger of God. You cannot but say, that these are from God. Many conversions have been brought about in our day by something very like the enchantments and tricks of the Egyptian jugglers. But they prove to be superficial, hollow, worthless things, a discredit to the very name of conversions, and in the end a stigma upon their authors. But look at the conversion of Saul of Tarsus, and of the multitude on the day of Pentecost, and of the Corinthian believers, some of whom had been given to the most loathsome vices. Look at the conversion of Augustine, and Luther, and Edwards, and Brainerd, and John Newton, and Henry Martyn and others of like kind. You will find them to be what the Apostle calls them, *God's workmanship*. Here, you will say, *here is something from above. Here is the finger of God.* And here, in the work itself, is the very image of God. This gives it a manifest superiority over other divine works. All the works of creation and providence show that God is the author. But here a work is done, which not only shows God to be the author, but does, in its own nature, bear the *moral image* of God. It makes the soul of man a partaker of "the divine nature." You see that in every point of view, the true, saving conversion of a sinner is far above that which is accomplished by mere human power. It is a change of another and higher kind. It is a change which a man never comes to by the very best operation of reason, conscience, or self-love, or by the power of the will, or by the desire of pleasure or the fear of suffering, or by the working of superstition or enthusiasm, or by the dreams of imagination, sleeping or waking, or by human persuasion, either in the way of allurement or terror, or by the mere influence of instruction, or education, or example, or experience, or external rites, or events of providence. A saving conversion is entirely above and beyond what can be effected by any or all of these, *without the divine Spirit.* It is a change to which no one ever attains, unless he comes under the special operation of God.

But it must be remembered, that this special, supernatural, divine work, though so much above what the mere agency of man can of itself ever attain, does not put a *stop* to man's agency. It puts a stop to his *sinful* agency; but at the same time it influences him to a *holy* agency. It changes his *bad* agency to a *good* agency. The converted sinner continues to put forth as real an agency, and as great an agency, as before. What then is the difference? It is this. His agency now is of another and better kind. The true convert wills or chooses as really and as often as before. The difference is, he now chooses *right.* He now has a will *truly free.* Before, his will was free from compulsion — free in every sense necessary to his being a moral, accountable agent. But after all he was a slave to sin, and his will was enslaved under the bondage of corruption. Now he is free, and his will is free, in the best sense — free from the slavery of depraved passions and desires. The work of God in conversion *emancipates* the sinner, and emancipates his will from this degrading bondage, and brings him into subjection to the will of God. This is true liberty, " the glorious liberty of the sons of God.

There never was a more palpable mistake, than to suppose, that the efficacious operation of the Holy Spirit in the conversion of a sinner interrupts or impairs his agency or takes away his freedom. What converting grace does, is not to interrupt or impair a man's agency, but to improve it, to make it what it should be; not to paralyze or embarrass the *will,* but to correct its irregularities, and bring it to follow truth and righteousness, instead of error and sin, to act for God, rather than the wicked one; — not to take away freedom, but to give freedom — freedom worthy of the name. This man never obtains of himself. He may change his posture and his place, but he keeps on his fetters. He may act with vigor — he may work hard; but he is a *slave.*

I remark further; that, in accomplishing the work of man's conversion, God does *just that which needs to be done.* A skilful physician always aims to discover the nature and seat of the disease in his patients — to discover what needs to be done in order to a thorough cure. And he well knows that, how far soever he may be able to check or vary the outward symptoms or the visible operations of the disease, he will fail of effecting a cure, unless his medicine reaches the seat of the distemper and removes the radical evil existing there. Now in the dispensation of grace, God undertakes to *convert* the sinner. And in this work of his Spirit, he does *that very thing* which needs to be done in order to a thorough and saving change. Now why or for what purpose is the special operation of God necessary? What is the great work to be accomplished, and which can never be accomplished, except by the divine Spirit? I reply, first — if any one needs such a reply — that the special influence of the Spirit is not required to make men moral, accountable beings; for they are so before their conversion as much as after. It is not necessary, in order to furnish them with any power or faculty of mind, which goes to constitute them moral beings, or to put them under obligation to obey the divine law; for they have every such faculty and are under such obligation as really and as completely in their natural state, as when renewed. The influence of the Spirit is not always necessary to a man's outward reformation; for this may be brought about by the exercise of his natural powers and dispositions. It is not necessary in order to excite strong emotions, apparently religious and devout, such as Rosseau sometimes felt, and such as many now feel in view of the natural beauty and sublimity of divine objects, or under the influence of solemn rites, or awakening events of providence. There are, as we have seen, many and very remarkable things which men may do, and remarkable intellectual acquisitions and external ornaments to which they may attain, without regeneration. Very powerful and diversified are the operations of self-love, and natural conscience, and the inclinations and instincts which belong to our mental and corporeal constitution. The disorder which has seized upon us does not destroy or supersede these natural principles of action, though it perverts them. This disorder is of a moral or spiritual nature. It affects us in our relations to God and his holy law. It lies in *the heart*, the seat of moral action. The heart is deceitful and desperately wicked. It is turned away from God and is wholly inclined to sin. Out of this evil treasure of the heart, Christ says, man brings forth evil things. Here then is *the very thing which needs to be done, and which must be done*, in order to a saving conversion. The heart must be changed — changed from enmity to love, from rebellion to submission, from disobedience to obedience — from sin to holiness. So it is represented in Scripture. God gives a *new heart*. He takes away the heart of stone, and gives a heart of flesh. He gives a heart to love God — a heart to believe in Christ — a heart to obey the gospel. This is the great thing which needs to be done, and which the divine Spirit does. Nothing else will answer the purpose. But when God changes the heart — when he gives a new heart; the essential work is done. There is a saving conversion — and ultimately a *complete* conversion. The change, in its essence is internal, but in its developments it reaches all that is external. The cause of the outward irregularities is removed, and of course those irregularities cease; — they *immediately begin* to cease, and in the end they cease entirely. This new heart, this *new principle of action*, is "the seed" planted in the renewed, and which an apostle says "*remaineth* in them." It is an abiding principle. And ultimately they will cease to sin, "because they are born of God." This renewal of the heart is the commencement of a spiritual change, which, according to its own nature, and the appointment of God, is to be continually advancing, and finally to be made perfect.

I have now touched upon another characteristic of that conversion which is the work of God, namely, that it is a *permanent* change. I do not mean that the change would be permanent, *independently* of divine influence. But it is, in fact, permanent. When God gives a new heart, he gives it effectually. He that begins this good work, will carry it on to perfection. Its continuance depends on the same cause as its commencement; and we could not know that it will continue, did we not know from the word of God, that he will continue to work in the believer to will and to do, till he is made perfect in holiness. That conversion, that religion, which is "of the will of man," has no security for its continuance. And if it should continue — if those who assume the appearance and the profession of godliness without regeneration, should persevere in their superficial, self-made religion — as some doubtless do; they would still be numbered with hypocrites and unbelievers. But the general fact is, that false converts *draw back*, and thus make it evident that they are not born of God. Their goodness is like the morning cloud and early dew. Not so the goodness of those whom God turns by his effectual grace. They have within them an incorruptible seed. They have a well of water, which never fails, but springs up to eternal life. The divine power which works in them is superior to all other powers and cannot be overcome. Their governing affection, their principle of action, though opposed by so many contrary influences, will hold out and be victorious, because it is in alliance with omnipotence. God is greater than all, and no one can pluck his people out of his hand.

My brethren, the subject which I have introduced is one of great extent and of inexpressible importance, and I can do but little towards a just and adequate discussion of it. I might go over the common Scriptural views which are set forth by evangelical preachers and writers, and which are all of great importance. I might say, that those whom God turns by his special grace, have a new spiritual discernment; and that they have an affection for God essentially different from natural self-love, and entirely above it. They have new desires, new hopes, new joys, and new sorrows. They have new views of themselves, and of the preciousness of Christ and his salvation; and they live a new and spiritual life. These topics are all important; but I cannot dwell upon them at the present time.

And now, my hearers, it must be evident to you, that all conversions, which are merely the work of man, are worthless in themselves, and worthless and pernicious in their results. Let them be multiplied ever so much — let hundreds or thousands of sinners be converted, *in this way*, in a short time; and let it be published and sounded abroad, that so great and wonderful is the number of converts. If the conversions are merely the work of man, they may for a time, be to the *glory* of man; but they are not to the glory of *God*. God will not own them. They are all worthless, like chaff which the wind driveth away. A thousand spurious conversions are of no more value than one, and one is of no value at all. Every one is a counterfeit. And you know that counterfeits are without value, and that multiplying them does not give them value. The counterfeit coin is all cast away, and the authors of it must answer for their dishonesty and fraud. A minister, from mere love of honor, may desire a revival of religion; and may pursue such a course as will enable him to count a large number of conversions. But conversions, without *regeneration*, are entirely worthless. They are worthless to those who are the subjects of them; — worthless to ministers, and to the church. Spurious conversions are really worse than no conversions. In the end, they are both worthless and *calamitous* to all concerned.

But, who can duly estimate the worth of a real, saving conversion? Who can tell what blessings are involved in it — what peace and joy in this life, what hope in death, what blessedness without end in heaven? Who can tell what a crown of rejoicing it is to a gospel minister, and what benefits it secures to the church; — what joy it awakens among the angels in heaven, and what glory redounds from it to the grace of God! A minister, who has added to his church hundreds of persons, who have been born only of *the will of man*, has done nothing to purpose. His ministry has been barren. But if, through the grace of God, a gospel minister may be the instrument of really converting a few sinners, and preparing them for usefulness and comfort on earth, and rest in heaven; he will not have labored in vain. He will stand and gaze upon those few souls, freed from the bondage of corruption, and adorned with the beauties of holiness, once enemies to Christ — now cleaving to him as the chief among ten thousand, and striving to be like him ; — he will fix his eye upon them as they move forward in the Christian life, and as they finish their course on earth, and as they go to enjoy the end of their faith, the salvation of their souls ; and he will be constrained to say, oh ! what work of God in the vast creation around us can be compared in real worth, and glory, with the work of his Spirit in the conversion of sinners !

And if the conversion of one sinner is of such excellence ; what will be the conversion of a great multitude which no man can number ? What will the angels say, and what will you say, when all nations shall be converted ? You may have wept for joy over the work of God, in the conversion of a beloved child, or a dear friend, for whom you had travailed in birth. How then will you adore and praise the grace of God, when you look from the heavenly world, and see the whole human family turned from sin and adorned with the beauties of holiness. What powerful reasons then have we to come daily to our God and Saviour and to offer up the fervent prayer for the millions who are perishing in sin — *turn* them, O God, and they shall be turned. Amen.

GENERAL INDEX.

INDEX OF TEXTS.

www.ingramcontent.com/pod-product-compliance
Lightning Source LLC
LaVergne TN
LVHW021231110826
845150LV00002B/298

* 9 7 8 1 4 2 5 5 6 3 0 8 0 *